Praise for **THE WOMEN WITH SILVER WINGS**

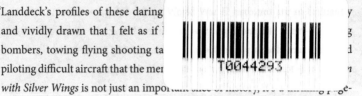

"Landdeck's profiles of these daring [women] are so [thoroughly] [researched] y and vividly drawn that I felt as if [ ] bombers, towing flying shooting ta[rgets] d piloting difficult aircraft that the men [ ] n *with Silver Wings* is not just an impor[tant slice of history], [it's a thrilling pa]ge-turner that explores the patriotism, sexism, and camaraderie of the WASPs' world."

—KAREN ABBOTT, *New York Times* bestselling author of
The Ghosts of Eden Park

"Historian Katherine Sharp Landdeck's highflying debut *The Women with Silver Wings* chronicles a cadre of fearless women whose wartime sacrifices were nearly forgotten. . . . [This is] a powerful story of reinvention, community and ingenuity born out of global upheaval."

—*Newsday*

"*The Women with Silver Wings* starts with a dramatic takeoff, introducing a personal story that author Katherine Sharp Landdeck, also a pilot, uses effectively to historicize a little-known, important part of U.S. military aviation. . . . The book is a prime opportunity to admire women in service."

—*San Francisco Chronicle*

"*The Women with Silver Wings* is the true story of America's unsung heroines of World War II. Katherine Sharp Landdeck has written a beautifully researched tribute to the courageous women who bravely served their nation in a time of need."

—FANNIE FLAGG, *New York Times* bestselling author of
Fried Green Tomatoes at the Whistle Stop Café and
The All-Girl Filling Station's Last Reunion

THE WOMEN WITH
SILVER WINGS

Nell "Mickey" Stevenson Bright, class 43-W-7, poses in front of the B-26 she flew at Biggs Field in late 1944. *Nell Stevenson Bright Collection. Courtesy Texas Woman's University*

THE WOMEN WITH SILVER WINGS

The Inspiring True Story of the
Women Airforce Service Pilots
of World War II

KATHERINE SHARP LANDDECK

CROWN
NEW YORK

For the Women Airforce Service Pilots
Thank you for trusting me with your stories.

And for my family.

CONTENTS

THE WOMEN WITH
SILVER WINGS

Cornelia Fort shares the story of her experiences at Pearl Harbor for a war bond drive on Nashville's WSM radio, not long after her return from Hawaii in early 1942. *Courtesy Nashville Public Library*

Prologue

In the quiet early morning of December 7, 1941, Cornelia Fort was teaching takeoffs and landings. Cornelia was a flight instructor at the civilian John Rodgers Field next to Pearl Harbor in Hawaii. She and her regular Sunday morning student, a defense worker named Ernest Suomala, liked to fly the little two-seater plane at dawn, when the air was calm and the beauty of Oahu revealed itself below them. Cornelia was twenty-two years old and had been flying for nearly two years. A former debutante from Nashville, Tennessee, she had recently escaped from polite society to follow her dream of flying professionally, moving to Hawaii, where she had been living for the past few months.

That morning, when Cornelia first noticed another aircraft flying in her direction, she wasn't immediately worried. Sundays were a busy day for pilots, as they flew students and sightseers alike, and it was not uncommon to see other airplanes nearby. Then she realized the plane was making straight for them, and fast. Cornelia acted quickly, jerking the controls away from Ernest and jamming the throttle open, willing their own plane upward. As she later remembered, their little blue and yellow Interstate Cadet narrowly missed colliding with the other plane, which "passed so close under us that our celluloid windows rattled violently." Cornelia looked down to see whose airplane had come so close to hitting them. She was stunned to see the red circles of the Japanese flag painted on the tops of the wings.

Then she looked back at the harbor. Thick black smoke was billowing below, a sight that sent shivers down Cornelia's spine. When she looked up again, she could see dozens of planes in formation ahead, their silver fuselages glinting in the morning sun. The skies over Pearl Harbor were now thick with enemy aircraft. "Something detached itself from an airplane and came glistening down," Cornelia later wrote. "My eyes followed it down, and even with the knowledge pounding in my mind, my heart turned convulsively when the bomb exploded in the middle of the harbor."

Quickly recognizing they were in danger, Cornelia hurried to land the tiny plane as the shadow of the Japanese Zero went over and bullets splattered off the ground all around them. She and her student leapt out of their cockpit and ran to the hangar as enemy planes dove toward them, strafing the airfield with bullets. They spent the rest of the morning huddled in the hangar, watching helplessly and anxiously counting as other planes from the airfield came in to land. "Two never came back," Cornelia remembered. "They were washed ashore weeks later on the windward side of the island, bullet-riddled. Not a pretty way for the brave little yellow Cubs and their pilots to go down to death." By midday the American fleet in the Pacific lay in ruins, and more than 2,400 Americans were dead.

The next day Cornelia's friend Betty Guild came to see her at the airfield. Betty was a pilot, too, and had been home sleeping when the attack began. She'd woken to her brother's screams: "It's the real thing! It's the real thing!" Betty dashed to the balcony as the sound of dozens of airplane engines bombarded her ears. From there she could see the dense clouds of black smoke obscuring the harbor. Betty's boyfriend was a Navy officer who had slept in the guest room after getting her home from a late party the night before, and her father offered to drive him down to his ship, which was already burning. Betty wanted to go with them, but the two men snuck away while she ran upstairs to get her purse, not wanting her to be exposed to strafing Japanese planes overhead. Betty's boyfriend survived that day, but many of their pilot friends did not.

At the airfield with Cornelia, Betty was still in a daze, her friend's close call only adding to her sense of dismay. The two women went to look over Cornelia's little blue and yellow plane, realizing that the bullets from the Japanese fighter had only just missed the gas tank or the plane would have certainly exploded.

After their experiences at Pearl Harbor, Betty and Cornelia were inspired to do whatever they could to help their nation in a time of war. The next year, when both women were invited to fly as civilians for the U.S. Army Air Forces, or AAF, they jumped at the chance. Cornelia Fort became part of the Women's Auxiliary Ferrying Squadron, a small group of elite women pilots led by the well-known commercial pilot Nancy Love. Betty Guild joined the Women's Flying Training Detachment, or WFTD, which aimed to train thousands of pilots under the direction of the famed air racer Jacqueline Cochran, and feed them into the WAFS. Later, these two parts of the same program were given one name, the Women Airforce Service Pilots, or WASP.

More than 25,000 hopefuls applied to join Nancy and Jackie's program, with 1,102 women completing training and earning their silver wings. They went on to be stationed at 126 bases across the United States. From September 1942 to December 1944,

WASP ferried new military planes from factories to points of embarkation for the war on two fronts. They flight tested planes. They towed targets behind aircraft to help train male gunners, who fired at them with live ammunition. All told, the WASP transported 12,000 planes over 60 million miles, released more than 1,100 male pilots for combat flying overseas, and proved beyond a doubt that women pilots were just as skilled and tenacious as men.

In the years after the war, however, the story of the WASP faded into the distant past. The women moved on with their lives, busy growing their careers and taking care of their families. Many managed to keep up with their flying, but others were kept grounded by lack of jobs or opportunities for women in the aviation field. It was only as the women grew older that they realized that their time serving their country had been forgotten.

They would spend the last decades of their lives fighting for their place in history.

Teresa James wears a full parachute as she prepares for her stunt flight in an open-cockpit biplane in the late 1930s. *Courtesy Texas Woman's University*

CHAPTER ONE

Airminded

Only a few short weeks after the attack on Pearl Harbor, Teresa James stood on the freezing platform of Pittsburgh's Union Station saying goodbye to the love of her life. They were an attractive couple: Teresa a pretty, curly-haired brunette with brown eyes and a ready smile, and George—who went by Dink—looking so handsome and clean-cut in his new uniform, with his cropped hair and square jaw. The couple had been preparing for this moment ever since America's entry into the war, but even so, they hated that the time for goodbye had come so soon.

Both Teresa and Dink had spent years anxiously following the news, waiting for the moment when their country might finally

join the fight. They were children of European immigrants—
Teresa's mother was from Ireland and Dink's was from Hungary—
and perhaps, as a result, they took events overseas personally.
Dink was a well-qualified pilot with 2,100 hours of flying time,
and the Army's Air Transport Command wanted him to join their
Ferrying Division. But by the time the telegram from the Ferrying
Division arrived, he had already gone with a friend and enlisted.
He was now Private Martin, headed to training at Keesler Army
Airfield in Biloxi, Mississippi.

Seasoned pilots like Dink were in high demand in January
1942. A sleeping nation had finally woken up to the fact that
America was woefully underprepared for war. In the weeks that
followed Pearl Harbor, the nation's military began a fevered rush
to train and recruit new personnel, especially pilots. It was clear
that this new conflict was going to be fought, and won, in the air.
In the years since the end of World War I, advancing airplane
technology had transformed the nature of armed conflict, with
newly developed combat aircraft enabling both sides to enact swift
and deadly violence. In particular, the might of the German air
force—the infamous Luftwaffe—drew the awe and respect of all
who knew airplanes. In order to counter it, the United States
would not only need to train thousands of pilots to fight overseas
but also to manufacture and deliver aircraft in vast numbers.

Across the country, pilots were being called up to serve. Many
didn't wait to be asked and, like Dink, simply enlisted. These patriotic Americans came from every state in the nation, from every
race and social class. But they had one thing in common. They were
all men. In 1942, the draft applied only to males ages twenty-one to
forty-five, and while the military did recruit women volunteers as
nurses and for other positions, it did not admit them as pilots.

On the icy train platform, Teresa and Dink said their goodbyes
and promised to write. Teresa wanted to know all about Dink's
training. After all, she was an accomplished pilot in her own right,
well-known for her stunt flying, which she had only recently given

up to make her living as a flight instructor. Teresa had been flying for nine years, during which time she had amassed almost 1,200 hours in the air, teaching scores of young men to fly and to improve their flight skills in preparation for war.

The couple had met on the airfield in 1937. Dink noticed Teresa right away, but it took him a while to pluck up the courage to ask her out. Then, one summer day all flying stopped for a sudden rainstorm. Dink took the opportunity to invite Teresa over to his family home for lunch. That day they spent time talking and getting to know each other. Teresa always asked her new students if they were good dancers: she had a theory that people who were light on their feet would likely turn out to be light on the airplane controls as well, making them good pilots. Teresa soon learned that although Dink couldn't jitterbug, he loved to slow waltz with her and that he was a natural in the air. She had met her match.

After Dink's departure, Teresa went back to work as an instructor, but the busy airfield now felt lonely. The year before, Teresa had helped to set up a local division of the Civil Air Patrol, a civilian auxiliary organization that was preparing to surveil the surrounding area from the air in the event of war. Although she continued to volunteer for work in the air patrol, Teresa felt at loose ends. She wished she could do more. She missed Dink terribly. The couple wrote to each other, sending letters back and forth daily.

Then an opportunity arose. Teresa learned that one of her flying friends, a local pilot named Helen Richey, had received a telegram two pages long signed by the prominent aviator Jacqueline Cochran. In the telegram Cochran explained that since the attack on Pearl Harbor every front in the war was now an American front and it was time for patriotic American women to step up and do their part. She was taking a group of women pilots to England to fly for the war effort there, and she wanted Helen to come with her. Helen was already beginning to prepare to leave for Canada, where she would be put through rigorous flight and medical tests along with the other potential recruits.

Teresa wrote to Cochran, hoping for her own invitation to join. In her letter Teresa touted her credentials: she was thirty-one years old, had been flying for nine years, had 1,200 hours of flight time, was an active flight instructor and a member of the Ninety-Nines, the all-women flying organization. She desperately wanted to go with Helen to Canada, but it wasn't to be. That same month her mother suffered a heart attack. Teresa wasn't about to leave her side. When Cochran's offer arrived a few weeks later, Teresa turned it down.

Stranded in Pennsylvania, Teresa took care of her mom, who slowly recovered her health. Dink was now in Colorado. In July 1942, after seven months of separation, he asked Teresa to come and see him and to bring along his mother and Teresa's sister Betty, too. The three women made the long drive west in Dink's Buick across two-lane highways with their windows down and hot summer air blowing. Finally, Teresa and Dink were reunited, with Dink able to get a two-day pass to spend time with his visitors.

It was in Colorado Springs that Dink proposed. He explained to Teresa that he didn't want to leave to fight overseas without marrying her first. Although Teresa was Catholic and had always dreamed of a big church wedding, Dink convinced her to agree to a more modest setting, at least for the short term. The couple was married at the Colorado Springs City Hall, with a private from the 6th Photographic Squadron as best man. Instead of a wedding gown, Teresa wore her Civil Air Patrol uniform. Her sister Betty was maid of honor in her own uniform, as she was also a pilot and had joined Teresa in her air patrol work. Dink's mother served as witness. The couple had planned to keep the wedding a secret and to have their traditional church wedding after the war, but a local journalist gave away the game, running the headline FAMOUS STUNT PILOT MARRIED, much to the shock of Teresa's stunned mother—who learned of her daughter's wedding from the newspaper the following day.

There was little time for romance or celebration. After two weeks of day trips to the mountains and evenings with Dink, Teresa returned to Pennsylvania with her sister and Dink's mother. She went back to work at the airfield, taking on even more hours as a volunteer pilot in the Civil Air Patrol while continuing as an instructor training men to fly for the war, still hoping that the time might come when she could do the same.

Then on September 6, 1942, Teresa received a telegram that was the answer to her prayers. It was from the well-known commercial pilot Nancy Love and Colonel Robert H. Baker of the U.S. Army Air Forces' Ferry Command, inviting her to join a newly formed Women's Auxiliary Ferrying Squadron at New Castle Army Air Base in Wilmington, Delaware:

> FERRYING DIVISION AIR TRANSPORT COMMAND IS ESTABLISHING GROUP OF WOMEN PILOTS FOR DOMESTIC FERRYING STOP NECESSARY QUALIFICATIONS ARE HIGH SCHOOL EDUCATION AGE BETWEEN TWENTY ONE AND THIRTY FIVE COMMERCIAL LICENSE FIVE HUNDRED HOURS TWO HUNDRED HORSEPOWER RATING STOP ADVISE COMMANDING OFFICER SECOND FERRYING GROUP FERRYING DIVISION AIR TRANSPORT COMMAND NEWCASTLE COUNTY AIRPORT WILMINGTON DELAWARE IF YOU ARE IMMEDIATELY AVAILABLE AND CAN REPORT AT YOUR OWN EXPENSE FOR INTERVIEW AND FLIGHT CHECK STOP BRING TWO LETTERS OF RECOMMENDATION PROOF OF EDUCATION AND FLYING TIME STOP

With her mother returned to good health, there was nothing standing in Teresa's way. She made plans to leave for Wilmington immediately.

Like the other women who went on to serve as Women Airforce Service Pilots, Teresa James grew up in a time of national obsession with aviation. She was born in 1911, only eight years after the Wright brothers' first flight, and she came of age at a point in history when the world seemed to have gone airplane crazy. This was an era when aviators drew massive crowds, inspiring the popular imagination as they broke record after record: for the highest altitude flown, the fastest trip across country, the first flight to just about anywhere. Couples were getting married in airplanes. They were naming their daughters "Aerogene." Opera singers gave concerts in the sky. Americans gathered at air shows by the thousands, spending their afternoons watching brave—or perhaps foolish— young aviators climbing out of the cockpit and onto the wings of the biplanes, performing stunts that made the crowds gasp with pleasure or look away in horror. Air shows of the era garnered higher attendance than professional or college sporting events. The airplane wasn't just a technical innovation; it was seen as a sort of mechanical messiah heralding a new chapter for humanity.

Aircraft manufacturers wanted attention, too, and were optimistic that this obsession would translate into the purchase of airplanes for private and commercial use. The air was the new frontier, and the era saw more rapid changes in aviation technology than almost any other period in history. Airplanes went from fragile, open-cockpit biplanes with 45-horsepower motors to passenger liners with two engines over 1,100 horsepower each, capable of flying to over 20,000 feet at speeds of well over 200 miles per hour. Companies like Seversky and Grumman competed to sponsor the brightest air show stars, hoping to see their latest model discussed favorably in the newspapers.

Although the majority of pilots during this time were male, the "air-mindedness" of the 1920s and 1930s certainly wasn't limited to men. Women had been part of the story of aviation from the very beginning. Katharine Wright, Harriet Quimby, Matilde Moisant, Blanche Stuart Scott, and Bessie Coleman were all well-known pilots in their own time. Then there was Amelia Earhart, who broke records and made headlines throughout the late 1920s and 1930s and who, in 1932, became the first woman (and only the second person after Charles Lindbergh) to pilot a plane solo across the Atlantic. For Earhart, her transatlantic flight was symbolic of women's freedom and independence, offering proof that women could succeed in nontraditional roles and that they were equal in "jobs requiring intelligence, coordination, speed, coolness, and willpower." This was an era that came to be known as the Golden Age of Aviation, and Teresa grew up in its glow.

Unlike so many of those budding women pilots, however, it took Teresa James a while to get up the wherewithal to climb into a cockpit. Flying was—and is—an expensive hobby, and the James family was not at all wealthy. Teresa's parents owned the local flower shop in Wilkinsburg, Pennsylvania, a town of around 30,000 people just east of Pittsburgh. Her father was a third-generation florist and Teresa grew up working in the store, helping make wedding bouquets and funeral wreaths. Although the James Flower and Gift Shoppe was popular around town, the Great Depression hit her family's business hard. Teresa remembered walking to school in the cold, wearing cardboard in her shoes to cover up the holes, and eating potato soup and oatmeal for dinner. She would joke that her family even cut out onions as "too expensive."

But money wasn't the only thing keeping Teresa from flying. She was also frankly terrified of airplanes. As a young teenager, she had witnessed an Army plane crash in which the two pilots were killed, and she never forgot it. A few years later, in 1933, when she learned that her brother Francis was taking flying lessons, Teresa was horrified, certain he would be killed, too. Not long after Francis got his license, Teresa's fears were confirmed when her brother stretched a flight too long in strong winds and ran out of gas, crash-landing in a field. Francis ended up seriously injured, spending six weeks in the hospital and almost losing a leg. While her brother was still recuperating, he managed to talk Teresa into driving him over to meet his friends at the airfield; with his broken leg, he couldn't drive himself. Although reluctant, Teresa agreed, still believing he was crazy.

It took a handsome pilot to convince Teresa to leave solid ground and take for the skies. One afternoon at the airfield, while her brother and his friends indulged in some "hangar flying"— swapping flying stories—a silver plane pulled up and a local pilot named Bill Angel jumped out. Teresa was the first to admit she fell in love with a different boy every week, but when she saw Bill, she was smitten. She thought he was the best-looking guy she'd ever seen.

Bill was clearly just as impressed with Teresa. He asked her out on the spot, telling her he was flying in an air show in nearby Latrobe, about sixty-five miles away, and invited her to fly over with him. Teresa reluctantly declined, but she didn't tell him it was because she was too scared to get in an airplane. Not long after, Bill asked her out on another flying date. This time she said yes. Up in the air, hundreds of feet above the ground, Teresa was petrified from the beginning of the flight to the end, unable to even look out of the window. Even so, she was determined to overcome her terror, spending the rest of the summer going on flying dates and group picnics as Bill's passenger.

At the end of the summer, Bill left to take an airline job flying out of Chicago. Now that he was out of the picture, another pilot at the airfield, Harry Fogle, hoped to woo Teresa himself and suggested he teach her to fly so that she could surprise Bill when he got back from Chicago. Teresa agreed. Harry knew Teresa was a nervous flier and so was sure to take her up in the early morning when the air was calm and still. They flew in a Travel Air OX-5, an open-cockpit biplane with tandem seating, with Harry sitting in the seat behind Teresa. Student and instructor didn't have radios, nor did they have Gosport helmets—a primitive communication system that enabled the instructor to issue instructions directly into the student's ears—and so Harry had to sit in the back, cupping his hands around his mouth, shouting out instructions as loud as he possibly could:

"Get the wing up! Get it down! Put the nose down! Put it up! What's the matter with you?"

After a good deal of shouting—and plenty of swearing—from Harry, Teresa began to master the basics of flying. For his part, Harry must have believed Teresa was getting the hang of things, because after just over five hours of dual instruction he decided it was time for her to fly solo. Early one Sunday morning, after they had made a couple of landings, Harry got out of the plane, turned the tail around, and said, "Take it off, you're okay!" So Teresa pushed the throttle in and the airplane jumped in the air, free of the 160 pounds of her instructor and easily gaining altitude. Teresa was soaring. She thought, *Oh my God, I'm up here!*

The biggest problem was, without the weight of Harry in the back, the plane was behaving in unfamiliar ways. Teresa was so scared that, while flying the landing pattern around the grass airfield, she missed her altitude marks. All of a sudden she was at 800 feet when she should have been at 600 feet. She began to panic. What if she couldn't get down or landed too fast to stop?

Teresa's lack of experience and her desperation to get back on the ground now combined into an act of pure daring. Another pilot was coming in to land ahead of her and she watched as he performed a slip, an advanced maneuver where the pilot banks the plane while using the opposite rudder, allowing the plane to quickly descend without adding airspeed. Teresa, who had never practiced a slip before, decided to give it a try. She made her rapid descent, almost flying over the edge of the field, but landing just in time and taxiing up to the fence. She jumped out of the plane, relieved but shaken to her core. She promised she would never go up in a plane again. She was done with flying.

Other pilots on the field were convinced that Teresa really

could fly, and they worked to persuade her to get back in the air again. One of the guys pointed out that she had gotten up and down by herself; a little more time with an instructor and she would be just fine. Teresa reluctantly agreed. Over time, she began to gain confidence and started to appreciate the joy that comes from flying once the fear fades away. Alone up in the clouds, a pilot has a feeling of powerful independence, as if nothing can touch her, and only she can control her fate. For a young woman living in the 1930s, when so much of what happened on the ground seemed intended to restrict or limit her scope, Teresa found a place of escape, empowerment, and freedom in the air. By the time one of the guys on the field received a letter from Bill telling them that he had met a pretty schoolteacher in Chicago and gotten married, Teresa had found a new love: airplanes.

Teresa had started flying to impress Bill, but she continued flying for the sheer pleasure and challenge of it—and for the cash. Around this same time, a local pilot named George Heller took note of Teresa's skill and pointed out that she could make good money as a stunt pilot at local air shows. Almost every Sunday of the year, there was an air show somewhere in Pennsylvania or Ohio, and stunt pilots could make up to $50 a weekend. That was a lot of money for Teresa, with her family's flower shop still suffering the effects of the Great Depression—a time when the average amount spent on flowers for an entire wedding was just over $13.

Teresa began to practice aerobatics: spins, loops, and her favorites, hammerhead stalls. She proved to be a virtuoso stunt pilot, and once she got used to the sensation of flying upside down and in circles, she even started to enjoy herself. Teresa's mother, while in general supportive of flying, was less pleased with her daughter's newfound passion for stunts. After Teresa finished her aerobatics practice in the afternoons, she always made sure to fly low over her family home before pulling the power off and shouting to her mom, "I'll be home for dinner, don't worry!" Some days her parents would squeeze into the plane and fly to her shows with her so they could watch, half proud, half terrified.

Flying was a way for Teresa to prove her mettle and make money in the bargain. But it was also a social activity. If you could fly a plane, you could grab a picnic and spend the day exploring the world from above, meeting new people at every airfield where you came in to land. Some of the pilots Teresa met ended up becoming her dance partners, taking part in (and winning) dance marathons, a popular cheap form of entertainment in the 1930s where the dancers kept going until they dropped. Some of Teresa's pilot friends goaded her into ice-skating as well; she enjoyed it so much she went on to win a bronze medal in speed skating at the Pennsylvania Skating Association championship in 1934.

For the most part, these other pilots were men, and Teresa enjoyed their attention. She loved going to the airport—often still wearing the dress and heels she'd worn to the flower shop or to mass—and sitting around with the guys talking about airplanes, sometimes until after midnight. It was only when she decided to join her local chapter of the Ninety-Nines in 1938 and started attending their meetings that Teresa realized she was also part of a flying sisterhood.

A group of active women pilots, including Amelia Earhart, had founded the Ninety-Nines in 1929, when women made up barely 1 percent of licensed pilots and had very few opportunities for camaraderie and support, something that their new organization hoped to rectify. (The women came up with their name based on the number of charter members: ninety-nine.) The organization was extremely active across the country, staging air shows, holding meetings, and providing social connections for its members while sharing news and updates in their regular newsletters. The Ninety-Nines also played an important role advocating for women and removing barriers to flying at a time when many air events and air races were for men only. Ninety-Nines president Betty Gillies had even led a successful fight against the Air Commerce Department's proposed ban on women flying during their menstrual cycles.

One of the members of Teresa's Western Pennsylvania chapter

of the Ninety-Nines was Helen Richey. Teresa and Helen had already met through their flying, and although Helen was a few years older, they had much in common. They were from neighboring towns—Helen from McKeesport, Pennsylvania, about a thirty-minute drive from Teresa's hometown of Wilkinsburg. With their dark, curly hair and irresistible sense of humor, they could almost have been sisters. What's more, both women were determined to make their living through flying. Helen's family had hoped she would train to be a teacher, but after dropping out of college she had begged her father to let her learn to fly. Eventually, with some cajoling from Helen's mother, he agreed. Helen earned her pilot's license in 1930 and since then she had paid her bills as a stunt pilot by performing at air shows, breaking records, and entering racing contests.

Even before meeting Helen, Teresa knew all about her exploits: her name was often in the newspapers. In 1933, together with her fellow female pilot Frances Marsalis, Helen had broken the air endurance record, a stunt sponsored by Outdoor Girl cosmetics. Helen and Frances spent ten consecutive days airborne over Miami, taking turns flying the airplane and resting. The women even had to refuel the plane while airborne, one of the most dangerous aspects of the stunt. This involved Helen climbing out on the wing to grab the fuel nozzle from a supply plane as it flew just close enough for her to reach without crashing into her plane. Then she would push the fuel nozzle into the gas tank, an experience she later described as like "wrestling a cobra in a hurricane."

During one such refueling exercise, the supply plane got too close and tore the fabric covering the wing of Helen and Frances's plane. At this point the women were just one day shy of breaking the record, and if they didn't repair the ripped wing immediately, they would have to land. Both Helen and Frances were exhausted, but they were also determined. Helen climbed out on the wing, found the tear, and carefully repaired it in midair using a needle and thread, sewing as fast as she could while the wind fought to snatch the needle from her hands. Finally she climbed back into the plane, much to the relief of her fellow pilot and the reporters watching from below. After fighting heavy rains all night long, the women finally broke the endurance record. Deciding a hot bath and soft bed constituted time better spent than tacking onto the record, they landed safely after remaining in the air for a total of 237 hours and 42 minutes.

A year after her endurance stunt, Helen made headlines again, this time for a very different reason: she was the first woman to be hired by a commercial airline as a pilot. In these early days of commercial aviation, the role of airline pilot was a new and highly desirable position, but it was strictly an all-boys club. Until Helen came along, no woman had been able to break into the profession. Then Central Airlines decided to hire Helen as a copilot on their Washington, D.C.–Detroit airmail route, which would also carry passengers if there was room. As accomplished as she was, Central Airlines likely hired Helen for the positive publicity she would bring them, rather than for her piloting expertise. Her first flight warranted a big story in the *New York Times* and a few months later *Collier's,* a popular national magazine, published an article that began, "This is Pilot Richey. Yes, she's a girl. She's young. She's pretty. She's a good flyer. But she's more than that . . ."

Despite the excellent press Helen brought to their company, Central Airlines' male pilots were not supportive of a woman pilot in their midst and refused to admit her into their pilots' association. Soon the federal government's Bureau of Air Commerce— apparently goaded by Helen's male colleagues—made an "informal suggestion" to the airline that perhaps Helen was too weak to fly the twelve-passenger Ford Tri-Motor plane in bad weather. Thanks to the "suggestion" and the refusal of the male pilots to admit her into their union, Central Airlines allowed Helen to fly only a dozen round-trips in over ten months. Frustrated and disappointed, Helen resigned, giving up the dream she had worked so hard to achieve.

At the time, Amelia Earhart spoke out about Helen's predicament and the pilots' union's refusal to allow such a qualified pilot to join their ranks "not because of lack of ability, but because she was female." Earhart called for the creation of a fund to "help woman to gain her proper place in aviation." Suffragette Alice Paul picked up Helen's cause as well, lambasting the Department of Commerce for having made "Miss Richey's position as co-pilot impossible." But despite the support, Helen was done flying for the airline, and it would be another four decades before a regularly scheduled airline would hire another woman pilot.

Although Teresa and Helen became good friends and allies, there was one significant difference between them: While Helen had financial support from her family, Teresa did not. Helen's father was the superintendent of her local school district, and although her family was not exceptionally wealthy, they were well-off. When Helen first started flying, her father bought her a four-seater plane, which she was able to use to start her career as a stunt pilot. Helen's financial cushion also allowed her to enter air races, giving her the chance to win substantial financial prizes and a measure of fame. Teresa was competitive by nature, whether she was skating, dancing, or playing tennis, and would have loved to join the world of women's racing alongside Helen. But without a plane or a sponsor, the sport remained out of her reach. Being a woman pilot was hard enough; being a woman pilot without money or connections was even harder.

While Teresa was never afforded an opportunity to race in the 1930s, she did continue to make a living from flying. Although the aviation industry restricted the jobs that were available to women—as evidenced by Helen's attempt to fly for the commercial airlines—one out of five women pilots in the 1930s did manage to turn flying into a profession. These women tended to find jobs as flight instructors—essentially teachers, a culturally accepted role for women—but they also worked as aerial photographers; fixed-base operators, providers of fuel, minor repairs, weather information, and other flying services; or saleswomen peddling planes. For her part, Teresa decided to become a flight instructor. By the summer of 1939 she had earned her commercial license and was able to support herself with a relatively steady income. The following year she decided to train in Buffalo, New York, to teach others to fly.

In Buffalo, Teresa was the only woman in the instructors' ground school and, as she later remembered, "the guys weren't too friendly." Despite her easygoing nature and knowledge of flying, the men shut her out of their conversations. They weren't interested in having a woman join them, whatever her experience. Teresa went home from class each night and hit the books for the next day, knowing she had to be twice as prepared as the male students in order to prove herself. In July 1940, all her hard work paid off and she earned her primary instructor rating. After that, Teresa had long lines of students signing up for classes and went back for her advanced instructor rating so she could teach inverted flying. She soon spent some of her time teaching Dink advanced maneuvers.

That same summer of 1940 marked a significant turning point in America's attitude toward the conflict in Europe. Until now, the isolationist viewpoint had prevailed—with the majority of the American public preferring to stay out of the fight. Then, in May 1940, Germany began its invasion of France. Within six weeks it was complete. In June the British stood alone after having barely escaped with their lives at Dunkirk. In July the four-month-long Battle of Britain began in the air over the English Channel. At this point the United States shifted its foreign policy, doing as much as it could to help Britain remain standing short of sending men to fight.

Dink soon joined Teresa in her flight instruction duties, preparing as many pilots as possible for what everyone feared was

America's now inevitable entry into the war. Teresa and Dink both flew sunup to sundown, doing whatever they could to be ready. Days after the Japanese attack on Pearl Harbor, Dink enlisted, and within weeks he left for training. Seven months later Teresa received her telegram from Nancy Love inviting her to join the group of women pilots in Wilmington. On September 17, 1942, Teresa returned to Pittsburgh's train station, this time leaving for her own part in the war.

Some of the first women pilots for the AAF pose for the cameras in a September 1942 media shoot in Wilmington. From left to right, back row: Aline Rhonie, Helen Mary Clarke, Teresa James, Adela Scharr. Front row: Esther Nelson, Cornelia Fort, Betty Gillies, Catherine Slocum. *Courtesy Getty Images*

CHAPTER TWO

The Experiment Begins

Teresa had been home only a few weeks since her wedding to Dink in Colorado; now she was getting her chance to fly for the Army, too. As she watched the glass and steel of the train platform disappear into the distance behind her, it wouldn't have been lost on Teresa that if Dink had waited just a bit longer before enlisting, he would have been in the Ferry Command, too, and they might have served together.

On the three-hundred-mile journey east to Wilmington, Teresa decided to pass the time by starting a diary. "Here I am on my way and I still don't believe they will let us ferry airplanes for Uncle Sam!" she wrote. "Could it be that I lack faith? Imagine it.

The Spirited Woman, Powder Puff pilots, Bird Women, Sky Menaces trying to get in the Army. Well, at any rate: WHEREAS, they have decided to let us try, be it resolved that come hell, high water and insulting criticism, we will not let Washington down. Amen."

After finally arriving in Wilmington station, she made straight for the Hotel DuPont downtown. At thirteen stories, the DuPont was the grandest hotel in the city, and as Teresa stood in its vast lobby under the gilded ceiling, she was nervous. She had seen photographs of the women's commander, Nancy Love, but she had never met her before, and she didn't know anything about Colonel Baker or very much about the Ferry Command. With her 2,200 hours of flight time, she was well over the 500-hour minimum required for the new program, but even so, she wondered if she would make the grade. Teresa spent a worried, mostly sleepless night, waking before dawn and looking out over the quiet city, marveling at the fact that a place that had made the first iron sailing vessel and the first steamship was about to be home to another first: a women's ferrying squadron. Teresa just hoped she would be one of the chosen ones.

At 6:30 A.M. she went down to the hotel coffee shop, where she met fellow hopefuls Aline Rhonie and Helen Mary Clark. Aline was a well-known aviator and fine artist who had recently completed a 106-foot-long mural of aviation history at Roosevelt Field near Garden City, Long Island, and had only just returned from war-torn France, where she had driven ambulances and flown to raise funds for the war. Helen Mary was a married mother of two from New Jersey who was good friends with Nancy Love and had been flying for over eight years. As the three women shared a cab to the nearby New Castle Army Air Base, Helen Mary tried to reassure Teresa that she had nothing to worry about. But Teresa still found herself "afraid I'll be afraid."

At the base, Teresa was ushered into a room where she met with Nancy Love, Colonel Robert Baker, and other staff from the Ferry Command. Teresa handed over her paperwork and waited as Nancy Love and Colonel Baker reviewed her logbooks and asked her questions in order to determine if she would be a good fit for Army flying. Teresa was immediately struck by Nancy's beauty and her warmth. Nancy was a pale, youthful blonde, with almond-shaped eyes and long, elegant fingers that she moved around as she spoke. Something about her calm, smiling demeanor settled Teresa's nerves.

After passing the interview, Teresa was told she still had to undergo a flight check in order to win her place in the squadron. Her check ride was scheduled for 11:00 A.M., and she struggled to fill the time as she waited. In the hope of distracting herself, she wrote in her diary:

> This Base is new and not at all what I had expected an Army Base to be. Buildings and roads are under construction and mud is knee-deep all over the place. I don't know what I expected, probably old red brick buildings with ivy clinging all over . . . Nancy Love is everything I thought and more! Beautiful, capable and charming. Wish she would show up right now. Twice already she has put me at ease, and I could stand it again.

Teresa hoped with "fear and trembling" that she wouldn't have to fly the strange, low-winged aircraft she saw in the distance. When her turn finally came, she was relieved to discover her check ride would be in a Taylorcraft L-2B Grasshopper, a lightweight liaison and reconnaissance plane in which she had 115 hours of experience flying. A Lieutenant Saccio was her check pilot, but he did little to relieve her anxiety as he climbed into the seat behind her. Strictly professional, he didn't indulge in chitchat, instructing Teresa to climb to 2,500 feet before beginning a standard test including "lazy eights" (two 180-degree turns in opposite directions), chandelles (180-degree turns combined with climbs), power stalls, 720-degree turns, and more. Teresa felt good about her performance, but as she landed and rolled to a stop, Saccio climbed out without a word.

Her check ride completed, Teresa made her way to Colonel Baker's office, where she sat outside "sweating out a couple of eternities" until Nancy finally called her into the room. There, Baker told her she had indeed passed, and Teresa felt a rush of pure relief. Nancy welcomed her into the program, making Teresa the eighth woman to join the newly formed Women's Auxiliary Ferrying Squadron, or WAFS.

That afternoon Teresa met some of her fellow recruits, including Cornelia Fort, the debutante from Nashville who had barely escaped the attack at Pearl Harbor. Since that horrifying day, Cornelia had been traveling the country, telling her story and raising tens of thousands of dollars for the war effort. Like Teresa, Cornelia had received Jackie Cochran's invitation to join her in England, but she couldn't get back to the mainland in time. When she finally received her telegram from Nancy Love inviting her to join the WAFS, she wrote in a letter to her mother: "The heavens have opened up and rained blessings on me . . . The army is going to let women ferry ships and I am going to be one of them."

Then there was Betty Huyler Gillies, "a wee person with the merriest blue eyes," as Teresa described her in her diary. At five foot one and one hundred pounds, Betty was one of the smallest pilots in the group but also one of the most experienced and well-known, having served as a president of the Ninety-Nines, the organization for women pilots founded by Amelia Earhart and her friends. Although Teresa could not have realized it on first meeting, Betty's sunny demeanor masked a deeper sadness. The previous winter Betty had lost her youngest child, only four years old, to leukemia. With the support and encouragement of her husband and mother-in-law, who moved in to take care of her other children, Betty decided to join the WAFS. It would be a way to support Nancy and her fellow women pilots—and perhaps a welcome distraction from her grief.

That same day Teresa also met Adela Scharr, a policeman's daughter and former schoolteacher from St. Louis, Missouri. The two women quickly discovered they had something in common: they both had husbands in the armed forces. When Nancy's telegram arrived, Adela's husband, Harold, had been getting ready to ship out with the Navy. Adela had leapt at the chance to serve along with him.

After passing an Army physical to confirm she was healthy enough for military flying, Teresa headed to the subdepot and spent the next three hours drawing her equipment. Like all the new recruits, she received a flying jacket, helmet, goggles, boots, and coveralls— gear that was clearly designed for men, as it didn't really fit. "I never was sure of my size," Teresa wrote in her diary later that day. "Now I never will be. If those coveralls are a 36, I am evidentally [*sic*] a size 13½."

That same afternoon Nancy showed Teresa where she'd be living for the next few months. The women were assigned to BOQ 14, short for Bachelor Officer Quarters—yet another reminder that the women were filling roles originally intended for male pilots. Construction on the building was barely finished, and the women had to teeter across a series of planks laid across a drainage ditch to get into their barracks without falling into the mud. Light shone through the cracks in the pine-board-and-tar-paper walls. Nancy apologized for the Spartan surroundings, reassuring Teresa that it wouldn't be so rough forever and that she was working to improve their living conditions. In the meantime Teresa chose a corner room on the second floor, furnished with an iron chair, a cot with an Army blanket, a simple maple bureau, and a pine wardrobe. Before falling asleep that night, she made a final entry for the day in her diary:

THINGS I BET I NEVER FORGET: Astonishment at the sunlight peeking through cracks in the walls of my room in the BOQ . . . the sagging of the cot and the sheer discomfort of the one iron chair . . . Sensation of sitting on one side of a closed door while your destiny is being tossed about on the other side . . . Relief when Colonel Baker said I was accepted for training . . . Friendliness I saw registered in Adela Scharr's large eyes . . . I look forward to knowing these girls better. From all appearances and conversations, I do not have my doubts.

The Army Air Forces had decided that the main mission of the WAFS was going to be ferrying light aircraft from the factories where they were produced to the Army bases where they were needed. In the wake of the Pearl Harbor attack, President Franklin D. Roosevelt had demanded new production goals from America's aircraft manufacturers: 60,000 new aircraft in 1942 and 125,000 in 1943. Normally, the task of ferrying all those planes would fall to men from Robert Baker's ferrying division, which hired male pilots as civilians and, after ninety days of probation, commissioned them into the AAF as second lieutenant service pilots. Now those pilots were being called to serve overseas, and the women of the WAFS were stepping up to fill their shoes.

From the beginning, there was confusion about where the women fit within the structure of the AAF. Unlike their male counterparts, the women were considered civilian pilots, employed under civil service rules, despite having "Squadron" in their name. They also had to meet a higher bar for admission, with more experience and education than was asked of men—and initially received lower pay. But the Ferrying Division repeatedly emphasized the equality of the position: the women pilots would have the same privileges and responsibilities as U.S. Army Air Forces officers.

It soon became clear to Teresa that reality was a bit more complicated. Despite being among the most accomplished pilots in the country, she and her fellow WAFS still had to prove they were worthy. The women spent the next thirty days demonstrating they were competent enough to pilot the light trainers—small, forgiving planes generally used for beginners—that the AAF was allowing them to fly. Nancy Love had required WAFS pilots to have a 200-horsepower rating, but many of these planes had engines as low as a 40 horsepower—similar to the Piper Cub that Teresa had more than 1,000 hours of experience flying, and the Interstate Cadet that Cornelia had used to teach her flight students. In other words, the women were incredibly overqualified.

Life on base took more adjustment. Mornings began with breakfast at 6:30 A.M. in the officers' mess, followed by standing formation and roll call at 8:00 A.M. and not a minute later. After roll call, the women went off to flight training, where they reviewed standard flight maneuvers and cross-country navigation. When not flying, they sat in a classroom learning about meteorology, navigation, and military communication. The women were also schooled in military courtesy, military forms, and military laws, and were even made familiar with a .45 pistol. If they were to live on military bases and fly military planes, they needed to be fluent in every aspect of Army life. Altogether they would receive nearly a hundred hours of instruction—far more than the men on base. As much as Nancy hoped her pilots would be treated as equals of the men, she was even more determined to make certain they would be ready.

Although the women's living quarters left something to be desired, the location had its perks: a new officers' club had conveniently opened right next door. The club soon became an end-of-day gathering place for the WAFS, and the squadron members were welcomed there from the beginning, each one allowed to keep her own bottle behind the bar. Needless to say, the women attracted a certain amount of attention at the club, which was frequented by male officers. Teresa later remembered the officers' heads turning, especially when Nancy made her entrance, cigarette in hand. With her regal beauty, she was known for stopping men in their tracks.

Not long after arriving in Wilmington, Teresa was about to turn in after a quick drink at the club, when Nancy Love and Betty Gillies called out to her, inviting her to come up to one of their rooms for a nightcap. Until then Teresa had been a little in awe of the two women, who, in addition to being well-known in aviation circles, were close friends. That evening Nancy, Betty, and Teresa, along with three other women from the WAFS, sat around on the bed, side chair, and floor, chatting and getting to know one another. They soon got around to talking about where they were raised and where they went to school.

Nancy had gone to Vassar, and although she dropped out after her first year due to a downturn in family finances, she still carried with her a certain amount of Seven Sisters cachet. Another woman had attended Smith and another had gone to Wellesley. Next it was Teresa's turn. Teresa wasn't rich, and her education had ended after high school; her loving parents had never harbored any expectation that she would go to college. She took a deep breath. "Oh, it was one of the classic schools in Pittsburgh, Pennsylvania," she bluffed. "Unique. A very exclusive school. Thorn Hill. It's well known."

The rest of the women nodded, pretending they'd heard of it. What Teresa didn't tell the others—or at least not until she got to know them much better—was that Thorn Hill was actually a correctional school for boys.

It wasn't until later that Teresa learned that Betty Gillies was an heir to the Huyler's candy fortune, that Helen Mary Clark had married into a well-known New Jersey real estate family, and that another member of the WAFS, Barbara Donahue, was a Woolworth descendant. In fact, the majority of the early WAFS pilots came from upper-class backgrounds, with families who could pay for both their college tuition and their aviation exploits. Fortu nately, when the women were trudging through the rain in mud-stained flight gear, they looked pretty much the same, at least to Teresa. The makeshift bachelor's quarters and ill-fitting coveralls may not have been the most comfortable, but they did have a decidedly equalizing effect.

Nancy Harkness (Love) poses with her plane, not long after earning her pilot's license. She is likely sixteen or seventeen in this photo. *Courtesy Texas Woman's University*

CHAPTER THREE

She Will Direct the Women Pilots

Nancy Love was twenty-eight years old and under tremendous pressure. She knew the success or failure of her squadron would determine the future of women's involvement in the U.S. Army Air Forces, and her handpicked group of pilots did, too. "All of us realized what a spot we were in," Cornelia Fort later explained. "We had to deliver the goods—or else . . . there wouldn't ever be another chance for women pilots in any part of the service."

In total, Nancy had chosen twenty-eight women for her WAFS. Keeping the program small meant she could be highly selective— the women's flight time averaged 1,162 hours, far exceeding the initial requirement of 500 hours—and maintain close control. For their part, the WAFS were pleased to have Nancy as their leader. "No better choice could have been made," Cornelia later wrote. "First and most important she is a good pilot, has tremendous enthusiasm and belief in women pilots and did a wonderful job in helping us to be accepted on an equal status with men."

Indeed, in many ways, Nancy was ideally suited to lead the WAFS. She had caught the flying bug early, at sixteen, while on summer vacation in her hometown of Houghton, Michigan. It was August 1930, and Nancy had been riding her horse, Daisy, near her house, when the sound of a low-flying plane caught her attention. In those days the thrum of a plane overhead was still a novelty, and so she looked up. This was a time when barnstormers were beginning to become a regular sight in towns across America. These young men—and sometimes women—would go from place to place hoping to make enough money to fill their plane with gas and put food in their bellies by selling airplane rides and performing stunts, often flying in old biplanes that were relics from the Great War. Some barnstormers had sponsors to help cover costs: locals could "win" the chance at a flight by buying the sponsor's product. Others depended on charging their passengers for the pleasure of a flight. The pilot who landed near Houghton that day charged a "penny a pound" for a sedate takeoff and landing and five dollars—a significant sum at a time when a loaf of bread might cost a nickel and a new wool sweater only one dollar—for a stunt ride. Nancy stepped down from her horse, gave the barnstormer her pennies for a short ride, and climbed aboard.

Within seconds the plane was accelerating along the bumpy field, and as it lifted up from the ground, Nancy felt herself sink into her seat, a sensation that took her breath away. Suddenly they were aloft. Nancy leaned over the side of the cockpit to see the field fast receding away from her. The pilot banked left as he climbed, then left again so they were flying in the opposite direction, now parallel to the runway. They flew just past the runway before the pilot turned again. As he made his final approach, Nancy watched as the earth rose up to meet her. Then they gently touched down, bouncing until they slowed to a stop.

Nancy knew she wanted more. She quickly found five dollars for the longer flight, and the pilot took her up for a second ride. The sensation of the wind on her face reminded her of being out on her horse, the sheer freedom and exhilaration of riding, but with an even more powerful thrill. The purr of the engine and the rush of the air silenced the world below, the streets of her little town all connected, and she, high in the air, was a part of it all and yet separate. As she grinned back at the pilot, she knew that their view was one few were privileged to see. "A ride in a barnstorming Fleet was my undoing," Nancy later remembered, "and from then on I knew what I wanted."

That evening she went home and told her parents she wasn't going back to boarding school in the fall. Instead she was going to learn to fly. Nancy's mother was not at all pleased with her daughter's declaration. Alice Chadbourne Harkness was a member of a prominent Boston family who had first settled in the area in the 1630s, and she had sent Nancy to Milton Academy back east so that she would get a decent education and then marry well. Flying did not fit at all with Alice's—or society's—idea of what a well-bred young lady should do.

Nancy's father, meanwhile, was the youngest son of Scottish immigrants who had settled in Pennsylvania. Robert Bruce Harkness went to Germany to complete his medical education and had returned to Michigan, where he established a thriving practice. He saw his own spirited independence in his daughter and encouraged it. When Nancy announced that she would fly rather than return to school, Robert found a way to appease both the women in his life. His daughter had less than a month until the start of term, but if she promised to go back to Milton, he would pay for her to learn to fly in the weeks she had left.

Nancy agreed. On August 26, 1930, dressed in riding breeches and boots, she climbed back into a Fleet biplane for her first lesson. Her instructor was eighteen years old and had only recently learned to fly himself. Nancy was his first student and the biplane was "rather broken down . . . with prop held together with tacks." Nancy later remembered the experience as "a classic example of the blind leading the blind . . . but we made it. It was wonderful fun and quite routine at the time. I don't think he knew what made the plane stay in the air. At least he never told me. My instructions were just to 'keep up the flying speed.' " Five days after her first lesson, with only four hours and thirty minutes of flight instruction, Nancy flew her plane solo for the first time.

"I wanted to fly right off, and I just about did," she later explained. "I'm no supergenius, you understand, but I concentrated hard and I learned fast." She garnered twenty-three hours of flying time—nearly ten hours of it solo—before she kept her promise to her father and headed back to Boston. That fall, her mother seems to have either come around to support Nancy's flying adventures or to have realized it was too late to do anything about it. In early November, Alice Harkness accompanied Nancy to Chicago to take her written flight test and then on the short train ride up to Milwaukee, Wisconsin, for her flight test. It was 1930, and at sixteen years old Nancy was officially a private pilot.

Nancy returned to school with her license in hand. By now she was obsessed with airplanes, doodling "Stearman" (a popular airplane at the time) and "Aviation" on her school notebooks. She kept flying as often as she could, becoming notorious at Milton for one adventure in particular. The academy had two separate schools, one for boys and one for girls. On a dare from her older brother, who rode along as her first passenger, she decided to fly low and fast over the boys' part of the academy. Nancy swooped in for the stunt but badly misjudged her timing as she pulled the plane up, rattling the slates from the roof loose and barely making it over the bell tower. She narrowly escaped expulsion, in large part because Milton Academy had rules forbidding the girls only from driving cars, not from flying airplanes.

When she wasn't aloft, Nancy took her studying seriously

enough to be admitted to Vassar College in Poughkeepsie, New York, in the fall of 1931. Soon after arriving, she began lessons at a nearby flight school, determined to earn her commercial license, even though very few women had one. Nancy had already decided to make a career out of flying, and a commercial license, along with the experience and knowledge it brought, would help make that possible. Once she earned the license, she would be able to charge her fellow students at Vassar for joyrides over the Hudson Valley or to transport them from place to place. The very idea that the next level of license just sat there, waiting to challenge her, was likely a strong motivation for someone like Nancy.

Even Nancy's first crash, a serious one in early April 1932, wasn't enough to discourage her flying plans. That day she was flying with her flight instructor, John Miller, in a Great Lakes bi-plane trainer, when the motor quit as they were landing and they ended up in the top of a tree. The plane tipped backward and dropped another thirty feet, landing upside-down over a stone wall. Shaken but miraculously unharmed, Nancy then made the mistake of hastily unbuckling her seat belt. She fell out of the plane headfirst into the stone wall. Nancy walked away with a concussion and a new thin stripe of gray hair she would carry with her for the rest of her life. Three weeks later she headed to New York, where she earned her commercial license, becoming one of only fifty-six women in the United States to achieve that feat. She was eighteen years old.

Nineteen thirty-four marked a turning point for Nancy: the country was in the throes of the Great Depression, and that year it hit the Harkness family hard, leaving no money for Vassar. Nancy dropped out of college and moved to New York, where she attended a secretarial school paid for by a benevolent uncle. Nancy's plan was to learn shorthand, typing, and filing, but she really hoped to find a job as a pilot. She began spending two days a week commuting to Newark Metropolitan Airport to practice flying, writing her uncle, "I do not want to take time away from my studies, but I feel very keenly that I must be in a position to make my own way as soon as possible and to do this I must have a job." She joined the Ninety-Nines and began to network with other pilots, and by April she got a position working for Inter-City Aviation, a small flight service that offered flight instruction, charter flights, aerial surveying, and aircraft sales in Boston.

Nancy's job at Inter-City Aviation was as a saleswoman, demonstrating to customers that the company's planes were so easy to operate "even a woman" could fly them. The owner of the company, Robert Love, had started the business in 1932, the nadir of the Depression, with financial help from his sister Margaret. Bob was the son of a New York banker and after surviving polio as a child had become fascinated with flying. Tall and broad-shouldered with pale blue eyes—Nancy later called him "homely handsome"—he was quickly taken by his new pilot. The feeling was mutual. When the couple announced their engagement in 1935, the newspapers ran the headline "THE ROMANCE OF THE GLAMOROUS YOUNG SOCIETY COUPLE MEETS THE ROMANCE OF THE SKY."

After their wedding in January 1936, Nancy and Bob departed for their honeymoon in their own plane, spending three weeks flying around the West Coast, across to Palm Beach, Florida, and finally home again to Boston. It was on their honeymoon that they experienced their first argument of married life: Bob insisted they had enough fuel to make one of the legs of their flights but Nancy claimed they didn't. In the end they had to make an emergency landing thirty minutes short of their destination when they ran out of fuel. Bob learned that when it came to flying, his new wife was the expert.

Throughout the 1930s, Nancy continued to work as a professional pilot, including stints as a test pilot and in the federal government's air-marking program, an effort to paint navigational signs on rooftops to help other pilots find their way, led by fellow Ninety-Nine Phoebe Omlie. By the end of the decade Nancy was one of the country's most prominent women pilots and the frequent subject of newspaper profiles. A naturally private person who actively disliked having her photograph taken, she was ambivalent about her newfound fame. She avoided being the center of attention and the subject of headlines when she could, preferring to leave the spotlight to air racers and stunt pilots. She hoped that, before long, she and Bob would start a family.

After war broke out in Europe, Nancy and Bob followed the news closely. Everyone who understood aviation knew that more qualified pilots would be needed when the time came for America to join the fight. Some of Nancy's flying friends had already organized a group of aviation clubs encouraging women to fly in preparation for war, and so the part women pilots might be able to play was very much on Nancy's mind. In May 1940—with the Battle of France raging in Europe, and the French and the British struggling to hold their own against the might of the German army—Nancy took her ideas about women pilots to an acquaintance. His name was Lieutenant Colonel Robert Olds, and he worked in the Plans Division of the Office of the Chief of the Air Corps.

Lieutenant Colonel Olds was not quite forty-four years old, with a world of experience behind him. He'd been a pilot ever since joining the Army in 1917 and had helped develop the American bombing strategy for future wars, leading in the 1930s the first operational unit of B-17s, four-engine bombers that would be essential to the war in Europe. Olds was well-known in aviation circles for his own flying, his longtime aviation advocacy—he was a leading advocate for an independent air force—and his initiative and drive. Accustomed to taking risks, he had confidence in his own ideas and was known for making quick decisions, not out of haste or arrogance, but because he had the brilliant ability to look at a problem, analyze it, and make a choice. Perhaps Nancy sensed that Olds would be receptive to her ideas, or perhaps she simply thought it was worth a shot.

Nancy's suggestion to Olds was this: in the event that the United States entered the war, a small group of qualified women pilots might prove very useful to the military.

Olds was intrigued. He asked Nancy to find out what she could about how many women might be available to fly on the home front if men began to be sent away overseas. Nancy quickly began compiling a list of qualified pilots. She placed stars beside the names of those women she knew personally and who "had a good deal of experience in heavier ships, cross-country, etc. . . ."

Nancy was confident in women's ability to do whatever Olds might envision, including work ferrying planes from factories and other domestic flying tasks. "As you see, I've been able to find forty-nine I can rate as excellent material, including the Privates [those holding private licenses]," Nancy wrote. "There are probably at least fifteen more of these whom I don't know about and so haven't starred. I really think this list is up to handling pretty complicated stuff. Most of them have in the neighborhood of a thousand hours or more—mostly more, and have flown a great many types of ships." Nancy starred her own name, recognizing that she met the guidelines she'd held the other women to, but noting with a degree of self-effacing humor: "Incidentally, you can take my name off—I was only obeying orders."

Days after Nancy submitted her report to Olds, news arrived that British and French troops had only narrowly escaped with their lives at the Battle of Dunkirk. Nancy and her husband were horrified by the Nazi advance and wondered how they could help. Together with two other Inter-City Aviation pilots, they joined an effort to transport American planes to aid the French cause. In early June, thirty-three pilots departed Boston and New York in three-month-old Stinson sport planes. They rendezvoused in Houlton, Maine, on the Canadian border. Because laws of American neutrality prevented them from flying into Canada, the pilots climbed out of their cockpits and watched as the planes were towed across the international border by truck. Upon rejoining their aircraft, the pilots then flew to military airfields on the country's Atlantic coast, where they left the planes behind, ready to be sent over to Europe. Nancy and the other pilots returned to New York via steamer. It was exactly the type of ferrying work Nancy and Robert Olds had talked about the month before, and Nancy's participation offered evidence that women pilots really could help in the war effort.

Unfortunately, this time the efforts of these "neutral" ferry pilots were too little, too late. The official surrender of France to Germany on June 22, 1940, was a harsh wake-up call for Americans. The United States recognized that a Europe dominated by a single hostile power was a dangerous possibility, and preparations for war needed to be made. Olds wrote to the chief of the Air Corps, Major General Henry H. Arnold, proposing they hire one hundred women pilots to ferry planes, releasing men pilots for other duties. The Navy was already debating authorizing women to fly as commissioned pilots, Olds wrote. Why not the Army?

Despite the slight smile almost permanently fixed to his face, "Hap" Arnold wasn't as gentle as his mien would suggest. He could be impertinent and contrary, even with superiors. At fifty-five, Arnold was an old-time flier, military-style, and had been a vocal advocate for an independent air force. He had learned to fly at the Wright brothers' flying school in Ohio, taught by Orville and Wilbur themselves, becoming one of the first two men to be trained as a military pilot. In other words, Arnold wasn't just there for the beginning of military aviation; he *was* the beginning of military aviation. Fiercely intolerant of incompetence and failure, he held himself and those around him to a high standard for success.

Whether or not to bring women into the military as pilots was Arnold's call to make. He said no. Despite the growing crisis in Europe, which had spurred the Army to expand the Air Corps by an additional 7,000 pilots per year, the United States was not actually in the war yet and had not made use of all available men. Arnold believed he had no need for women pilots and no time for the logistical challenges integrating them into the Army would bring.

Disappointed but not particularly surprised, Nancy went back to her day job flying for her husband's company, Inter-City Aviation.

After Pearl Harbor, Nancy and Bob found their lives upended. Bob was forced to close Inter-City Aviation when every airfield within fifty miles of the coast was ordered to be shut down. Formerly in the Army Reserves, he had already moved to active duty in the U.S. Army Air Corps before the declaration of war. Now, he was to report to General Robert Olds with the Ferry Command in Washington, D.C.

Both Nancy and Bob were patriotic and ready to serve, but even so, they were sad to leave their home. They had only recently bought an old farmhouse on a leafy, secluded lane just outside Boston and were looking forward to fixing it up and starting a family. In February of 1942, Nancy turned twenty-eight, and although the couple had been married for six years and very much wanted children, she had yet to become pregnant. Now all plans to settle down were put on hold.

In Washington, Bob went to work at the Pentagon. Nancy found a new job opportunity as well. At the suggestion of Robert Olds, she started work as a civilian administrator in the new Domestic Wing of the Ferry Command in nearby Baltimore. Although Nancy was pleased to have the work, for the first time in her professional life she found herself stuck at a desk, pushing paper, mapping ferry flights, and learning about the ways of the military. Out on base, male pilots were getting to fly the latest and greatest planes available, and Nancy, who had always flown for her living, was green with envy. At least she could still fly her commute from D.C. to Baltimore in her own single-engine Fairchild

24, even if that little aircraft paled in comparison to the gleaming new combat planes outside her window.

At the time Nancy began working for the Domestic Wing, the division was brand-new, having only just been established in January of that year. Nancy's boss was a dynamic veteran of World War I named Major Robert H. Baker, who saw that the need for ferry pilots was increasing with every passing day and took steps to meet that demand. In March of 1942, however, Nancy's division underwent a serious upheaval: her ally Lieutenant Colonel Robert Olds suffered a heart attack and was temporarily relieved of duty.

General Harold George took over from Olds while he recuperated. Under his leadership the Ferry Command was reorganized and renamed the Air Transport Command. George brought in C. R. Smith, the former president of American Airlines, as a colonel and his chief of staff to help with the enormous effort of moving thousands of planes and the men to go with them. In the ensuing reshuffle, Nancy's husband, Bob, was promoted to major and made deputy chief of staff for operations. Meanwhile, Colonel William Tunner was given the job of commanding officer of the Ferrying Division. Tunner was younger than Arnold, George, and Olds, energetic, and determined to innovate. He knew it wouldn't be long before pilot shortages would slow or even halt the work of the Ferrying Division, and he was determined to get ahead of the problem.

Tunner worked down the hall from Bob Love in Washington, D.C. One morning the two men were chatting in the hallway of their office, which was housed in an old munitions factory. Bob happened to wonder aloud if his wife had landed safely in Baltimore. It was spring and the weather had been stormy, and Bob hoped her commute hadn't been affected.

"Good Lord," Tunner exclaimed. "I'm combing the woods for pilots, and here's one right under my nose. Are there many more women like your wife?"

"Why don't you ask her?" Bob suggested.

Tunner did.

That June, Nancy began working with Colonel Tunner to bring women pilots into the Ferrying Division. She immediately dusted off the list of pilots she had put together with Olds two years earlier and prepared to sell her plan all over again. Nancy's idea was to put together a unit of fifty skilled women pilots with five hundred hours of flight time, between twenty-one and thirty-five years old, with a high school education at a minimum. These women could then be commissioned as second lieutenants in the newly formed Women's Army Auxiliary Corps (WAAC)—a support arm of the military, which was already recruiting women as cooks, drivers, typists, and clerks—or perhaps directly into the Army Air Forces. Nancy worked quickly and diligently. If she got this right, perhaps she could finally escape her desk job.

Colonel Tunner and General George were equally anxious to get Nancy and other women ferrying planes. American factories were building new aircraft at a frenzied pace, and those planes couldn't just sit idle after they rolled off the assembly line. Tunner called Nancy's old boss, Colonel Robert Baker, now the commanding officer of the Domestic Wing of the Air Transport Command. Baker had recently moved to New Castle Army Air Base in Wilmington, where the 2nd Ferrying Group was stationed. The base, he reported, had housing that would be suitable for the women pilots, including a barracks that was separate from the other buildings and could be converted easily into a women's dormitory. The women could use the new officers' mess, too.

The push to bring women in as military pilots was moving fast, but the most basic of logistical realities soon stalled the program. The barracks where the women were supposed to stay didn't have suitable toilets, as they had been originally designed for enlisted men and had a wall filled with urinals. Modifications would take at least six weeks. More crucially, it turned out that the women couldn't be commissioned via the WAAC as Nancy had originally proposed: among other problems, the bill authorizing the WAAC bill did not include any provisions for women to receive flight pay. Instead, the women pilots would have to be brought in as civilians. This wasn't without precedent: the Ferrying Division was already recruiting civilian men as service pilots, making them second lieutenants after ninety days' probation. Together with her boss, Nancy submitted a detailed proposal for a women pilots' squadron made up of civilians. Although the women would be working for the military, they would not be members of the military per se. Not yet.

Now that they had decided on bringing the women in as civilians, Colonel Baker hurried to solve the housing problem by moving a group of officers out of their quarters with bathrooms that required only "negligible modification" and into the enlisted barracks, promising the men they'd be moved into new planned officers' quarters soon. Nancy and her superiors finally had everything in place. They even came up with a name for this squadron of civilian women pilots: the Women's Auxiliary Ferry Troop, with the fitting acronym WAFT.

Nancy submitted her proposal and waited. Surely there was no longer any reason to delay: everyone knew that ferry pilot shortages were imminent. But in July 1942, General Arnold stalled again. Before any action could be taken to hire women as pilots, he explained, they needed to contact the Civil Aeronautics Authority (CAA) and Civil Air Patrol one last time to make sure that the existing supply of male pilots had been completely exhausted. Only when it was certain that every possible male pilot was already being used would Arnold consider the women. Nancy must have felt exasperated. Why did Arnold continue to delay? At least he seemed to recognize that the time was nearing to bring in women pilots, as he asked General George to estimate how many of them he would need and could reasonably bring on.

At the White House, Eleanor Roosevelt was firmly in support of women flying for the war. On September 1, 1942, in her newspaper column, "My Day," the first lady wrote about the women pilots and their cause: "I believe in this case, if the war goes on long enough, and women are patient, opportunity will come knocking at their doors. However, there is just a chance that this is not a time when women should be patient. We are in a war and we need to fight it with all our ability and every weapon possible. Women pilots, in this particular case, are a weapon waiting to be used." It seemed Arnold, too, was ready to move forward.

Two days later George wrote to Arnold telling him now was the time. He reassured Arnold that plans were sufficiently advanced that they would be able to activate within twenty-four hours. In his memo George was very clear about who would lead the women. It needed to be a woman director who was a qualified commercial pilot "with over 1,200 hours flying experience over a period of twelve years." Just in case there was more than one woman who fit that bill, he added that person should also have worked in the Air Transport Command in administrative roles. If there has ever been a case of a job description being written around the specific qualifications of a favored candidate, this was it. George wanted Nancy Love to lead the women pilots.

On September 5, 1942, Brigadier General L.S. Kuter, deputy chief of air staff, signed approval for the recruitment of the first women pilots to fly for the U.S. military to begin within twenty-four hours. That same day Nancy Love humbly and happily accepted the job as the director of the Women's Pilot Group, an extraordinary promotion for a young civilian administrator. They had a new, easier on the ear name: the Women's Auxiliary Ferrying Squadron, or WAFS. Right away, Nancy began sending telegrams to qualified women pilots, including Teresa James, asking them to report at once to New Castle Army Air Base.

On September 11, 1942, the *New York Times* ran a photograph of Nancy Love wearing a light-colored suit and pillbox hat, holding up one hand as she took her oath of allegiance while using the other one to shake hands with General Harold George of the Army

Air Corps. The headline above the photo read: "SHE WILL DIRECT THE WOMEN PILOTS." By the time the *Times* article appeared, Nancy was already in Wilmington, welcoming the first of her applicants and putting them through their ground tests.

Throughout the summer, Tunner, Baker, and George had urged Nancy to work as quickly as possible to get her program up and running. In this respect, they weren't motivated only by the emergency of war. They had another reason to fast-track the women's flying program. They knew very well that General Arnold had already selected someone else to lead the women pilots when the time came, and they were not at all happy about his choice. This other person was Jacqueline Cochran, and she was currently in England, leading American women flying with the British Air Transport Auxiliary. They wanted to have their program ready—with Nancy installed as leader—before Cochran could arrive back in the United States to stop them.

If men like Tunner, Baker, and George were going to bring a woman into their fold, they wanted her to be an insider, someone who understood the workings of their organization and who wouldn't overstep the rules. Nancy fit the bill in every respect. Not only was she already working within the Ferrying Division, where she'd shown herself to be personable and graceful in her dealings, but, thanks to her husband, she also socialized with the men after hours. They knew they could get along with her.

Jackie Cochran was an entirely different prospect.

Jacqueline Cochran, with her many aviation trophies, shortly after returning from flying the Lockheed Hudson bomber to England. *Courtesy Getty Images*

CHAPTER FOUR

Outstanding Woman Flier of the World

Jacqueline Cochran was famous. Even with war raging in Europe, her exploits were rarely out of the headlines. A glamorous curly-headed blonde (and sometimes redhead) with large brown eyes, Jackie had first learned to fly in 1932, soon discovering she had a formidable talent for air racing. Throughout the 1930s, Jackie competed regularly in all of the major air races, setting multiple records, including the world's unlimited speed record for women in 1937. Married to the millionaire tycoon Floyd Odlum, one of the richest men in America, she had a constant source of funding and support for her often expensive flying adventures as well as for her company, Jacqueline Cochran Cosmetics. Since the death of her close friend Amelia Earhart, Jackie had stepped into Earhart's shoes, eventually becoming the leader of the Ninety-Nines, the organization her friend had helped to found.

Jackie wasn't shy about her accomplishments, either. When she noticed that the script of a 1940 radio program described her as "one of the world's outstanding woman fliers," she scratched the line out and wrote instead, "the officially recognized world's outstanding woman pilot." When she learned that American women pilots were going to fly for their country—and that Nancy Love was going to lead them—Jackie was furious. The idea that Nancy—someone younger, less notable, and (at least in Jackie's estimation) less worthy—had been given the coveted director's position was unacceptable to Jackie.

Throughout the spring and summer of 1942, Jackie had been in England, leading a group of American women pilots who were serving in Great Britain with the Air Transport Auxiliary, which ferried military aircraft and personnel from factories to air bases and important delivery points on the domestic front. The ATA had been founded soon after the outbreak of war in Europe, and British women had been part of the work since the beginning, flying alongside women from thirteen other nations, including a group of Americans led by Jackie. Jackie had not always been well received while abroad. She had, for example, arrived at the air base in a Rolls-Royce and wearing a fur coat, rankling British pilots who were suffering under the wartime deprivations of gasoline and clothing rationing. Nonetheless, her time in England had proven that she had the necessary skills to put together a group of qualified women pilots to fly for the war and to lead them to success.

For the past two years Jackie had been encouraging the U.S. Army to recruit women pilots and positioning herself to lead them. In January, just before she sent her telegrams recruiting women for England, she had learned that a plan was indeed coming together. Jackie made waves by threatening to pull out of her trip to England so she could lead any American program. Wanting to avoid a diplomatic crisis with an important American ally, General Arnold reassured Jackie that he would wait for her to return from Europe before he mobilized any kind of program for women pilots. When she did come back from her travels, the job of leading the women would be hers.

Now hearing rumors that Nancy was being installed in her place, Jackie made plans to leave England immediately. On September 10, after being delayed by a commander who she later suspected of waylaying her on purpose, Jackie boarded a military plane bound for Washington, D.C. That same day, the War Department announced that the Air Transport Command was establishing a unit for women pilots and that Nancy Love would serve as their leader. Jackie was too late to stop the announcement, but she was determined not to be left out in the cold.

The next day, the *New York Times* published its story on the WAFS, complete with the photograph of Nancy shaking hands with General George of the Air Transport Command. That might have marked the end of Jackie's ambitions to secure a leadership position of her own. But Jackie Cochran was not a quitter. After arriving on her plane from London, she marched into General Arnold's office, reminding him that he had promised her the job. Arnold attempted to placate Jackie, then called in Harold George and his assistant, C. R. Smith. He informed everyone in the room that he couldn't have two separate groups of women flying for the Army Air Forces and ordered them to get together and work something out, making certain that Jackie was included in the new configuration.

The day after this meeting, George sent Arnold a three-page memorandum with his recommendation. As he saw it, there were two options. The first was Nancy Love's newly formed WAFS—up to fifty highly qualified women fliers fully integrated into the larger group of Air Transport Command ferry pilots and considered equal to their male counterparts. The second plan was Jackie Cochran's, and it was much more ambitious. Jackie wanted to take less experienced women pilots, put them through Army flight training, and have them do flying jobs for various commands across the country. She also wanted the women to be segregated, designated as "women pilots" instead of simply "pilots." According to Jackie's research, there were nearly 3,000 women available for this type of work. She wanted to train all of them and then go on and train even more. George worried about logistics. This flight training program of Jackie's would be an extensive undertaking and one the ATC was not interested in or capable of running. In his memo to Arnold, George made it clear that the Air Transport Command preferred Nancy and her plan.

Recognizing Arnold's support of Jackie, George suggested a potential compromise. Neither Nancy nor Jackie would be the sole leader of the women. Instead, Nancy Love could lead the WAFS and Jackie Cochran could be in charge of recruitment and training of less experienced pilots. When Jackie's women completed their training, they would move on to Nancy's group— essentially different stages of the same program, which he hoped would keep both General Arnold and the women happy.

On September 15, the *New York Times* ran a new article, this one announcing Jackie's appointment as director of women's flight training, just as George had proposed. "In this all-out struggle women must more and more take on noncombatant burdens as to free men for combat service," Jackie told the reporter. There was no mention of the wrangling that had gone on behind the scenes.

Jackie and Nancy had been born just a few years apart, at opposite ends of the country. What they had in common was their love of flying and desire to lead women pilots during wartime. In almost every other way, they couldn't have been more unlike. Nancy was coolheaded and personable, but she had an ambitious, passionate streak and could be stealthy and strategic in achieving her own aims. Jackie, meanwhile, was a born fighter, hungry for attention and unabashed about seeking it, someone who often ruffled feathers and made enemies in the pursuit of her goals. Whereas Nancy's class background smoothed her way wherever she went, Jackie's path was very different. Throughout her life, she'd had to fight for the gentle acceptance that was Nancy's birthright.

These two women would never have described themselves as friends, but there is no doubt they knew each other, even before the war. As women pilots, they moved in the same aviation circles and they were both members of the exclusive Long Island Aviation Country Club. Located in Hicksville, New York, in the 1930s and '40s the club was the epicenter of social activities for a moneyed class who loved to fly. It was similar to a regular country club, with a pool and tennis courts, but instead of playing golf, its members all flew airplanes. Those members included many of America's elites: several du Pont heirs, Marshall Field III (heir to the Marshall Field empire), Henry Sturgis Morgan (grandson of J. P. Morgan and cofounder of Morgan Stanley), as well as aviation greats such as Charles Lindbergh, Walter Beech, and L. R. Grumman. The social scene at the club was a heady mixture of power and pleasure, and Nancy Love fit in easily. Nancy had a sophisticated elegance and charming personality that drew people to her with little effort.

Jackie's experience of the club would have been very different. No one could have failed to notice the more famous Jackie whenever she swooped into the room, but, even so, she had to work much harder for acceptance. Despite her attempts to hide her Southern accent, Jackie's voice retained a twang that marked her as someone who didn't belong. What's more, Jackie had married into the wealth of her husband, Floyd Odlum, who had been nicknamed "the Farmer" by his fellow Wall Streeters due to his own humble beginnings. As such, Jackie and her husband were forever considered "new money."

When people who knew Jackie and Nancy describe them, they

often mention their hands. Nancy gesticulated with her hands as she spoke; they were long-fingered, feminine, and lovely. Her hands confirmed that she was a "lady," someone with breeding and refinement, even in times of her life when she didn't have any money. Jackie rarely wore rings, although she had a giant diamond from Floyd that she wore when she wanted to emphasize her power, and often seemed to hide her hands, which were large and strong with short nails, the hands of a woman who had done physical work since a very young age. No matter what Jackie did or how wealthy and successful she became, her hands sent a message to people about where she was from and what she had left behind. Her upbringing was as different from Nancy's as can be imagined.

Throughout her life, Jacqueline Cochran spun stories about her past, telling people she was an orphan adopted by foster parents to obscure her true origins. In fact, she was born Bessie Lee Pittman on May 11, 1906, in Muscogee, a small town in the Florida Panhandle. Her father, Ira Pittman, was a dirt-poor millwright whose work in the sawmills took him from one Florida or Alabama logging camp or mill town to another. Her mother, Mary "Mollie" Pittman, also worked in the factories, or wherever she could. Bessie grew up in towns without electricity or paved streets, dropping out of school for good at eight years old. She was often hungry as a child and wasn't above stealing potatoes, corn, or squash from nearby gardens, or even a neighbor's chicken for a little meat to add to the family pot.

When the family moved to a company town in Georgia named Bibb City, Bessie began working at the mill, making six cents an hour. Although the men at the mill pinched her and touched her in all the wrong places, Bessie was a fighter. She was also a smart worker and quickly was promoted. By age nine she was supervising other children in the inspection of cloth and making just over $5 per week. From an early age she knew that money could get you what you needed as long as you had power to go along with it. Once, when she won a pretty china doll as a prize in a raffle, buying the tickets with her own money, her mother took the doll from her, said she was too old for it, and gave it to Bessie's two-year-old niece. Bessie never forgave her mother, and many years later, after she had changed her name to Jackie Cochran—transforming herself into the aviator and businesswoman of legend—she offered to pay to maintain the Pittman family if they gave her the doll back. They did.

At the age of ten, Bessie started working for a family who owned three beauty shops, learning the tricks of the beauty trade, making wigs, helping with the permanent waves, giving shampoos, and running errands. Soon she graduated to operating a permanent-wave machine in a department store salon in Montgomery, Alabama. That same year Bessie learned she was pregnant. She was fourteen years old.

Little is known about Robert Cochran, the father of Bessie's child. Some sources say he was a twenty-year-old salesman; others suggest he was twenty-four and worked as a machinist. We do know they were married in Georgia, a state that would allow a fourteen-year-old girl to marry with parental consent—or perhaps Bessie had lied about her age—and that, three months later, on February 21, 1921, their son Robert Cochran, Jr., was born. Jackie left her son with her parents and went back to work in Montgomery, visiting when she could. Then, in late May 1925, Jackie's son died while playing alone in the backyard at his grandparents' home in DeFuniak Springs, Florida. He was just four years old and lit some paper with a match he'd found. The paper set fire to his clothes, and within moments he was engulfed in flames. They buried him in the cemetery just east of town under a small, heart-shaped headstone. Bessie stayed with her family for a time, then fled once again to become a new woman and to start a new life.

By twenty Bessie was divorced and working to build her reputation and business as a beautician. It was at this point that she decided two things: She was going to move to New York. And she was going to change her name. In 1929, at the age of twenty-three, Bessie took the money she'd saved and boarded a train bound for New York City. She left Florida as Bessie Pittman Cochran. By the time she arrived at Grand Central Terminal, she had decided on a new name: Jacqueline Cochran. Why she kept her ex-husband's name, nobody knows. What is clear is that she was determined to wipe out the past altogether. For the rest of her life, she never spoke of her son publicly. She simply blocked him out. The day Jackie arrived in New York, illiterate Bessie Pittman ceased to exist and sophisticated and ambitious Jacqueline Cochran appeared. She began telling people she was an innocent, hardworking orphan who had picked her name out of a phone book because her "foster family's name wasn't really mine anyway." Jackie hadn't just arrived in New York with a new name; she had arrived with a new history. The stories she told about herself for the next fifty years were designed to obscure her origins completely.

In New York, Jacqueline Cochran went in search of a job and landed at Antoine de Paris, a Saks Fifth Avenue salon founded by the celebrity hairdresser Monsieur Antoine, whose clients included Coco Chanel and Greta Garbo. Before long, Antoine decided to send Jackie to Miami for the winter season. She had clearly proven herself to be among the best on his staff, and he trusted her to keep his Florida clientele happy. In Miami, Jackie began socializing with her clients, moving in sophisticated circles. She began to affect an aristocratic tone to her speech, imitating the mannerisms of those to whose station she aspired, rejecting her Southern origins even further. She was desperately trying to fit in—and stand out, seizing any opportunity for money or fame. By the early 1930s she saw those opportunities in aviation.

Jackie learned to fly as part of a bet. She had been at a party at a Miami hot spot, hosted by one of her clients, when she met the millionaire tycoon Floyd Odlum. Like Jackie, he'd grown up poor, picking berries to eat and digging ditches; once he'd even ridden an ostrich in a race to win a few dollars. Floyd had built his fortune from nothing and, after anticipating the stock market crash of 1929, became one of the few people who actually made money during the Great Depression, generating millions for himself by speculating in utilities and general securities. He was also married.

That night, Jackie told Floyd she was thinking about taking a traveling sales position with a cosmetics company as a way to see the country and "be out in the air." Floyd wondered if the best way to beat the competition covering the sales territory might be *in the air*. What if she learned to fly? Jackie thought about it, imagining herself soaring over the competition, beating them to the next town, and outselling them before they even had a chance to knock on the first door. Eager to begin, she told Floyd that she would learn to fly and earn her pilot's license during her six-week vacation from the salon. Knowing it usually took three months to earn a license, Floyd liked her spark and promised to pay the cost of the license if she actually succeeded. Jackie accepted his wager.

Jackie took her first flying lesson in July 1932 at Roosevelt Field on Long Island. She was twenty-six and didn't have time for frivolous novelties. Some of her clients were members of the exclusive Long Island Aviation Country Club and she'd heard tales of their exploits. She had a vision for what her life could be: bigger, grander, and more successful, putting her at the center of an elite crowd. Learning to fly could help her achieve that, and the quicker she managed it, the better.

Only a week after her first lesson, Jackie was allowed to "solo" the plane for the first time. Before she knew it, she was soaring up in the clouds, looking down on Long Island below, feeling the intoxicating, adrenaline-fueled surge of power and independence that comes from being the only one in control, the sole master of a machine aloft alongside the birds. "There are so many wonderful things one can see while flying that earthbound souls miss," Jackie later wrote. For the rest of her life, she would seek the thrill, the freedom, the speed, and the escape of flying.

On August 11, Jackie passed her flight test, just seventeen days and fifteen hours of flight time after she had begun her training. But she still had to pass the written test, not an easy task for someone who had dropped out of school at age eight and struggled to read and write. Hard work had gotten her this far, but now she needed to draw on her powers of persuasion. Talking the examiner into an oral rather than written exam, Jackie passed the test, and on August 17, 1932, she earned private pilot's license No. 1498. "It was a thrilling thing," she would say later. Her reward for her success came in part in the form of $495 from Floyd Odlum, who was delighted to make good on his bet with the young beautician. Jackie had earned her license in three weeks and three days.

Overnight, she went from obscurity to the headlines. Stories of girl fliers were popular in the press, which couldn't seem to get enough of the novelty of women flying, and Jackie's speedy license made the pages of the *New York Times*. The reporter wrote that while "most working girls look forward to sleeping late during their weeks away from the job," hardworking Jacqueline Cochran "has set herself the task this summer of becoming a licensed pilot in three weeks . . . for there is a bet with a friend involved." She was having, according to the report, "the time of her life." Jackie had seen the fame and renown that flying had brought other women pilots of the era; it was impossible to miss. They were given ticker-tape parades, their names in the headlines of the papers and their faces on the covers of magazines. Someone like Amelia Earhart sat at the same table as First Lady Eleanor Roosevelt. In a time when there were very few high-level professional opportunities for women, flying offered Jackie a direct path to success. "Flying was now in my blood as a career of its own," she said.

With Floyd's encouragement and financial support, she quit her job at Antoine de Paris and reached for more. Jackie began competing in air races in 1933 and the following year launched Jacqueline Cochran Cosmetics, with its "Wings to Beauty" line. With Floyd's financial help, she leased an office on Fifth Avenue, near Rockefeller Center, along with a laboratory. She also hired a cosmetic chemist and opened a salon on North Michigan Avenue in Chicago. Even with the country still deep in the Great Depression, Jackie began her business in full force and with the complete expectation that it would be a success—as she did everything else in her life. Now she had an even greater reason to race and win: to promote herself and her beauty business.

In 1935, Floyd's wife finally divorced him on grounds of cruelty, ending his twenty-year marriage. He was relieved she did not name Jackie in the divorce papers. The following year Jackie and Floyd were married on Jackie's thirtieth birthday, May 11, 1936, at the office of the justice of the peace in Kingman, Arizona. Jackie kept the name Cochran, using Mrs. Floyd Odlum only when it suited her.

Floyd and Jackie had very different personalities—he was unpretentious and witty and disliked publicity, while she was ambitious, dramatic, and attention-seeking—but they were a good match. Although in many ways they lived in separate worlds, with Floyd focused on his business dealings and Jackie always running from one place to another, they idolized each other, and Floyd became the biggest booster of Jackie's flying career.

Jackie also became close friends with Amelia Earhart. The two women met through mutual friends and, within days of their first encounter, Earhart asked Jackie to fly cross-country with her in her new Electra plane to pre-position it for the upcoming Bendix Trophy Race. Bad weather and a poorly running plane meant that the trip took two weeks, offering the women plenty of time to bond. "Those first few days with Amelia gave me an opportunity— even more than in the months that followed—to get to know her well," Jackie recalled, "and to know her was to love her."

Amelia often visited Jackie at the desert ranch she had bought with Floyd in the Coachella Valley of Southern California, and the two women competed against each other in the major air races. Over the brief years of their friendship, they often spoke about what would happen if one of their planes went down in a remote area. Jackie believed she had the gift of extrasensory perception, so that in the event Amelia had to crash-land, Jackie would be able to pick up the coordinates of her location via psychic messages. The women carried out a number of tests, with Jackie apparently accurately pinpointing landing locations while Amelia was on her cross-country flights. When Earhart decided she wanted to circumnavigate the globe, Jackie warned against it, arguing with Earhart's husband that Amelia was taking on too much. Jackie knew Earhart's navigator, Fred Noonan, and thought he was qualified, although she worried about the rumors that he had been fired from Pan American for alcoholism. In any case, she believed it was too ambitious to expect Noonan to find tiny Howland Island in the middle of the ocean with the navigational aids available at the time. Jackie claimed to have told Amelia in no uncertain terms that it was a suicidal trip.

After Jackie learned that Amelia's plane had gone missing over the Pacific during the final leg of her trip, Jackie did her best to use her powers of perception to find her. For the first few days Jackie was convinced that she knew where Amelia had gone down, that her friend was still alive, and that the plane was afloat. "I followed the course of her drifting for two days . . . ," Jackie remembered. "On the third day I went to the cathedral and lit candles for Amelia's soul which I then knew had taken off on its own long flight." Jackie spoke at Amelia's memorial, saying, "The Amelia I knew was soft, sweet, educated, refined and a rather shy person—feminine, able and without fear." Jackie knew she would miss Amelia, one of the very few women who seemed to understand her.

A month later Jackie flew in the Bendix race, the only female racer to enter that year. She placed third, ahead of Amelia's fifth place the year before, winning not only the women's prize of $2,500 but another $3,000 for the feat. That September she won the world's unlimited speed record for women, flying 301.66 miles per hour in an airplane designed by the Russian pilot and airplane designer Alexander de Seversky. The same month, she set another speed record for a flight from New York to Miami, beating Howard Hughes's record from the year before by eight minutes. For these achievements Jackie was awarded the highly competitive and prestigious Harmon Trophy established by real estate developer and aviator Clifford B. Harmon. Past winners had included Charles Lindbergh, Amelia Earhart, Wiley Post, and Louise Thaden. Now Jackie was about to enter their ranks. In just five short years she had gone from trainee pilot and beautician to prominent businesswoman and award-winning pilot. Flying had afforded her everything she craved: escape, excitement, recognition, and power.

There's a photograph from April 4, 1938, taken at the White House, the day that First Lady Eleanor Roosevelt presented Jackie with the Harmon Trophy. In the photograph, Jackie is shaking Mrs. Roosevelt's hand and looking determinedly in the first lady's direction. She's wearing a swipe of red lipstick and a stylish, tailored, dark-colored coat with wide lapels, her curling blond hair tucked under a matching hat set on her head at an angle. By winning the award, she had reached the pinnacle of aviation achievement.

Standing directly behind Jackie in the photograph, looking over her left shoulder, is another woman, slightly younger, with sloping eyes, blond hair, and a refined beauty. She is Nancy Love, a guest at the event. While Jackie is center stage, Nancy is looking off to one side, quietly observing Jackie's moment of triumph from the background.

The following year, in the spring of 1939, Jackie won her second Harmon Trophy for "outstanding woman flier of the world for 1938."

These two visits to the White House brought Jackie a new and valuable connection, Eleanor Roosevelt. Soon the elementary school dropout from the Florida Panhandle was exchanging letters with the First Lady herself. Jackie knew Mrs. Roosevelt was a longtime supporter of women in aviation and had been good friends with Amelia Earhart. Mrs. Roosevelt had even applied for her student pilot's license, although she was never able to begin lessons; her husband didn't approve.

Immediately following France and Britain's declaration of war on Germany in September 1939, Jackie decided to write to the First Lady with a suggestion. The letter was marked September 28, and it was written from Jackie's lavish townhouse on East Fifty-Second Street in Manhattan. Jackie knew that if America was to join the fight, there would likely be a bottleneck in pilot training. Women pilots could help solve the problem. While the male pilots were occupied with combat flying, Jackie wrote in her letter that America's "lady birds" could do all sorts of helpful "back of the lines work. Every woman pilot who can step into the cockpit of an ambulance plane, or courier plane, or commercial or transport plane can release a male pilot for more important duty."

It is significant that Jackie didn't suggest women should *replace* men—only that they should *release* them. While she wanted women to fly in case of national need, she didn't want it to be at the risk of upsetting the gender hierarchy. Throughout her life and career—despite her own success as a pilot and a businesswoman—Jackie would remain constant in her belief that women should take supportive, traditionally feminine and submissive roles to their male counterparts.

Eleanor Roosevelt received Jackie's letter in the days after the news of the fall of Warsaw to the Germans. On October 11, 1939, the First Lady replied, promising to share Jackie's ideas with the Army, Navy, and Coast Guard. In fact, she shared Jackie's letter with President Roosevelt, too. The secretary of war, Harry Woodring, soon informed the First Lady that, with 25,000 licensed male pilots in the United States, there would be no immediate shortage of pilots for military service and that "the organization of the Air

Corps and the Air Reserve does not provide for or contemplate the organization of units including women pilots." Even if the timing wasn't right for Mrs. Roosevelt to push further, Jackie's idea would not be forgotten.

In June 1941, on General Arnold's recommendation, Jackie began finalizing her plans to fly a Lockheed Hudson bomber across the Atlantic to Britain. The flight would help publicize the need for pilots to fly planes to Great Britain while the United States was still technically neutral. It would also enable Jackie to go on a fact-finding mission in Great Britain, where women had been flying for their country as ferry pilots for the past three years. Lastly, it would make her the first American woman to fly a bomber across the Atlantic Ocean, yet another feather in her cap. (Ultimately, Jackie was able to pilot the plane, but not during takeoff or landing; male ferry pilots had threatened to strike if she did so, arguing that her presence might be dangerous, as the Germans might target her, and that it would hurt the prestige of their work if a woman was allowed to do it.)

In England, Jackie met with one of the leaders of the Air Transport Auxiliary (ATA), Pauline Gower, who had been instrumental in bringing women pilots into the group. Inspired, Jackie returned to New York determined to start a similar operation in America. The morning after her return, she was summoned to the White House for a luncheon. According to Jackie's memoir, after lunch President Roosevelt invited her into his office, where they spoke for over two hours about her trip to England. Jackie was invited to Hyde Park for another meeting with the first lady a few days later.

Not long after her visits to the White House, apparently at the president's request, Jackie attended another meeting in Washington, this time with General Henry H. Arnold; Robert A. Lovett, the assistant secretary of war for air; and Lieutenant Colonel Rob-

ert Olds, head of the Army Air Forces' Ferry Command. The purpose of the meeting was to discuss the possibility of using women
pilots to ferry aircraft during wartime in order to release combat
pilots for duty—the very same idea Jackie had written about in her
letter to Mrs. Roosevelt nearly two years earlier. Jackie left the
meeting that day with a new job. In the coming months she would
serve as "tactical assistant" to Olds, helping him collect data to
determine whether using women pilots to ferry military planes
while male pilots were overseas was actually feasible. Jackie's careful maneuvering seemed to be working.

Olds immediately encouraged Jackie to gather information on
all women pilots in the United States, asking officials at the Civil
Aeronautics Authority (CAA) to allow her to view their files, explaining that he was particularly interested in the one hundred
pilots with more than five hundred hours of flying experience. For
the next several weeks Jackie worked out of Olds's office, bringing
seven of her own clerical assistants from New York to help her
search through thousands of CAA records.

Olds had already put together a list of qualified women pilots
the year before while working with Nancy Love, but he clearly felt
it was necessary for Jackie to complete a more up-to-date list.
While Jackie was working in his office, Olds decided to invite
Nancy Love to meet with them, perhaps hoping that the two
women would get along and collaborate on the project. Nancy,
Jackie, and Olds already knew each other from aviation circles,
and Olds likely felt that talking through their ideas together might
be helpful. It was not.

That day at Olds's office, it quickly became clear that Nancy
and Jackie did not share a vision for the women's flying program.
Nancy wanted a small program of fewer than one hundred highly
experienced women pilots, an elite group that would be able to
step into flying for the military as needed. Jackie wanted something much bigger and more democratic: she wanted to potentially train thousands of women to help with all kinds of flying.

Equally confident, equally stubborn, they were both certain they were right.

Jackie labored for some weeks to craft a successful proposal to incorporate women pilots into the Army Air Forces, even sending a questionnaire to women pilots asking about their willingness to serve. On August 1, 1941, Olds presented his argument to Arnold, pushing forward both Nancy's and Jackie's plans and suggesting Jackie should be hired as chief of women pilots in the Ferry Command. The general was still not ready to bring women into the fold. Jackie was furious. She was sure that Olds had misrepresented the proposal—not realizing he had actually recommended her for the job—and insisted on meeting with General Arnold herself. Arnold reassured her that although he wasn't ready for women pilots yet, when he was, she would be top of his list to lead them.

Only a week later Arnold asked Jackie to return to Washington. He had a new job for her. The British had approached him asking him to recruit qualified American women pilots to assist in the work of the ATA ferry pilots in Great Britain. Anxious to prove herself, she agreed to lead the effort. After months of preparation, on January 23, 1942, she sent her telegram to seventy-six women, telling them that if they were good enough, she had an opportunity for them to do more than knit for the war effort. She had a chance for them to fly. In England, twenty-five American women donned dark blue ATA uniforms, beginning training with Jackie as their "honorary flight captain." Before long, they were ferrying planes to the four corners of the British Isles.

They had been in England for four months when Jackie received word of Nancy Love's impending appointment as the director of the American women pilots, sending her dashing back to the United States to confront General Arnold. At Arnold's urging, General George had created two stages of one women's flying experiment: Nancy's ferrying squadron and Jackie's training program.

It was Arnold who gave Jackie's program its name: the Women's Flying Training Detachment, or WFTD. He also gave Jackie less than two months to get everything organized before training began in mid-November. There was no time to lose. Not only did Jackie have to recruit her women pilots, she had to find instructors to train them, planes for them to fly, and places for them to live—and she had to do it all in a matter of weeks.

Several WAFS prepare for their first ferrying flight in PT-19s, open-cockpit trainer aircraft, in November 1942. Teresa James is third from the right. *USAAF photo. Courtesy Texas Woman's University*

CHAPTER FIVE

Ferry Pilots

Back in Wilmington, Teresa James prepared for her first mission alongside four of her fellow WAFS pilots: Cornelia Fort, Helen Mary Clark, Aline Rhonie, and Adela Scharr. Betty Gillies, who had been recently appointed as Nancy's new executive officer and second-in-command, led the group. The date was October 23, 1942.

The women had officially graduated from training four days earlier, on the nineteenth, and had been cleared for ferry pilot duties. Since then, they had traded in the borrowed coveralls for new gray-green WAFS uniforms, complete with shirt, pants, and cap. As the Ferry Command didn't have any existing patterns for women, Nancy found a tailor in Wilmington to custom-make the uniforms—but it must have been his first time making pants for the feminine body, because when he came to measure Teresa and the other members of the WAFS, he was too afraid to go between their legs to measure the inseams properly. When the women finally received their finished uniforms, the pants were so baggy in the rear that, as Teresa later described, "you could put a watermelon back there with all the excess material."

Teresa was excited to get to work. After thirty days of training and flight checks, she was more than ready. The women grabbed their parachutes and climbed aboard an Army transport plane that was going to take them to Lock Haven, Pennsylvania, home of the Piper Cub factory. It was an appropriate departure point for their first mission: factory owner William T. Piper was a great advocate for women pilots. When they arrived in Lock Haven, the women were surprised to find a crowd waiting. It looked as if the entire factory had come out to greet them on this windy October day. The flight dispatcher was ready for them when they arrived, and after a quick photo op he assigned them to ferry six brand-new light trainers to Mitchel Field on Long Island. After gaining clearance for the flight, the women climbed into the planes and one by one taxied them into position. Despite the 25-knot wind, they each made a precise takeoff and were on their way. As flight leader, Betty Gillies flew at the rear of the group, to watch over the others. Cornelia, as sub–flight leader, was in charge of navigating the group from the front over the Allegheny Mountains, what she later described as an "awe-inspiring" task. As they had planned, the women flew in a V echelon formation, like birds on the wing.

Ferry pilots weren't allowed to fly after dark, and so the women landed before the skies could turn dusky, spending their first RON (remain overnight) in Allentown. Cornelia wrote home, "All of us felt practically historic—the first female ferry pilots to have active duty." Their RON at the hotel was hardly "roughing it," however. The hotel had hot baths rather than cold showers, big soft beds rather than stiff Army cots, and a telephone call to wake them rather than someone pounding on their door. The only downside was that they got to see themselves in their uniforms in a full-length mirror for the first time. "With those ill-fitting uniforms we were certainly the prize," Teresa wrote. "And our spirits fell right on down into our shoes."

The next day the six were up again at dawn. They took off again at 8:00 A.M. to make the short hop from Allentown to Mitchel Field, just east of New York City. Teresa looked down over Manhattan, marveling at all of the buildings, but grew sad as she flew over Roosevelt Field. Once the busiest airport on the East Coast, it was now deserted, closed to all flying because of its proximity to the coastline.

The women arrived at their destination just an hour after taking off to find another crowd. The men at Mitchel Field had heard that women were ferrying the planes and wanted to watch them land. "They probably thought we would ground loop, bounce all over, and run into a couple of buildings," Teresa wrote. "but EVERYONE MADE A PERFECT LANDING!" To celebrate their success, Betty took her pilots to her country club, where they slipped out of their flight suits and into skirts and enjoyed a pre-lunch sherry. It wasn't a long first mission, but it had been uneventful, just as they wanted it to be.

After lunch, Betty Gillies gave the women the afternoon to themselves. Helen Mary took the opportunity to go see her two children in New Jersey. Cornelia called some friends and hurried into New York to attend a concert at Carnegie Hall. Aline dashed away as well, so Teresa and Adela decided to go into New York City to explore. It was Adela's first time in the city, and Teresa showed her the sights, taking her down into the subway, up and down Broadway, and to Radio City and the Rainbow Room. Despite their better-fitting uniform skirts, their outfits still lacked any official insignia, and so they continued to provoke "stares, wild looks and questions" wherever they went, with people trying to guess if they were air-raid wardens, WAACs, Red Cross volunteers, or even Girl Scouts.

Then it was back to the train station for the ride home, their first mission completed. Back at the Wilmington base, the women who had been left behind swore the first six pilots had been gone a week. "It was fun," Teresa wrote in her diary on her return. "In fact so much fun that we were anxious to go right back out the next day."

The next few weeks were spent trying to get their uniforms fixed. Teresa had hers taken in five times, and it still wasn't right. She didn't mind, though—at least, not much. "The thing, I guess, is for each of us as individuals to do our job the very best we can," she wrote. "I love my job. All of us do. The motors make music in their different ways—roaring, droning, purring and growling. They are loud, but they don't say anything they have to explain or apologize for."

Teresa couldn't wait to capture the feeling again.

When it was too rainy or the clouds were too low to fly, the women learned close-order drill, the movements and formations used for military parades and marches. As commander, Nancy was responsible for leading the women and calling out the commands. Unfortunately, shouting was not among Nancy's many talents. The women all knew Nancy dreaded the days when she had to make them march. In the beginning, especially, they didn't usually go well. Not only were the women new to military life and learning the drill formations for the first time, many of them were quite short—at least two were only five feet tall—which made the long strides necessary to stay in line particularly challenging. It wasn't unusual for the male personnel on base to gather to watch and enjoy the "spectacular comedy" of the women struggling with their marching.

Teresa didn't care for the marching much, either. She found the drills boring and tedious, but at least she had experience with them from her time in the Civil Air Patrol. She felt bad for Nancy, who had to "bear the brunt of our zigging when we should have been zagging." It didn't help matters that the fall of 1942 was a particularly wet one. "All I can remember was the miserable rain and mud, mud, mud!" Teresa later recalled. Meanwhile, the base was still under heavy construction, as roads and new buildings went up in every direction. "Things are going awfully fast around here," Teresa wrote in her diary. "Houses, for instance. There are lines drawn in the mud at dawn and inhabited dwellings at sunset. Roads become paved thoroughfares in the twinkling of an eye."

In her corner room, Teresa James found ways to make herself feel at home. She decorated the place with a lamp, comfortable sheets, and a nice bedspread from her mother; a chaise longue from home, and the RCA radio that Dink had given her as a birthday present. Before long, she had fancied up the place so nicely she began calling it the "Waldorf Astoria." When pilots came in after a long flight, they'd often stop by the "Waldorf." Like most of the women, Teresa always kept a bottle of something in her room so that she could make herself and the other girls a cocktail. Then they'd sit together on the bed, catching up and describing the day—where they'd been, how the aircraft had handled, what the weather had been like along the way—with cigarettes and drinks in hand.

Whenever Teresa could—and if she didn't have to get up at 5:00 A.M. to leave for a flight—she went out dancing. Back home she was known as an excellent marathon dancer, an expert at the jitterbug. Often Teresa and a group of the women pilots would land somewhere en route to deliver a plane, and if it looked like the weather would keep them grounded, they'd go out jitterbugging for the night. Although Teresa missed having her Dink as a partner, she wasn't going to let the fact that he was training out in California stop her. Dancing gave her a pure form of release, and she loved it almost as much as she loved flying.

It was dancing that got Teresa in trouble with Nancy Love. One morning, she was told to see Nancy in her office right away. Apparently, Nancy had received a report that Teresa had been out dancing with another woman. Teresa gladly admitted it was true. Her younger sister Betty, a pilot herself, had come to visit, and the two had gone out together. Nancy admonished her, insisting that dancing with someone of the same gender "wasn't proper" and "was not the thing to do." Teresa was flummoxed. "Back in Pittsburgh, we did it all the time," she later recalled. "A lot of the guys won't dance. The only way the women can get out on the floor is to dance with each other." But Nancy firmly asked Teresa to be more careful about appearances when in public.

The reality was that Nancy was under a huge amount of pressure. She had watched as the Women's Army Corps struggled to fight public sentiment that the women in the military were either prostitutes or lesbians—as far as the American public was concerned, the two were equally indecent—and knew that anything that fed that perception could mean the end of the already tenuous program.

It didn't help that the women of the WAFS were under near-constant surveillance by the press. From the week they arrived in Wilmington, the media was fascinated by their every move. As they began flying more and more, they became even more newsworthy. Initially, the Army Air Forces resisted requests from the media, concerned that if the program failed, it would be harder to simply move on and forget it had ever happened if it had been widely publicized. But as the women began to prove themselves, the Army saw an opportunity for positive headlines. In 1943, over a dozen stories about the WAFS appeared in national magazines and newspapers. Film crews were dispatched to make newsreels about the women, which were shown at local movie theaters.

In early December, reporters with *Look,* a semi-monthly competitor to *Life* magazine with more than 2 million subscribers during the war, came to the base. They spent about eight hours taking pictures of the "girls" in their winter gear—which weighed about twenty-five pounds—standing next to their planes, plotting courses on the maps, drinking coffee together. They even took a photograph of Florene Miller in her flying gear, daintily applying her lipstick. By the end of the day the women were all ready for bed, hoping they would actually get to fly tomorrow rather than pose for pictures. Meanwhile the Ferrying Division was only too aware of the media attention and became increasingly worried that the WAFS, pilots they were beginning to count on, would be portrayed behaving improperly, particularly when the women were working in such close proximity to men.

The women pilots were serving during a time when the daily lives of unmarried men and women—at least, ones who weren't related to one another—were still strictly segregated. Single-sex colleges kept women sequestered in single-sex dorms; many cities still had single-sex hotels, and landlords forbade their single female tenants from entertaining male visitors. In keeping with the mores of the era, the Ferrying Division began to put in place a number of restrictions specially designed to prevent any semblance of impropriety. One of the most frustrating prohibited the women from hitching a ride on a military plane after they had completed a mission, a regular practice for male ferry pilots. Joyriding in a new type of plane—a favorite activity of pilots everywhere—was likewise prohibited for the women but not for the men. They would be largely restricted to simple, single-pilot training and liaison planes with limited range—and no male co-pilot. As the war went on, practicality often won out. The women did end up flying with men—and they went for joyrides, too. But in these early days of the program, they had to prove themselves, even if it meant jumping through a few hoops.

Although flying a plane from point A to point B might seem like easy duty, in reality, things were rarely that straightforward. Teresa seemed to spend an inordinate amount of time waiting. Waiting for the weather to clear for takeoff. Waiting for factory workers to add the final nuts and bolts to a plane on days when they were expected to fly only minutes after the aircraft came off the assembly line. And then waiting to get back to base once the planes were delivered, only to be sent out again. Ferry pilots could fly one plane in the morning and a completely different one in the afternoon. Some flights were a short hundred miles, lasting under an hour. Others were thousands of miles and could take all week. Weather was a constant factor, but to varying degrees, depending on the type of aircraft. A light liaison plane could be grounded by clouds, while heavy twin-engine transports or bombers might not be affected a bit. Pilots were expected to work around the unexpected and to do whatever it took to deliver their planes on time.

By December, WAFS pilots were being sent out on longer and longer missions. Teresa kept hoping she might get sent as far as California, where Dink was now stationed for training. In December 1942 she came close. That month Teresa, together with five other women and twenty-four male flying officers, was sent to Great Falls, Montana, where they were on orders to fly PT-17s, Boeing-Stearman Model 75 biplanes, to Jackson, Tennessee. It was a 1,700-plus-mile trip in December, in open-cockpit planes going nearly 100 miles per hour—promising to be a numbingly cold series of flights. But Teresa and the others were so excited for the trip, they couldn't sleep. They finally arrived in Great Falls by train three days after their departure, on December 7, one year after the bombing of Pearl Harbor.

Upon their arrival they discovered that their planes weren't ready for them, so again they waited. The women shopped and wrote Christmas cards, and Teresa taught them and several of the men how to ice-skate. (She had been a champion ice-skater back home.) Soon after, Teresa and a few others came down with the flu. Teresa drank orange juice and grape juice until it practically ran out of her ears in an attempt to speed her recovery. They all slept, willing themselves well, as they waited.

With the planes finally ready and the women recovered enough to get out of their sickbeds, they finally left Great Falls on December 12, in their fur-lined flying suits with their new masks made of chamois leather and with straps of elastic over their faces to prevent frostbite. They flew south instead of east, despite the rugged terrain, to get out of the frigid temperatures as soon as possible. Teresa was the flight leader but struggled to see the women as they flew away; the planes were yellow and the snow was bright in the sun. Teresa "worried and watched and worried and kept flying in circles" as she tried to gather her flock. Florene Miller, a twenty-two-year-old Texan, was navigating. Like most pilots back then, Florene worked from a simple paper map denoting rail lines, rivers, and towns along their routes. It was flying "by the seat of your pants," which required a careful watch on the effect of the winds on the compass, airspeed, and gas gauge as they made their way.

These were far from ideal conditions for navigation, as the ground was covered in snow, with highways, rivers, and roads hidden under the same layer of white, making them impossible to differentiate. Those celebrated air markings on barns and railroad stations, meticulously painted during the 1930s to help pilots find their way, had already been covered by war-worried brushes to prevent enemy planes from finding their targets, and it would be another decade before radar and radio technologies would transform cross-country navigation. Fortunately, Florene was a talented navigator. Even when her maps blew out of the open cockpit only twenty miles after leaving Great Falls, leaving her with only her compass and watch, she never took the women more than ten miles off course. After they landed in Billings, Montana, Teresa was still rattled and went to bed in a "wringing my hands and tearing my hair mood," wishing she could write a poem, "Ode to a Navigator," to express her thanks for Florene's skill.

On December 14, Teresa flew over Colorado Springs, where she and Dink had gotten married just six months earlier, and reminisced about "the happy hours I had known in that place." But new challenges emerged when the engines on the planes started cutting out over the Colorado–New Mexico border at 10,000 feet. At one stop an aircraft mechanic put his boot through one of the plane's fabric wings and the women got their tanks filled with dirty oil, which caused the planes to sputter and stop all the way to Amarillo, Texas. The following evening Teresa managed to get a call through to Dink in California: "I talked to Dink, thinking I would probably not be this close to him again before Christmas. Seems funny wishing somebody you love a merry Christmas and happy New Year on the 15th of December. But if you get down to stranger things—what about telling somebody you love you hope to see them sometime? The whole world is an abnormal place right now." Two days before Christmas, they had made it only as far as Little Rock, Arkansas. "Although little is said about it, we had all hoped to eat Christmas dinner at the base," Teresa wrote. "At least we would have felt more at home. We are all really down in the mouth. All are threatening to get pleasantly plastered." The women spent a glum Christmas day in 80-degree temperatures, drinking eggnog at the hotel coffee shop. The café had run out of turkey and chicken, so they settled for pot roast.

On December 31 the women finally delivered the planes to Jackson, Tennessee, where the lieutenant on the field asked, "Well, did you finally get here?" He had been expecting them every day for the past two weeks; such had been the delays due to winter weather.

After a commercial flight home, the women arrived back on base just in time to celebrate New Year's and to a raucous welcome by Andy, their house mother, and the other women, who greeted them with hugs. "Gee, it was just like coming home to your family," Teresa wrote in her diary. There were stacks of letters and packages waiting for her, including gifts from Dink, still training out in California, who sent her a beautiful silver identification bracelet and a teddy bear. She had been away for so long that his letters were "piled sky high."

By the end of 1942 the WAFS pilots' ninety-day contracts had come to an end. The program was deemed a success. The Wilmington women had flown nearly 1,600 flight hours without incident, delivering sixty-four L-4Bs (Piper Cub variants), and another twenty primary trainers (PT-19s and PT-17s). Plans were already in motion to expand the experiment. Nancy Love had visited bases at Long Beach, California; Dallas, Texas; and Romulus, Michigan. All three locations were home to major aircraft factories in desperate need of pilots to fly their planes to training bases or points of embarkation for a war on two fronts.

Nancy, too, was ready to leave the 2nd Ferrying Group. Teresa and the other women at Wilmington understood very well why she was ready to be stationed elsewhere. As director, she wanted her women to do their part for the war effort, but as a pilot herself she was bored, "dissatisfied" with the limitations on the types of small, light trainer airplanes the women were being allowed to fly. The base at Wilmington was focused on the lighter planes in part because so many of the nearby manufacturers made those types of aircraft. By contrast, the other bases at Long Beach, Dallas, and Romulus were all near manufacturers of pursuit aircraft and bombers. Nancy was ready to fly those more sophisticated planes and open those cockpits to her women by her example.

Teresa knew this change was coming. She had seen Nancy when the women were on their never-ending trip from Great Falls. After days of being bedridden with the flu, Teresa finally felt well enough to take her handwritten diary notes down to the hotel's stenographer to be typed, when she was mortified to see Nancy Love. Teresa was terribly embarrassed to be fully dressed when she had reported herself ill. But Nancy didn't seem to mind. She asked Teresa to come to her room so they could talk.

Nancy only had an hour before she had to go back out with the three Army officials she had flown in with, but she wanted to fill Teresa and the other women in on the news. She changed clothes while she chatted with Teresa. Nancy told Teresa that the women would probably have to start wearing ties, which Teresa took to mean that they were in line for commissions. Then Nancy explained she was on a cross-country flying trip to all seven of the ferrying groups, evaluating potential quarters for the women. In other words, the program was expanding. Teresa immediately asked to move to Long Beach. She would be only an hour or two from Dink. "Anybody with one eye would know I would do this," she wrote in her diary.

In the new year, Nancy left to help settle in the new WAFS members at the 5th Ferrying Group in Dallas, taking a select group of the original women with her and leaving Betty Gillies in charge in Wilmington. Teresa stayed behind, too, sad to say goodbye to Nancy and some of her friends. Although she asked Nancy if she could be transferred to the new base at Long Beach in California so she could be closer to Dink, Nancy ended up selecting Cornelia Fort, Evelyn Sharp, and Barbara Towne for Long Beach duties. The historical record does not reveal why Nancy didn't let Teresa make the move despite her desperate hope to go, but the story goes that Betty Gillies wanted Teresa to stay: she wanted to keep the best pilots for herself. Teresa tried not to be too jealous and remained grateful that she was close to home, continuing to work with people she liked.

Dedie Deaton with Jean Ross Howard and Jean Pearson, in Dedie's office in Houston. Note the Fifinella on her wall calendar. *Dora Strother McKeown Collection. Courtesy Texas Woman's University*

CHAPTER SIX

The Fabulous First

While Nancy's group was established in Wilmington and expanding to new bases, Jackie was working hard to catch up. First she had to find an airfield where her women could train. She ended up selecting busy, crowded Houston. The city was humid and often foggy—terrible weather for flight training—but the Howard R. Hughes Airport was available, it was wartime, and it would have to do. At least it was a relatively quick flight to the Army Air Forces Flying Training Command headquarters in Fort Worth, where she could have her offices.

With her usual bravado, Jackie began interviewing and recruiting women for the new 319th Army Air Forces Flying Training

Detachment even before she knew where she was going to train and house them. After years of running her cosmetics business, she knew a personal touch always helped to close the deal, so she rented a suite at the Mayflower Hotel in Washington, D.C.—where her husband Floyd's company kept an apartment—and invited a group of local Ninety-Nines to a cocktail party. She hired waiters to ply the women with drinks as she regaled them with stories about the American women now flying for the ATA in England. One of the women in attendance that evening was Jane Straughan, a twenty-nine-year-old from Washington, D.C. Years later Jane remembered how impressed the women were by Jackie's tales of wartime flying. After they'd all had a few more drinks, Jackie turned to the crowd and asked: "How many here would be willing to fly for your country?"

"Of course everyone, by then, would fly for their country," Jane recalled.

In a few short weeks, Jackie managed to recruit thirty well-qualified women for her first class. These women were selected with enormous care. Jackie wanted pilots with unimpeachable character, excellent flying experience, and—this being Jackie—appropriately feminine good looks.

There's no doubt Jackie was under an intense amount of scrutiny during this time. Nancy Love had set an impressive precedent with her WAFS. The Ferrying Division was happy with Nancy's existing twenty-eight pilots. They were happy with Nancy. They did not particularly care for Jackie's assertive style and likely would have been untroubled if Jackie's program failed. Jackie knew she had to get it right or her program would be over—and over fast.

In Houston, Jackie knew she needed to find someone to fill the role of "establishment officer," whose job it was going to be to manage the women's housing, well-being, and general discipline. Less than a week before the trainees were due to arrive, Jackie still hadn't found anyone to handle the logistics, which were becoming complicated. There weren't any barracks available near the airport, and so Jackie was being forced to find rooms for her recruits in private homes and hotels around the city. Meanwhile, housing in Houston was in high demand, with thousands of men and women flocking to urban centers in the hope of securing wartime jobs. Jackie needed someone to figure out a solution before the women started arriving to find they had nowhere to sleep. Jackie's secretary at the time, Jean Holloway, had a cousin in Wichita Falls, Texas, who she thought might be perfect for the role. Jackie asked Jean to give this cousin a call.

Leoti Deaton was in the middle of hosting a formal tea honoring the national secretary of the Camp Fire Girls—a children's organization for which she energetically volunteered—when the telephone rang. Ordinarily, "Dedie" would have ignored a ringing telephone while giving a tea for such an important guest, but it was wartime, and you never knew who might be calling. Her husband, Cliff Deaton, was in line for a direct commission to the Marines, and her nineteen-year-old son, Cliff Jr., was waiting to be summoned for training in the Army. As she picked up the receiver, the thirty-nine-year-old housewife and mother had no idea that she was the one who was being called upon to serve.

It was Dedie's cousin from Fort Worth on the other end of the line. Jean implored Dedie to come to Fort Worth right away. There was a top secret wartime experiment going on in Houston, and Jean's boss, Jacqueline Cochran, was looking for a capable woman to organize and administer it. Dedie said she would do whatever she could to help. After her party guests left, she quickly washed her teacups, letting them air-dry so she could pack a bag. She planned to go and meet with Miss Cochran the following day and give her names of people who might be a good fit for the role.

The next morning, November 8, 1942, Dedie took the early train to Fort Worth, arriving by 10:00 A.M. Petite and trim, with a round face and short dark hair in neat waves, Dedie was the kind of smiling, amiable woman who rarely said no when asked to help a worthy cause. Besides her volunteering work for the Camp Fire Girls, she was active in any number of local organizations, including the Boy Scouts and the YWCA, and served on the faculty of the National Red Cross's aquatic schools, where she had long been a swimming instructor. After stepping off the train, she made straight for the Army Air Forces Flying Training Command headquarters.

Dedie's first impression of Jackie was that she ought to be in the society pages rather than flying planes and organizing military missions. Jackie was dressed and groomed to impress, wearing a pretty dress and a hat with a feather, golden earrings in her ears. Throughout their meeting, Jackie held a gleaming gold cigarette case decorated with diamonds, rubies, and emeralds in her hands. Dedie couldn't help but stare at it, and when Jackie noticed Dedie's interest, she showed it to her, explaining that the jewels marked the route of every major flight and air race she'd ever taken.

Dedie went into the meeting ready to give Jackie a list of names of women who would be perfect for the role of establishment officer. What she didn't realize was that Jackie had already decided, based on Jean Holloway's recommendation, that Dedie was the person for the job, and all that remained was to close the deal. That day in the meeting, Jackie spoke about the Women's Flying Training Detachment with such passion and enthusiasm that Dedie couldn't help but get swept up in the excitement. Dedie's husband and son were going to be serving soon; why shouldn't she also do her part?

Jackie's instructions to Dedie were simple: "Go down there and take care of the girls." When Dedie asked what authority she had to do so, Jackie was firm: "The military has absolutely no authority as far as they are concerned. This is your job; you take care of them. Place them, get them a place to eat, see that they go to [a] beauty parlor once a week. See that they stay out at the airport and have a study hall every night from 7:30 to 9:30."

After a relatively short interview, Jackie then turned to her assistant, Susie Covington, an employee of the U.S. Civil Service Commission, and said, "Ms. Covington, take Ms. Deaton to Dallas and get her certified for Civil Service." Powerless to resist, Dedie found herself agreeing to get the next train to Dallas to sit for her civil service exam.

A little over an hour later, Dedie arrived in Dallas, where she went straight to meet with the Civil Service Commission administrator for her test.

The administrator was livid.

"Who is this Cochran woman?" he barked. "She is crazy as she can be! This woman [Dedie] has no qualifications whatsoever!"

It was true, Dedie had yet to hold a position in the civil service, but she was capable, having worked as her father's secretary during his time as a school superintendent. She didn't see why this man had to be so rude.

The administrator stormed off to call the regional office but soon returned even more furious.

"Who is this Cochran woman?" he asked again. "She thinks she can rule the world!"

Clearly, Jackie had been pulling some strings on Dedie's behalf, because that afternoon, despite the continued protestations of the administrator, Dedie earned a Civil Service Commission classification of CAF-6 (for clerical, administrative, and fiscal work).

With her rating secured, Dedie got on another train, this time the 3:00 P.M. to Houston. She made her way to the Ben Milam Hotel, close to the station, where she had been told to stay the night. She'd been hosting an afternoon tea party only the day before, and now she was in charge of women pilots in a military training program. She'd barely had time to put her teacups away.

Thankfully, the next morning an Army lieutenant by the name of Alfred Fleishman offered to show Dedie around town and help her find a place to live. Tall and tan, with hair graying at his temples, Fleishman had been put in charge of the subdepot in the aircraft hangar in Houston because, at thirty-eight, he was too old to serve in combat. Although he was under no official obligation to help Dedie, Fleishman took it upon himself to do whatever he could to get her situated. That day he drove her to the home of an elderly Jewish couple who offered Dedie a well-appointed room in their apartment. He even managed to borrow a little Mercury Club Coupe so that she could drive herself around town. In the coming days, Fleishman worked with Dedie to find other private homes where the trainees could stay so that when the women began arriving a week later, she would be able to give them a list of names and addresses where they could obtain a room. This was just the beginning of Fleishman's involvement with the training program. In the coming months, he continued in his role as Dedie's close ally and the women's supporter.

As Dedie was soon to discover, the other men on the field were not quite as helpful as Fleishman. Before long, she met with commanding officer Captain Paul C. Garrett and his adjutant, Captain Jessie L. Simon. The open hostility of these two men left her taken aback. Garrett had already told Jackie to "keep the girls happy and out of my hair" and that he wanted nothing to do with Dedie or the trainees. Together with his adjutant, he simply didn't think that leading women pilots was a respectable way to spend the war—and he would have rather been almost anyplace else than in Houston running an Army Air Forces training detachment made up of women. Dedie later described Garrett and his men as "devils" and wondered if she could have ever made a go of it without the help and encouragement of Alfred Fleishman.

Now that Dedie had arrived in Houston, Jackie sent her new recruits a telegram, letting them know to report on November 16 to the city's Rice Hotel at their own expense.

The Rice was the busiest hotel in Houston, and when Dedie arrived to meet the women that day, the lobby was packed with men in uniform: Army cadets, Marines, Navy and Coast Guard officers. Women were there, too: Red Cross volunteers, military women, others selling war stamps—"all thrown together in the lobby like jackstraws." Dedie tried to spot the women pilots amid the crowds. Jackie's telegram had instructed the women to report to the commanding officer, but before that could happen, they were sent to a room at the hotel to process their paperwork. Dedie found the women crowded around a small coffee table, using whatever flat surfaces they could find to fill out the Civil Service Commission forms in quadruplicate. Some of them were dressed in neat tailored suits, others in simple print dresses, and still others in pressed slacks and sweaters.

Finally, Jackie swept in with contractors from Aviation Enterprises in her wake. Initially the plan had been to run the women's training through the Civilian Pilot Training Program, a government program that had begun teaching Americans to fly in the years leading up to the war. But the CPTP was already overwhelmed, so Aviation Enterprises, a civilian contractor, had been found to do the job. Jackie was wearing a tailored outfit with a brooch on her lapel in the shape of a petite silver propeller with a large rosette diamond at its center. Miss Cochran, as she was known to all, greeted the women and casually leaned on the arm of a chair as she told them what to expect, and what she expected of them. She made certain that the women of newly named class 43-W-1 were aware that the weight of the program rested on their shoulders. "You girls are the first women to be selected for training by the Army Air Forces," she explained. "You are all experienced pilots. There isn't a girl in this room who has less than two hundred and fifty hours, and most of you have much more. If things don't run smoothly at first, just remember that you will have the honor and distinction of being the first women to be trained by the Army Air Forces. You are very badly needed, and I hope that you will all be out of here in two and a half to three months at the most."

Jackie then introduced the women to the Aviation Enterprises contractors and to Dedie Deaton. All of a sudden Dedie found herself standing in front of a roomful of pilots eyeing her skeptically. Squaring herself up to the task, she told them about the housing situation and offered up the list of recommendations she and Lieutenant Fleishman had compiled. She also explained in no uncertain terms that they were forbidden to tell their new hosts and landladies exactly why they were in Houston. If anyone asked, the women had to say they were a part of a girls' basketball team. Jackie was so terrified of bad publicity that she had told Dedie she needed to keep the entire training program a secret.

As the trainees left the Rice Hotel that day, Dedie assumed they would make straight for her suggested accommodations. In fact, while some did look into Dedie's recommendations, others were determined to do as they pleased.

It turned out that the women Jackie had selected were a wildly mixed group divided by class, economic status, and background but with at least one thing in common: none of them was a pushover. Most of the trainees were in their late twenties and many had had careers before joining the program, either as flight instructors or in other professions: government employees, radio announcers, secretaries, reporters, and photographers were all represented. Others had been full-time wives and mothers.

Some were illustrious. The heiress Marion Florsheim, of the Florsheim shoe empire, had swept into the lobby of the Rice Hotel with her two Afghan hounds and seven trunks, wearing a bright green bow in her hair to match the bows around the necks of her dogs. Twenty-seven-year-old Mary Lou Colbert was the daughter of Rear Admiral Leo Otis Colbert. Others, like Marylene Geraldine "Geri" Nyman, came from more modest backgrounds. The daughter of an itinerant barber and a fruit packer, Geri had learned to fly after offering the local flying school her services as a bookkeeper in return for lessons. Before long, she was earning her living as a flight instructor. Geri had spent the early months of the war writing letters to her elected officials, asking why the military couldn't use women when they claimed there was a shortage of men to fly the planes. Another new recruit from this first group was Betty Guild, who had witnessed the Pearl Harbor attack from her balcony and was friends with Cornelia Fort. She had since married her Navy ensign boyfriend and was now known as Betty Tackaberry.

Each of the women was strong-willed; as Mary Lou later remembered, it was "pretty hard to boss that group around." Some, including Mary Lou, decided to stay in the home of Colonel Oveta Culp Hobby, the director of the Women's Army Corps (WAC), who was away in D.C. Jane found a room with Hobby's neighbor but took her meals—reputed to be excellent—at Hobby's. Other women took up lodging at the Rice Hotel. Marion Florsheim moved into an apartment in the posh Warwick Hotel, bringing her dogs and seven trunks with her. A few of the others who could afford it booked themselves penthouse rooms at the Plaza, while others who didn't have quite that level of funds, including Betty Guild Tackaberry, joined forces and rented their own apartments. The cover story that Dedie and Jackie had asked the women to use with their new landlords caused some problems. As Mary Lou later recalled, some of the women were barely five feet two inches, hardly believable as basketball players, so it was a "ridiculous" ruse, raising suspicions that the women were trying to hide something scandalous.

Now that the women were housed, there were other issues for Dedie to fix. The women's homes and hotels were up to fifteen miles from the Houston airport, and most of the women didn't have cars or ration coupons for gasoline and tires. Once they arrived at the airport, they faced yet more challenges. Building work at the airfield wasn't finished yet, so there were no facilities for the women trainees: no ready room, no restroom, no dining hall. Their first morning at the field, the women learned that they were going to have to walk over a mile to the Houston Municipal Airport Terminal to eat or use the bathroom. In the coming weeks the women trekked across the crushed-shell road so many times each day they shredded the soles of their shoes and struggled to find ration coupons to replace them. When they finally made it to the bathroom, they discovered that cleanliness was not a priority at the busy airport. At least one trainee was reported to have caught crabs from the terminal toilet.

Food was another problem. The café itself was dirty and crowded with workers from the nearby plants, and Geri later described the meals at the airfield café as "abominable." Most of the women avoided eating there whenever possible and often ended up fasting all day. Dedie later cited the lack of decent food as a "serious factor" in her ability to keep flight instructors and other employees.

To make matters worse, the men at the airfield were not at all happy to see them. Their first day at the field, the commanding officer, Captain Garrett, greeted them with a gruff speech. "The best way to get along here is to be where you're supposed to be and do what you're supposed to do," he warned them. "And just because a thing isn't specifically forbidden, it doesn't mean it's all right to go ahead and do it. There's no specific regulation against putting an elephant in the baggage compartment. But it wouldn't be very smart to try it." Garrett and his men were "just determined that these girls were not going to make it," one of the women noted.

But Dedie Deaton was nothing if not determined. She tackled the transportation issue head-on, working with Aviation Enterprises to locate a bus to get the women to and from the airfield. The only problem was that the bus had recently been used to transport a Tyrolean orchestra, so it was white with red-and-white-striped awnings and decorated all over with edelweiss. As there was no time to repaint it, the women had to travel around in a bus that turned heads wherever they went. So much for the secrecy of their mission.

Then there were the planes the women were going to fly. The

contractors at Aviation Enterprises were still waiting for their contract with the Army to be signed to have priority in acquiring military aircraft, so in the meantime they had gathered as many civilian planes as they could find. There were twenty-two different types at the airfield, including Stearmans, Wacos, Pipers, and Beechcrafts. Jackie had been hoping for military training planes and turned up her nose at the hodgepodge of aircraft, later describing them as "claptrap equipment." But the trainees felt very differently. Stearmans, Wacos, Pipers, and Beechcrafts were the planes they knew how to fly. In fact, the women all had at least two hundred hours of experience flying these exact types of planes. Many of them had worked as flight instructors before joining Jackie's program and had taught others to fly these planes. For these women, climbing into the cockpit of a Stearman was like meeting an old friend.

As it turned out, the men who had been hired as the women's instructors were the ones who needed to be shown the ropes, as they mostly had experience flying military planes—and so the women ended up having to instruct the men rather than the other way around. As Geri later remembered, "That's what saved us, because we were able to more or less show them how to operate those planes . . . so they would have had a rough time washing any of us out."

Dedie did her best with the first class, but she was really just making it up as she went along. She had so little time to get things put together; a commanding officer who didn't want to deal with women pilots and who actively encouraged them to rebel against Dedie's orders; a demanding boss in Jackie, who expected her to work miracles; and a group of women who didn't listen to her. Jackie urged her to take command, but Dedie was unsure of herself. She was a little over a decade older than the pilots but had not been out of Texas much, while many of the women in the first

class were from the East Coast and big cities and were well educated and well traveled. While some were kind to her, several of
them were unimpressed with the former Red Cross swim instructor. Meanwhile, Dedie was supposed to police the women even
when they weren't at the airport, making sure they didn't leave
their rooms—scattered in houses, hotels, and apartments all over
town—after 8:00 P.M. and that they went to a beauty parlor once a
week.

Dedie did what she could to find the trainees better food,
warmer clothes, and airplanes to fly, but many of them could only
see her failures, going as far as complaining to Captain Garrett
and asking him to make Dedie leave them alone. Mary Lou later
admitted, "It sounds very undisciplined of us, but we just did our
job and nobody particularly bothered us." These were stubborn
young women, confident that they would easily pass the training
course and become ferry pilots. They weren't inclined to let anyone slow them down.

Early trainees march from classroom to field in Houston. Note the Aviation Enterprises' "Flying is Fun" on the side of the building. Dora is third from right. *Dora Dougherty Strother McKeown Collection. Courtesy Texas Woman's University*

CHAPTER SEVEN

A Chance to Serve

Dora Dougherty was reading her morning newspaper at her family's home in Winnetka, Illinois, when she turned the page and saw an announcement that the Army was recruiting women for flight training. Round-faced, with a broad smile and wavy light brown hair that she kept neatly pinned to her head, Dora immediately sat up in her seat. It had been almost a year since the events of Pearl Harbor, and since then she had been waiting for a chance like this one.

Dora read the announcement carefully. She met the minimum age for training—twenty-one—and had recently acquired the required two hundred hours of flight time. Those who were interested in applying should meet with Mrs. Ethel Sheehy, recruiting officer and assistant to Jackie Cochran, at the Palmer House in downtown Chicago. As soon as she could, Dora put on her Sunday best and boarded a train.

At the Palmer, Dora was ushered into a room where Sheehy was interviewing prospective trainees. Dora dutifully answered each question she posed. Satisfied with the responses, Sheehy assured Dora that all she had to do was pass her physical with the Army and she was in. Dora was young and in good health, so she wasn't worried. She made straight for the Congress Plaza Hotel in Chicago, where the examinations were taking place. But as she entered the hotel, Dora became flustered. The hallways were full of young men in various stages of undress as they waited to be examined. Dora had barely dated a boy, let alone seen one in his underwear. By the time it was her turn for the physical, her heart was pounding from a combination of adrenaline and shock. The technician couldn't find a steady pulse, so he suggested she lie down on the cot to try to calm herself. Dora's heart was still racing when an Army doctor came to examine her. He told her to come back the next day, with a warning that she would fail the medical exam if she couldn't show a normal pulse. Dora returned home dejected, but after reassurance from her family doctor that she just needed to relax she again took the train to downtown Chicago and waited her turn. This time, to her great relief, she passed.

On January 10, 1943, Dora took the overnight train from Chicago to New Orleans, where she stayed for a few days with a friend from college, then went on to Houston, ready to join the third class of Jackie Cochran's Women's Flying Training Detachment.

Airplanes had been a part of Dora's life for as long as she could remember. Like so many of the future WASP, she had grown up with her eyes on the skies, always looking out for a plane overhead, dreaming of her own chance to fly.

She had been born in Minnesota, but when Dora was five, the family moved to a house in Garden City, Long Island, that was "practically in the back door of Roosevelt Field," as Dora later described it. Roosevelt Field was one of the most prominent airfields of the day: aircraft were manufactured there, record-setting flights began and ended there, and the most famous aviators of the day flew in and out all the time. Dora could stand in her backyard, her head tipped back, watching the planes come and go. Dora's father, Jonathan Dougherty, shared her excitement. He had served in the U.S. Army infantry during the First World War, had gone up as an observer in an open-cockpit biplane, and had been fascinated by flight ever since.

Like so many Americans in the 1920s and 1930s, Dora's family spent their Sundays at their local airfield watching airplanes for recreation and entertainment. Airplanes were less than three decades old—still a wonder to behold. Then there were the adventurous and brave pilots who flew these awe-inspiring machines themselves: no wonder people, particularly young people, were intrigued by the possibilities that the life of an aviator could bring. Each weekend Dora and her family climbed into the family's old Oakland Motor Car for the short drive to Roosevelt Field. In 1931 they were at the field to witness aviator Wiley Post and his navigator, Harold Gatty, return from their record-breaking flight around the world in eight days in the airplane *Winnie Mae*.

They weren't alone. After eight days of nonstop coverage of the flight in newspapers and on the radio, more than 10,000 people were gathered at Roosevelt Field to watch and wait. Even the famed aviator Charles Lindbergh and his wife, Anne, were in attendance. Post flew over the field three times, rousing ever more lusty cheers from the crowd, before finally landing. A group of motorcycle policemen quickly encircled the plane to escort it to the hangar. But the excitement was too much, and soon the crowd broke through, knocking over the policemen on their motorcycles in an attempt to get a glimpse of the pilots. While it is unlikely that

Dora and her family were part of the mob being beaten away from the pilots with clubs, they all surely spent time the next day reading the coverage of Post and Gatty's flight, landing, and celebration throughout the first seven pages of the *New York Times*. Pilots like Post, Gatty, and Lindbergh were celebrities—and Dora's heroes when she was growing up.

Later that year the family moved again—this time to Winnetka, near Chicago—but they kept up with their Sunday outings at Curtiss-Reynolds Field, a popular airfield that was just a mile or two from their new home. Each week there was a parachute jump at the field, and members of the public were encouraged to guess the height of the jump, with a free airplane ride as the prize. Despite repeated guesses, Dora and her brothers never did get the answer right. Eventually their father decided to buy the whole family an airplane ride. Dora's father was a white-collar worker and his family was middle-class, but they still didn't have a lot of extra money for frivolities. The airplane flight was a real treat.

The day of their flight the whole family walked down through the gate that read PILOTS ONLY, excited to be going up in the air. But when the pilot added up the weights of the five Dougherty family members, he determined that, together, they would exceed the weight limitations of the plane. He offered to take them in two flights instead. Dora's mother wouldn't hear of it, stomping her foot and saying, "We're all going to die together or we're not going." The pilot recognized a mother's determination and recalculated the weights to take the entire family on one flight in his old high-wing plane. For Dora, it was just the beginning of a lifetime of flying, and she never forgot it.

After graduating high school, Dora enrolled at a small two-year women's college, Cottey College, in Nevada, Missouri. Dora's mother, Lucille, was determined that her daughter would get an education equal to her brothers'. Lucille had lived through the women's suffrage movement and was a rebel in her time, graduating from Coe College in Iowa with a double major in physics and chemistry, subjects that were not considered "ladylike" in that era. Whereas Dora's mother needed to fight for her education and then was limited as to what she could do with it, Lucille expected that Dora would have a chance to do anything she pleased. Dora had been born in November 1921, one year after the ratification of the Nineteenth Amendment, which granted women the vote, placing her among the first American women to consider enfranchisement her birthright.

It was an exciting time to be a young woman in America as new technologies shrank the world and brought people together. The automobile meant young people could be more independent of their families, going for dates in the car instead of sitting on the front porch. The radio meant they heard the same news, soap operas, and music in Chicago as they did in New York, New Orleans, Denver, and Seattle, opening their minds to the world beyond their own hometowns. Airplanes were very much part of this shift in perspective. Flying was modern, exciting; it expanded the freedom that the automobile had brought the decade before. The airplane meant you could go anywhere and see anything you wanted. And there were just enough women flying planes that young women like Dora—smart, curious, eager—might believe that there was nothing stopping them.

In the summer of 1940, after finishing her freshman year, Dora knew that she was going to be kept busy, even while on vacation from school. Every year her mother insisted that Dora and her two brothers go to summer school. Lucille didn't mind which courses her children took, as long as they were occupied and learning. Dora decided to sign up for classes at Northwestern University in Chicago. She wasn't sure what to take, but when she saw there was a course in aviation, she signed up immediately. It was run by the Civilian Pilot Training Program and, best of all, it was free, paid for by the government.

The Civilian Pilot Training Program played a crucial part in a generation of young women like Dora learning to fly. Until the

CPTP came along in 1939, flying had been an activity limited primarily to women who were either wealthy, exceptionally brave, or lucky. After the CPTP was established, the opportunity was opened up to thousands of Americans, men and women, including 42 percent of those who would go on to serve as WASP.

The program was conceived in 1938 when it was obvious that war in Europe was imminent and that America was in danger of being utterly unprepared when the time came to join the fight. The Civil Aeronautics Authority (CAA), the precursor of today's Federal Aviation Administration (FAA), estimated there were only 3,800 commercial pilots and 3,600 private pilots between the ages of eighteen and thirty in the United States in 1939, many of whom would not be physically qualified to fly for the military, leaving a serious shortage in case of a national emergency. Robert H. Hinckley, the head administrator of the CAA, initiated the new pilot training program to help increase the number of pilots before war broke out. After all, learning to fly took time. But Hinckley had to be careful. The isolationist movement in the United States was strong and vocal, and even as Nazi Germany began invading its neighbors, there were many who were determined to keep the United States out of another global war. So, from the beginning, the program was promoted to the public as a Depression-era effort to help the struggling civilian aviation industry. Another way to send a signal to the isolationists that this was not a war-preparedness program was to admit women, who clearly wouldn't be asked to serve in a war.

Dora was a direct beneficiary of that choice. That summer of 1940 she earned her pilot's license. Dora always strove to do her best, dreading the possibility of disappointing herself or her family, but although she had always succeeded in her studies, flying offered her something else: freedom. Up in the skies, she felt separated, both literally and figuratively, from the rest of the world. When she was flying she was never bored: being in control of a plane was always stimulating, requiring her complete presence and attention to so many things, or there might be dire consequences. Dora's time in the Civilian Pilot Training Program sparked the beginning of a lifelong love.

That fall Dora returned to Cottey with her brand-new pilot's license in hand, longing to fly but never expecting that she would be able to afford it. Her family didn't have any money to spare, and as a college student she needed every penny for her studies. Soon enough, she learned that the local mailman had bought a little Piper Cub, renting a field on the east side of town and building a T hangar where he kept his plane. There were horses and cattle in the same field as this makeshift airport, and they loved to chew on the fabric of the plane's wings. Despite these challenges, the mailman rented out the plane to fellow enthusiasts. Dora spent all of her allowance and any other money she could find to fly that Cub high over southwestern Missouri, the soft, beautiful mountains at the northern end of the Ozarks unrolling below her.

The college administrators at Cottey soon found out about Dora's exploits and wired her parents. "Dora has gone to the airport," they wrote. Dora's parents wired back and said that was fine; they approved. The administrators didn't know quite what to do with this information, and so they turned Dora over to the student council. The council didn't know what to do with Dora, either, so they ended up confining her to campus for two weeks. Even in a progressive environment like Cottey, young women were expected to be ladies. You had to wear hats, hose, and gloves to town. You had to attend chapel. You had to behave. Dora could see why a woman flying a plane was confusing to them.

It just wasn't going to stop her flying. In that field in Missouri, Dora had found where she was happiest, chasing a horse away from the airplane or flying high above the world, separate from the rules below. While she appreciated the education at Cottey, she never quite fit in there. She would have to wait until she joined the WASP to find others who understood her passion—women who, like her, squirmed in their hose and gloves and would rather be in slacks and saddle shoes, striding toward the runway.

After leaving Cottey College and returning to Northwestern to continue her studies, Dora signed up with her local Civil Air Patrol. War was on the horizon and she wanted to play her role in being prepared. But she soon learned that, as she didn't own her own plane, she would spend most of her time learning to march and hardly flying at all. Frustrated, she helped her mother bake cookies and serve them with coffee to the local boys heading off to war from the Chicago and North Western railroad station. She was happy to do it. But Dora didn't want to be the one left standing on the platform, waving goodbye to the departing troops. She wanted to join them.

In the early fall of 1942, a friend who was a pilot with the Army Air Forces tipped her off about a program for women pilots out of New Castle Army Air Base in Wilmington. Not long after that, the Chicago papers reported that Nancy Love was starting the WAFS. Dora was still just a little too young, and with only 180 hours of flight time she wasn't nearly experienced enough. Even so, she didn't let that stand in her way. She told her parents she wanted to apply—and that she planned to drop out of college to focus on building her flying time. Her parents were concerned. They had always taught their daughter to put education first, but they also understood that it was wartime and the usual rules did not apply. When Dora promised them she would return to her studies once the war was over, they reluctantly agreed to support her.

Dora took a job as an assistant bookkeeper at the airport. Bookkeeping was not the ideal job for Dora, as her handwriting was virtually illegible; but the airport paid her in flight time, and with her savings she was able to pay for additional hours in the air. Her plan was to reach five hundred hours so she could join the WAFS, but at times those five hundred hours felt like an insurmountable goal.

Then came the announcement about Jackie's program in the local newspaper. Dora was accepted and, a month later, summoned to Houston to join the third class of Jackie's Women's Flying Training Detachment.

———————

After a long train ride south, Dora made straight for Houston's chamber of commerce, where she was to meet Dedie Deaton and commanding officer Captain Paul C. Garrett. The next day she joined another sixty-seven new recruits gathering that day, standing in the hot sun, all ready to serve. On average the women were younger than the women in the first two classes, ranging from twenty-one to thirty-five, and they came from a wide array of backgrounds. Pilots from fourteen states were admitted to training, with the greatest numbers hailing from California and New York, and Dora was happy to see that quite a few others were also from the Chicago area. Some were married with children; others were students or flight instructors. One woman worked at a casino in Reno, another was an actress on Broadway, yet another was a graduate aeronautical engineer.

Commanding officer Garrett's mood had evidently not improved since the arrival of the first class in Houston. Garrett gave Dora and the rest of 43-W-3 a speech designed to put them in their place: "A lot of you girls have come down here with a lot of [flight] time and you may think that you are pretty hot pilots," he declared, "but, let me tell you that just because you may have three hundred or five hundred hours—you may have a thousand hours—it doesn't mean that you can fly. Maybe you haven't got anything but a collection of bad habits. So, if you think you're hot pilots, my advice to you is to forget it. You're here to learn to fly the way the Army flies."

The women of the first class had been confident enough to dismiss Garrett's attempt at deflating them, but Dora immediately began to doubt herself. What if Garrett was right and she couldn't make the grade? The commanding officer concluded his speech with another stern warning: "There are three things for which you can be washed out in this course. The first is that you can't fly. The second is that you can't do the ground-school work. The third is that your attitude isn't good." By the end of the speech, Dora was no longer certain that she'd finish this new adventure without being sent home in disgrace.

After the meeting was finally over, the women left for their various accommodations. The situation had progressed somewhat since the arrival of the first class, and in general the administrators of the program—both military and civilian—seemed to have a much better idea of what they were doing. By now Dedie Deaton had arranged for the women to stay together in groups of cottages called "camps" or "tourist courts," located a fifteen-minute drive from the airport. These cottages typically housed travelers or itinerant workers, and "decent folk" often described them as "dens of iniquity," filled with people of questionable character. Jackie had been horrified by the reputation of the tourist courts and seriously considered firing Dedie for even thinking of housing "her girls" there, but eventually acquiesced when she realized there was no other option.

Dora was sharing a room in the Oleander Courts, where conditions were less than ideal. In her letter home on January 14, Dora wrote: "The rooms are quite small, have pine paneling, our own telephone, ice cold running water (they say), our own shower, etc." On the other hand, they would have maid service, which was an unexpected perk. Dora also thought that her roommate, a woman from New Jersey named Marge Clarke, seemed very nice—which was good, considering they would be sharing the one old double bed. Dora wrote home that Marge was Episcopalian, too, so maybe they would try to go to church together.

Following a sleepless first night, Dora, Marge, and the others were picked up by a bus and taken to the field for more speeches. While the first class had ridden around in a bus painted with edelweiss, by the time Dora and the third class arrived, Aviation Enterprises had found a large moving van with windows and homemade benches along the sides. That day the bus was so freshly renovated that Marge got blue paint on her new coat when she sat next to one of the windows.

Under the warm Houston sun, Lieutenant Alfred Fleishman climbed on a table while the newbies stood smartly at attention. Dora glanced around at the other women, feeling young and inexperienced. She noticed one of her classmates wearing a fashionably tailored gray flannel suit with a matching hat bearing a fresh orchid. Dora was, by her own estimation, a "country girl" and felt conscious of her own simple clothes and saddle shoes.

Fleishman began his speech, reminding Dora and the others that they were in the Army now, even if they were technically still civilians. His message was serious and tough-minded, similar to Captain Garrett's, if delivered in a slightly more sympathetic tone:

> If you are a normal individual, you are probably in a great state of confusion by this time as to just what you are going to do here; what is to be expected of you; what kind of life you are going to lead for the next 4, 5 or possibly 6 months; and—as if that weren't enough—what you are going to do after that . . . If you thought you knew anything about flying before you came here, you may find out when the Army starts teaching you flying the Army way, that you don't know anything about it at all . . . You will wear clothes that might not fit too well. You will probably lose every bit of glamour that you thought you had . . . [Y]ou will be required for the time being, to sleep two in a bed, but you will please remember there is a war going on and our soldiers are sleeping 50 to 100 in a room, many of them with no beds at all—and you are just as much a part of that army as they are . . . [F]orget your down couches back home, and make the best of what you have, including the cold water, which inevitably runs in the showers . . . [Y]ou will have dust kicked up in your face when we exercise; you will wear out your shoes on the rock roads; the noise will be deafening; it will

be wet; there will be fog; the Sun won't shine when you think it should shine; you'll be hauled back and forth in busses; your instructors will be tougher when you think they ought to be easier and there will be many an evening when you just know you won't be able to stagger home to bed. But you will. And you will overcome all of it; get up the next morning and be here on the job again.

Fleishman—together with Dedie—had evidently learned a lesson from the first two classes, because they were determined to make clear from the outset that no "prima donnas" would be tolerated. "We are not concerned here with your previous social, or lack of, position," Fleishman said. "Here you stand on your own feet. If your father is a General, or your grandfather was an Admiral, you will stand or fall based strictly on your ability to fly or ability to conform to the standards which have been set up . . . You are part of an experiment that will do more to advance the cause of equality for women, than anything that has been done so far."

For the duration of the war plus six months after, the women were obligated to do their part no matter how rough it got.

As Fleishman went on for nearly twenty minutes, Dora felt herself moved by his words. "My heart and my determination swelled," she later recalled. But after all the talk about the Army way came a reminder that as far as the Army itself was concerned, the women were still civilians. They filled out Civil Service Commission forms in quadruplicate, had their fingerprints made, then lined up for their oath of office. Now officially Civilian Student Pilots, Unclassified, the women stood in line again to get their supplies, including the clothes they were going to wear during training. Each recruit got a baggy mechanic's jumpsuit (the women dubbed it a "zoot suit"), a leather flight jacket (if they were lucky; the Army ran out, so not everyone got one), and a heavy sweater that smelled like it had been on mothballs since 1941. Dora managed to get the smallest size left, a 40, which fit her terribly; Marge arrived later, only managing to find a 42, which drowned her tiny frame.

That evening Dora, Marge, and some of the other women gathered in one another's rooms, modeling their ill-fitting clothes. There was Elsie Dyer of Virginia, who felt lucky to have made it into the program at all; she was just five feet two inches, the minimum height required, and a month away from turning thirty-six. (Thirty-five was the age cutoff.) Laurine Nielson, who went by Rene, had been raised in the backwoods of South Dakota, where she'd developed a strong work ethic and a no-nonsense attitude. Betty Deuser was a tall, long-legged blonde from California who had grown up near the Oakland airport. She had learned to fly the same way as Dora: thanks to the Civilian Pilot Training Program.

That evening the women waltzed around, giggling in their new oversized clothes. Some of the taller women had pants that were too short, while the smaller women were swimming in coveralls so big that their feet and hands disappeared. They laughed at the sight, sharing treats left over from their travels to Houston as they began to get to know one another.

Over the weekend, Dora and her classmates got a tour of the field, settled into their rooms, and ventured out to explore Houston despite the surprising January heat. That Monday, after a restless night, they awoke to the bitter cold rain of a Houston winter. The new recruits weren't going to be able to fly due to the weather, but they headed out to the field anyway, getting their first taste of ground school as well as Lieutenant Fleishman's calisthenics class. Fleishman had decided the women of the first class needed to do something with the time they spent waiting between ground school and flying besides sitting around and drinking Cokes. With Dedie's blessing he'd begun a fitness program, leading them from atop a table through an hour of exercises in the grass. The women grumbled, some participating while others sat on a nearby fence smoking cigarettes and watching the others sweat.

Now Dora and her classmates in the third class were being subjected to Fleishman's routine, this time in the freezing cold in what felt like twenty pounds of bulky G.I. clothing. But while many of the women in the first class had derided Fleishman, Dora liked him, describing him to her folks as "tall and tan and military to a degree, plus a wonderful sense of humor."

Not that it made her any less stiff and sore.

After the rain of that first Monday came a record-breaking cold, just 18 degrees, a crisis for a Southern town like Houston. Water pipes burst and muddy holes froze up. The wind made the women's fingers freeze despite their newly issued gloves. The ground crew had trouble starting the "ships"—as aircraft were often called—so much of the morning was spent waiting until they could get the engines warm. The next struggle was going to the bathroom in so much heavy clothing. The women knew by now that there were only two toilets available to them, one down the road at the Houston Municipal Airport Terminal building and another at the old Civil Air Patrol barracks—and that by the time they managed to get there, they still had to take off a jacket, sweater, zoot suit, and slacks in order to do their business.

Despite the lack of bathroom facilities, the third class had new amenities that hadn't been afforded to the first class. Aviation Enterprises, the civilian contractor hired to help administer the program, opened a new mess hall, converted from an old theater, less than a mile from the flight line. Dora, never one to complain, later wrote home about the food that they were being served: "Sometimes it is pretty well disguised and we can't tell what it is or what it is supposed to be but it is nourishing and most of us are staying pretty healthy." They still faced civilian rationing, meaning they got only one cup of coffee each meal, and milk at only lunch and dinner—and they missed butter altogether—but it was a far better experience than the food at the airport terminal, and Dora optimistically believed "we are having it easy compared to civilian life."

Then there was ground school, where the women were put through the same basic classes as the male recruits. Dora, just shy of her degree from Northwestern University, was a strong student and was bored silly by the math class in particular, taught by a man she thought was "kind of stupid." To distract herself, Dora used the time to write letters home. However, some of her classmates struggled, especially with the Morse code class, where the goal was to get them to a point where they could decode ten words per minute. The class was widely disliked, but Dora excelled and was one of only two who got 100 percent on her first test. She wrote, "Most of the gals are having a terrible time with their code and I am so glad I know mine."

The following Wednesday, a week after her arrival, Dora finally got her chance to fly. Her instructor that day was named Banks. He was in his late twenties, good-natured, with nails bitten down to the quick. He sat behind Dora as she settled into the cockpit and surveyed the controls of the Taylorcraft Tandem no. 255. She had never flown the plane before, and it was different from those she was used to flying—with control wheels instead of a stick—but she was determined to do her best. She taxied into position and paused for incoming traffic before taking her foot off the break and pushing in the throttle. The tail lifted off the ground and Dora carefully corrected for the wind (knowing the light plane was particularly susceptible to it), heard the hum of the engine giving everything to the takeoff, and was up in the air at last.

She flew for an hour and fifteen minutes while Banks showed her the lay of the land, including the two auxiliary fields used for takeoff and landing practice. Next they soared over the coast of the Gulf of Mexico, with its beige beaches and clear blue waters. Banks made sure to point out the rice fields planted near the coast, wet with mud and what appeared to be ditches filled with water around the sides. Dora concluded the fields would be "very bad for forced landings" and resolved to stay away from them.

Dora began writing home on her new Army Air Forces–headed notepaper, in tiny script to make the most of the limited wartime supply. She told her family that her first flight was "swell," but despite her over two hundred hours of flying time she found the stall—a maneuver pilots train for when the plane loses energy in a climb and essentially stops flying—confusing in the Taylorcraft, and by her next hour of flying on Thursday she was feeling "very dumb." The women weren't able to fly on Friday due to the weather, but on Saturday she got an hour in a Piper Cub, a plane she'd flown before, and felt a little better.

At the end of a long day of flying, ground school, and calisthenics, the women boarded buses back to the tourist courts they were beginning to call home. Once back in their rooms the women would write letters, listen to music from rented radios, and have a beer or two. Often Dora and Marge would go into town for dinner and a movie. On days when the frequent Texas fog kept them grounded, they would find themselves waiting in their rooms or lingering in the mess hall, playing cards or writing letters, while the nickelodeon played Glenn Miller and the Ink Spots. The women were constantly behind in their flying— waiting, waiting, waiting for the weather to clear. Diaries and letters home were filled with laments about the fog; Dora wrote that some days it was "so thick it is almost raining." Whenever the sun did come out, the women had to catch up, which meant flying on weekends if necessary. For some reason the fog often cleared just at the end of the day. One of the women wrote a song about the phenomenon, which they used to sing as they marched:

> We get up at six in the morning—regardless of where we have been.
>
> But at quarter of eight—it won't hesitate,
>
> *The fog rolls in.*

We hurry our eating at lunchtime—get out our chute,
    check the pin.

But at quarter of two—there is nothing to do,

The fog rolls in.

At dusk, when daylight is waning—'tis then at the end of
    the day,

You can hear us all sigh—it's too late to fly,

And the fog rolls away.

A group of WASP serving with the 6th Ferrying Group in Long Beach takes a moment for a group photo. Betty Blake, who witnessed Pearl Harbor, is at the bottom right. *USAAF photo. Courtesy Texas Woman's University*

CHAPTER EIGHT

Carrying On

By the beginning of 1943, the remaining women at New Castle air base in Wilmington had grown to be close friends, spending most of their downtime with one another. The exception was Adela Scharr, whom Teresa used to teasingly call "Miss Goody Two-shoes" because she spent her evenings on base, writing to her husband, Harold, in the Navy. Teresa was all for writing letters to your husband in the service, but not at the expense of having fun.

Before long, everyone was calling Teresa by her nickname, "Jamesy," and she quickly became known as the queen of the practical jokes. She left a Limburger cheese on the radiator in Betty Gillies's room just to "stink it up," short-sheeted Betty's bed, and once enlisted other women to put a bucket of water over her door so that, when Betty opened it, she got a proper dousing. Betty called them all "brats" but soon got even with them, taking their uniforms and sewing the sleeves shut.

Like the rest of the Wilmington women, Teresa adored Betty, calling her "Mother Gillies" or "Mother Hen." But as caring as Betty was, she also wasn't a pushover. It didn't matter what time you went to bed, according to Betty: you had to get up at daybreak ready to go, even if you had to put matches in your eyeballs to keep your lids open. No wonder the women also called their tiny leader "the Mighty Atom."

Betty did her best to keep the women's spirits up during what was turning out to be a brutal winter. It was bitterly cold in their quarters and no one could keep warm: those cracks in their walls let in freezing blasts of air. On February 15, 1943, Teresa wrote in her diary: "Only two girls went to breakfast today. It was 10 degrees below zero. No one could sleep. They got up and put their clothes on and then went back to bed. Water pipes are busted by the dozen. What a day." When she learned Betty was sending her on a solo trip to Burbank, California, she was so happy, she could barely breathe. Dink was still training in California and she would get to see him after many months apart. As a plus, she would also get to escape the freezing temperatures.

Teresa left New Castle on February 17, bound for Hagerstown, Maryland, where she picked up a PT-19. The plane needed to be delivered to Major Paul Mantz, who ran the 1st Motion Picture Unit in Burbank. Mantz had made his name as a stunt pilot in movies during the 1930s; he was also a close friend of Amelia Earhart's and had started a flight school with her just before her final, fateful trip. Now he was making educational and propaganda films for the military. Teresa was excited to meet him, but not half as excited as she was to see Dink.

The plane Teresa was assigned to deliver had an open cockpit, and it was February, so she braced herself for the cold, dressing in her heavy leather flight suit and giant leather boots, which made finding the right pressure for the rudder pedals so much more challenging. It was a long, lonely cross-country trip, but Teresa had a "rip roaring time" along the way, skimming along at fifteen feet over a highway, playing chicken with a train as she flew low over the tracks, scaring a farmer off of his tractor as she buzzed his field—liberated to play because there were no identifying numbers on her plane and she knew she wouldn't be caught. As she flew over the desolate West, she was awed by the beauty of it and wrote in her diary as she flew, "I feel so all alone up here right now. Nothing but vast space . . ." Some ten days after she left, Teresa delivered the plane to Mantz in Burbank, who then generously helped her borrow a plane to fly to Santa Maria and her Dink.

At last, at 8:00 P.M. the night of February 26, the long-awaited moment arrived. Teresa was overjoyed to be reunited, but there was a problem: Dink's commanding officer would only give him a twenty-six-hour leave, starting the next day. When he begged for a three-day leave instead, the CO claimed it was impossible: "There is a war going on," he said, as if Dink and Teresa needed reminding. Later that evening Teresa found herself a room in a nearby hotel, writing in her diary that "I was so damn mad I could have bombed the place. Here I am with a week's leave and I can only see Dink for 24 hours . . . Went to bed early, still cursing the Army."

She spent the entire next day waiting to see her husband. Finally, at 6:00 P.M. he was free. They had dinner and spent the rest of the evening together. The next day, they sat around drinking beer with some of Dink's "pals" until evening, as Dink had to be back on base by 8:00 P.M. "I was one unhappy soul when he left," Teresa wrote. "After coming across the continent, I could only see him for such a short while." Frustrated and sad, she fled by train to Burbank.

The next morning, Paul Mantz invited her to tour the studios with him, putting her up in the manager's suite of the Beverly

Hills Hotel, where Katharine Hepburn and Spencer Tracy were also staying. Teresa spent the rest of the week backstage, meeting Cab Calloway, Bill Robinson, Ingrid Bergman, Gary Cooper, Ginger Rogers, and other famous faces. The movie stars were just as thrilled to meet her, a real-life "girl flier." "The uniform caused more sensation than Garbo walking down the street naked," Teresa later wrote.

Bob Hope enjoyed Teresa's company, too, taking her around to meet people, introducing her as "Jessie James, his little WAF." He wanted Teresa to join him on his broadcast on Sunday night, but Teresa had other priorities. She'd already stayed in California a full week—long enough for Dink to have another day off from duty. She returned to Santa Maria, where she spent a "precious evening" telling him all about her adventures. When she returned to Los Angeles the next night, there were dozens of phone messages for her. She had skipped her rehearsal for Ginny Simms's show to have more time with Dink. Eventually, on March 9, Teresa—feeling so nervous her knees actually buckled—was featured on the national radio program. Simms was a popular singer and movie star, and on her show she interviewed service personnel from all over the world and let them send messages to their families. The women in Wilmington sent Teresa a telegram letting her know that they would be listening.

With her star turn on the radio over, Teresa left for home on a commercial airliner, sleeping as much of the flight as she could. When Teresa finally rolled into Wilmington, Betty Gillies was there to share some big news: she'd soloed the P-47, one of the most advanced pursuit planes of the day, and every guy on the field had come out to watch her do it. The P-47 was a seven-ton aircraft. At only five feet tall, Betty was so tiny, she had to put blocks over the rudders so she could reach the controls and still see out of the cockpit. But she was an excellent pilot, and although the men held their breath, Betty flew the magnificent plane beautifully. The leap Betty had just made for the AAF from 40-horsepower, 75-mile-per-hour Piper Cubs to the 2000-plus-horsepower P-47—capable of flying over 400 miles per hour—was a bit like going from driving uphill in a broken-down truck to zooming along a highway in the latest sports car. Teresa knew the fact that the Ferrying Division was beginning to trust the women enough to throw them the keys was very good news for the program. The night of her return, she washed her clothes, had a hamburger for dinner, and fell into bed—hardly believing her adventure, grateful for the extra time with Dink, and wondering when she, too, might get to fly that fast new plane.

While Teresa continued flying out of New Castle, Cornelia Fort was getting settled in her new base in California. The 6th Ferrying Group in Long Beach was among the oldest and most prominent of the ferrying groups and handled a wide range of aircraft—exactly the kinds of challenging airplanes that Nancy and her WAFS pilots dearly wanted to fly.

Predictably, the Army had struggled to provide even the most basic accommodations for the women on base, hastily emptying out a hospital ward in order to house them. In a letter to her mother, Cornelia wrote, "When I arrived there wasn't a chair, a towel or anything. Just a 60-foot-long gaping room." The women assessed the situation and went to the Villa Riviera hotel downtown instead. When the bachelor officers' quarters were finally ready for them, they settled in, personalizing their space with rugs and pictures. Besides the balmy weather and the terrific officers' club, the most noticeable difference between Wilmington and Long Beach was the friendliness of the people. Cornelia wrote to her mother, "People stare at us as we knew they would but they are friendly stares. Pilots say 'Welcome' and seem to mean it." The fact was, the 6th Ferrying Group needed pilots—any pilots.

Still, the commanding officer at Long Beach, Colonel Ralph E. Spake, was initially skeptical of all these women coming into his command. "Any girl who has flown at all," Cornelia wrote home, "grows used to the prejudice of most men pilots who will trot out any number of reasons why women can't possibly be good pilots . . . The only way to show the disbelievers, the snickering hangar pilots, is to show them."

The women flew their first mission, from Long Beach to Dallas, less than a week after their arrival. Cornelia wrote home after their first night on the road, a beautiful stop in Palm Springs, California: "The moon was full and the desert smelled of all the wonderful flowers I ever imagined. That was one of the times when I knew clearly the reason for my love of flying, why I wouldn't change jobs for anything else in the world. The reasons are many, I know them in the beauty I see, in the freedom of the air, in the pride of skill and the joy of self-sufficiency."

Cornelia and the others made good time overall, and Colonel Spake was impressed. "He was delighted at our delivering to Dallas in such speed and safety," Cornelia reported. "He was nearly purring this morning." Spake quickly became one of the women's biggest advocates.

Nancy wasn't surprised by the Long Beach women's success, but she was pleased by it and happy that Spake had come around. Long Beach was home to dozens of important airplane manufacturers and was the busiest of the domestic ferrying bases. A commanding officer who believed in the women's abilities as pilots—and who was desperate to move thousands of planes out of the area—meant the women would really get to fly.

But California WAFS soon learned that not everyone was quite so delighted to see them. It turned out that the wives of the male pilots on base were working themselves into a panic, convinced that the WAFS pilots were plotting to steal their husbands. They went to the commanding officer en masse to demand that he do something. Colonel Spake agreed to send one of his deputies to talk to the wives at their biweekly luncheon at the officers' club.

The women pilots were duly invited to the same luncheon.

Cornelia described the experience as "the most desperate ordeal I ever saw. Talk about being stared at and appraised and in a decidedly unfriendly fashion. Whew! They are in a frenzy of jealousy that we will co-pilot with their husbands. Of all the damned, stupid, female rot!" The deputy made a speech in an attempt to reassure and quiet the wives, explaining that men and women would not copilot and that "no mixed operations orders would be issued." In fact, pilots out of Long Beach often flew in the same direction, stopping for dinner together along the way whether they were copilots or not; but this nuance was lost on the wives, who were pleased with the news that their husbands would not be tempted by sitting next to a woman in an airplane. Cornelia wrote home, "And can you believe it, the rude women applauded right in front of us! I was so livid at an exhibition whose equal I'd never seen that I got up and walked out, whereupon the other girls followed me. I hope they had the grace to be ashamed of their rudeness if not their feelings."

In February, Nancy decided to pay the new California base a visit. She had recently visited the new 5th Ferrying Group in Dallas, where she jumped on the chance to get checked out in the AT-6 Texan, a 600-horsepower advanced trainer with a cruising speed of 145 miles per hour—quite a leap from the 40-horsepower Cubs and 220-horsepower PT-17 Stearman biplanes she'd been flying out of Wilmington. After arriving, Nancy had a chance to catch up with Cornelia and the other women stationed there. Cornelia had just bought her dream car: a gray Chevrolet convertible with both a radio and a heater. She couldn't wait to drive it with the top down in the California sunshine that summer.

While in Long Beach, Nancy had a chance to climb into the cockpit of a new pursuit plane known as the P-51 Mustang. The P-51 had been designed in 1940 to compete with the Luftwaffe's fast, powerful pursuits that were doing so much damage in Europe. But with 1,800 horsepower and sensitive controls, only pilots with both experience and confidence dared to fly it. It was also a single-seat plane, which meant that Nancy would go up for the first time alone. The check pilot, Major Samuel C. Dunlap, was an old friend now serving as operations officer at Long Beach. He stood on the wing of the plane while Nancy sat at the controls, demonstrating she knew where the various instruments were to prove she was ready. And with that, Dunlap sent her to the end of the runway and watched as she held the brakes for a moment before hurtling down the asphalt.

Up in the clouds, Nancy felt "the same lonely but wonderful feeling you get on your first solo." She returned to the ground an hour later, exhilarated. She called her husband, Bob, to tell him all about it. Just two weeks past her twenty-ninth birthday, she was flying one of the fastest planes in the world. Bob wrote to her that night, genuinely happy for his wife but a little worried, too. "Boy what news your call brought! You've just about reached the top!" He continued: "I'm so afraid you will be so famous and involved with things that you won't care for the things that we have longed for before." Flying gave Nancy a chance to live in the moment rather than worry about the future, about settling down and having kids. That seemed to be what Bob was afraid of. He wondered whether she was beginning to imagine a career as a military pilot.

The Air Training Command was beginning to take notice of Nancy's ambitions. Within one month of her arrival at Long Beach, she'd checked out in sixteen different types of aircraft, squeezing her flying in between her administrative duties.

Nancy much preferred being in the cockpit to being on the ground. She didn't have much patience with paperwork or bureaucracy. She was proud to lead a group of such qualified and dedicated women pilots, but she was much more interested in flying. Every time she checked out in a new airplane and mastered its intricacies, she had a sense of accomplishment that only made her hungry to try another, and then another.

Other WAFS pilots quickly followed Nancy in the more advanced planes, partly because the women had proven themselves to be competent pilots, but primarily because the demand for qualified pilots at the aircraft factories was at an all-time high. In other words, the "experiment" of women flying for the military was working. Beginning in January 1943, the United States had finally begun bombing raids on Germany, using the kinds of airplanes that Nancy's pilots were ferrying out of factories in Long Beach, Dallas, and Romulus, Michigan. By mid-February, daily aerial battles in the Pacific theater helped the Americans defeat the Japanese at Guadalcanal, enabling them to move on to the Solomon Islands. More women pilots on the home front meant that more planes could be shipped out and more men released for the fight.

Everything was going so well for Nancy and the WAFS. Then, on March 21, 1943, she received the worst of news from Long Beach. Cornelia Fort had been killed. She had been flying in formation with six male pilots ferrying BT-13 Valiants to Dallas when one of the men accidentally flew into Cornelia's plane, sending her plummeting to the earth. According to witnesses, Cornelia made no effort to recover the plane from the spin, so it was possible she was unconscious after the initial impact, or so her friends and family hoped. The plane hit the ground vertically and with such force that the engine was buried two feet in the ground. The young male pilot's plane had been badly damaged, but he managed to make an emergency landing in nearby Abilene, where he reported the accident.

Cornelia, who had so narrowly survived the Japanese attack on Pearl Harbor, who had such a passion for flying and for life, was dead. She was the first WAFS casualty, and the first time Nancy had to bear the responsibility of losing one of her own.

Cornelia's funeral took place four days after the accident, on March 25. Nancy was on a ferry trip to North Carolina along with WAFS pilot Barbara Erickson and their operations officer, Major

Dunlap, but got permission to make a stop in Nashville along the way. After flying through gray, rainy weather, they arrived at 5:30 A.M., found a hotel, and cleaned up as best they could after a sleepless night, putting on their gray-green uniforms. At the church the casket was draped with an American flag. Cornelia's mother, who had only recently lost both her husband and her family home in a fire, quietly begged Nancy for more information on Cornelia's death. She was such a good pilot. How could it have possibly happened? Nancy knew so little but reassured Cornelia's mother that her daughter wouldn't have suffered. The service was packed, and while Nancy helped lead the processional, she did not dare give a eulogy, worried that her official demeanor would crack and she would break down in front of the congregation. Cornelia's death would stay with her the rest of her life. Nancy had recruited her and she was responsible for her. Now Cornelia was gone.

After leaving Nashville, Nancy flew to Washington, D.C., where she was able to spend a day with Bob. It must have been a comfort to finally let down her guard after days of keeping her emotions in check. Because the WAFS pilots were considered civilians, the Army did not pay for Cornelia's funeral expenses, and Cornelia's mother was to receive only a $200 Civil Service Commission death benefit. Nancy was furious. All she had ever asked for her women was that they be treated fairly. It was bad enough that they were paid less than men, but their treatment in death was like a kick to the stomach. Cornelia had contributed just as much as a male pilot, and the Army was effectively saying her life was close to worthless. Nancy later wrote to Cornelia's mother expressing her deep condolences. "My feeling about the loss of Cornelia," she wrote, "is hard to put into words—I can only say that I miss her terribly, and loved her . . . If there can be any comforting thought, it is that she died as she wanted to—in an Army airplane, and in the service of her country."

Cornelia's death haunted the women, but the report of the accident compiled by the Air Transport Command testifies to their resilience: "It is remarkable that this first fatality among so small a group of women pilots, all bound together by ties of friendship and common interest in flying, had no serious effects on the morale of the WAFS. There is no indication that the death of Cornelia Fort caused any resignations from the organization or any reluctance to carry on with the ferrying missions assigned."

Dorothy Swain (Lewis) was trained as a flight instructor by famed pilot Phoebe Omlie. After teaching some of the women in Sweetwater and seeing them get the chance to fly faster and more powerful planes, she decided to join the program herself. *Photo by and courtesy of Dot's student Flora Belle Reece*

CHAPTER NINE

The Army Way

On January 27, 1943, Dora and her classmates were about to march the mile from the hangars to the mess hall for dinner, when a car stopped next to them and Jacqueline Cochran climbed out. She was wearing a glamorous fur coat, which Dora thought might be mink, and carried an over-the-shoulder bag. Dora had been in training for about two weeks, but this was her first time meeting Miss Cochran. She'd expected someone much older, based on the photographs she'd seen, and was surprised by how young and feminine Jackie looked. Jackie reassured the women that she hadn't forgotten about them and promised to share a meal with them the next day.

The following afternoon Jackie joined the women for lunch. She told them she was looking for constructive criticism and that she was going to install a suggestion box on base so that they could submit their comments. Jackie also explained that she intended to fly with each one of them and invited them to bring any personal problems they might be having to her. Dora was impressed, writing home that "[Jackie] looks wonderful today, has beautiful blonde hair and a very business-like appearance" and that she had recently learned from instructor Banks that Jackie had sent each instructor a two-pound box of candy from California. (Jackie no doubt wanted to keep the instructors happy, as they were putting up with less-than-ideal conditions and had plenty of other opportunities to teach elsewhere during wartime.)

A week after her initial visit, Jackie returned with a big announcement. Together with the Army brass, she had taken note of the delays caused by the weather, the ongoing housing headache, and other troubles caused by the Houston location. They had spent weeks exploring other options, and while it was all still top secret, she had just learned that the Army was going to open a second flight school for women, this one at Avenger Field in Sweetwater, Texas, west of Abilene and far from the coast and the fog. Jackie had flown Dedie Deaton up to Sweetwater in her green-colored Beech biplane to show her the field, and Dedie had pronounced herself "delighted" with the facilities.

Ten days after the suggestion box was installed, Jackie returned to Houston. Dora, all the other students and their instructors, as well as the contractor staff, stayed on the field until 10:30 P.M. listening to Jackie address all 75 comments submitted by the 140 trainees on base. While promises were made to build barracks and other facilities, the thing that mattered most to Dora was that they were finally going to get access to more military planes, AT-10 Wichitas and AT-17 Bobcats included, because those who met the standards were going to go directly into the Ferry Command after the training program.

Aviation Enterprises was also beginning to work with the Army to find ways to entertain the women when they weren't on duty, including getting them access to the local YMCA swimming pool each Monday evening and giving them opportunities to play volleyball, basketball, softball, and Ping-Pong. Lieutenant Fleishman often led the activities, offering music and lectures on various topics. The women helped put together evening entertainment in the mess hall, including weekly movies—both full-length features and shorts. The haphazard early days of the 319th were becoming a thing of the past.

That February, the first issue of the women's newsletter was released, underwritten by Aviation Enterprises. It included reports about what was happening at the field, short biographies of staff members and women in aviation history, movie timetables, a section on aircraft identification, and original poems and cartoons. There was also a letter from Walt Disney, giving the editors of the newsletter permission to use the name "Fifinella" for their new publication. At the time, Disney was making Roald Dahl's children's book *Gremlins* into an animated movie and had released artwork from the film, including the cartoon of a zany blue-winged creature named Fifinella. The character was based on the mythical imps who had caused mechanical problems for Royal Air Force pilots until they were convinced to become loyal helpers of all fliers. With her large goggles, yellow flight cap, and giant red boots, Fifinella quickly became the women's mascot.

Dora offered to help out with the *Fifinella Gazette* and soon became the paper's humor editor. She also kept writing letters home, often multiple times in a single day, as she listened for the drone of planes coming in to land, a welcome signal that her turn might come soon. In one letter home Dora described the weather improving long enough to go up. "There was the usual thick fog in the morning, but it blew away and there were huge clouds that seemed high enough," she wrote home. "I went up with my instructor Banks and we had a wonderful time flying through clouds and chasing ducks . . . I had never flown through a cloud before. It was swell, but gave one a rather lost feeling, being all alone with nothing at all around you." Ever the loyal and diligent daughter, she assured her parents that she would try to include every detail of her time in training. "If there is anything you would want to know please write for I am sure nothing that I could tell you would be divulging a secret and the only reason I don't tell you things is that I forget or think I had told you before. You know I would keep nothing from you and I want you to know what I'm doing."

As the days went on, Dora must have wished there were aspects of her time at Houston that she *could* keep from her parents. The reality was that, despite her skill in the classroom, Dora was struggling with the flying. After around fifteen hours flying in light trainers, the women had to go through a spot check with a civilian instructor. On February 6, 1943, Dora passed hers, but barely. "I had my check ride or spot check this morning and didn't do so well," she wrote home that day. "I passed but just by the skin of my teeth I guess . . . golly, I really messed the thing up." In the same letter she explained that she wasn't alone. "There are several girls that are about ready to be washed out. It makes me feel so terribly for they are the nicest girls down here and those that are so darned conceited are the ones that are hot," she wrote, adding with uncharacteristic rancor, "It really burns me up and hope I can stay here only long enough to make them eat their own conceit."

Three days later it was her turn to go up again. This time she was going to be examined by a lieutenant from the Army and things did not go so well. The evening of February 11, she wrote home to her family:

> This letter is going to begin on a rather dismal note for
> I got an unsatisfactory mark on my Army progress
> check today. It was rather a shock for I felt sure that I

would pass it but I really did stink it up . . . I will get some more instruction and then another chance and sure hope that I do better. The Lt. was very nice and helpful. I don't seem worried somehow and maybe that is bad and I should be more concerned . . . I really don't know. An awful lot of the girls have flunked their Army checks so maybe it is nothing new, but just the same it is not the best thing in the world that could happen to me. But don't worry, please, for I'm not and I know you love me no matter what happens to me or how terrible I am.

Dora's instructor was surprised that Dora had failed the test and was sure she'd pass the retake. Lots of girls failed their first check rides, but for Dora failure of any kind was unnerving—to the point that it affected her second ride. After ten days with another instructor who told her "there wasn't a thing the matter" with her flying, she went up with the Army lieutenant for another check ride. Again she wrote home to her family with bad news:

Am sorry that I haven't written more often but I kind of wanted to wait until I had some good news to tell you but for now it has been so long and I still have no good news. Yesterday I had another Army check which I messed up much like I did the first one . . . It made me kind of sad, I had no understanding family on whose shoulder I could cry . . . I was rather amazed at the terrible ride I gave the Lt., I knew that I was doing it while we were up but I couldn't seem to do anything about it . . .

But Dora was allowed to keep flying, and after ten more hours of training she had a final chance with a third attempt at the check ride. She passed.

Dora's spirits were lifted somewhat when the new fourth class began arriving and the existing trainees were allowed to pick new rooms. Marge and Dora chose a new, much bigger room in front of the tourist courts, with a bath "you can stretch your arms out in without hitting the walls," as she wrote home to her parents.

Only weeks after the new fourth class moved into their accommodations and began training, however, the women received the worst of news. It was late afternoon on March 7 when Dora's instructor, Banks, flew frantically to the field to report an accident. Immediately all the Army officers on the field left and the ambulance went out. No one knew what had happened until later that night, when Dedie came to the tourist courts to make the sad announcement. Margaret Oldenburg from Berkeley, California, was in the fourth class and had lived about five or six doors down from Dora. She went up in a PT-19 with her instructor, Norris G. Morgan. The weather report had been ideal; it was CAVU—ceiling and visibility unlimited—the best report a pilot can receive. Morgan was introducing Margaret to spins—how to get into them and out of them—so that when she was finally allowed to fly solo, she would be safe. At about 5:45 P.M. they were in the middle of a spin, when instead of pulling out, the spin tightened and they plummeted to the field below. It took less than half an hour for the Army ambulance and officers to arrive at the scene of the crash, but they were too late. Thirty-three-year-old Margaret and her instructor were dead.

Dora had been in a different class from Margaret and hadn't known her well, but she mourned her just the same. Margaret had had a dimpled smile and twinkling dark eyes; she had been married to an ensign in the U.S. Navy, Jack Oldenburg, and often entertained the other women singing songs she had learned when they were stationed in Hawaii. Apparently she had been feeling "swell" just before her flight, as she'd just gotten a rare chance to talk to Jack. Margaret was young and full of promise. She could have been any of them.

Dedie sent telegrams to Margaret's family and also implored the women to remain upbeat and levelheaded in their letters home, to avoid scaring their own family members. But on base the women mourned, asking one another the same question: *Why* had it happened? Margaret was a strong pilot and there was no reason for her to lose control as she did, especially as her instructor was with her. Did the instructor's lack of experience in the plane contribute to the crash? Morgan had had a reputation as a thoughtful, friendly fellow and was well-liked as an instructor, but he had only twenty-one hours in the PT-19 they were flying the day of the crash. Or had something gone wrong with the plane? That night Dora wrote in her diary: "Worst of all things—our first fatal accident—a girl in the fourth class and her instructor spun in, in a PT. There was no hysteria among the girls but all kind of down. As yet they don't know how or why. I was up solo 59 min and dual 1:27 but was down when the accident happened. It was a lovely day for flying."

Following Dedie's advice, Dora deliberately neglected to mention the accident in any of her letters home for a full week. For a young woman who had promised to tell her family everything, holding back information was agonizing, and she soon confessed: "There is something that has been preying on my consciousness all week and I have been trying to figure out how to tell you and whether to tell you or not," she wrote. "It is that last Sunday afternoon a girl and her instructor 'spun in.' They were in an old PT and were both killed instantly . . . It has put a terrible damper on everyone as you know a thing like that can . . . Since then everyone has been extremely cautious. The Army has ridden with all of the instructors again and it has cleared up a good many things like standardizing the sequence, etc."

Dora would sit grounded for a week while her instructors got additional flying time in the BT-13s, the basic trainer the third class was due to move into next. Meanwhile the women collected a quarter from each of the trainees to buy flowers for Margaret's funeral. A few days later there was a ceremony at the field, with the flag at half-mast and taps played in honor of the two who had been killed. "Nothing has been mentioned of it since then," Dora wrote home. "Even at that, we have a very low percentage of accidents compared to the cadets."

This first fatal accident left the women shaken, and it also drew stark attention to their lack of death benefits. With their pseudo-military and pseudo-civilian status, the women's insurance coverage was as haphazard as their housing. Aviation Enterprises was responsible for taking care of any accident or injury that took place as the women moved around in the buses coming to and from the field. For everyday concerns, the women had created a "Cadet Fund" into which they each put $3 and were covered up to $150 for health troubles—an emergency appendectomy, for example. The Army handled hospitalization if they were in a nonfatal aircraft accident. But if a woman pilot died in a crash, her family was not entitled to a cent from the Army. When Margaret Oldenburg's body was sent home to Alameda, California, Dedie sent an escort to go with the casket. Jackie paid for the extra ticket herself. The instructor, forty-one-year-old Norris Morgan, went home to the Galva Cemetery in Knox County, Illinois. His widow and three young daughters received the $10,000 benefit granted to instructors. Margaret's family would have received only a $200 benefit from the Civil Service Commission. After Margaret's death, Dora and many of the others looked into private death insurance, wanting their families to get something in case of a fatal crash. Despite it all, Jack Oldenburg, Margaret's beloved husband, wrote his thanks to the trainees for their kindnesses, urging them to "keep up the good work. I'm with you all."

Jeannette Gagnon (Goodrum) was a student at the University of New Hampshire when she joined their Civilian Pilot Training Program, and learned to fly in a Taylorcraft with skis to land on the snow. She was thrilled to have a chance to join the WASP and quit her job as dean of women at American University to join class 43-W-8. *Courtesy Sherry Dunn*

CHAPTER TEN

The Hopefuls

All across the country, young women who had grown up during the Golden Age of Aviation began reading about Nancy's Women's Auxiliary Ferrying Squadron and Jackie's Women's Flying Training Detachment. Inspired, they signed up for flying lessons in droves, working to increase their hours in order to be eligible to qualify for Jackie's training program.

Mary Anna Martin—known as Marty—was one of these women. In February 1943 she was sitting in her room, flipping through a copy of *Look* magazine. In her senior year at DePauw University, a small liberal arts college just west of Indianapolis, Marty was an avid reader of magazines, and that day she happened to turn to a page with the following headline:

"THE WAFS: A SQUADRON OF 25 GIRLS IS LEADING THE WAY FOR WOMEN FLIERS."

Under the headline was a photograph of eight women pilots wearing heavy leather flying suits, goggles, and boots, standing in front of a row of airplanes.

The article went on to describe the daily lives of the women ferry pilots of New Castle Army Air Base in Wilmington, Delaware. There were five pages of pictures of the women wearing their flying suits, sitting in front of maps and working on their navigation skills, checking aircraft before taking off, and wearing their gray-green uniforms while striding across the runway. According to the article, these were some of the most qualified women pilots in the country.

"They live in wooden barracks," the article explained, "sleep on iron cots, fly day and night, sometimes in open cockpits, in zero weather, perform their hazardous duties with the skill born of hundreds of hours of flying time. These women are the elite of America's auxiliary services."

Marty had gotten to know some male flying students who were training for the Navy while at DePauw, but she had no idea women could do the same. She could only imagine what adventures the women at Wilmington were having, whizzing around the country in their shining planes. These women looked strong; they looked like they were having fun. They also looked like they knew their own minds.

All Marty had ever wanted was to be her own person—not an easy feat for the daughter of a small-town minister. Although she adored her father, being "Reverend Martin's daughter" had its drawbacks. From an early age she resented that everyone in Liberty, Indiana, knew her name. Church members seemed to view her as a sort of extension of her dad, constantly calling on her to help out. The pianist couldn't make it? Mary Anna could do it.

Someone didn't come to teach kids Sunday school? Mary Anna could do it. Finally, Mary Anna had enough. She started attending another church on Sundays just to escape it all. She wanted to be herself, free of anyone else's judgments and expectations.

Even after she defected, her father knew better than to try to tame his daughter's independent spirit. Instead he supported her, teasing her gently about her attendance at the other church. While her father valued Marty's feistiness, her mother felt very differently. She worried about Marty and what would become of her. When Marty was still in high school, she had snuck in a flying lesson, making sure not to tell her parents. But it was a small town, and soon enough they found out and put a stop to her flying, telling her that it was far too dangerous (and not covered by their insurance). By then Marty was dating a boy they considered a little too "fast," and her parents were both worrying about the road she seemed to be heading down. They forced Marty to say goodbye to the boyfriend, hoping to redirect her down a better, safer path.

After graduating high school, Marty did her best to meet her parents' expectations. Following her mother's wishes that she pursue her studies in piano, Marty managed a year at MacMurray Women's College in Illinois on a music scholarship before switching to DePauw University as a major in piano. It didn't stick. She soon changed her course of study to sociology and criminology before finally settling on bacteriology. In early 1943, Marty began thinking about getting into the military. Perhaps this would be her chance to reinvent herself completely. She learned about the WAC (the Women's Army Corps, the women in the U.S. Army), the SPARs (for "*Semper Paratus*—Always Ready," the women of the U.S. Coast Guard), and the WAVES (for "Women Accepted for Volunteer Emergency Service," the women of the U.S. Navy). When she read that the WRENS (for "Women's Royal Navy Service," the British navy's women) were based in Hawaii, she considered joining them, too, because, after all, who wouldn't want to go and live in Hawaii? Marty didn't care which branch; she just knew she wanted to join.

With her college graduation just a few months away, Marty read the article in *Look* about the WAFS and made up her mind. The article mentioned a woman named Jacqueline Cochran "who directs the training of future women ferry pilots at Houston." Clearly, there was a training school for women who wanted to be pilots.

Marty was sure this was her chance. She told her bacteriology professor that she was sorry but she wasn't interested in the graduate fellowship he had found for her at the University of Michigan; she was going to join the military as a pilot. Her professor pointed out that she didn't have a single hour of flight time to her name. How was she going to get into the training program without any experience? But Marty was stubborn and stuck to her plan.

After graduation, she got a job at Eli Lilly's serology laboratory testing blood plasma before it went overseas; her goal was to earn enough money for flying lessons. Marty's mother thought the whole idea was "foolish" and a "very bad mistake," but by now her father had come around to the notion of his daughter as a pilot—and even lent Marty his car to get to the airport for her lessons. She arranged to take her flights at dawn so that her dad could still have his car during the day and she could go to work at the lab after she was done.

Marty was excited about her lessons, but she soon hit a roadblock. Every time she went up in the flight instructor's small Taylorcraft, she became airsick. This queasiness was a real problem. Although most new students at that time tended to solo (fly the plane alone) after around five to eight hours of training, her instructor wouldn't let her do so because she wasn't safe to fly the plane if she was feeling sick. Marty thought she had blown it. She had given up her graduate fellowship and wasted her time by not signing up with some other military service. But something inside her told her to keep going. She would simply have to will her body to cooperate.

Then one day her instructor forgot to bring his cigar along for the flight. For the first time since she'd begun her lessons, Marty felt fine. Once they realized that she was reacting to the cigar smoke, not the flying, the instructor stopped smoking during her flights and Marty excelled at her training. Soon enough, she had her thirty-five hours, the new minimum for WASP trainees. She was ready to apply.

Jackie received over 25,000 applications for the women's flight training program. She could have her pick of prospective trainees, choosing women who were between the ages of eighteen and a half and thirty-five (preferring those who were younger), with the right number of flight hours, some college education in most cases, and ideally a "good attitude" and girl-next-door good looks. She was also looking for women with light-colored skin.

In 1942 the armed forces remained resolutely segregated—and that included the Ferrying Division. Despite the war on fascism overseas, racial discrimination remained a fact of daily life in the United States, with hotels and restaurants often catering to whites only. Entire towns—thousands of them—were known as "sundown" towns, where black Americans faced arrest if they were found within the town limits after dark. In the face of such widespread discrimination, it would have been impossible for an African American woman or man to do the job of a ferry pilot, which entailed flying from place to place and finding your own room and meals as you went. As far as we know, not a single black pilot, male or female—not even the famed Tuskegee Airmen—flew with the Ferrying Division during the war.

While the racism of the day would have made it difficult for Nancy's WAFS to employ black women as ferry pilots—and as far as we know, none applied—it might have been possible for Jackie to admit them into her training program. The women in her program—and Nancy's, for that matter—were officially civilians and not automatically bound by Army rules about segregation. Jackie had already hired women of color at her office in the Pentagon, claiming others called her office "Little Harlem." She praised her black employees' work ethic and claimed not to have "given a damn" about their race. Now that she was in charge of her training program, she was imagining her women would do all kinds of work for the Army Air Force, not just ferrying. Women of color could have easily served in some of those roles. But Jackie decided she wasn't going to rock the boat. Furthermore, the women were training in the South, and Jackie was certain that integration of housing in particular would have posed too many problems for her.

Instead, she actively discouraged black women from applying. She warned one qualified African American woman pilot that she would have a rough time if she did apply, whether Jackie supported her or not, explaining, "I'm having enough troubles without adding blacks to it." According to Jackie, the woman withdrew her application.

Twenty-one-year-old Mildred Hemmons Carter was another black woman pilot who hoped to be accepted into the program. Like Dora, Mildred had learned to fly under the Civilian Pilot Training Program, which offered courses at six black colleges and universities. It's hard to overstate how radical this would have seemed at the time; less than two decades earlier, Bessie Coleman had to find her way to France to earn her pilot's license because no American flight school would train a black woman. Some airports across the country served only white pilots. But in 1939 the newly formed National Airmen's Association of America, which had been created by a number of black aviation enthusiasts in Chicago, successfully lobbied Congress to include an anti-discrimination provision in the bill creating the CPTP. Black women were admitted to the program at the same ratio as their white counterparts: one woman per class of ten.

Mildred had trained at Tuskegee University and met First Lady Eleanor Roosevelt during her visit in March 1941, watching as the black male graduates joined the Army Air Forces and became the famous Tuskegee Airmen. By the time she read about Jackie's program, Mildred was married to a pilot she had met while training at Tuskegee and was working as a civilian at the Tuskegee Army Air Field. Mildred was excited to apply, feeling confident she had a good chance of getting an interview at least. She was well qualified, with her private pilot's license and a bachelor's degree in business. But her résumé, with its Tuskegee credentials, gave her away. Reading her letter of application, Jackie's staff would have known Mildred was not white. By this point they had a standard reply:

> Thank you for your letter. Your desire to help your country in this time of war is very praise-worthy. Unfortunately, there is no provision for the training of colored girls in the Women's Flying Training program. However I would suggest that you investigate the Women's Army Corps since they enlist colored girls for various types of work. If that should not prove to be satisfactory, a war job in your own home town will do just as much to help your country at this time as any duties you might undertake in a military organization.
>
> Very truly yours,

Jacqueline Cochran's name was stamped at the bottom of the letter.

Mildred was furious with disappointment. She tore up the letter and threw it in the trash, having no desire to read it a second time. Instead of being able to use her skills as a pilot to serve her nation, Mildred kept working at Tuskegee, bulldozing trees to clear land for an airstrip, rigging parachutes, and taking on various administrative jobs. Black pilots in general had a difficult time finding opportunities to fly during the war; being a black woman made it all but impossible.

Women of other backgrounds fared somewhat better in their applications, but they remained the exception rather than the rule. Ola Mildred Rexroat, a member of the Oglala Lakota tribe who joined class 44-W-7, is considered the only Native American woman to fly for the military during World War II.

There were also very few Jewish women in the group. One of them, Julie Jenner Stege, had been a dancer in New York and grown accustomed to hiding her Jewishness, as she felt it kept her from getting hired. (Many clubs and other establishments were off-limits to Jews.) When Julie arrived at Sweetwater, she continued to keep quiet about her religion, telling the other girls that she would rather sleep in on Sunday morning than go to church services with them. Another Jewish woman in the program, Bernice "Bee" Falk, of class 44-W-7, was much more open about her background and insisted she didn't face any discrimination for it.

Hazel Ah Ying Lee from Portland, Oregon, was one of only two Asian women to serve in the program. In the 1940s, discrimination against Chinese Americans was rampant, with many towns keeping anti-Chinese Jim Crow–style laws in place decades after the Chinese Exclusion Act of 1882. However, now that China had become a vital ally of the United States in its fight against Japan, American attitudes were beginning to shift. While Japanese Americans were being forcibly interned in isolated camps, the U.S. government and media were working hard to convince the American people to accept their Chinese neighbors. As it turned out, it was just good politics for Jackie to be open to accepting a Chinese American pilot like Hazel.

Hazel had learned to fly ten years earlier, on Swan Island in Portland, where the city's Chinese Benevolent Society funded free lessons for young Chinese Americans in the hopes that they would go to China to fight the Japanese, who had invaded Manchuria in 1931. When Hazel began her flight training, she was twenty years old and working as an elevator operator. Her parents worked in a Chinese restaurant in Portland and retained many customs from

Hazel's father's village in the Toishan District, Kwangtung Province. Hazel learned to cook traditional Chinese meals and, along with her nine siblings, attended Chinese language school. She was well prepared, then, to head to China in March 1933 to serve as a pilot in the war against Japanese aggression. There, Hazel flew as a commercial pilot and was in Guangzhou (Canton) in the spring of 1938 when the Japanese bombed the city, killing hundreds of civilians. Later, she struggled to get back into the United States, as her Form 430, or Citizen's Return Certificate, had been destroyed in a Hong Kong fire, but with evidence from her family and even the Portland doctor who had attended her birth, she was finally allowed back into the country. Hazel went to New York to work for the Chinese government as it scrambled to gather matériel and aircraft to combat the Japanese military.

When Hazel learned about Jackie's training program, she was quick to apply, hoping she would be admitted despite the discrimination of the era. She was.

WASP Claire Callaghan (class 43-W-1) and Ellen Gery (class 43-W-2) take a break with some of their fellow ferry pilots. Romulus Army Air Base. *USAAF photo. Courtesy Texas Woman's University*

CHAPTER ELEVEN

Earning Those Wings

Nancy and Jackie corresponded from the very start of their respective programs, each woman keeping a careful eye on the other. Although they had been in the same flying circles for years, they had never become close. Their early interactions as leaders of the women were marked by a distinct courteousness, which may have masked a calculated wariness.

Nancy sent the first letter, mailed to Jackie from her offices at New Castle Army Air Base on November 4, 1942, to congratulate her on the new training program. "Just a note to tell you how swell I think your training program is," Nancy wrote. "It sounds grand and most thorough. I'm hoping to get out your way soon, and would like very much to see you."

Jackie wrote back from Fort Worth, thanking Nancy for her note. "This job entails a great deal of hard work with no glamor attached," she explained, somewhat defensively, "and I certainly hope the results will be satisfactory and will justify the effort that is going into it." She expressed her hope that they would see each other within the next few weeks.

On February 24, 1943, just before Nancy transferred to Long Beach, the two women spoke on the telephone. Jackie's first class of trainees was about to graduate and move on to Nancy's ferrying group, which would necessitate a new level of interaction between the two leaders. Jackie updated Nancy on the first class's date of graduation, which she said would not be until April at the earliest. Jackie made clear that she wanted to be present whenever Nancy visited Houston to observe the trainees there.

What they don't seem to have discussed in the call was the matter of militarization. By February 1943, Jackie was already working closely with General Arnold to figure out how the women pilots could be brought into the military—and starting to let the trainees know that this was her goal. Yes, they had started out as civilian volunteers, she told them, but that was just a temporary situation.

Jackie's idea was for the program to become a part of the U.S. Army Air Forces, with herself as its leader. Broadly speaking, she wanted the women in the military for purposes of discipline so she could have more control over them, eliminating the chance that they would resign if they didn't like an assignment or were just tired of the job. Insurance was also a priority. Currently the women were buying their own insurance, and if they were killed, their families only received the $200 Civil Service Commission death benefit rather than the $10,000 to which they would be entitled if they were members of the AAF. As it stood, it just wasn't fair.

At the same time, Jackie was clear that she wanted the women to be separate from the men. Again, for Jackie, this was a matter of control. With the women operationally segregated, she could have more say over their day-to-day lives, keeping a close eye on them at all times. Jackie was hypervigilant against any impression that the women might be of "low moral character" and was adamant about there being no question of their sexual propriety. She was determined to do whatever she could to protect the women's reputations—which included preventing unwanted advances and pregnancies—thereby protecting the reputation of the Army Air Forces as a whole.

Nancy also wanted the women to be officially brought into the AAF, but she had very different views from Jackie on how that should be done. From the beginning, Nancy believed women should be fully integrated into the Ferry Command. She simply didn't see the need to segregate the women from the men. In fact, she wanted them to be treated just like the men: civilian male pilots had ninety days of on-the-job training and probation, then took a final flight test before being designated as service pilots and made second lieutenants. Why shouldn't the women have the same? She trusted that her women could fly with male pilots and still retain their moral compasses and reputations. She was also convinced that pilots were pilots, and the women didn't need or want any special treatment—even to protect them from the men in their midst.

How to bring the women into the military had been a matter for debate from the start. General Arnold and other supporters of the women pilots initially believed that tying the women into the Women's Army Auxiliary Corps, or WAAC—which in 1943 was in the process of being militarized—would be the simplest way to go about it. In March of 1943, Congress began holding hearings on the WAAC to decide if it should become an official part of the military under the acronym "WAC"—it would no longer be an auxiliary—putting it in line with the Navy's WAVES and Coast Guard's SPARs, who were already full members of their respective branches. General Arnold was considering whether the bill to create the WAC should incorporate the women pilots.

As the WAC bill began to slowly work its way through Congress, Jackie had other problems to distract her. With a history of poor health care when she was young, she was afflicted with chronic sinus infections and terrible stomach troubles. She had been told by her doctors that she was suffering from abdominal adhesions, a condition in which bands of fibrous tissues form in the abdomen and around the organs, causing them to stick together. The adhesions were causing her intense pain and had gotten so serious that in March 1943 she had to be hospitalized in Los Angeles, not far from the ranch she shared with her husband in Indio. The doctors warned Jackie to slow down or she would require surgery.

On March 29, one of Jackie's secretaries wrote to Nancy Love to say that Jackie should recover and be back in her office by April 5. At that time she would call Nancy about meeting in Houston.

Meanwhile, Nancy and her pilots were experiencing new pushback. In late March 1943 the commander of the 3rd Ferrying Group in Romulus, Michigan, made a rule that limited the WAFS to flying light trainer aircraft only; it seemed calculated to prevent the WAFS in Romulus from making the kinds of advances the WAFS were making at Long Beach. The other rulings were even more bizarre. The women were to fly missions only individually, rather than in groups, which was the usual procedure. And the preference was for the women and the men to fly on alternate days. If the women had to fly on the same day as the male pilots, then they were instructed to fly in opposite directions. And finally, they were informed, "no mixed flight assignments or crew assignments [would] be tolerated."

By keeping the women segregated from the men, flying on alternate days and in opposite directions, the Romulus command was likely seeking to avoid scandal and negative press—and perhaps to frustrate the women, as the commanding officer resented their presence—but these new prohibitions effectively ended the women's ability to fly out of the Romulus base.

And just days after the Romulus directive, the Ferrying Division issued a new restriction of its own. On March 29, 1943, Air Transport Command headquarters sent a letter to all group commanders ordering that women remain grounded while pregnant or when they were having their periods.

Nancy and her flight leader in Wilmington, Betty Gillies, couldn't believe this was coming up again. Only three years earlier, when Betty was still president of the Ninety-Nines, she had led the fight against the CAA attempt to prohibit women from flying while pregnant or menstruating. Betty was the mother of three children and had continued to fly through her pregnancies and during her periods. She knew from firsthand experience that the ruling was nonsense. However, the Civil Aeronautics Administration (CAA) had recently issued their *Handbook for Medical Examiners* with guidelines for women pilots. With no science to support them, the authors warned that "all women should be cautioned that it is dangerous for them to fly within a period extending from 3 days prior to 3 days after the menstrual period." They added that "many women pilots have fainted when flying during this period with fatal results" and concluded that "pregnancy is a disqualifying condition for all grades."

At that time, Betty and the Ninety-Nines had successfully convinced the CAA to change their ruling. Now, three years later, they were prepared to fight again. They'd already had one pregnancy among the WAFS without any problems at all. Esther Manning had married in late 1942, and when she became pregnant, Betty simply allowed her to fly until she couldn't fit in the plane anymore, at which point Esther went home and delivered a beautiful, healthy baby. As for the restriction on women when they were menstruating, this seemed even less defensible—and much harder to enforce. The Ferrying Division would have to either trust the women to self-report or ask every single pilot whether she was menstruating on a daily basis. Nancy and Betty doubted the men of the Ferrying Division wanted to regularly ask the pilots if they were having their periods, and meanwhile, how many of the WAFS were going to report they were menstruating if that meant they couldn't fly? The whole idea was impractical and a waste of time, especially since the women had been flying during their periods—and while pregnant—without serious incident for years.

In the end Nancy managed to get the period ruling overturned by going over Tunner's head, taking the matter straight to General C. R. Smith. (That same month Bob wrote to his wife saying, "I hope you didn't get your head chopped off.") But she was even more concerned about the Romulus base's prohibition of women from flying in the same direction as male pilots, which would further limit which trips the women could make. She made a personal appeal to Air Transport Command headquarters protesting the restrictions, using the women's excellent flight record and her own and others' successful upgrade to more sophisticated aircraft as evidence of the women's capabilities. Finally, under pressure from Nancy, the Army Air Forces chief of staff sent a letter to the Ferrying Division explaining that the WAFS should be permitted to fly any aircraft they were capable of flying on any trip that needed to be taken. "It is the desire of this Command that all pilots, regardless of sex, be privileged to advance to the extent of their ability in keeping with the progress of aircraft development," the letter stated. "Will you please ensure that the terms of this policy are carried out insofar as it applies to ferrying of aircraft within the continental U.S.A."

Although the women had proven themselves, the policy change was also a matter of practicality. In the spring of 1943 the Ferrying Division became a part of the Army Air Forces training system, so the Air Training Command began using the Ferrying Division for advanced training of its combat pilots. The male pilots ferried light planes, then more advanced planes, to gain experience with the aircraft before entering combat. If women pilots were restricted to ferrying only light aircraft, the number of planes available for men to fly would be limited, and there would be a serious lag in their training cycle as a result. By allowing the WAFS to progress to the more advanced aircraft, the lag was prevented, the male combat pilots were trained, and the planes were successfully delivered. They were still restricted from flying with male pilots "except during training," but since delivery flights could be considered training flights when designated as such prior to takeoff, even that limitation could effectively be circumvented.

It was a testament to Nancy's skill and that of her women. If they had had anything other than a safe and efficient flight record when the decision was made, there is little doubt that the AAF would have ended the experiment. No one was about to risk the training of male combat pilots so a few hundred women could ferry trainers. Fortunately, the WAFS' track record was immaculate. And with the first class of Jackie's trainees about to graduate, the experiment was about to get much bigger.

By April 1943 the women of the first class of trainees readied themselves for graduation. The "Famous First" were initially told they would move up to the Ferry Command by February 1943. February became March. In March, just days before they expected to be done with training, graduation was moved once again and the women began referring to "the day we knew would never dawn." Dedie watched as the first class, which had never had much regard for authority, grew more impertinent each day. They found loopholes in the drill manual so they could saunter, skip, and hop to class—anything but march. They buzzed the tourist courts during night flights, flying down low over the women's housing just for the fun of it, and sneaking back into the landing pattern before they could get caught. Dedie, who was splitting her time between the two fields at Houston and Sweetwater, was ready for them to graduate and be gone.

By now Jackie had seen to it that the women's hostile commanding officer, Captain Paul C. Garrett, and his adjunct, Jessie Simon had been moved to another command; Dedie later claimed it was the Aleutians, a very undesirable post, but evidence is lacking. Garrett's replacement, Major Walter W. Farmer, had started on the job in February 1943. One of his first moves was to give Lieutenant Fleishman an official title. Fleishman had been helping the women pilots in a voluntary capacity as their "visiting fireman," but after Major Farmer took over, he was known as the 319th's "Tactical Officer, Special Services Officer, and Physical Education Director."

In his new capacity, Fleishman helped spearhead preparations for graduation, which he was determined to execute with military precision. He sent the second and third classes through so many marching drills that they wore through their shoes. But as the day approached, a problem presented itself. When Army Air Forces pilots graduate, they were always given silver wings, which were pinned to their uniforms. But there weren't any wings for the women. Firmly believing the women had earned those wings, either Lieutenant Fleishman or Dedie Deaton picked up the phone and called Jackie at her ranch in Indio. Jackie was still in the hospital, recovering from her abdominal problems, but Floyd answered for her, giving them permission to buy the wings and send him the bill.

Lieutenant Fleishman went to the post exchange at nearby Ellington Field, Houston, to buy twenty-three pairs of silver pilot wings, which he brought to a local jeweler. The jeweler embellished the shield symbol, signifying that the wearer was a pilot, and engraved "W-1" in the center, for the women's class. A banner above read "319." As promised, Jackie and Floyd paid for it all.

Jackie left St. Vincent's Hospital in Los Angeles in time to spend a day or two resting at the ranch in Indio before her flight to Houston for the graduation ceremony. She was still in considerable pain but wouldn't miss it for the world. Unable to sit up, she hired a mortuary's "meat wagon" to take her the two hundred miles to the Phoenix airport for her flight to Texas.

On graduation day, April 24, 1943, despite leaving the hospital only a few days earlier, Jackie got dressed, put on her makeup, and readied herself to face the cameras. She wore a bright floral print dress and was hatless, her hair in loose curls. Carefully, she stepped up onto the speakers' stand, flags fluttering in the breeze behind her, military men flanking her on either side in their uniforms and caps. No one would have ever known how sick she was as she stood there, surveying the scene, reveling in her achievement. She had fought to start and lead the program, to find the women housing, to get them out of that hodgepodge of civilian planes and into military aircraft. She had told her pilots that they just needed to get through it, thereby proving to the world that women could fly. And she had made it to graduation, beautifully turned out as ever, despite a journey of many miles while in considerable pain. Jackie was nothing if not a fighter. Although Nancy had been invited to graduation, she chose not to attend.

The names of the twenty-three graduates were called, and Jackie watched as each strode up to the podium, where Jackie and Colonel Walter H. Reed, the commanding officer of Ellington Field, pinned on the women's wings. "I've done this for hundreds of cadets, but never pinned wings on a woman before," Reed whispered to one of the women. "If I stick you, for heaven's sake don't jump. My wife is in the front row, and I'd never live it down." The newsreels "gummed up" the whole process for nearly twenty minutes as they maneuvered to get just the right pictures. Rear Admiral Colbert, the head of the U.S. Coast and Geodetic Survey, proudly pinned the wings on his daughter Mary Lou while the media swarmed. Jackie quietly handed each graduate a small box with a silver disc inside inscribed "43-W-1, April 24, 1943" as her own commemoration to them. The entire ceremony was complete in under two hours. Finally the guinea pigs, the "Famous First" class 43-W-1, had their hard-earned silver wings.

With the first graduation behind her, Jackie began to think of the future. Just days before her graduates were to report to their ferrying bases, Jackie wrote to General Arnold. In the letter she reminded him that the number of women in the Ferry Command was about to double and would only grow from there. As the women were moved to multiple bases, she argued, they needed a woman to coordinate personnel issues. Jackie presented herself as a solution to the problem:

> You need eyes and ears in whom you have confidence, and they must be feminine. That's the job I would like to do, and which I think I can do well.

Jackie was humble enough, or perhaps clever enough, to urge Arnold to choose one woman for the job, even if it wasn't herself:

> While this is the job I have foreseen for myself from the beginning, and I think you have too, I would feel the same way about the need for this kind of overall coordination even if you should select someone else. I would rather lose my identity with the women's flying project and see it go well, than have all the rank and power you could give me in a set-up that could produce only mediocre results by comparison . . .

Despite her modesty in the letter, there's no doubt that Jackie wanted to be the women's only leader. The WFTD and WAFS were already two parts of one program: training and active duty. As her first class of trainees graduated, Jackie might have begun to realize she was going to eventually work herself out of a job. Her letter to General Arnold was her way of asking for her role to be elevated and for her to retain some control over the women pilots even after they were done with training, just as she had planned before the Ferrying Division installed Nancy as the leader of the WAFS in September 1942.

After graduation, the twenty-three women of the first class left for their new stations. They were split among the bases at Wilmington, Long Beach, Dallas, and Romulus. When Jane Straughan, who was headed for Wilmington, learned that she was joining another group of women pilots, she was surprised: she thought the members of her class 43-W-1 were the first women pilots to fly for the Army Air Forces. The fact that she had no idea about Nancy's existing group reveals just how keen Jackie must have been to promote the idea that she was the women pilots' lone leader.

By all accounts, Nancy's women were initially uneasy about "Jackie's girls" joining their ranks and questioned whether these new recruits had the skills to match such an elite group of fliers. On some bases the new graduates felt insecure in the beginning. In Wilmington, at least, the women held a welcoming party for the new pilots, and it didn't take long for Jane and her classmates to prove they fit in. Before long, they were telling stories and sharing experiences as if they'd known one another all their lives.

Madge Rutherford (Minton) and Violet Thurn (Cowden), 43-W-4 in Sweetwater, show the tall and the short of it. For her medical exam, petite Vi raised her hairdo and ate a dozen bananas to meet height and weight requirements. She went on to fly P-51s throughout the war. *Madge Rutherford Minton Collection. Courtesy Texas Woman's University*

CHAPTER TWELVE

Avenger Field

Hazel Ah Ying Lee was one of the first women to arrive at Avenger Field, the new base Jackie had found in West Texas. She was a member of the fourth class, which had been split in two, with half the women beginning at the new base in Sweetwater and half the women beginning in Houston, about four hundred miles away. Sweetwater was quite the change from Houston, with its wide plains that slowly rose into shallow plateaus, its dry khaki-colored earth covered with dry grass and scrubby, squatty mesquite trees. Like the rest of the trainees, Hazel got her first glimpse of Avenger Field from the distance, its rows of shining silver planes lined up neatly, visible through a haze of heat and dust.

Although Hazel and the other women were excited to get settled into their new base, the townspeople of Sweetwater were less enthused. For the past few years the locals had grown accustomed to having an all-male Army Air Forces training school for cadets and British pilots located within a few miles of their town. These young men spent their money at local businesses, adding a boon to the local economy. Sweetwater's young women were especially pleased to have an airfield full of pilots for dances and dates with men from all over the country—and even from England—transforming a backwater into a little bit of social heaven.

After the women pilots arrived on the field, however, the men no longer wanted to go into town, as they very conveniently had a large number of women, all of whom knew more than a little bit about airplanes, right in the same mess hall. The townspeople of Sweetwater didn't know what to think. Who were these women pilots? The reputation of women serving in the military at the time was not a good one: the prevailing assumption was that if women were stationed on an Army base, they must be camp followers, or prostitutes meant to serve the men. And if they weren't prostitutes, then they must be lesbians. Why else would they want to spend time at an Army base wearing uniforms with so many other women doing "men's" work?

Dedie was put on high alert by Jackie to quash any fraternization between the trainees and the men. However, this was a challenge, as the women seemed to enjoy the camaraderie and competition of having members of the opposite sex on the field, even if there were some privacy concerns. The men's barracks were only a few short feet away from the women's, and—in an effort to preserve the modesty of the women pilots—Aviation Enterprises had painted the windows on their barracks black. But in the searing Texas heat, the women soon opened their windows in the hope of a breeze, privacy be damned. They'd crouch low beneath the windows as they snuck from the showers to their lockers, hoping none of the men would decide to peek. In the mess hall, the men were supposed to sit at one end and the women at the other. But pretty quickly everyone would arrive for meals looking his or her best, with the cadets spending much of their mealtimes trying to impress and entertain the women. Dedie watched the coed group closely, on alert for even a whiff of scandal, only allowing movies on Friday and "dates" for dinner on Saturday and Sunday.

While meals provided a chance to mingle, when it came to flying, competition was the game. Each group worked hard to make certain the other didn't achieve a better flying record. The male cadets were in the hangar just south of the women's, and each flying period the two groups would race to the taxi line to see who could take off first. On any given day there could be nearly one hundred planes trying to take off, find a piece of sky to practice various maneuvers, and land, all in the same time window. It was guaranteed that whoever taxied out last ate the first group's dust. Madge Rutherford of Greensburg, Indiana, remembered the air being full of sand all the time and wrote home, "I wake up every morning with Texas between my teeth." Often, the women watched the cadet "upperclassmen" enviously as they flew solo for the first time. A plane would come in to land and taxi to a stop, the instructor would clamber out across the wing, and the plane would take off again, this time with the pilot flying alone. The women could almost see "the instructor's hands clasped in fervent prayer," as the plane went up. They couldn't wait until it was their turn to go up solo and make their instructors pray for their safe return.

After the men finished their training and left for good, Avenger Field had women trainees and became a popular spot for "emergency" landings—the men training at nearby bases apparently wanted to see these women pilots for themselves. Jackie quickly cracked down, forbidding unauthorized flights from landing at Avenger, which soon came to be known as "Cochran's Convent."

———

Hazel Ah Ying Lee seems to have been universally well-liked by her classmates. She was smart, had a great sense of humor and an infectious laugh, was a terrific storyteller, and was compassionate by nature. Hazel was also a highly experienced pilot, which made the training course fairly easy for her, and so she was always willing to help a classmate in need. Yet, as the only Chinese American on base, Hazel faced unique challenges. At the time, anti-Japanese sentiment was at a high: the United States was imprisoning some 117,000 Japanese Americans in internment camps, and Japanese mini-submarines were patrolling the West Coast. As someone of Asian descent flying around in an airplane, Hazel ran the risk of being mistaken for a Japanese invader. *Life* magazine addressed the problem of Americans confusing the Japanese with their Chinese allies, devoting a stunning article in late December 1941 complete with pictures delineating the supposed differences between people of the two nations, down to the color of their complexions and the shape of their noses.

One day Hazel found herself caught up in a terrible hailstorm and so she quickly landed in a field. As she climbed out of the cockpit, she was met by the farmer with a pitchfork, who was certain he had captured a Japanese pilot. Hazel tried to calm him down, as she later regaled her bay mates with the story, by playing directly to stereotype, putting on an accent and protesting: "Wait a minute, wait a minute! Me Chinaman, me no Japanese!" After one of Hazel's friends and classmates, Madge Rutherford, learned about what had happened, she wrote home to her parents, explaining how worried she'd been that "some ignorant Texas farmer or rancher would shoot her for a Japanese spy."

Madge wasn't the only one worrying about mistaken identities. Dedie Deaton soon learned that a group of prostitutes claiming to be pilots from Avenger Field had set up shop in Sweetwater's Blue Bonnet Hotel. Dedie made the discovery on a bus to Sweetwater after a brief trip home to Wichita Falls when some men from Camp Barkeley, about fifty miles from Avenger Field, mistook her for one of the Blue Bonnet women and propositioned her. When Dedie told them in no uncertain terms to leave her alone, the men warned her not to get so "high and mighty," as they knew all about the women pilots at Avenger. In response, Dedie did the only thing she could think to do to protect and preserve the reputation of her women trainees: she prohibited overnights off the base (unless a woman could prove her mother or husband was visiting), setting a midnight curfew on Saturday and 9:00 P.M. on Sunday, and then published announcements in the Sweetwater paper specifying this.

For her part, Jackie was outraged about this slight on the women's reputation—and concerned. She called on the mayor of Sweetwater, using all the charm and grace she could muster to convince him the women pilots were innocent. After the Blue Bonnet incident, Jackie began encouraging her trainees to go to the local churches to convince the locals they were good, upstanding young women. It rapidly became obvious to the townspeople that the women at the hotel were not the same as the women training to fly for the Army Air Forces, and the prostitutes were hurried out of town. Soon the people of Sweetwater decided to host a "hospitality day" for the pilots, where each of the trainees signed up to go to a church of their choice, then home for dinner with a church member. Not all of the women were thrilled with this arrangement—particularly the Jewish women—but Jackie was determined to send a message.

It wasn't long before the Army decided that two different training bases for women pilots was one too many. They would abandon humid, foggy Houston altogether and move all the women to Sweetwater. Dedie was determined that the Sweetwater trainees would have a smoother transition into military life than the first few classes had had. As a result, life at Sweetwater was strict. Each morning at 6:00 A.M. the women awoke to the sound of reveille played on a trumpet by Nelle Carmody, a trainee from 43-W-6, who had led a swing band before joining the WTFD. Once up, the women had to clean their barracks and get to breakfast by 6:30. They had an hour for breakfast, but with a fifteen-minute wait in line for food, it was shorter than it seemed. At least the food was a happy improvement over Houston: there were eggs, bacon, toast and jam, milk, and real butter; that, with the endless coffee and even pink lemonade, made it easier to forget there was even a war on. But their metal trays with little dividers helped remind them, as each one had to be scraped off by hand over a giant trash can, which gave the women the sense they were really in the Army. Then they were off to ground school and flying. In addition to the actual flying, the women also had ten hours in the Link Trainer, a primitive flight simulator devised in the 1930s that let them practice flying while still on the ground. After all that, the women were still required to have one hour per day, six days a week, of calisthenics and some 230 hours of ground school before graduation.

What's more, Sweetwater was a "dry" town, which meant no beer in the evenings or on weekends as Dora and the Houston crowd had become accustomed to enjoying. In late May the second class, 43-W-2—the last women pilots left in Houston, since Dora's class had left weeks earlier—arrived for their graduation, bringing with them some six cases of liquor for their planned wet party. The graduation ceremony was simple and successful. The band from the bombardier school at Big Spring, Texas, came to play. The newsreels recorded it all. The non-graduates stood on the hot pavement of the runway, trying to stand at parade rest and not to squirm as the heat burned through the soles of their shoes.

Few families of the women pilots were able to make it to the ceremony, because of the rationing of tires and gasoline and the limited availability of train travel for personal purposes. Instead, the people of Sweetwater showed up in droves. Dedie and Jackie had invited them on purpose, determined to lay to rest any lingering rumors and to prove that the smartly dressed women of

Avenger Field standing to attention were patriots first and fore-most, doing their part to help win the war.

Just as the second class was graduating and leaving, the seventh class of trainees began arriving at Sweetwater, dutifully reporting to the Blue Bonnet Hotel to check in and await further instruc-tions. The hotel, built in 1927, was seven stories tall, a regular sky-scraper by Sweetwater standards. The ground floor hosted a drugstore that the women from the field frequented when they went to town on the weekends; there they could buy soap, paper, and cold cream, and even sometimes have their laundry done if they missed the truck from the field. Despite the earlier fuss with the prostitutes posing as women trainees, the store owners took good care of the girls so far away from home, helping them send mail when the post office was closed and often refusing to take money for the postage. On a few occasions they even shipped home the women's unneeded suitcases, dragging them over to the Railway Express Agency office when it opened on Monday morn-ing. At one point the store obtained the pilots' birth records from the field office, sending a decorated cake to each one on her birth-day. The generosity and kindness of the people at the Blue Bonnet Hotel drugstore kept the women coming back.

Most new recruits spent their first night in Sweetwater up late with the rest of the new arrivals, excitedly learning who was from where, figuring out people they knew in common, and trying to determine who was the hottest pilot among them. Each woman had a different story: some came from money, while others worked for a living; some had scraped together just enough for the train ride down, while others bought expensive airline tickets or drove their own cars. The one thing they all had in common was that they loved airplanes. Back home in Ohio, twenty-one-year-old Caro Bayley had felt so isolated, usually the only woman on the field. All of a sudden she could talk about airplanes as much as she wanted and no one thought she was strange or boring—quite the opposite. For the first time Caro had a feeling of belonging, of being among women who loved to fly as much as she did. She remembered thinking she'd "died and gone to heaven." Meanwhile Katherine "Kaddy" Landry, twenty-five and a "Rosie the Riveter" from Michigan, good-naturedly grumbled, "Good Lord, I've never seen so many women in one place in my whole life. I'm gonna get awful sick of seeing nothing but females," and then kept talking airplanes until 3:00 A.M. with the rest of them.

The next morning at 8:00 A.M. sharp, a cattle wagon came to take the new recruits to Avenger Field. As the truck drove closer to their new home, they clamored to look out the small windows as planes roared overhead. It was hard for them to believe how many aircraft there were in the skies and that a woman was flying each one. Would they be up to the same challenge? Winifred "Winnie" Wood remembered seeing a big, colorful Fifinella sign welcoming them from the top of the administration building as they neared the field. Then the women were shown the field itself. One can only imagine the enormity of emotion they must have felt at the sight of an airfield full of planes that they—*women*—were going to have a chance to fly. It must have been the same kind of heart-racing joy of an excited child with a new bicycle on Christmas morning.

For her part, Dedie prepared herself to face yet another group of young women under her command. She had been on the job for over six months, and she recognized the kind of person she needed to be if her program was going to succeed: someone who took charge and set rules. By June of 1943, Dedie was using the thirty-three-page "delinquency list" of the Gulf Coast Army Air Forces Training Command to discipline the women. The trainees received demerits for everything from lint on their clothing to the more egregious playing of the radio when not authorized. The women of the unruly first class would have laughed at these regulations, but Dedie was learning her way and following the path set by the Army Air Forces male cadets.

An Army officer came and regularly inspected their rooms. The Sweetwater women worked themselves into a frenzy getting their bays ready, as it took only seven demerits to confine you to base, and too many demerits had you kicked out of the program altogether. Some used rulers to smooth and pat out the bedcovers. Others crawled under their cots, pulling the sheets and blankets tight from underneath. As the lieutenant entered the room, they all did their best to stand at attention at their bunks, carefully palming the tissue they had used for last-second dusting. They may have been serving as civilians, but at moments like this the women certainly felt like they were in the real Army now.

Dedie wasn't merely responsible for ensuring that the women adhered to impeccable military standards; she was also expected to hold them to Jackie's behavioral standards. Jackie cared deeply about the public and military perception of her women. She knew that it would take only the smallest of scandals—a pregnancy or an affair with one of the married officers—to reach the press for the whole program to be put in jeopardy. As establishment officer, Dedie found herself having to walk a fine line between enforcing Jackie's ideals and accepting that no matter what she did, the young women were going to want to have a bit of fun. As a result, Dedie regularly turned a blind eye to parties held at nearby Lake Sweetwater—initially even when instructors attended—but she strongly drew the line at the sort of fraternizing with the men that could lead to a full-blown scandal. As a result, she bore down hard on any drinking on base. Throughout the early months of the program, Dedie found she could keep Jackie's confidence and full support in running the school—as long as she kept the women in line and out of the newspapers.

Dedie also added to her duties as establishment officer, giving the women regular swimming lessons at the Sweetwater municipal pool, which helped her to keep an eye on them when they weren't flying or in classes. At first the women had gone to the pool to have fun and escape the Texas heat, but Dedie, who was certified as a water safety instructor, realized she could keep her certification current by offering lessons to the women. Soon she had them at the pool three days a week. At one point Dedie decided the trainees needed survival swimming classes and threw them into the pool in their coveralls.

On base and at the pool, Dedie had the women under control with her uncanny ability to be everywhere at once. But beyond those areas, it was harder for her to extend her supervision. Lake Sweetwater was about five miles south of town, and if the women could talk someone with a car into going, they would drive out to the lake on the weekends to cool off and relax—and escape from Dedie's eagle eye. Sometimes they would camp out at the lake or even rent a cabin. Often their instructors joined them, along with officers from nearby Camp Barkeley. Despite the fact that Sweetwater was a dry town and drinking was strictly forbidden by Dedie, the women managed to lay their hands on alcohol for their trips to the lake, some of it sourced from an old woman in town who made moonshine and sold it out the back door of her little house.

Dates became a regular occurrence, and Jackie began to grow concerned about the fraternization going on between the women pilots and the men, either at the lake or in town. Meanwhile the newsreel crews kept coming throughout that summer of 1943, contributing to a growing collection of stories about the women. The press attention only heightened Jackie's anxiety that there would be a scandal and the program would be disgraced.

Another consequence of all the publicity was that Jackie arranged for the women to coordinate their physical appearance. When a *Life* magazine spread showed the women in a hodgepodge of outfits, wearing everything from strappy, open-toed sandals to Spalding tennis shoes to leather oxfords, Jackie decided that wouldn't do. The newsreels taken of the women doing calisthenics later that summer showed them in matching navy blue rompers. By that time the novelty of the publicity had begun to wear off. When *Life* first came to the field, many of the women were excited about the attention and had fun posing for the camera. Now they dragged their feet when they had to go outside in the heat to pretend to exercise or sunbathe for the newsreels. (All of the photographers wanted them to sunbathe to show they were just "ordinary girls" who happened to be pilots.)

In August 1943, Dedie stepped up her campaign to rein in the women. She began keeping records of "board hearings," a type of tribunal where women who were in some kind of trouble were assessed and often dismissed from the program. For the most part, the women were pulled in front of the board for lack of flying ability. During the hearings the women were assessed for their mistakes as well as their looks and general demeanor. Dedie and the board seemed to have looked favorably on girls who had a "nice attitude" and a neat appearance. These girls were sometimes given a second chance in the form of extra time or an additional check ride. But if trainees cried too much—if they had a "poor attitude" or were sloppily dressed—they would be described in the notes as "mentally unstable" and denied a second chance.

Then there were the women who were called before the board for drinking or fraternizing with the male officers on base. Dedie looked much less kindly on these kinds of violations, which had the potential to generate bad press and potentially bring down the program altogether. These women were quickly eliminated and sent home with sternly worded notes to their families. To Dedie, it didn't matter whether a woman had been the victim of harassment by men on base; she still had to go. In one case a young woman came before the board after her instructor made a pass at her, she rejected him, and he failed her. Dedie knew what had happened but maintained that her hands were tied. She sent the woman home.

Dedie was especially intolerant of any signs of lesbian activity and later recounted that she was more likely to put up with fraternization between a man and woman than she would between two women. When reports came back to Dedie that two of the trainees were dating, sleeping together in the bay after lights-out, she quickly had both women dismissed. One woman tried to take the blame, saying she had instigated the relationship, so that her girl-friend could continue to fly. But Dedie still made them both pack their bags. She admitted later that she couldn't stand even the thought of homosexuality and that "when I see a butch, I gag."

Although there are no known official records on the matter, by Dedie's account at least two women became pregnant during the course of the program. In an era before reliable birth control, it was perhaps inevitable that this would come to pass, but when Jackie received word of the pregnancies, she hit the roof. Preserving the women's reputation was tantamount to preserving her own. She came to Sweetwater immediately.

Several of the women reported that Jackie had arrived on base and was "making herself disagreeable and unpopular." Although the women didn't seem to know what was going on, they did get wind of Jackie having "a scandalous fight with the Major." Tensions were high and the trainees were "tip-toeing around for fear something will crack." Soon enough, the twelve Army men on base were summarily shipped out, to be replaced with older married men who would not be so much trouble. One of the trainees, Madge Rutherford, reported home, "It seems Miss Cochran thinks we have too many privileges, that the present personnel has been too lenient with us in matters of weekends and dates." While unhappy with the loss of the instructors and command that she liked, Madge admitted that "unfortunately it's true." New trainee Caro Bayley could already see why the men were all leaving: "They are too susceptible to the girls." And while the *Avenger*, the new name for the women's paper now that they were in Sweetwater at Avenger Field, wrote a warm farewell with "deep regret" to the

Army men, Dora was relieved. "We got word that the entire Army personnel up here is going to be moved out and it is a good thing too for they couldn't get in anything that could be much worse no matter what so at least our class is satisfied." The officers had been resentful toward the women who came to Sweetwater from Houston, showing clear favoritism to those who were at Avenger Field from the beginning of the training. As far as she was concerned, it was good riddance.

Dedie would later claim that two officers on the field fathered two children. She also recalled that one of the pregnant women trainees left, got an abortion, and returned after a sixty-day leave. Dedie had the woman's references checked when she found out about the pregnancy, and as all reported her to be a "nice girl," Dedie concluded that perhaps she had simply made a mistake. She decided that when the situation had cleared, the woman could return—and although she was "washed back" to a later class because she was behind with flying, her classmates were never the wiser. And the woman's reputation remained intact.

At Camp Davis, pilots towed targets behind war-weary planes, training the ground gunners to fire live ammunition at a moving target. Dora Dougherty (top) was among them. *USAAF photo*.

CHAPTER THIRTEEN

Expansion

As Jackie's trainees were successfully moving their way through the program, the Army Air Forces realized that as the number of women flying for them on active duty grew, it was becoming more difficult to document their work for the experiment—and it was sometimes unclear who was actually in charge. They were moving toward making the women an official part of the AAF as well. Under pressure from Jackie, they decided it was time to formally bring the women under one leader. On July 5, 1943, General Arnold made the news official. From that point on, Jacqueline Cochran would serve as the director of women pilots—all of them. Jackie was finally in charge, just as she'd always hoped.

Not everyone was happy with the news of Jackie's appointment. Colonel Tunner, the man responsible for Nancy's women ferry pilots, had tried to shut Jackie out of a leadership role from the beginning, and he actively resisted Jackie's new appointment. The Air Transport Command had very different qualification standards for the women—namely, higher minimum flight time—and Tunner believed he should be able to control his own pilots and have some say over their selection, training, and duties. In an attempt to undermine Jackie and likely with Arnold's blessing, he made his own appointment, also on July 5, announcing that Nancy Love was now a part of his staff, as executive of women pilots in the Ferrying Division. This set off a media frenzy, with headlines reading "COUP FOR COCHRAN" and the appointments presented as a catfight between the two famous pilots. But Jackie and Nancy—publicly, anyway—smiled and said it all made perfect sense.

That same month, the women learned they would not be joining the Women's Army Auxiliary Corps, as many had thought they might. In mid-June 1943, General Arnold had sent a memorandum to the Army chief of staff, General George Marshall, who was in charge of coordinating the Allied war effort in Europe and the Pacific, explaining that all of his commanding officers working with the women pilots wanted them to be militarized but independently of the WAAC (or the soon-to-be-legislated WAC). Arnold explained that the "Director of Women's Flying Training [Jackie Cochran] urges this procedure, which is overwhelmingly favored by the women pilots and trainees, themselves." General Arnold strongly advocated for the women pilots remaining separate and under the Army Air Forces.

There were, in fact, several problems with the pilots joining the other women in the Army. The women of the Women's Army Corps, while important volunteers for the war effort, did not have the same qualifications as the women pilots. The AAF had discovered it was easier to train younger pilots, men and women as young as nineteen; meanwhile the WAC minimum age was twenty-one. The AAF pilots needed one year of college or the equivalent, with some exceptions based on flight experience; the WAC only had to have two years of high school. Arnold reported that, in 1943, 20 percent of the women actively flying had children under fourteen, and some 15 percent of trainees had children; the WAC didn't allow their women to have any dependents under the age of fourteen. There were other practical reasons, too, among them that the WAC had no provision for flight pay. Most important, Arnold argued, the women pilots were pilots first. They were doing the same jobs men pilots were doing. Having them administratively and operationally controlled outside of the AAF simply did not make sense.

Ever the pragmatist, Arnold had an alternative to bringing the women in via the WAC—and a precedent for it. Just months earlier Congress had passed Public Law 38, which allowed women physicians and surgeons to become part of the Medical Corps of the Army and Navy, making them full members of the military without having to join the WAC or WAVES. Arnold believed the precedent had been set for women with special skills to be brought into the AAF with independent legislation. He was betting the fate of his women pilots that he was right.

Less than two weeks after Arnold sent his memo to General Marshall, he sent Jackie to have a face-to-face talk with Colonel Oveta Culp Hobby, the head of the WAC. During this meeting, Arnold wanted Jackie to determine how much control Hobby would have over the women if the WASP were to become part of the WAC. Jackie and Hobby had met before, and it hadn't gone well: there seems to have been an immediate and lasting antipathy between these two powerful women. When Hobby suggested that the women would have to go through her basic training as well as AAF pilot training, Jackie simply told her: "I don't think so." When Jackie informed Hobby that pilots were "temperamental" and needed to be handled by people who understood them—the implication being that Hobby did not—Hobby coolly responded:

"There is no use in our discussing it as the decision will not be made at my level. Nor will the decision be made at your level in the Air Forces."

The resistance of both General Arnold and Jackie Cochran seemed to be enough. In July 1943, a week after Jackie and Colonel Hobby met, the Women's Army Auxiliary Corps became the Women's Army Corps, without the women pilots written into the law. Jackie was determined to keep it that way. It was a gamble to throw away a chance for the women to be in the military, but, fully confident that she had General Arnold's support, Jackie told her women pilots they would still be in the Army Air Forces within the next ninety days—with her in charge.

That same July, Dora Dougherty completed her training and graduated to active duty, finally earning her silver wings. Immediately after her graduation, she went back home for July 4 celebrations with her family, driving back down to Texas with a friend and arriving at her new station—Love Field, just outside Dallas—on July 16. Dora had chosen Romulus, Michigan, as her top choice, as it was so close to home, and listed Love Field last, as it was farthest away. However, when assignments came out the day before graduation, Dora learned she had been assigned to Love Field. As her father told her, "You're learning about the real Army now."

Dora had barely unpacked her bags in Dallas before she was informed by the squadron leader, Florene Miller, that she was off to D.C. on a classified mission. Via the Air Transport Command, Jackie had directed Nancy to assign her women to report at once for two weeks of temporary duty. The ATC made phone calls seeking clarification from Jackie, but they were told that the matter was "too secret to divulge." Only a few days into her new role as director, Jackie was already wielding her power. Nancy and the Ferrying Division resentfully issued the orders as instructed.

Soon, twenty-five graduates of Jackie's training program, including Dora, assembled at the Mayflower Hotel in Washington, D.C., where Jackie was staying. Jackie began to explain in guarded terms why they were there. The women were going to be part of an experiment to see just what women pilots could do outside of the Ferrying Division. Jackie promised they were going to fly B-26 bombers and other bigger, faster planes, and that she would give them more information over the next few days. She urged them to keep quiet about the change in their duty, as she was still working out the details. If they failed in their mission, they would be returned to the Ferrying Division, and Jackie indicated she didn't want the embarrassment of the Air Transport Command knowing the women were unable to fly more advanced aircraft.

Jackie and the Army Air Forces had decided to expand the women pilots' role to encompass jobs beyond ferrying: what Jackie described as "aerial dishwashing"—work no one particularly wanted to do but that had to be done. Her move was strategic. General Arnold wanted to bring the women into the AAF as military pilots, but he knew it would be a tough fight in Congress. The new expansion of the women's duties was a way to demonstrate their capacity and thus make them more valuable to the Army. Much was riding on the success of these twenty-five pilots, and Jackie knew it. The reality was that General Tunner of the Ferrying Division and the Air Transport Command didn't want too many of Jackie's graduates; it was not because they were women—he loved the work the WAFS were doing—but because he was worried the new women did not have enough flying time, even after training. He didn't care for Jackie's forthright style, resented the authority she had been given, and much preferred Nancy. The tension between Tunner and Jackie only got worse, and she knew that if her gamble to expand the women's duties failed, Tunner would be first in line to seize the opportunity to discredit her.

After the meeting at the Mayflower, Dora was assigned to room with her friend and classmate Isabel Fenton—or "Izz"—at the Dodge Hotel, just one and a half blocks from the U.S. Capitol. The women stayed up late, beyond excited at their good luck. The next morning the twenty-five of them piled into buses and made their way to Jackie's office in the newly built Pentagon, which had just opened in January 1943. Dora had never been to the nation's capital before. She loved the wide streets, the parks, and the river, and strained to look out the windows as they passed the Capitol, the Smithsonian, the White House, the Washington Monument, and the Lincoln Memorial before going across the Potomac River into Arlington. Once inside the Pentagon, the women were led through a maze of stairways, ramps, and passageways until they found Jackie's office. Jackie then guided them a short distance down the hallway for a meeting with General Henry "Hap" Arnold, now a four-star general. The women waited in a large conference room with a glass-topped table and red leather chairs, jumping to attention when Arnold entered the room.

As Dora later described, Arnold had the "aura of a man in command." He complimented the women on the job they were doing and explained that he had a new task for them: he needed their help finding out if women could be counted on for other piloting jobs besides ferrying. Dora and the rest of the pilots were thrilled to meet him and hear him say their country needed them. Even so, the details of what they would actually be doing remained cryptic. After the short meeting, Jackie hurried the women back down the hall to her office, where they crowded together, hanging on her every word. Now that she had wowed the women with their visit to the Pentagon and meeting with Arnold, she told them where they were going.

Their destination was Camp Davis Army Air Field, in Onslow County, North Carolina. It wasn't going to be pretty. Camp Davis was surrounded by swamps, mud, and mosquitoes. They would live in the simple nurses' barracks and eat from a small, unappealing mess hall or field kitchen. On the plus side, the women would be near the ocean, and Jackie promised the experiment would only last ninety days, after which they would be transferred someplace less dismal.

The following day, the women boarded General Arnold's camouflaged C-47 Skytrain. Aside from the two Army pilots and a crew chief, they had the ship to themselves. (The women had fun calling the crew chief "hostess," Dora wrote in her letter home, although "he didn't like it very well.") Despite its size, the young pilots had a tough time finding the Army's 45,000-acre Camp Davis, which was hidden in swamps. They ended up landing in Wilmington, North Carolina, to ask for directions, then learned they had flown a humiliating thirty miles southwest of their destination.

Finally, Camp Davis came into view and the plane began its descent. Even though they knew they were only a half hour's drive from Wilmington, the base looked completely isolated, its long rows of low, red-roofed wooden buildings surrounded by the dark trees and thick vegetation of the looming swamp. As they taxied toward the big square hangar with a control tower sticking out of its roof, reminding Dora of a child's building blocks, she eagerly looked at the rows of planes. She later remembered, "The planes were painted a dull, khaki color with the star of our country on their sides. Here were the warplanes we had come to fly. They were not new and shining. They looked dark and dirty, but big and exciting nonetheless." As the women pilots climbed out of the plane, sweaty in their uniforms but wearing their wings as badges of honor, they found a line of men squinting to get a look at them. Commanding officer Major Lovick Stephenson, whom Dora described in her letter home that evening as a "stubby, balding man," met them "with a forced smile and a too-eager handshake" and welcomed them to the 4th Tow Target Squadron of the Third Air

Force. Waiting with him were a number of captains and lieutenants and a group of mechanics.

It was hard not to feel as if they had just landed on another planet where they were not particularly welcome. The Army base was home to some 20,000 men—including a group of British combat pilots—spread among the airport and three different camps, of which the air field was just one. The women later found out that there had been a small rebellion on the field before their arrival, with the enlisted men who worked on the flight line rushing to get transferred out to avoid serving with "girl" pilots. The commanding officer had persuaded the men to stay only by agreeing to transfer them later, after they'd helped him get adjusted to the women's arrival.

While the pilots at Camp Davis were skeptical, the waiting mechanics were thrilled to have young women on the desolate base and gave them each a soap and towel as a welcome gift. Next, the women were taken to their rooms in the nurses' barracks, which were furnished with Army cots, desks, chairs, open lockers, and shelves, all of it appearing quite hastily thrown together from unvarnished wood. The mechanics had kindly covered the windows of their rooms with shades so they'd have privacy—a luxury that didn't extend to the shared toilets, which were without doors. The women were also given mosquito netting, a necessity in the swampy climate. As Betty Deuser wrote in a letter home, "They say the mosquitoes fly in formation—two come in and pull the covers off and two more do the stinging. They're fast too. Can't swat 'em."

The morning after they arrived, the women took a tour of the base, learning that those low wooden buildings with their red roofs housed everything from barracks and mess halls to chapels and the base exchange. They were also pleased to learn of the "War Room," a space filled with maps and newspapers where they could follow the Allies' progress. Afterward they met with Major Stephenson, who explained why they were stationed at Camp Davis:

they were there to join the 3rd and 14th Tow Target Squadrons. Tow target squadrons helped train newly drafted men learn to fire at enemy planes. This required the pilot to fly steadily along a pre-set route dragging a large fabric target at the end of a long cable so that men on the ground could fire color-coded ammunition at it. Although flying the route was relatively straightforward and sometimes quite tedious, it could be a hazardous job, as live fire was employed and the people doing the firing were still in training. In addition to the target towing, the women would also go on night searchlight tracking missions without their lights on, to provide training for searchlight crews, as well as strafing missions, during which they would pretend to be enemy planes diving at troops and gun positions. Dora knew it would be exacting work and initially assumed she would hate it, but once she realized it was going to be challenging and she would accumulate a lot of flying time, she began to believe it was going to be "a very good deal indeed."

In the coming days, Dora checked out in Piper Cubs and other light trainers in preparation for her new role. But then all of a sudden the women were grounded. It turned out that Jackie had been in such a hurry to get them there that they didn't actually have official orders, and the commanding officer at Camp Davis didn't want the liability of them flying without proper clearance. So the women sat. And sat.

The women's transfer to Camp Davis had been problematic from the start. The new graduates were now under the command of the Ferrying Division, which still hadn't been told why they had to transfer twenty-five of their new women pilots to temporary duty with Jackie Cochran—even after receiving bills for several thousands of dollars for transportation costs. Lieutenant Colonel James Teague, who had boldly expressed his distrust of Jackie the previous year, refused to pay the bill, claiming the expense was unauthorized. Phone calls between AAF headquarters and the Ferrying Division led to more grumbling and pressure from Headquarters to pay the bills and put the women pilots on detached service, which the Ferrying Division argued was not allowed for civilian employees. The battle continued until the Army Air Forces finally sent to the Air Transport Command written orders to transfer Dora and the rest to Camp Davis. Now that they knew the reason for the transfer, Lieutenant Colonel Teague and the Ferrying Division were even *more* enraged. There was no legitimate reason to keep the transfer a secret; that's just the way Jackie wanted it. The debacle became known as the "Camp Davis incident."

Matters only got messier. The AAF headquarters decided that, since the ATC had agreed to take all of Jackie's graduates, they should continue to employ them, including paying them out of their own funds, even when Jackie plucked some out for ninety days at a time to conduct her experiments. This new directive created a huge mess: the ATC had only agreed to take Jackie's graduates under duress, and they did not have funds to pay the women who were now regularly graduating from Jackie's training program. Even if they did have the money, they did not have the legal authority to pay women pilots who were working for other agencies. All of this travel and expense was done during wartime, when budgets were tight and competition for funds and resources was high. The suspicion about Jackie within the Ferrying Division seemed to have been confirmed: she created more work and more expense for them and simply refused to follow regular procedures. In other words, they believed Jackie didn't know what she was doing and was putting at risk everything they had worked so hard to achieve.

Now the women were stuck on the ground while they waited for their official orders. In the meantime they took code classes in ground school. They memorized the cockpits of the planes they were going to fly and took blindfold tests to prove they knew where all the instruments were by heart. They practiced the routes in flight simulators. Frustrated and concerned, not to mention bored, Dora and some of the others went swimming at the nearby beach, feeling as if they'd had the whole ocean to themselves.

Some ten days into the standstill, Jackie decided to take matters into her own hands. On August 5 she flew down to Camp Davis from Washington, D.C. She was as friendly as ever with "her girls," chitchatting with Dora about how nice her hair looked and how she wished she could wear hers that way. But once she began speaking with the officers, Jackie got straight to the point: the women needed to fly. By the time Jackie left, the women of Camp Davis were grounded no more.

The women were finally allowed to fly again, and, after their training, Dora strode out onto the runway, ready to fly her first official tracking mission. She was going to be flying a Douglas A-24 Banshee, a dive-bomber. The plane was a dirty khaki color with an American star on the side, and, like many of the planes at Camp Davis, it was far from new. At this point in the war, new planes and parts were immediately being shipped overseas to men in combat, and the mechanics at Camp Davis often had to resort to cannibalizing wrecked planes for their parts and repairs. There were frequent engine failures and tire blowouts. It seemed that pilots at Camp Davis were never certain if they would fly that day or which planes would be ready for them. There had been three engine failures that Dora already knew of since she'd arrived.

Despite the war-weary plane, Dora was happy as she climbed into the cockpit again. She loved being up in the air. She took off from the Camp Davis runway, quickly climbing to 10,000 feet before flying back and forth in figure eights along a four- to five-mile stretch while men on the ground trained guns or radar on her, learning to track her as she flew. Dora described the flying as "mighty monotonous" and "a little tiring," but her view was beautiful. From that altitude she could see the spot of the beach where they had gone swimming weeks before. A Marine base and the town of Jacksonville were just in sight, too. It was cold at that altitude—a relief from the stifling August heat below. Later that day Dora wrote home to her family that finally "it seems as if we are really doing something to help with the war and it is a very satisfying feeling."

The women received dog tags and were each fitted for their very own parachutes, which made Dora "feel like a real flyer." Jackie had hinted they might someday go to England, and at that point the experiment of women pilots was so fluid that the women didn't know what possibilities their future held.

In the following weeks the women took an Army truck into Wilmington, North Carolina, to buy items for their rooms. Dora bought large but inexpensive red bandanas, which she used to make curtains, adding one atop her dresser and another to form a sort of red ruffle around her mirror. The other women decorated, too: some bought blue curtains with a pattern of white AT-6 Texans and red-and-white Army Air Corps wings on them. Jackie, wanting them to be happy enough to stick it out, helped, too. She found them space for a "ready room," where they could wait to be called out on flights without crowding the male flight officers out of their own space—or being harassed by men who, initially at least, weren't too happy to have them there—and gave them money to buy furniture so they would be comfortable. The women kept busy flying throughout the early fall, and a month after their arrival they continued to gain more training, including flying in formation and at night.

Jackie had warned them that they were to behave as officers and therefore not to date enlisted men. She also advised them to use discretion when dating officers, as fraternization was not allowed. But the women were civilians and not strictly bound by military rules. Besides, there were twenty-five WASP and six hundred men on the airfield alone, so they were never short a date if they wanted one. To keep track of the "wolves," the women kept a notepad next to the telephone that was in the hallway of their barracks with the names of the men they dated. Separate columns listed those who were "ok to date" and those who came under the category "don't advise."

The evening of August 23, 1943, some of the women were assigned to go out on a familiarization flight, which would make them aware of what the swampy area looked like at night—especially necessary with the war-mandated blackouts. Although they were tired after four hours of flying tracking missions earlier in the day, Dora and pilots Lois Hollingsworth and Marion Hanrahan were called up for the night flight. However, as Marion got to dinner late, her old classmate from 43-W-3, Mabel Rawlinson—a bright, friendly young woman from Kalamazoo, Michigan—offered to take her spot so she could have a chance to eat. Dora, Mabel, and Lois walked together to Operations, where they would be assigned their plane and check pilot. With hundreds of pilots on the field, it was a chore for Dispatch to get the pilots the right plane for the right mission. Dora climbed into a waiting A-24, wearing her cloth helmet and headsets, and buckled her parachute and lap belt. Her check pilot, a Lieutenant Cerwin, climbed in the back. Dora fired up the motor. As she and Cerwin prepared to taxi, Dora attempted to call the tower but got only silence: the plane's radio was dead. Not wanting to fly into a busy night sky without a radio, she shut down the motor and she and Cerwin walked back to Operations to request another plane. Dora watched as Mabel and Lois took off, the blue flame from their exhaust pipes showing their path in the moonless night.

It was twenty or twenty-five minutes before Dora and Lieutenant Cerwin were back on the west ramp to try again. They were standing on the wing of their new plane, when they heard it. Everyone on the field did. A plane coming in too low, its motor clearly struggling to make power—catching, then quieting again as the pilot thrust the throttle in and out, desperate to get the motor to catch. It was Mabel Rawlinson and her check pilot, Second Lieutenant Harvey Robillard, in their A-24. Dora had tried to take a flight in that very plane just five days earlier, but it wouldn't make proper horsepower, so she marked it for repairs. Now Mabel and Robillard were having the same trouble, except they were already airborne and crossing the field at under 700 feet—too low to parachute out. In the dark night, it was hard to tell whether yellow flames were coming from the engine or if it was normal exhaust.

The nose of the plane hit the ground first, in a swampy area some three hundred yards from the end of Runway 4. Robillard was thrown from the plane. He had cuts and bruises all over his face and was delirious but alive. Mabel was still strapped in. The wide drainage ditch, junglelike trees, and undergrowth of the swamp slowed the men from the field in their efforts to reach her. The plane had caught fire when it crashed, the high flames burning the trees around them. The rescuers were powerless to do anything but watch, horrified, as Mabel burned with the wreckage. While some witnesses later recalled hearing her scream, Dora and others who were close by remembered nothing but the roar of the fire.

Lois and her young check pilot were flying overhead when they saw the fire. The tower called and told them it would be an hour before they could land on that one lit runway, so they flew in circles and did figure eights until they were finally cleared to land, quietly wondering who had gone in.

Meanwhile, Dora stood frozen on the wing of her plane, then silently returned to Operations in shock, going by rote as she turned in her things and walked slowly back across the dark field to her barracks near the end of Runway 4. She sat on the wooden steps and watched the swamp burn. It was the first time one of her friends had been killed, and she was numb at the horror of it. One of the nurses who lived in the barracks next door, an off-duty captain, came outside. She, too, was stunned by the crash and whispered, "Honey, I'm so damn sorry! God!" She offered Dora one of the two beers she'd brought with her. Dora declined, but the nurse sat down next to her. As she opened her second beer, the nurse began softly singing "Nearer My God to Thee" and "Shall We Gather at the River" in a whiskey tenor voice, the old hymns floating out into the night over the sounds of the quieting fire, until dawn finally broke.

A group of WASP pause from their training as B-17 first pilots while at Lockbourne Army Air Base in 1943. *USAAF photo. Courtesy Texas Woman's University*

CHAPTER FOURTEEN

The Women Airforce Service Pilots

Amonth after General Arnold's surprise announcement putting Jackie in charge of all the women pilots, there was more news. On August 5 the women learned the names WAFS and WFTD were no more: they were now all members of the Women Airforce Service Pilots, or WASP. The women had always been two parts of one whole, but now their name reflected that reality and the new work they were doing. It also reflected the Army Air Forces' determination to bring the women into the military along the same lines as male civilian pilots—who were brought into the AAF as service pilots and then commissioned after ninety days—but under a separate program just for women. In keeping with Jackie's view that her pilots should stay separated from the men, they were called women service pilots. Ever conscious of the need for simple acronyms, "Airforce" was likely added to the name of their organization at least in part to make them the easier to say "WASP" rather than "WSP."

Needless to say, the Ferrying Division resisted the new name. They loved Nancy and wanted her small group of highly experienced, elite pilots to be directly integrated into the Ferrying Division with the men—even if that plan was officially dead in the water. By now Colonel Tunner had been promoted to brigadier general, but when it came to the women pilots, he had lost control. Nearly all matters concerning the women pilots, whether in the Ferry Command or another part of the Army Air Forces, now went through the director of women pilots, Jacqueline Cochran. Undeterred, Tunner continued to fight against each new policy change that came across his desk, and his letters have the tone of a man in a permanent state of annoyance.

Meanwhile, Jackie and AAF headquarters continued to work on expanding the "experiment." In reality, Jackie did not bother Nancy's "original" women much and did not try to move them into new jobs or have them transferred to other bases. Instead she focused on controlling the movements of the women who had gone through her training program. But the fear of what Jackie *could* do—and the loss of power, real or perceived—only increased the level of tension between Tunner and his nemesis.

While Jackie began sending pilots to Camp Davis, General Tunner was working on expansion plans of his own. By now Tunner had begun to actively prefer women pilots. "Women, I found, would do what they were told to do," Tunner later recalled. "The young men we had hired with little military training often found excuses and generally, I might say, they were not as good. They were not as well trained. They were not as knowledgeable as the women pilots."

Tunner decided to both trust and test Nancy Love and Betty Gillies and in August 1943 sent them to Lockbourne Army Air Base in Columbus, Ohio, for training in the mighty B-17 Flying Fortress. One of the best-known planes of the war, the B-17 was a 25,000-pound tail dragger with four engines. First designed in the 1930s, the Fortress was a workhorse that would be used successfully to bomb German industrial and military targets throughout the war. Tunner believed that if the women could fly the Fortress, they would prove his conviction that they could fly anything.

On their first day in the plane, the women made the long climb up the body of the plane and toward the cockpit, which sat nearly two stories above the ground. While the plane carried a crew of ten, it was still narrow enough that they could have stretched out their arms and reached both sides of the long, skinny fuselage— which is quite extraordinary, considering that the plane regularly carried up to 8,000 pounds of bombs. After balancing their way through the bomb bay and scooting around the seat for the top-turret gunner, they climbed into the cockpit, with room for a bombardier to climb down to the plane's Plexiglas nose. The throttles for all four engines sat between them. It nearly took two of them to push the throttles up as they pulled the big yoke back for takeoff, but the more they flew, the more they could feel their arms strengthening, and their instructors, certain they could do it, taught them techniques that helped make the B-17 a joy to fly despite the size. It wasn't long before the women were flying it by themselves. After thirty-one hours of rigorous training, Nancy and Betty were officially allowed to ferry B-17s across the country, delivering three different B-17Fs between the factories, modification centers, and any delivery point in between.

But General Tunner had bigger things in mind: he wanted the women to fly the B-17 across the Atlantic to England—an active war zone. At this point in the war, the young men flying to Europe had little flight time and were nervous about making the Atlantic crossing. Nancy and Betty, meanwhile, had plenty of flight experience (Nancy with nearly 1,500 hours, Betty even more). As Betty later explained, having the women make the flight "was just to make the boys think, 'surely the work can't be that hard . . .' " On September 1, together with their crew of four men, Nancy and Betty picked up a B-17 in Cincinnati and flew to New Castle Army Air Base in Wilmington before heading to Gander, Newfoundland, to refuel and rest before the big trip across the North Atlantic. After a few days waiting out bad weather, they finally received a positive forecast. That evening Nancy, Betty, and the crew ate dinner and made plans to turn in early before the long flight the next day.

Meanwhile, unbeknownst to them, their careful plans were slowly coming undone. The women had radioed General Tunner and Nancy's husband, Robert Love, who worked for Tunner, to let them know of the delay. But because of the poor weather at Goose Bay—aggravated further by the active aurora borealis, or northern lights—radio signals weren't getting in or out. As a result, on the eve of the flight, Tunner and Love assumed that the pair were well on their way to Scotland.

Only then was General Arnold informed that Nancy and Betty would be piloting a B-17 across the ocean. The task of informing him should have fallen to General C. R. Smith, deputy commander of the Air Transport Command, and General Harold George, head of the Air Transport Command—both big supporters of Nancy and the WAFS. We may never know for certain whether their failure to inform Arnold before the women took off was an oversight or whether they intended to keep the mission secret until the women were already in the air. But after hearing that the women should be on their way to Scotland, Smith sent a telegram to Brigadier General Paul E. Burrows, commander of the European wing of the Air Transport Command, telling him to expect a delivery of a B-17 piloted by Nancy Love and Betty Gillies, and to inform General Arnold. Burrows received the message while at dinner and casually handed it to Arnold, who was sitting nearby.

Arnold's response was swift and unequivocal. He immediately sent a message of his own to Lieutenant General Barney Giles, chief of Air Staff of the Army Air Forces in Washington, D.C. The trip had to be canceled immediately—and Giles needed to get control of his generals, who were acting autonomously. When Giles received Arnold's telegram, he wired up to Goose Bay right away, canceling the flight. Sadly, the weather and northern lights abated just enough for the message to come through. The women were still at supper when somebody came in to break the news. They were officially grounded. Betty's reaction was a simple "Damn!" As she later remembered, "We had plenty of time to go to the bar and drink our sorrows out that night." A dozen years later the canceled flight still stung for Nancy, who in 1955 wrote that her dream of flying to Europe in a B-17 had been "shattered" and that "the disappointment is still with me." The women weren't the only ones disappointed. Over thirty years later, General Tunner described himself as "heartbroken" about the canceled flight.

Once the message had been received, it couldn't be ignored. At Goose Bay the next morning, Nancy and Betty posed for pictures in front of their plane with the crew who had been so proud to fly with them. In an attempt to raise the women's morale, the men had painted the acronym "WAFS" on the nose of the B-17 during the night. Beneath Nancy's window, they painted the name they'd chosen for the plane in her honor: *Queen Bee*. As grateful as they were for the crew's kindness, Nancy and Betty couldn't bring themselves to smile in the group photo, instead looking glumly at the camera, hands shoved dejectedly in their pockets. Still, they exchanged fond farewells with their male crew members, who were continuing on to Great Britain in the B-17 with a replacement pair of male pilots. Together, the two women stood near the desolate runway at Goose Bay, at the very edge of the Atlantic, and watched their *Queen Bee* lift off for Scotland. Later that day they boarded another plane as passengers and headed back to the United States.

Jackie's response to Nancy's and Betty's achievements in the B-17 was typical of her style. She immediately set out to prove that any skilled woman pilot—not just an elite few—could fly a bomber. To prove her point, she sent seventeen women to Lockbourne Army Air Base in Ohio to be trained as first pilots (or captains) in the B-17, just as Nancy and Betty had been. One of them, Blanche Osborn, wrote home that she was "simply nuts about the airplane. It's funny, I don't think of it as an airplane—but more like something alive." She and twelve others made it through the program to become known as the "Lucky Thirteen."

Jackie, ever aware of optics and perhaps in an attempt to overshadow Nancy and Betty, made certain an Army Air Forces photographer was there to capture the women's success. One picture went on to become one of the most iconic photos of the WASP ever taken: in the black-and-white photograph, four women are walking toward the camera, away from a B-17 painted with the name *Pistol Packin' Mama,* after the popular 1943 song performed by Bing Crosby and the Andrews Sisters. The women are wearing their leather flight jackets and boots and carrying their parachutes. They're striding along, close together, shoulder to shoulder, smiling, confident, with a clear sense of purpose. General Tunner was livid about the publicity the women received, seeing it as another slight by Jackie and the AAF, and wrote a terse memo reminding the AAF's office of public relations that his women had actually flown the B-17 first.

Few seem to have noticed.

Helen Richey, airline pilot and air racer, smiles as she climbs in for a flight as a pilot for the Air Transport Auxiliary in 1942. *Photo courtesy San Diego Air and Space Museum*

CHAPTER FIFTEEN

England

In September, Teresa James received some good news: Helen Richey, her old friend from Pennsylvania, was soon going to be stationed at New Castle.

Since the last time they had seen each other, Helen had been working as a ferry pilot with the British ATA. For the first few months of her time in England, Helen was in her element. She never knew which type of aircraft she would be assigned to fly next, making each day more exciting than the one before. Like the other women flying for the ATA, Helen was trained and rated to fly specific classes of planes ranging from the light trainers of Class 1 to heavier, faster, and more complex planes, culminating in the four-engine bombers of Class 5. Helen quickly moved up to the more advanced planes, competing with the other women to fly and "collect" as many different aircraft types as she could. The ATA pilots often boasted that every plane the Royal Air Force flew had already been flown by them first—twice. They weren't exaggerating. Most new airplanes had to be ferried to an RAF maintenance unit where they were fitted with extra equipment before being delivered to the RAF squadrons. Women were an important part of that effort.

By July, Helen was flying the Spitfire, one of the most prominent of the British fighter planes. For Helen, lifting off in the Spitfire was "like flying in a beautiful dream." As she described it to her friend, the journalist Ernie Pyle, who published an article about Helen in October 1942, the plane moved as easily "as a fish through water." According to Helen, Pyle wrote, "It's a sharp knife through soft butter, it's a bullet through the sky—there simply was never such an airplane, ever before." On one flight she delivered a Spitfire to a field before she was asked to fly back in a Walrus, a plane she had never flown. Pyle described the Walrus as "an old-fashioned, cumbersome, pusher-type amphibian plane," a complete contrast to the "sleek nothingness of the Spitfire." Helen was quoted as saying, "It was just like flying a hotel. About three stories of hodge-podge sticking up there above you. It all looked so domestic and old-lady-like I felt I ought to get out on the wing and hang out a washing."

In September 1942, when Jackie returned to lead the women's training program in the United States, she appointed Helen as her replacement. Helen was a superb pilot, smart and personable; her fellow pilots described her as "gay-hearted and level-headed," and she was particularly popular with the American women. She was also famous, which meant that she would continue to draw positive attention to the women's work in England.

But after Jackie left, Helen's time in England took a different turn. While Helen was glad to be flying for the British, there was no doubt that the wartime conditions were far from ideal. The pilots were expected to fly all types of aircraft, in all conditions, to the point of exhaustion. They flew six days a week, fifty-one weeks per year, even in English fog and rain, all the while dodging barrage balloons—giant balloons anchored to the ground by cables and meant to bring down low-flying German planes—which were raised and lowered upon their departures and arrivals. Living conditions were equally challenging: under rationing, the food was terrible and heating fuel was in short supply. Perhaps most troubling was that many of the planes were badly in need of repair and downright dangerous to fly.

Helen's early reports back to Jackie in America were newsy, cheerful, and upbeat, but in the days to come they became less positive in tone. As she began to face the realities of flying during an English winter, Helen wrote to Jackie on the women's progress and began to repeatedly ask when Jackie was returning to England. She also wondered if there would be room for her in the Ferry Command soon. By the end of October, Helen was sick with a cold and feeling wretched. The American women she was closest to were being posted to new bases and split up. "We are heartbroken about it," she wrote to Jackie, "but there seems to be nothing we can do about it. It brings back all the old homesickness which I was just beginning to lose." The following month she cabled Jackie asking for "Scotch for Christmas."

Then, in late December, Helen learned her mother had fallen gravely ill. On January 8, 1943, Helen sent a desperate cable to Jackie: "Want to see mother before she dies. Seems to be some question about leaving [for the United States] what do you think?" Jackie, who had kept in close touch with Helen, replied that it was incredibly difficult to get eastbound passage, what with the war and the weather, but that she would see what she could do. The next day Jackie cabled back to say that she had done her research and there wasn't any way to get Helen out of England for the time being. She closed the note with a single word: "Sorry."

Helen's last flight with the ATA was that same day, January 9, 1943. It seems that after the news of her mother's illness, she experienced some kind of nervous breakdown or "crack up." She'd had her fourth accident just days earlier—the third for which she'd been found responsible. On January 23, 1943, her contract with the ATA was canceled and she was instructed to undergo medical testing. The chief medical officer of the ATA wrote to Jackie that Helen had endured "considerable mental strain by virtue of her anxiety over the health of her Mother, who I believe is a very ill woman. The strain of ferrying in winter months in this country, superimposed upon a background of mental anxiety has rendered Miss Ritchey unfit to continue duty as a ferry pilot in this Organisation." According to the medical officer's letter, Helen wanted to continue to fly despite her "disability," but he, along with Air Transport Auxiliary women's leader Pauline Gower, recommended "prolonged rest."

Helen's dismissal from the ATA threw the program into crisis, and it is clear from telegrams between Jackie and Helen's other friends that people who cared about her were very worried. From mid-January to mid-March, Helen dropped out of contact with her family altogether. Helen's sister had to wire Jackie in Texas to find out if she'd had any word of her. Eventually, on March 19, Helen returned to the United States by ship. She had been in England for exactly one year. She went home and saw her mother, who was by then recovering from her illness.

The following month Helen received a letter from Jackie in which she apologized for being out of touch. She herself had been sick in the hospital and had only just been released. Then, on June 7, 1943, Helen telegrammed Jackie, "Where are you. Hope your not ill again stop. Like to join WAFS. Do I have to take training course first. If so how can I make application and when do I start. Sorry we haven't got together yet. Take Care of yourself. Love Helen Richey."

Jackie informed Helen that before she could fly for Nancy and the Ferrying Division, she would indeed have to go through Jackie's training program first, even with her wealth of experience. Perhaps Jackie simply wanted to have the glory of a famous pilot like Helen graduating from her program, but it's just as likely that she wanted to keep an eye on Helen after her problems in England. The one concession Jackie did make was putting Helen in the fifth class in Sweetwater, which was already going into advanced training, so that she could skip the basics.

Helen began her training in July 1943, and as she approached the field at Sweetwater for the very first time, the arid surroundings would have provided quite the contrast to damp, war-torn England, which she had left by ship just a few months earlier. When the other trainees realized Helen Richey the famous pilot had joined their ranks, it caused quite a stir. In July 1943 the *Avenger* ran a profile of Helen, expressing surprise that a woman of her experience was required to undergo training. After all, in England she had been flying Spitfires, among the hottest planes in the world at the time. But as the article explained, "It's a rule—no woman pilot may now enter the Ferrying Division of the Air Transport Command without receiving training by the Army at Avenger Field . . . because no other training is as highly specialized and thorough."

Helen spent the next two months in Sweetwater. At thirty-four, she was among the oldest of the women, and because she came in later, she kept herself somewhat separate from the rest of the class (although one classmate, Mary Parker, became a friend to the end of her life). In September 1943 Helen finished her training and prepared to graduate and move on to active duty. Her time at Sweetwater had not been all smooth sailing, however. In a letter on August 27, 1943, Dedie wrote to Jackie about the 43-W-5 graduation plans, saying, "Helen Richey also overcame her difficulties and will be graduating with the Class." The record is silent on what those difficulties might have been, but it's clear that Helen had not yet fully recovered from her struggles in England.

After her graduation, Helen wrote to Jackie: "Since I may not see you for some time I want to thank you for the wings and tell you how much I appreciate everything. Some day we'll go over the whole story if you're interested . . ."

Wings in hand, Helen was transferred to the 2nd Ferrying Group at New Castle, where she was reunited with Teresa.

That same fall, Teresa left New Castle, saying farewell to Helen and the other women. This time, she was headed out west to visit Dink in Roswell, New Mexico, where he was serving as a B-17 instructor. It had been months since the couple had last seen each other in California, and although Dink had sent Teresa an invitation to his graduation, she had been too busy ferrying to attend. In Roswell, Teresa and Dink were happily reunited. At some point the two of them had their portrait taken at a local photography studio. It shows two handsome, first-generation kids, both in uniform, both smiling, and both obviously very much in love.

During Teresa's visit, Dink told his wife he had something important he needed to discuss with her. He was thinking of volunteering to fly combat in Europe. Dink was a valuable B-17 instructor and could have stayed on in that role in the United States, but the Allies were preparing to invade France and expand their bombing of Germany, and he wanted to join that fight. One can't help but wonder if he was thinking in part of their future: a veteran with combat experience would be better paid and more highly respected than one who had stayed in the States for the duration of the war. Or perhaps it was the same enthusiasm that carried him to enlist rather than waiting to be a service pilot, as his older brother was. In any case, Teresa knew she couldn't stand in his way. After saying goodbye to him, she returned to her base at New Castle.

In early 1944, Dink was accepted for combat flying and started preparing to leave for Europe. When he hit the East Coast at the end of March, he got a forty-eight-hour pass before shipping out. Betty Gillies gave Teresa time off to go see him, and he and Teresa shared one last dance before he left for England.

In the weeks to come, Teresa missed Dink more than ever. She devoured his letters when they arrived, which was almost daily. Dink was now with the 337th Bombardment Squadron, 96th Bombardment Group, stationed at Snetterton, in Norfolk, England. He was one of thousands of American and Allied aircrews flying out of England that spring, taking their bombing runs deeper and deeper into Germany as the Luftwaffe fought them off with fewer and fewer aircraft. This marked a significant shift. When the war in Europe had begun in 1939, the Germans had the best air force in the world; their planes were the fastest, their pilots the most experienced, and their tactics the most brutal. However, after three years of fighting, the Luftwaffe was in bad shape. While the Allies took losses as well, they were able to recover and strengthen because American factories were catching up to the needs of the war. Staffed mostly by women, they built more than 84,000 airplanes in 1943 alone—nearly 300,000 over the course of the war—and were constantly improving their technology. By contrast, the Germans, their factories often filled with slave laborers, built only 94,000 planes during the entire war.

In other words, the Allies were overwhelming the Germans with equipment. It was the same equipment that the WASP were now working to test fly, train men with, and ferry from the factories to the ships that would take them to war. The work of Teresa and her fellow WASP was beginning to pay off.

As flight instructors began to fight for jobs by pitting themselves against the WASP, the USAAF unintentionally undermined the women by highlighting their femininity. Flora Belle Reece (left) felt a little silly when asked to pose for this picture, but thought it turned out pretty well. *USAAF photo. Courtesy Flora Belle Reece*

CHAPTER SIXTEEN

Aerial Dishwashers

On September 17, 1943, Jackie Cochran walked to her closet and picked out an immaculately tailored designer suit jacket and skirt. She needed to be perfectly turned out for the day ahead. The women's program was almost a year old, and with plans for militarization in place, she had finally gotten General Arnold to agree that the Women Airforce Service Pilots needed a uniform of their own. Later that day she was due at the Pentagon to meet Generals Arnold, Giles, and Marshall for approval of her designs. She just had to make sure that Arnold and his generals allowed her to use the uniform of her choosing.

Jackie had already rejected the leftover brown WAC fabric she had been offered for her new WASP uniform, selecting instead a bright navy color she dubbed "Santiago blue." She knew that General Arnold and others who supported an independent air force hoped one day to have blue uniforms for their branch and that the color would have a special appeal to them. Then, too, dark blue had looked so good on the women of the ATA, she knew it would work for her women as well. Jackie approached the luxury department store Bergdorf Goodman in New York, commissioning the fashion designers there to create three designs to her specifications.

Before she made her way to the Pentagon to meet with the men, Jackie went to the quartermaster general's office and found two women of average build and looks to serve as models. She asked these women to put on the first two uniforms she'd commissioned. Then she put the uniform that she wanted on "a beautifully proportioned Greek fashion model" she had found especially for this purpose. The uniform on the Greek model included a neat skirt and tailored jacket in blue, worn with a light-colored shirt, black tie, and beret. Then off the women went to show Generals Arnold, Giles, and Marshall their outfits. At the Pentagon, the three men carefully surveyed the women in their tailored suits. As it turned out, Marshall liked the designer suit Jackie was wearing the best, but when she explained how much it cost, he joined Arnold and very practically chose the blue uniform on the Greek model.

Jackie needed to have the women look like uniformed members of the military for good reason. That same month, September 1943, California representative John Costello submitted House Resolution 3358 to bring the women into the Army Air Forces as service pilots with the same pay, rights, and benefits as male pilots. Costello's bill was written exactly as Jackie and General Arnold wanted it to be, with the women remaining independent of the WAC and on equal footing with their male counterparts in the AAF.

When the bill was made public, Betty Deuser—who had been posted with Dora at Camp Davis but was now at Liberty Field in Georgia, learning to fly top secret radio-controlled aircraft— joined a group of WASP who wrote to Congress advocating for its passage. Despite the women's good intentions, they were soon in trouble. Jackie was adamant: she wanted the women to stay out of the politics and do their work. She called down from Washington and, as Betty wrote to her family, "bawled out the C.O., so he bawled us out," accusing them of being subversive and telling them they had "no right" to contact their representatives. It didn't make sense. The women thought they were helping. But the point had been made, "so we had to call all the four ferry bases and tell them to disregard the telegrams (asking them to send wires too)."

Jackie believed the women needed to sit quietly, do their jobs well, and let the political process work. She informed them they were not allowed to write publicly about militarization—period. Jackie had put rules in place from the beginning to make sure her women pilots would be perceived as nonthreatening. Now she was terrified that any negative press would mean the end of the women's chance to fly—and her own chance to lead. Dora, still under the impression that the women might be brought into the Women's Army Corps, speculated that maybe Jackie's reaction meant that she had "something cooking that would be spoiled by such." Jackie reassured Dora and the other women that even if they were eventually brought into the WAC, they would still be WASP and have their own uniform.

When at the next Sweetwater graduation, on February 11, 1944, Jackie stood surveying the scene at the ninth class of trainee graduates, her women looked quite different from the first graduating classes. Back then the trainees had worn their own tan slacks and white shirts, with caps borrowed from the boys at Ellington Field. This time, class 44-W-1 marched out onto the field proudly wearing their smart new dress uniforms, including skirts and jackets, black ties and berets. They had new silver wings, too. No longer would there be a panicked rush to create wings for each particular class at graduation; instead there was a new standard set of silver wings that all the WASP would wear.

In every respect, the women were ready for militarization. By now Jackie and her team had a much better idea of what they were doing with the women, not only when it came to uniforms, but in all aspects of accommodating, managing, and training them. The barracks at Avenger Field were finished by December 1943, including new sidewalks instead of muddy pathways, and a gymnasium for calisthenics classes, games, and graduation ceremonies. Now that hundreds of women had gone through the program—not to mention thousands of men who were going through a nearly identical training cycle in the AAF—the training had stabilized, too, increasing from four months for the first class to nearly seven months for the latest classes, including some sixty additional hours on military training. The reason for the extra training was simple: the Army Air Forces wanted the women to be ready when they were finally officially made a part of the military, which was expected to happen at any moment.

The bill that Jackie kept promising would have the women in the Army Air Forces by Christmas died in committee before the holidays began. A redrafted bill was quickly introduced to replace it. In February 1944, Representative Costello proposed H.R. 4219 to incorporate the WASP directly into the Army Air Forces. This new bill was more complicated than the first one, establishing the women pilots on similar grounds as women in the other branches of the military, including the WAC. Among other things, it determined that the highest rank a woman pilot in the AAF could earn would be colonel, and that there would only be one—presumably Jacqueline Cochran, although she wasn't named in the bill. Once they finished training the women, they would be granted commissions as second lieutenants in the Army Air Forces, where they would be "entitled to the same rights, privileges, and benefits as are accorded to said members of the same rank, grade and length of service." In other words, just as Nancy Love had fought for from the beginning, the women would be U.S. Army Air Forces pilots and would have the same rights and responsibilities as the men pilots—evenly across all bases.

On paper, the new bill was very good news for the Women Airforce Service Pilots. In practice, it was the beginning of the end. Despite all of Jackie's efforts, when the news of Representative Costello's bill to bring the WASP into the Army Air Forces reached the press, the backlash she had always feared finally arrived.

Ever since the start of the program, Jackie had been terrified that her women pilots might appear threatening to men and their jobs and that this would lead to the end of women flying for the war. She'd worked so hard to ensure that the women's public image didn't conflict with socially acceptable ideas of femininity. She spoke of women pilots who were "relieving" men rather than "replacing" them. She often referred to the women as "aerial dishwashers" who were "helping out" until they were no longer needed, at which point they would step aside. She even stipulated that the women trainees should visit the beauty parlor at least once per week (although this rule was hard to enforce, and many of the women didn't go).

Now Jackie's worst fears were coming true. A group of soon-to-be-unemployed flight instructors of the War Training Service (WTS) learned about the WASP bill and decided that women were indeed taking away their jobs. They began to agitate.

The WTS had hired civilian instructors to train pilots as they prepared for induction into the Army. However, in January 1944, because losses of pilots had begun to drop, the AAF announced that it no longer needed the additional pilots produced through the WTS and would be ending the program later that summer. The AAF decided they wanted to train their pilots themselves, from the very beginning, rather than use this preparatory-type program. Hundreds of WTS men were about to be out of work. Not only that, the end of the men's program meant the end of their draft deferments, which meant that many of them ran the risk of being inducted into the ground forces. When they heard the news about the bill to bring the WASP into the military, they realized there were women flying for the AAF and immediately set their sights on the WASP and their jobs.

The WTS men began to organize, taking their complaints to the press. Why was the AAF accepting women with only thirty-five hours of training and then spending millions of dollars to train them to fly when men were already trained and available? Suddenly the media shifted from lauding the valiant war efforts of the WASP—as they had in *Life* magazine and countless other outlets—to accusing the women of stealing men's jobs. In January 1944 the editor of *American Aviation* magazine scolded the WASP: "One cannot blame the women for wanting to participate somewhere in the flying end of the war, but the fact remains that they are not as suitable for ferrying work as men, and now that men are available there is every reason to use them effectively." Just as thousands of "Rosie the Riveters" would be pushed from their factory jobs after the war, the movement had already begun to oust the WASP.

As the WTS men worked to get their message out, they focused their energies on the media and on Congress. One target of their efforts was Democratic representative Robert Ramspeck of Georgia, who quickly sat up and took notice of the men's complaints. Ramspeck was active in the airline industry, and he was also majority whip and head of the House Committee on the Civil Service. He immediately ordered an official investigation of the WASP and whether the Army Air Forces had proper authorization for all the money that was being spent to train the women pilots. With Ramspeck on their side, the male flight instructors and their supporters began inundating their members of Congress with letters and visits protesting their loss of deferment status and objecting to the use of women pilots when men were available. The American Legion joined the men in their fight, rallying their members to mobilize, calling for the end of the WASP training program and the removal of WASP on active duty as well. They wanted no women pilots flying for the AAF at all.

On March 22, 1944, the House Committee on Military Affairs held a hearing on H.R. 4219. They already held a letter from Secretary of War Henry Stimson recommending that the committee approve the bill to militarize the WASP; now they wanted to hear from General Arnold himself and invited him to testify. The hearing was initially convened to talk about getting the WASP into the AAF, but it quickly shifted to pacifying concerned representatives and their worries about vocal—and politically active—unemployed male pilots.

After Arnold's hour of testimony, during which he adamantly advocated for the women and sternly dismissed concerns about the men, the Committee on Military Affairs went into executive session to discuss the proposed bill. They emerged with a three-page report unanimously recommending passage. But in the weeks to come, the men of the WTS continued their lobbying. It was at this point that members of Congress began to wonder why they weren't hearing from the women pilots themselves. Why were they so quiet when so many were beginning to speak out against them? Did they even want to be a part of the military?

In fact, the women had been effectively gagged by Jackie. Although some of the women did write to their representatives, their telegrams were few and far between, and Jackie would have been furious if she had found out about them. Even the Army Air Forces and other supporters of the bill remained relatively quiet on the topic throughout the spring of 1944. For their part, the War Department declared a halt to all publicity concerning the WASP. There was an apparent belief that the less exposure the WASP received while militarization was hanging in the balance, the better. The War Department firmly believed that the prestige of General

Arnold and Secretary of War Stimson supporting the women would be enough; they just had to sit tight and keep the women out of Washington. Unfortunately, the result of that decision was that the only press the WASP received during this time was fed to the media by their opponents.

Tellingly, the Ferrying Division did not come out and publicly support the women's bill, either. They desperately wanted their women to be a part of the military; they just didn't want them to be under Jackie. By not vocally supporting the bill, they were following orders to keep quiet to avoid negative publicity. But they were also taking a chance. If Jackie's bill was defeated, they hoped to bring their ferry pilots into the Ferrying Division directly, as they had planned to do all along—and under Nancy Love's control instead of Jackie's.

Throughout the spring of 1944, members of Congress publicly questioned the necessity and quality of the women pilots, and the media followed suit. The women worried as they worked, writing home and asking their parents what they thought about it all. Some were anxious to serve; others wondered whether they should get out before they were stuck in the military. Jackie continued to drop the hammer on anyone she suspected of speaking out against the bill, reportedly asking that those opposed to it resign and keep quiet so the rest could get their commissions.

Finally, the War Department began to wake up to the fact that, despite support of the bill by the Committee on Military Affairs, their effort to bring the WASP into the AAF was in danger. In early May 1944, Secretary of War Stimson publicly and vocally began defending the work women pilots were doing and trying to fend off the opposition by declaring "neither the existence nor the militarization of the WASP will keep out of the Army Air Forces a single instructor or partially trained civilian pilot who desires to become a service pilot or cadet and can meet the applicable standards of the Army Air Forces." Stimson was trying to reassure the congressmen and the American people that women were not replacing men but only releasing them, Jackie's mantra from the beginning of the program. But as the male WTS pilots got louder, even those who had supported the WASP joining the AAF began to backpedal.

Kentucky representative Andrew J. May, chairman of the House Committee on Military Affairs, which had unanimously recommended the bill, pressed the Army Air Forces for more information about the women pilots. The AAF defensively explained that one of the primary reasons the program was created, in addition to releasing men for combat duty, was to "determine the manner and extent that women pilots can be effectively used in the Army Air Forces" for any future need. They went on to make the second point that "if we are going to test the project completely and fully we must have enough WASP so that the groups allocated to various phases of non-combat service will be large enough for us to reach definite conclusions. Without the enlargement of the present WASP training program, we will have the numbers necessary early in 1945." It seems Chairman May might have been trying to work out some sort of a compromise with his colleagues about the growing number of women pilots.

Meanwhile, the articles in the press about the women pilots took a new and often vicious tone. A May 1944 article in the *Idaho Statesman* speculated that the women were allowed to fly because of the "sentimental softness of American men in regard to their women." The article continued: "In colleges the smooth, good-looking gals can get A's without a lick of work; and in the armed services it may be that dimples have a devastating effect even on the generals." In late May, the gossip columnist Austine Cassini went after Jackie and Arnold in the *Washington (D.C.) Times-Herald*. In her column she described Jackie as a "shapely pilot" with "an attractive composition of wind-blown bob, smiling eyes and outdoor skin" and accused General Arnold of gazing into Jackie's eyes and taking "her cause celebre very much 'to heart.'" The article concluded with a snide and utterly unfounded analysis of Arnold's interest in Jackie: "It's whispered he's battling like a knight of olde, or olde knight, for 'the faire Cochran.' So the announcement can be expected any day that Jackie's commission has been approved, if the captivated general is victorious in his tournaments."

The women seethed as they read the lies printed about them. But rather than fight back, they did as they were told and kept flying, hoping that their work would speak for itself.

In January 1944, just before Representative Costello proposed the new version of his bill, Nancy Love learned that four of her pilots—including Betty Gillies—had snuck off to Washington, D.C., to try to find a way into the military. Betty and the others met with Jackie Cochran for two hours to "try to feel her out" about what was happening with militarization. But as Betty wrote in her diary later that day, they got nowhere, even if it was "an interesting experiment!" The women spent the rest of that afternoon and evening talking with various Army officers in the Pentagon, learning that there didn't seem to be any reason why the women couldn't go into the Army as service pilots under the existing laws. The next day Betty was able to talk herself in to see General Hall, the deputy chief of staff in charge of personnel. She and Barbara Erickson proposed that the women ask for a commission in the Army of the United States (the service component of the U.S. military during national emergencies) and a rating of service pilot. As Betty wrote in her diary, Hall nearly jumped out of his chair.

"By golly," he said. "If you can that would solve all our problems!"

While Hall was likely thinking commissioning the women via the Army of the United States would be an easy way to avoid the headache of going through Congress, Betty and the others had a slightly different motivation. "If we can go into the Army in this way, it will get us out of Cochran's clutches and will need no legislation!" Betty wrote, adding, in a parenthetical: "We are definitely going to be militarized one way or another and this is the way *we* want it done." Hall told the women to come back in a day or two; he would see what he could do.

When Nancy found out that the women were working back channels against Jackie, she was furious, chastising them for wandering the halls of the Pentagon, searching for someone to help them escape Jackie's leadership. Even when those around Nancy professed to actively dislike Jackie, Nancy continued to publicly promote the impression that all was well between them, mindful of Bob's advice not to fall into the tabloid trap of feuding with Jackie. Only in letters to him did she criticize her flamboyant colleague, at least in writing. She wanted the WASP to fly, and she knew their fate, and hers, was tied to Jackie's. When a member of Representative Ramspeck's investigative team asked if there had been a "battle" going on between Nancy and Jackie, as was so often suggested behind closed doors, Nancy quickly shut him down: "Miss Cochran's was an administrative job and mine was an operational one, and there was no battle between us."

What she didn't tell Betty and the other women was that she had also been working behind the scenes to oppose Jackie's plans. The previous November, Nancy and her ally in the Air Transport Command, General Tunner, had tried to circumvent both Jackie and General Arnold by writing a letter directly to Oveta Culp Hobby, head of the WAC. In the letter, they encouraged Hobby to bring the pilots into the WAC with commissions. The Air Staff, an administrative arm of the AAF answering to Arnold, stopped the letter from ever reaching Hobby, but Nancy's intention was clear: she wanted to be a part of the military and she did not want to be under Jackie.

Soon enough, General Hall came back with the news that direct commissions into the Army of the United States would not be possible: the volunteer forms called for "persons," and the military defined "persons" as "men."

In February, shortly after Nancy's thirtieth birthday, her husband, Bob, left for a new station halfway around the world, in Australia. At least Nancy had an opportunity to see him before he left. They'd gotten the chance to renew their instrument ratings in Long Beach, where they were able to spend some time together talking about their plans for the future. Now they were going to be separated by many thousands of miles. At Long Beach they said a sad farewell.

In the weeks to come, Nancy did her best to adjust to having Bob so far away. She worried about him. She also simply missed him. From the beginning of her time in the Ferrying Division, Nancy had counted on Bob as a sounding board. Nancy rarely showed her emotions publicly. At work she was always careful to present herself as cool and implacable. But that didn't mean she didn't feel frustrated and upset at times—and when she did, Bob was the one person she could trust to listen. If Nancy was finding Jackie difficult and exasperating, she could vent to him. When she felt thwarted in her desk job, he provided an open ear. And when she needed advice on how to navigate the world of the military, he was the one who could give her counsel from the inside. As the male pilots leading the anti-WASP campaign became more vocal, Nancy was beginning to question her strategy of watching and waiting. With Bob so far away, she could no longer call him up and ask him for his point of view, regular international phone calls being a luxury that no one could afford during wartime. Instead, Nancy had to wait for his responses to arrive via letter, which could sometimes take weeks.

Not only that, she was sick. She had caught the chicken pox, an illness that can be quite serious when contracted as an adult. The timing couldn't have been worse. Class 44-W-2 was set to graduate on March 11, and at the ceremony General Arnold would be presenting Barbara Jane Erickson, one of Nancy's original WAFS pilots, with the Air Medal for one of her long ferry flights. Nancy wanted to go to the graduation and award ceremony to recognize her friend BJ, the only woman pilot to receive the Air Medal during the war. It was also a political opportunity: General Arnold's testimony before Congress was set for March 22, and the Army Air Forces were determined to get some positive publicity about the women in circulation before then. Nancy knew that Jackie would be in attendance as well, and that this would be a chance to demonstrate to the press—which desperately wanted to play up any perceived conflict between the two women—that all was well between them.

The morning of graduation, Nancy dressed in her new Santiago-blue WASP uniform. She was wearing it for the first time. Fortunately, she had passed the contagious stage of the chicken pox, but her face was still covered with spots, so she was self-conscious about attending the graduation ceremony and having her photograph taken by the Army Air Forces and the press. As Nancy stood with the other women before the ceremony, she complained about the marks on her face. Jackie happened to overhear. Jackie could be ruthless and she could be stubborn, but she could also be tremendously kind, even to someone she counted as her rival. Right away Jackie reassured Nancy her spots could be fixed. She sat Nancy down in front of her, grabbed her expansive bag filled with Jacqueline Cochran Cosmetics, and went to work covering Nancy's blemishes. After Jackie finished her work, no one would have known that Nancy had been sick.

While the future of the WASP hung in the balance in Congress, the Army Air Forces continued to make preparations for the women to join the military. General Giles had issued a directive stating that since the WASP was due to become "an integral part of the Army Air Forces," the women pilots should have training comparable to that of the Army Air Forces officers. Giles began sending the women to Orlando to the Army Air Forces School of Applied Tactics for a thirty-day officer training school, where they would learn the tactical and operational methods of military aviation, something male officers learned as a matter of course. Once again Nancy, Betty, Teresa, and other women from the WAFS would be the guinea pigs. Soon enough, they left for Orlando, quickly becoming as well qualified in the ways of the military as they were at flying military planes.

Dorothea "Didi" Moorman (left) and Dora Dougherty join Lieutenant Colonel Paul Tibbets posing in front of their B-29, *Ladybird,* after the women had been checked out by the CAA and earned their type rating as first pilot in the plane. *USAAF photo*

CHAPTER SEVENTEEN

A Secret Little Deal

On June 20, 1944, the public-address system at the officers' club at Eglin Field in the Florida Panhandle announced "a call for a WASP." Dora answered.

By now Dora was one of the most experienced pilots on active duty. At Camp Davis the previous fall, she had towed targets behind planes so that male gunners on the beaches could practice firing on her using antiaircraft guns. Within a few weeks she and her fellow women pilots had proven themselves to the men at Camp Davis, who had initially been so resistant to sharing an airfield with them; when offered the transfers they had been promised, most of the men chose to stay put. After leaving Davis, Dora had transferred to Liberty Field in Georgia, where she learned to fly top secret drones and radio-controlled planes—a new technology for both Dora and the Army Air Forces—which could be flown remotely from a chase plane while gunners fired upon it.

At Dora's new station of Eglin Field, she continued towing targets—often in the powerful and fast A-20 Havoc—and flying the radio-controlled planes, while also test-flying AT-6 Texans that needed or had been repaired for the gunnery group. The day the phone call came in, she was tired and hot after a full day of flying, and had hoped to grab a quick snack before heading back to the barracks for a cold shower. Instead, she found herself faced with an opportunity she could hardly believe. On the line was another WASP named Dorothea "Didi" Moorman, whom Dora had gotten to know while they were at Camp Davis together. Didi explained that Colonel Paul Tibbets had been looking for the women. He needed their help.

Tibbets was a renowned pilot and leader known for his flying in Africa and Europe. He'd piloted the lead B-17 in the Americans' first daylight bombing run in Europe in August 1942, ultimately flying forty-three combat missions in Europe. General Arnold had recently put Tibbets in charge of a training program for the B-29 Superfortress. The B-29 was a massive aircraft, the largest in the American fleet, with four engines and a wingspan of 141 feet. With its pressurized cabin, it could fly to an altitude of over 31,000 feet and cover a distance of more than 5,000 miles—attributes that were critically needed during the Pacific campaign, when U.S. forces had to cover great distances, mostly over water, and evade Japanese fighters.

Tibbets had been among the first pilots to fly the B-29 and knew it could help turn the tide of the war. But he had a problem on his hands. When the newly designed B-29 was first flown in 1942, the prototype had a design flaw: the engines tended to overheat, often causing dramatic fires. This contributed to a deadly crash that killed ten crew members, including famed Boeing test pilot Eddie T. Allen, and another nineteen people on the ground. The defects were fixed, but the Army Air Forces men remained spooked. Tibbets's pilots were avoiding training in the B-29 at all costs, refusing to fly a plane with such a deadly reputation.

Tibbets had to find a way of getting the men back into the B-29 again. One day he happened to be on the runway at Eglin Field, where he witnessed a pilot stick a tough crosswind landing in the A-20, a temperamental plane. That pilot was Dora. This gave Tibbets an idea. He knew women had been used to prove to men that the Martin B-26 Marauder, known as the "Widow Maker," was safe and easy to fly. If he could persuade a woman to fly the B-29, male pilots refusing to fly the plane would look "chicken." Dora and Didi were the perfect duo for the task. Besides being excellent pilots, they were slender and both about five feet five inches; their success in the giant plane would show the male pilots that they didn't have to "manhandle" the B-29 and that, with careful attention, anyone—"even a woman"—could fly it well.

Tibbets talked with Dora and Didi, convincing them that they were the pilots he needed to do the job. They hurried to pack their bags. The next day the two women found themselves on the ramp of the modification center in Birmingham, Alabama, standing right in front of the mighty B-29. The plane was so massive, the nose wheel alone very nearly came up to their waists. Dora and Didi climbed up the ladder into the flight crew area of the plane. It was roomy up front with the two pilots in their seats, a flight engineer directly behind them, and the navigator and radio operator seated slightly farther back. Down below, in the distinctive Plexiglas nose of the plane, sat the bombardier. Even with six people already aboard, there was still plenty of room for Dora and Didi to stand upright behind the pilots and observe them while in flight. Dora later wrote home that it was like a "flying apartment building."

That day Tibbets taxied the plane toward the runway "with the ease of someone driving out of his driveway on a Sunday morning," as Dora described it. In the coming week the women underwent exhaustive training in which Colonel Tibbets taught them everything from the proper way to recover from a stall to flying and landing on just one of the four engines. The responsibility for flying the giant plane and flying it well weighed heavily on both Dora and Didi, who knew they were representing all of the women pilots.

Less than a week after they'd first talked to Colonel Tibbets, the women met Dean Hudson, a flight examiner from the Civil Aeronautics Authority in nearby Birmingham. Tibbets had asked Hudson to give Dora and Didi their flight check so that the women could have the horsepower rating put on their civilian pilot's licenses (despite the fact that Hudson had never even been in a B-29 before). Dora sat in the left seat while Hudson had her demonstrate a stall, an engine-out procedure, and other standard tests. But as she headed in to land, the number two engine began smoking. The flight engineer pulled the fire extinguisher on the engine as Dora calmly lined up her approach and safely landed, the fire trucks screaming after them down the runway as she did. Dora pulled the plane into the grass beside the runway and quickly told the others to deplane as she shut down the remaining three engines. The airport's fire trucks were already spraying down the flaming engine and the fire was soon extinguished.

While the crew later downplayed the event, the incident report makes clear that they'd avoided a close call, listing among the "considerable damage" from the fire that "the main gas line was nearly burned through." Although both Dora and Colonel Tibbets were disappointed that the flight had been cut short, they were pleased with how she'd handled the emergency, further reinforcing Tibbets's belief that the women were safe pilots—and that it was possible to fly and land a B-29 even with an engine on fire.

Once the training was complete, Tibbets asked for a volunteer crew to travel with him and the women to the air bases in New Mexico and Nebraska where male pilots were refusing to fly the

B-29. All the men of the crew who had trained with Dora and Didi except one, who was about to be a father, signed up. For the tour, the monstrous plane had been named the *Ladybird*. Tibbets's plan was to have the women stand in front of it and powder their noses before climbing aboard and taking off.

At one of the bases, there was a colonel who happened to have been an airline captain before the war started. When Tibbets told him that women were going to fly the B-29, the colonel replied, "Goddamned, I got to see that." He asked to go up in the first flight to see what the women could really do. When they landed, Tibbets later remembered, "the Colonel got out of the airplane and he had a big smile on his face. He thought that was neat and congratulated Dora and all that and thought it was great, and the other boys did the same thing."

The colonel had been convinced, but the four male pilots who were refusing to fly the B-29 were not so easily swayed. Tibbets had no sympathy for the men, later gruffly describing them as "the ring leaders in this pen of sheep." He wanted Dora and Didi to show the men up close "that they could fly the damn airplane." The men apprehensively got in the plane, and Dora and Didi took them out flying for about an hour. After the flight, the men exited the plane, their faces ashen. One of them walked off the runway and into the operations office, threw his wings on the table, and tried to quit. The commanding officer quickly reminded him he was in the Army and could not quit. Years later, Tibbets recalled his disgust at the man's attitude. "You talk about chauvinism," he pointed out. "I mean with airplane drivers they are the worst in the world. They thought nobody else could do it. I knew damn well they [the women] could."

While some of the recalcitrant pilots were upset by the women, many others were genuinely scared of the plane—some having been a part of the accident board that reviewed the earlier B-29 accidents. Dora and Didi flew one pair of pilots at Clovis Army Air Field near Clovis, New Mexico, whom she would remember.

"After lunch a test flight crew went up with us—Capt. McKeown, (pilot) and Lt. Osburn (eng.) and some crew—They turned out to be very nice, all were terribly leery of the ship at first and wore their parachutes, but gradually relaxed." Soon enough, a telegram came from Washington ordering Tibbets to "stop those women from flying that B-29." According to Tibbets, they felt that he had proven his point. By then Dora and Didi had logged approximately fifty hours in the B-29. Despite being cut short, the experiment had been successful. Tibbets would later laugh about how effective the women had been in getting the male pilots back into the B-29. It was a "secret little deal that we pulled," he said, and "it worked so well."

Two 44-W-10 trainees, Marguerite Jean Terrell and Suzette Van Daell, take a break to sun themselves and laughingly lament the fact that they are in "Cochran's Convent." *Courtesy TWU*

CHAPTER EIGHTEEN

The Lost Last Class

Throughout 1944, women trainees continued to arrive at Sweetwater. Among them was Mary Anna "Marty" Martin, the minister's daughter from Indiana, who had first read about the women pilots in *Look* magazine a year earlier.

Marty had worked hard to get to Sweetwater, persisting in her flying lessons so she could get enough experience to join the program even when her instructor's cigar made her airsick. As soon as she had her hours, Marty wrote to Jackie Cochran, asking to be considered for her program. In October 1943, Marty got on the train to Chicago, where she met with Ethel Sheehy, Jackie's "chief recruiting officer," at the Palmer House, the same hotel Dora had been interviewed in the year before. Marty brought with her let-ters of recommendation from her instructor and church mem-bers. With her bachelor's degree, traditional upbringing, and upbeat personality, Marty must have impressed Ethel, because she immediately earned a spot in the first class available, starting in June 1944. Marty just had to take her flight physical, which she could do at her local Army airfield in Indiana.

Marty anxiously awaited her turn to fly. She didn't have to wait long. In March she received a telegram inviting her to join an ear-lier class, in April. Marty quit her job and packed her bags. Her mother, who had disapproved of her flying from the start, was so upset that she wouldn't even come down from her room to say goodbye. She was convinced Marty was going to be killed and didn't want to have anything to do with her leaving for Sweetwa-ter. Perhaps she thought that if she was stubborn enough, she could change her daughter's mind. But Marty wasn't going to let anyone stand in her way.

Marty boarded the train and headed south but soon had to turn around and come back again. At a stop in Kansas she re-ceived a telegram from the program at Sweetwater explaining that her file was incomplete and that she would be deferred until a later class. It turned out that the flight surgeon at her local airfield who had performed her physical decided it was inappropriate for a young woman to fly Army airplanes and never sent in Marty's medical report. Marty was livid. She returned home and stormed into the flight surgeon's office, yelling that he had no right to make that choice for her and accusing him of ruining her life. The doc-tor heard her out, sighed, and finally said, "Young lady, you don't talk to Lieutenant Colonels that way. You are in the Army now."

The following month, Marty got back on the train and headed for Texas. She arrived at Sweetwater on May 26, 1944, and finally got her first glimpse of what would be her home for the next seven months. She was now a member of class 44-W-10. "Gee, what a long day this has been," she wrote in a letter home to her parents that evening. "We came out [to the field] in 2 huge semi-trailer trucks with benches arranged in the trailer, and have spent the *entire* afternoon marching here and there and in lengthy lectures from the chief of staff, the primary training flying officer and the physical training teacher. So far I am thrilled."

Marty wrote home multiple times each week, explaining that she was going to use her letters as a kind of a diary to keep a record of her time in training. Her tone was one of unrestrained happiness and excitement. "Well, I still love it!" she wrote on May 28. "This seems like dreamland down here." She spent her first week of training getting the lay of the land, attending lectures, and befriending her bay mates. The earlier classes were helpful to the newest gals and even lent them their primary flight manuals so Marty and her classmates could spend time "sun-bathing between thunderstorms and reading about flying the army way." She also took note of the natural camaraderie among the women. "There's a wonderful spirit among the girls down here," she explained. "All the girls try to be so friendly—almost to the point they outdo themselves. They have a lot of cute songs for the W.A.S.P. We just heard a serenade from Class 44-W-9," a reworking of an old military song for a new era:

We are Yankee Doodle Pilots,

Yankee Doodle, do or die!

Real live nieces of our Uncle Sam,

Born with a yearning to fly.

Keep in step to all our classes

March to flight line with our pals.

Yankee Doodle came to Texas

Just to fly the PTs!

We are those Yankee Doodle Gals!

Marty's class was determined to keep up with the songwriting and spent free time creating new songs of their own to sing as they marched, hoping to impress the upperclassmen. As freshmen, their days were rigorous. They were up at 6:00 A.M., then they cleaned their bay, dressed, and got in formation to march to breakfast by 6:25. By 7:00 A.M. they were in ground school for three hours, then it was on to drill. They were on the flight line by 1:30 P.M. and didn't sit down for dinner until 7:30 P.M.

By June, Marty was writing home about the heat, the black widow spiders that stalked the bays, and the sand that seemed to get into everything. But even these discomforts couldn't dampen her spirits. She loved it all, but most of all the flying.

"Yesterday I got to land for the first time," she wrote home on June 4. "It was a scream! I didn't have the slightest idea where the ground was and bounced about 20 feet. Instead of recovering for me Mr. Bingham let me recover my own bounces. This is an idea of what it looked like \/\/\/\ I'm learning though."

When she wasn't flying or socializing, Marty kept one eye on what was happening in the news, always remembering why she was there in the first place. On June 6, 1944, the women received word that the invasion of France had finally begun. All hopes were with the young men storming the beaches and moving inland, pushing the Germans back toward their own borders. The following day, Marty and the rest of the WASP gathered as the new chaplain on the field talked with them during a special service for D-Day. The trainees listened to President Roosevelt's prayer on the radio and added their own. Everyone was amazed by the scale of the invasion, with hundreds of thousands of American, British, and Canadian forces landing on five beaches and inland along a fifty-mile stretch of coast in France's Normandy region. No one yet knew if it would work, but Marty was hopeful that her little part would help those men as they moved toward victory.

After two weeks of initial confinement on base, Marty and the rest of class 44-W-10 were allowed to go into Sweetwater, where they did some shopping and then got to visit the Avengerette Club. The club for the women pilots had opened earlier that spring and was situated above a shop in the downtown area. "It has a lovely club-room for dancing," Marty wrote home, "and then a separate room for girls who don't desire dates. The color scheme is yellow and blue (WASP colors) and the walls have cute cartoons painted on them . . . They have a lovely large dance floor with a jukebox, a Coke bar, and tables around the floor." Male soldiers could come to the club to dance and mingle, but only when accompanied by a woman trainee. "I met a very nice fellow from the 12 Armored Corps from Camp Berkely [sic] . . . ," Marty continued. "He was one of the smoothest dancers I have ever danced with. He's from N.Y. and knew a lot of the steps I hadn't done. Didn't take long to learn though."

Marty neglected to tell her family about the ambulance driver from Barkeley who would drive to nearby "wet" Big Spring and supply the liquor for the club in "dry" Sweetwater. She did, however, make sure to tell her family about the service at the local church she attended each Sunday morning; her minister father had sent notes of introduction to all of the pastors in Sweetwater so they would know his daughter was in town. Marty received invitations from many of the congregations and dutifully sent home the bulletins, offering commentary on the various pastors and their sermons.

For someone who lived in "Cochran's Convent," Marty spent so much time dating that she began to run out of going-out clothes and had to write home to her mother and younger sister asking them to send additional outfits. Each weekend she had dates with the men from Barkeley Field or other pilots who came in from their own training in Abilene to date the girls who knew all about airplanes. It got to the point where her parents were writing to her suggesting she should slow down on the dating and concentrate on her studies a bit more. But Marty always sent home those Sunday church bulletins.

She also started a scrapbook, "a nice leather one which will wear," in which she kept clippings and photos about the WASP, documenting everything that was happening, as if she could sense her training slipping away from her far too quickly. Marty's favorite days were those when she got sent out to do solo aerobatics and when she and a bay mate would rendezvous at the far end of the practice area and watch each other perform "loops, snap rolls, vertical reverse, slow rolls and inverted flight. It was really sport!" She wanted to preserve these memories forever.

Like the rest of the women, Marty closely followed the progress of the WASP bill as it was debated in Congress, hoping it would pass—in part because now that she'd seen those silver wings on the blue uniforms, she just had to have them.

But as the summer progressed and the end date of their program neared, the WTS flight instructors redoubled their efforts. They kept pushing both Congress and the media to listen to tales of their "plight." The Navy, which had produced more than 35,000 new pilots in 1943, had announced it was suspending its contracts with the Civil Aeronautics Authority WTS, too, instead pushing its aviators through a more stringent Navy-led program. Booted by both the Army and the Navy, the WTS instructors were now even more vulnerable to the draft. As summer, and unemployment, was upon them, they began to push harder against the WASP.

The media—once so positive about the women's efforts—now fully turned against them. *Time* magazine ran an article titled "Unnecessary and Undesirable?" The *New York Times* declared that male pilots with over 2,000 hours of flight experience "may soon be cleaning windshields and servicing planes for 'glamorous women flyers who have had only thirty-five hours of flying time.'"

One aviation publication that was particularly harmful to the WASP's cause was *Contact*. Written primarily for pilots, it strongly supported the WTS instructors. An editorial cartoon titled "How to Get into the AAF" showed a former War Training Service pilot striding out of a thrift store wearing a skirt and jacket with his old uniform now in the store window. The cartoon was reprinted in the *Washington Daily News* along with a sympathetic article about the WTS flight instructors. An accompanying editorial was titled "Wanted—Female Impersonators." It asked, "Who is throwing their weight around Washington? Is somebody making a play for the 1944 female vote?" Despite the support of the War Department and the AAF, it was tough to find a positive article about the WASP that year.

On June 5, 1944, right around the time Marty was making her first landing at Sweetwater, the Ramspeck Committee released its report on the WASP. The committee indicated that it did not intend the report to be an attack against the women but rather an attack on wasteful spending and an argument for the most efficient utilization of personnel. Despite the reassurance, the overall theme of the report was that the WASP were unnecessary. Why recruit or train women, specifically former "stenographers, clerks, schoolteachers, housewives, and factory workers," at great expense when there was a surplus of men to perform the same duties? The authors of the report dismissed the argument that the women were needed, a line of thinking they maintained was "as startling as it is invalid." The report was filled with allusions to the unemployed male pilots.

The Ramspeck Committee had other problems with the WASP as well. Their report addressed the high cost of training women and pointed out what the committee saw as questionable authorization for the original training program, which had never gone before Congress; the War Department had run the program under a 1943 act allowing expenditures for the training of civilian employees. For most of the 1930s and early 1940s Congress had allowed the president and the military to encroach upon its authority as a result of the back-to-back emergencies of the Great Depression and World War II. By mid-1944 Congress was beginning to reassert itself and its role in the government. The fact that the AAF had not specifically asked Congress for funding for its experiment with the women likely angered legislators, and it placed additional doubt upon the legitimacy of the WASP's claim for military status.

Citing the costs of training the women and the availability of male pilots, Ramspeck and his Committee on the Civil Service concluded that there was no justification for the expansion of the WASP program and suggested that "the recruitment of inexperienced personnel and their training for the WASPs be immediately terminated." Significantly, however, they recommended that "the use of the WASPs already trained and in training be continued and provision be made for hospitalization and insurance."

The release of the Ramspeck report in June and the debate in Congress about the women coincided with a turning point in the war. Hundreds of thousands of Allied soldiers and airmen had crossed the English Channel for the June 6 invasion of Normandy. By the end of June, American troops pushed the Germans farther, liberating Cherbourg. The Allies began to have hope. Back in the United States, the federal government started working to encourage "Rosie the Riveters" and other women who had been active in the war effort to think about returning to their former domestic duties. While these women may have been hailed as heroines earlier in the war, the message coming from the government and in the press at this later stage in the conflict was that it would soon be time for the women to step aside. Throughout 1944, most of the propaganda images put out by the Office of War Information emphasized the nuclear family as the primary reason for men to fight and sacrifice during the conflict. Women's role was to heal men's physical and emotional wounds after the war and to nurture the next generation. The overriding message was that when women went back to creating a safe, comfortable, happy home, they would restore humanity to the world. At the same time, negative articles about working women proliferated. The Depression was still fresh in everyone's minds, and no one wanted a return to mass unemployment for men once wartime manufacturing had slowed or stopped. Still, not everyone on the Committee on the Civil Service agreed with Ramspeck's unfavorable report. Six members of the committee filed a minority report disagreeing with the majority's conclusions, arguing that it was "beyond dispute" that General Arnold and Secretary of War Stimson both wanted the WASP militarized, that whatever happened to the WASP would not affect the fate of the WTS flight instructors, and that the House Committee on Military Affairs had unanimously approved WASP militarization. They argued that it was foolish and illogical to lose women pilots who were already trained or in the process of being trained.

On June 21, 1944, as the battle for France raged on, the House began a vigorous debate about the fate of the WASP. Most of the time was spent discussing the male flight instructors of the WTS who had done such an effective job making their case to certain members of Congress. As for the WASP themselves, many supported them, but others found the legislation "unpalatable." "I think it is time to forget the glamor in this war and think more of the gore of war," one congressman said, in reference to the women. The debate went on and on during the busy final day before summer recess, until finally a frustrated Representative Edouard Izac of California, a longtime opponent of General Arnold and a Navy Medal of Honor winner, moved to strike out the enacting clause of the bill, hoping to kill it. He wanted to move on to more important business—and if the women's bill was declared dead, that was okay with him, too. He didn't mind Arnold losing.

The enacting clause of H.R. 4219 was stricken by a roll call vote of 188 to 169, with seventy-three members abstaining. It was over. The House of Representatives rejected the request of the AAF to bring the WASP into the military by just nineteen votes.

The House vote was not the end of the WASP—there was still a live bill in the Senate—but it was the beginning of the end.

The news of the failed bill spread quickly among the women trainees at Avenger Field. No one knew what it meant, and even those who were neutral or didn't want to be in the military began to worry.

It was up to General Arnold to decide what to do with the WASP in the aftermath of the failed bill. Technically, nothing had really changed. The enacting clause had been stricken, but no action had been ordered instead. Meanwhile, the Ramspeck Committee's report stipulated that recruitment for the training program should end but those currently in training and active duty should remain and receive some benefits. If General Arnold ever hoped to get the women into the military, he needed to follow that recommendation. Even if he had hoped to continue bringing in new trainees, he would soon run out of funds for the program. He didn't think Congress had left him much of a choice.

Nearly a week after the vote, on June 28, Arnold announced that women who were currently in training would get the chance to finish, but no new classes would begin. Marty wrote home to her parents to let them know that she and her 44-W-10 classmates were to be the last class of WASP. "Isn't that awful?" she asked. "You can imagine what it will be like next December when we are the remaining ones. No one will be here to see us graduate . . . Whew! I'm glad I'm here. The officials have definitely assured us that *we will graduate*."

Marty knew that not everyone was so lucky. "There are about 30 girls here that were expecting to enter the June class," she noted. "I feel so sorry for them. They are all heartsick—especially after seeing Avenger Field. They looked like a good bunch of kids too. Just think, we will never be upper classmen, always the babies."

On June 27, telegrams were dispatched to the one hundred women of future class 45-W-1, letting them know that their class was canceled and to stay home. Unfortunately, for many of the women, the telegram arrived too late: they were already headed to Texas. Forty-two women from class 45-W-1 had managed to make it all the way to Sweetwater, arriving with the usual excitement, marveling at the planes on the field, anxious to get their chance to fly them. Dedie Deaton gathered them together and shared the devastating news. They would not be flying for the Army Air Forces. They had just missed their opportunity. Dedie promised the stunned women rides home in AAF planes, apologizing as she left them alone to let the news sink in. Most quietly picked up their unpacked bags and left, unsure where to go next. Many of these women had been waiting for six months to begin training; most had already quit their jobs and paid for travel to Sweetwater. Some of the women stubbornly refused to leave, demanding the chance to serve their country as pilots. Dedie was sympathetic, letting them stay in vacant bays and allowing them "the freedom of the field" as they awaited their rides home.

When Air Transport Command planes arrived on July 2 to take the young women back to their home states, twenty-year-old Winona Jeanne Marsh from Omaha was among the disappointed. But the days she spent on the field awaiting her ride home touched her, and she left the remaining trainees like Marty a song:

Silver Wings on Blue

Silver wings on blue, go soaring through the sky above,

Though we are but few, we're flying for the land we love.

Daughters of the sky, just listen to those motors roar,

Anxious then are we to fly and be on high once more.

Chorus:

We live in sun and sand,

Eyes on the stars,

There is no life that we'd trade for ours.

Victory will come and we'll be there to see it too.

We will be on hand to greet it, SILVER WINGS ON
    BLUE.

The majority of the rest of the class was still en route to Sweet-water when they received the news. Jackie tried to help as best she could, taking phone calls from worried mothers and distraught girls, reassuring them that anyone who made it to Texas would receive a free ride home. "It's sad and unfortunate, but General Arnold has been directed by Congress to stop all additional training of WASP, and he had no choice in the matter," Jackie patiently explained. As she took call after call, more than one young woman ended up in tears. "We're more sorry than we can say," Jackie told them. Jackie had a reputation for being tough, but she was kind to the disappointed young women. After all, she was heartbroken, too.

Teresa James and George "Dink" Martin, not long after they first met in 1937. *From Teresa's scrapbook. Courtesy of Catherine Mowry*

CHAPTER NINETEEN

"I Regret to Inform You . . ."

Teresa James was in the pilots' ready room at the Republic Aviation factory in Farmingdale, New York, when the telegram came in.

A telegram in wartime rarely meant good news. This one was from the U.S. Army Air Forces in England, where Teresa's husband, Dink, was serving as a bomber pilot. The language of the telegram was stark in its lack of any sentiment. It simply stated that Dink had left England for France three days earlier in his B-17 and still hadn't returned. Together with six other men in his crew, he was currently missing in action. This was all that was known for now. The Army Air Forces would keep her updated. It was just weeks after D-Day.

Not knowing what else to do, Teresa called Betty Gillies, who gave her leave to go straight home. Back in Pennsylvania, Teresa waited for news, each minute an agony of anticipation.

Soon, Betty called her back to Wilmington. Summer was a busy time at the factories, and Betty, who'd lost a child the year before, knew that being busy could help one deal with grief. Teresa agreed, later reflecting, "I was better off flying and being with the girls." The women welcomed Jamesy back with open arms, knowing they couldn't do anything but keep her busy and wait for more news with her.

Back on base, Teresa went immediately to check her mail as she always did, and found a letter waiting for her. It was from Dink. The date on the letter was June 21. He was writing from his base at Snetterton in England, explaining that they were keeping him busy flying—twelve missions already and he was "tuckered out." He was taking a lot of fire but told Teresa about it as a joke. "If these jerks would quit shooting at us, it wouldn't be bad, I think they're mad at us though."

The weather was another danger that some pilots might not have written home about, but Dink and Teresa were always straight with each other, and he knew as a fellow pilot she would understand. "I had a close one on takeoff yesterday morn," he wrote. The sky had been dark and under a heavy fog, leaving him to rely on his instruments to fly a plane heavy with bombs and fuel. "I just got into the murk and good and solid in a climbing turn on the gauges when the horizon [the indicator that tells the pilot if the plane is climbing or descending] went out. I rolled right out of the turn and went on needle, ball and airspeed and stayed on them till I broke out on top, wheh! What a sweat. Bill, my co-driver, turned about 40 colors when it went out, some fun." Dink then turned his experience into advice for her. "How are you getting along with the gauges, honey? Are you driving on them yet or not? Learn all you can about them honey, they're the best insurance in the world, next to a flak suit."

Despite his joking tone, Dink was lonely and missing her. He hadn't had any mail after two and a half months away, even though Teresa had been writing him daily. He didn't doubt her but was frustrated with the system. "It's plenty lonesome . . . I'd sure appreciate a letter about now. I don't know what's holding it up. I feel like a stinker, all I do is eat, sleep and fly. I haven't even had time to take a bath for a couple of days."

He finished the letter with "enough griping now, I'm tired now. Still love me as much as ever, honey? I love you more than anything in the world honey and I always will. I miss you more every day and can't wait till this mess is over and I can see you again. I'm going to grab some rest now, write soon."

He mailed the letter the next morning, just as he left on his thirteenth mission—the one from which he had yet to return.

Teresa spent the summer of 1944 in a kind of unbearable limbo, never knowing if she was about to hear the news she longed for—that Dink was safe—or what she dreaded—that he was not. The WASP bill had died in the House and the fate of the women pilots hung in the balance, but how could Teresa imagine that her time in the Ferrying Division might come to an end? Her one consolation was that she was at New Castle with her friends and flying as often as she could, working to bring her husband home.

All of the other women on base noticed the change in their friend. Until now, Jamesy had been known for her practical jokes, her easy laughter and ready smiles, but now she kept to herself. Her eyes no longer sparkled and her features seemed frozen in place from the anxiety of waiting for news.

In September, Teresa found a welcome distraction from her worries. For the past two and a half years, the Republic Aviation Corporation factory had been making P-47 Thunderbolts for the military at a furious pace, feeding the demand for fighter planes. The 10,000th Thunderbolt was about to come off the line, and Republic Aviation was planning a celebration. But first they needed to choose someone to fly the *Ten Grand*—as it had been proudly named—from the plant.

Betty Gillies pulled out a matchbook to see which of the women would pilot the plane, and everyone was pleased when Teresa drew the shortest match. They would have done anything to see her smile again. The bosses at Republic Aviation were equally pleased that Teresa had won the draw. She had flown hundreds of Thunderbolts by this time.

The day of the launch, a crowd of thousands—including civilians, workers, and military representatives—gathered in Farmingdale, Long Island, to witness Teresa taking off in the *Ten Grand*. Republic Aviation's shift workers cheered as generals and bureaucrats lauded their hard work. Under Secretary of War Robert P. Patterson regaled the crowd with stories of the damage the P-47 was causing to German supply lines in Italy and France. Republic's work at Farmingdale was nothing short of a manufacturing miracle, he said. The Wilmington women sat together, listening to at least half a dozen VIPs give their speeches, applauding the workers for the good job they were doing. A bit bored, the women perked up as one of the speakers began talking about the women pilots and how essential they had been in ferrying the P-47. Then he said that the WASP would be missed when they were disbanded. The women crossed their arms and frowned. What did he mean, "disbanded"? What was he talking about?

Before they could spend too much time wondering about their fate, the first round of speeches was over and it was time for the rollout of the *Ten Grand* from the factory floor. Teresa left the others and put on her flight suit over her uniform, waiting with her parachute and cigarette for her chance to fly. A dozen men dragged and pushed the heavy plane forward, aiming its nose toward a paper curtain emblazoned with the words "Republic Aviation" at the front of the hangar until the plane finally broke through the barrier to a roar from the crowd.

At the side of the hangar, Teresa watched as Jackie Cochran

stood waiting on a truck-lift platform to play her part in the drama, dressed for the occasion in the Santiago-blue WASP uniform complete with regulation beret. As the crowd cheered, Jackie held up a bottle proclaiming, "I christen thee *Ten Grand*," before smashing the glass down against the gleaming nose of the plane. A reporter at the scene later described Jackie stepping back as a cloud of mist, meant to symbolize "the element into which the plane soon will soar," wafted over the front of the new plane.

Soon enough, it was time for Teresa to get to work. She carefully walked around the plane as pilots do before every flight, making certain it was in good flying condition. Then, after posing for a few photos for the Republic Aviation and press photographers, she climbed into the plane's cockpit, ready to get going. As she waved to the crowd, she managed to smile despite her worries, and it was hard not to feel a rush of excitement as she buckled herself in and hit the starter switch. The Thunderbolt began to groan to life, its four-bladed propeller slowly beginning to spin. The engine smoothed out as she taxied toward the runway. With a final wave to the cheering crowds, Teresa slid closed the canopy, gave the Thunderbolt full power, roared down the runway, and was off.

It was a short twenty-two-minute flight from Farmingdale to Newark, New Jersey, where a U.S. Navy ship was waiting to transport the *Ten Grand* across the Atlantic to war. Teresa had flown so many Thunderbolts this route by now she'd lost count. She didn't mind these little hops, though. During a short flight like this she stayed low, giving her a chance to see the world beneath her: the farmers in their fields, kids playing baseball, women putting clothes out on the line. It could be a beautiful world from up above.

Before she knew it, Teresa was up and over the Empire State Building before dropping the landing gear and chopping the throttle until the plane landed on the runway in Newark. Once she was parked on the ramp, she filled out her aircraft arrival report as she always did after her delivery was complete, turning it in to the clearance officer to sign, acknowledging that she had, in fact, delivered the plane. But since today was a special day and this was a special plane, she paused and jotted a note in the Thunderbolt's logbook to the men who would be the next to fly it. "To the pilot of the 10 GRAND, you hit the Jackpot," Teresa wrote. "May every mission be a GRAND one and every chance a winner. Good Hunting." She gave her name and address, hoping the men might write back. They often did, their letters telling her about their escapades in Europe, reminding her of the role she was able to play in helping them succeed. If she could deliver enough planes to be shipped overseas, Teresa hoped, maybe the Allies could win the war and Dink would finally be able to come home.

In late October, after four months without any further news about Dink, Teresa's friend Helen Richey offered to help. She wrote to her old friend Lieutenant General Jimmy Doolittle, famous for his raid on Japan in April 1942, who was now based in Europe and had connections throughout the military. Nearly a month later Doolittle wrote back. He had dug up as much information as he could find, managing to obtain a detailed report of what the crews in the other planes saw the day Dink went out on his thirteenth mission. The plane Dink was flying had been hit. The number three engine caught fire, the ship was out of control, but three men with parachutes managed to get out. Then the plane leveled off. Somehow Dink had been able to regain control long enough to enable another four men to parachute out. In other words, at least seven of the ten-man crew made it out of the B-17 before it disappeared in its own smoke and out of sight.

Doolittle wrote: "While we have heard nothing further, you can see from the above that there is a good chance that George got out and is now a prisoner of war. Should we receive any more dope I will pass it on at once. Mrs. Martin will get some measure of comfort from the knowledge that George was well liked by his associates, was doing a swell job and had made substantial contribution to the cause for which we are all fighting. Please extend to her my sympathy and hope that George may yet show up."

Around the same time Helen received the letter, Teresa saw a photograph in the *New York Daily News* captioned "American Airmen Captured by Nazis." She could swear she saw the side of Dink's face and one of his crewmen. She recognized the crewman from her time in California, drinking beers with Dink and his friends that fabulous week that seemed like a lifetime ago. Teresa was convinced she had every reason for hope.

While Nancy Love and Jacqueline Cochran dealt with the logistical changes in the WASP, the women themselves continued doing their serious work for the USAAF. *Courtesy Flora Belle Reece*

CHAPTER TWENTY

Simple Justice

In the days after the announcement that the women's training program was coming to an end, Jackie continued to take phone calls from distraught parents and their daughters. While tight-lipped with the WASP themselves, Jackie doesn't seem to have lost hope that the women might still be militarized. A new bipartisan bill was going before the Senate, and when worried parents called Jackie, she told them about it. She even had her secretaries mail the parents details about the killed House bill, including pages from the *Congressional Record* and copies of General Arnold's testimony from the previous spring. Jackie was careful: she didn't insist that the parents contact their senators about the new bill, but she did give them information they needed to do so. She believed that if the public got behind the WASP cause—led by the women's parents, perhaps—it might still have a chance.

When one mother asked if "it might be a little past the hour for it?" Jackie replied that she wasn't sure:

> After all, the war isn't won in the Pacific;" she pointed out, "and as far as I'm personally concerned, it isn't won in the Atlantic yet. I don't know how the Powers-That-Be feel about it, because they never express their opinions to me. However, and I'm speaking from the standpoint of purely a private citizen, as long as we're fighting a war, you never know what turn it's going to take; therefore, if you sit down and don't continue to be prepared, how are you going to fight it? If it doesn't go the way you planned?

On another call with a Mr. Nevin of Providence, Rhode Island, whose daughter had been due to join, she got even more emotional. Mr. Nevin told her he knew some people who knew her well—he said they called her "Jack"—and he was going to tell them what a wonderful job she had done with the program. Jackie thanked him. "I've done the best I can," she told him. "I've fought pretty hard to get a place for women in aviation in this war, and I don't see why they shouldn't have it . . . I mean, what's the difference in letting women serve in that capacity and all the other capacities. You relieve just as much manpower, but you not only relieve manpower, but you relieve manpower of the very high level of intelligence." The anger, the disbelief that all she had worked so long for was in serious danger of ending, finally burst out of her: "Just because you're a man I don't see why you have an invested right to fly airplanes!"

Mr. Nevin, perhaps sensing the emotion, changed the subject, mentioning a young woman from Providence who was in Sweetwater and how happy she was to be there. They wished each other luck and ended the call. But Jackie—who so carefully projected the image of a conservative who always knew a woman's place (except for her own)—had said enough. Not only was she heartbroken, she was just plain mad.

The new bill in the Senate had its supporters. Civic leaders in Sweetwater put forward an "all-out fight to restore the women's pilot training program." They contacted not only senators but the General Federation of Women's Clubs in the hope that women across the country would unite to convince more senators that the work the WASP was doing was important to the war effort and "that it would be rank discrimination to bar them from the skies." The Ninety-Nines rallied, too, sending letters and making phone calls to save the WASP.

In the end, the bill never made it out of committee. The record is silent on exactly why, but there is one dark possibility besides the lingering concern about the male WTS instructors and the shift in the war. In the spring of 1944, Dedie and Jackie had kicked two WASP out of the program for drinking on the field. They weren't the first or last. One of the women, Wendy Barkley, protested mightily. "Don't you know who I am?" she asked Dedie and Jackie. In fact, she was the niece of Alben W. Barkley of Kentucky, the powerful Senate majority leader. As the story goes, Senator Barkley pressured Jackie to reinstate his niece. She refused and instead went so far as to expunge the young woman from the record as if she had never been any part of the program. In later years some of the women wondered if the fact that the bill never came out of its Senate committee was personal.

By early July, the needs of the Army Air Forces were changing. More pilots were surviving their campaigns overseas, and those who met their quota of combat missions were being rotated out of the theaters of war and sent back to the United States, where they worked as combat-experienced flight instructors and as ferry pilots. Because the Army needed fewer new combat pilots, it also needed fewer light aircraft to train them on. Aircraft factories shifted their emphasis from light trainers to more powerful pursuits and bombers. Flying these planes was challenging, and despite Jackie's efforts to revamp her training program, the women coming out of Sweetwater simply did not have the experience they needed to fly such powerful planes. The AAF was still making the Ferrying Division accept new graduates at a pace of fifteen women per month, but the division was having a more and more difficult time finding planes they were qualified to fly.

Tension between Jackie and Nancy had been growing as Congress debated the fate of the WASP. But they knew that if the program was going to survive, they would have to work together to make a change. On July 3, Jackie and Nancy spoke on the telephone about how best to move 123 women out of the Ferrying Division and into the Training Command, which needed pilots to tow targets, test-fly repaired planes, carry non-flying personnel where they needed to go, and perform other domestic flying jobs. They discussed women individually, never having to explain to the other who was who or where a particular pilot was stationed— remarkable, given that there were hundreds of women under their command—and quickly decided where each one would go.

Jackie and Nancy had quietly worked toward their own goals for years, their supporters often clashing behind the scenes in the attempt to move one woman or the other into a leadership position. But this "Great Transfer," as it came to be known, showed that they could put their differences aside for the good of the women, and their country—even if they didn't always agree on what that meant.

Soon Jackie began visiting the WASP at 50 of the more than 120 bases they served scattered across the United States, collecting information for a status report she had been commissioned to make to General Arnold. (She asked Ethel Sheehy to visit some of the bases, too.) The tour was inspired by a phone call from General Barney Giles, a great advocate of the WASP, who wondered if it was time to begin thinking of ending the program altogether. During the debate before Congress that spring, the AAF had explained to Representative Andrew J. May, chairman of the House Committee on Military Affairs, that one of the primary reasons the program was created, in addition to releasing men for combat duty, was "to determine the manner and extent that women pilots can be effectively used in the Army Air Forces," for any future need. The women pilots had always been a part of an experiment. Now Jackie was being asked to check the status of that experiment—and to determine whether the women were still needed for the war effort.

On August 1, 1944, as the WASP neared its second anniversary, Jackie Cochran submitted to General Arnold the report she and her staff had been working on all summer. The eleven-page document laid out the work the women were doing at all the bases across the country. Jackie strategically acknowledged that the women should step aside when enough men were available for domestic piloting again. But she also made clear that the WASP experiment was going well and she wanted more for her women, including military status. Jackie asserted that "simple justice for the WASPs themselves also dictates such a step," making the case that "they are entitled to equal pay and equal recognition for equal work."

"Under a civilian status," she wrote, "so many elements of the experimental project are lost or weakened, and there is such lack of control over permanency of work by individual WASPs after they are trained, that serious consideration should be given to inactivation if militarization is not soon authorized. If such action should be taken, an effort should be made to obtain military status, if only for one day, and resulting veterans' recognition of all who have served commendably."

As soon as the report became public, the press began debating Cochran's "ultimatum." One newspaper headline read: "FIGHT TO GIVE WASPS ARMY ROLE RENEWED BY JACQUELINE COCHRAN. REPORT TO ARNOLD ASSERTS WOMEN PILOTS SERVICE SHOULD BE DISSOLVED UNLESS IT IS ABSORBED BY AAF." Others suggested that Jackie's mention of inactivation might be a ploy to pressure Congress to take action. Jackie was horrified that her report was being interpreted in those terms: it was not at all her intention to suggest the women be dissolved or to publicly disrespect General Arnold. Arnold himself didn't seem to have been fazed by the report or the media's interpretation of it, but those in the Ferry Command didn't respond with the same equanimity.

Nancy read Jackie's August report with interest, but for her, one section of the report would have stood out. In it Jackie wrote that if militarization proved impossible, "all WASP should either stay or, to avoid preference as between commands or individual WASPs, go out of service altogether." Nancy had assumed that if the WASP failed to be militarized, she would continue as the leader of the women's Ferrying Division, with a small group of women under her command. Everyone else in the Ferrying Division and the Air Transport Command assumed the same. Now Jackie was saying that she did not think that would be good for the women's reputation. Either all the women should be militarized, or everyone should go.

The Ferry Command immediately sprang into action, desperate to separate their women ferry pilots from Jackie and the Training Command in the hope of preserving Nancy's small but valuable group. Ferrying Division public relations officer Captain William R. Geddings implemented an urgent publicity push to promote the great work of the women in the Ferry Command. In a memorandum to Nancy on August 9, 1944, Geddings revealed the disdain many in the Ferrying Division had for the "other"

leader of the women. "Cochrane [sic] is determined to take the
Wasp program down with her if she is turned down in her efforts
to militarize the Wasps. She is the main factor in the congressional
criticism." Geddings was walking a challenging tightrope—the
Ferry Command would need to show they could "build up
the Wasps as a whole by publicizing the achievements of Wasps
in the Ferrying Division," because if it became clear that they were
attempting to promote only the women under their command, "it
is probable that AAF would turn down approval due to Cochrane's
attitude." The tone of Ferrying Division memos to Nancy was one
of near desperation as Geddings and his colleagues scrambled to
position Nancy and the women ferry pilots as unique and therefore worthy of saving.

By the end of August 1944, it seemed the entire world was shifting
on its axis. On August 25 the Allies liberated Paris. Most Americans, including military leaders, believed Hitler, who had survived
a late July assassination attempt, was on the run. While the war
was far from over, the United States was making clear progress
on the Pacific front against Japan as well. As the Allies pushed
Germany back toward its own borders in the summer of 1944,
a group of American B-29s—the same plane Dora and Didi had
demonstrated—carried out the first bombing raid on Japan since
the daring Doolittle raid in the spring of 1942. American carrier-
based planes shot down over two hundred Japanese planes, losing
only twenty of their own, in what came to be known as the "Great
Marianas Turkey Shoot." Shortly thereafter, U.S. Marines invaded
Guam and Tinian. One of the WASP, Caro Bayley, stationed at
Biggs Field in El Paso, Texas, realized that, with the failed bill and
the shift in the war, things were changing. She wrote home that
"there's an awfully big chance of them disbanding the WASP" and
wondered if resigning would be the patriotic thing to do, "because
it seems we're taking a job away from a man."

At the end of August, Nancy's husband, Bob, who had been

lobbying hard to live closer to his wife again, finally achieved his goal. He was appointed deputy commander of the Ferrying Division and posted to Cincinnati, where Nancy had been stationed for nearly a year. Bob and Nancy were reunited. But for Nancy it must have felt as if she was under pressure from all sides: from her husband, who was proud of her but did not seem to want her to take a military commission; from her core ferry pilots, who wanted to be militarized but separately from Jackie; from the Ferrying Division, who wanted the women to stop agitating and do their work; and from Jackie herself, who had determined that the women should be militarized or the program should end altogether.

Despite the cooperative visits and phone calls of the past year, Nancy was now actively avoiding Jackie. The longer the bill sat in the Senate, the less likely it seemed any action would be taken to bring the women into the military. Jackie's report had dismissed the special work the ferry pilots were doing, declaring that the job of all the women was "to do the routine, the dishwashing flying jobs of the AAF," and suggesting that if some of the women were no longer needed, then all of them should go home. This was the last straw for Nancy. She had cooperated for the most part, initially talking with those in the AAF and Congress about alternatives to combining her program with Jackie's, but in the end putting on the blue uniform and the WASP wings believing that Jackie had enough clout to make militarization happen. Now it all seemed to be falling apart, and Nancy blamed Jackie. When they both happened to land at Long Beach on the same day, Nancy made sure their paths wouldn't cross. She was convinced there was no use arguing with Jackie—that Jackie would only take what she said and twist it toward her own ends.

On September 4, 1944, Nancy wrote to one of her flight leaders and originals, Delphine Bohn, reassuring her that—despite all the fuss with Jackie, the newspapers, and the failed bill—the ferry pilots were once again a small, select group of excellent pilots, thanks to the "Great Transfer" of the summer. The women who remained, like Delphine, just needed to forget "the whole damn mess" and get out and "fly!":

"The WASP situation remains in its usual SNAFU state," Nancy wrote,

but I've acquired a new slant on it, and have tried to transmit to the gals, ie we are now the long-sought-for, small select group. We've got one heck of a good record behind us and an even rosier one ahead, or should have with this bunch of good pilots . . .

If the WASPs are abolished, we're still civilian pilots and darned good ones, and though I've outgrown optimism in the last two years, I have it on pretty good authority that we who are left in the Ferrying Division are not to worry, but to keep our mouths shut, eyes on the ball, stop arguing and fly the pants off any and all planes assigned to us . . .

So that's the deal and I still have hopes—wouldn't it be nice not to be anything but civilian pilots again—no WASP or even WAFS.

Anyhow—there's no use in getting het up and having a nervous breakdown over the deal. When you get back, you'll find your squadron small and self-sufficient, and there's no reason squadron leaders can't get out and have fun—only one responsible person need be there. We've all gotten so violent about this that I think its broken down our health . . . I've had flu and now have trench mouth, of all things—and Erickson looks like a ghost. So let's stop worrying and have fun—and see what happens . . . Nancy (you know) POLLY-ANNA Love

Nancy and Jackie had much in common: their ambition, their love of flying, their concern for the women under their command. In the end, their ultimate falling-out seems to have been caused not by simple rivalry, as the press liked to assume, but as a result of the assumptions each one had about what would happen if militarization failed. Nancy believed that she would stay on and lead her small group of women pilots in the Ferrying Division. Jackie had other ideas.

Hazel Ah Ying Lee poses with her new husband, "Clifford" Louie Yim-qun (also known as Louie Yin-cheung), for classmate Madge Rutherford's camera. *Courtesy Texas Woman's University*

CHAPTER TWENTY-ONE

Disbandment

On October 1, 1944, the news that the women had been dreading finally arrived: General Arnold was ready to disband the WASP. He wrote to Jackie, telling her that "the WASP will soon become pilot material in excess of needs." Paris had been liberated and Germany was being pinched by the Allies. With the changing war situation, Arnold could no longer justify the use of women pilots. He praised the work the WASP were doing but reminded Jackie that their job had always been to "release male pilots for other work and not replace them." He ended his letter with "The time has arrived to plan the program's deactivation."

The Army Air Forces had always considered the women pilots

an experiment—a chance to see what women could do not only in this war but in any future wars—and they had already decided that by early 1945 there would be enough statistical information available to reach definite conclusions about women's piloting abilities. General Arnold decided December was close enough. In order to get the women home for the winter holidays, he announced he would shut down the WASP by December 20.

When they heard the news, Teresa James, Helen Richey, Betty Gillies, and the rest of the women in Wilmington could hardly believe it. They were flying P-47s as fast as they came off the assembly line. At Long Beach, where there were 3,000 new pursuits built each year of the war, the women were equally stunned. Most of the women ferry pilots volunteered to serve for a dollar a year, despite the personal cost. They knew they were needed. They knew they were doing a good job. It just didn't make any sense. It was such a waste.

At Sweetwater, Marty Martin and the other trainees first heard the news over the radio, the announcer flatly informing the nation that the WASP experiment was over. Marty wrote home that "it was quite a shock for all of us. All this training without a chance to use it." Marty had been so excited to graduate and begin active duty. Now she and her classmates wondered if they would ever get to do anything with their hard-earned training.

The next day Dedie Deaton called all of the Sweetwater trainees together and made the official announcement. Dedie had devoted the last two years of her life to the care of the women. She had barely taken a moment for herself for twenty-four months and hardly seen her husband or son at home. She'd devoted all her energy to making sure the women's needs were met and that they stayed away from even a hint of scandal, and under her watch they had flourished. But for once, efficient and capable Dedie had no answers for them. Instead, she reassured them as best she could that the training they were doing was still worthwhile. Then Dedie gave them news that cheered Marty and her classmates up just a little bit. Jackie had negotiated with the Civil Aeronautics Administration to recognize the WASP training and give all graduates a commercial license. Marty wrote home, "That means I can take anyone up for a ride and can charge them for it, and it also means I can work toward my instructor's rating which is pretty hard to get." She was pleased they would get to keep one of their uniforms after disbandment, too (although they had to pay for the leather jacket). If she wasn't going to have the chance to serve her country, at least the training she was getting was going to help her with her postwar flying goals.

Dora was stationed at a new base in Wendover, Utah, serving as a shuttle pilot, when she got the news. The work they were doing at Wendover was top secret, and she wrote home about flying the "blue-plate special"—often a three-day mission on which she wouldn't find out where she was headed until the last minute and wasn't allowed to tell anyone where she had been. She sent her folks Jackie's and General Arnold's letters that explained why they were "quitting the WASP" and expressed relief that they had at least remembered to help them convert their Army flying to CAA commercial licenses. She was disappointed and a bit embarrassed that the program was ending but relieved that she would take her experience with her.

When word of disbandment reached Hazel Ah Ling Yee, she was at her base in Romulus, where she flew P-39s and other pursuit planes to the west, many already wearing the paint they would need as part of the Chinese Air Force. Hazel was helping both of her countries at last. As soon as she learned about the WASP's disbandment, she began working to help the women find flying jobs in China. She had married Yin Cheung Louie, a fellow pilot she'd met while training in Oregon, just a year earlier. He was now a major in the Chinese Air Force and was working to help the women arrange a chance to fly for the Chinese. Hazel had already accepted an offer. In Wilmington, Teresa began getting her papers in order to apply. If she couldn't help end the war and bring Dink home within the United States, then she could at least go help a struggling American ally.

By the time the news of deactivation came in, WASP were stationed at more than 120 bases all across America. From Long Beach, California, to Wendover, Utah, to Sumter, South Carolina, the women struggled to come to terms with what December would bring and what they would do next. As they began to imagine life without the WASP, they started to make plans for the future, but no one knew quite what to do with themselves and all their flying experience. Whether still in training or on active duty, the women felt the same way: the war was still ongoing, the victory hadn't been won, but they were going home all the same. It didn't seem right.

On October 3, General Arnold sent letters to all WASP confirming the news and expressing his gratitude for their work: "You have freed male pilots for other work," he wrote,

> but now the war situation has changed and the time has come when your volunteered services are no longer needed. The situation is that, if you continue in service, you will be replacing instead of releasing our young men. I know that the WASP wouldn't want that . . . I want you to know that I appreciate your war service and that the AAF will miss you. I also know that you will join us in being thankful that our combat losses have proved to be much lower than anticipated, even though it means inactivation of the WASP.

Jackie also wrote to the WASP, telling them she appreciated their service and was proud of their record:

> I felt sure when this organization was in its infancy that, given the opportunity, women could prove themselves capable in any situation they might be called upon to face,

and you girls have corroborated my statement many times over. Thus it is with deep regret that I found it necessary to recommend inactivation of the entire program, for I know how sorry you girls will be to have to divorce yourselves from Army flying. But how grateful we can be to know that our disbandment is the result of unexpectedly low combat losses; and how great is our satisfaction to know that over 1,000 women have learned to fly "the Army way."

She ended her letter by reassuring them that she hoped to stay in touch and sending her best wishes and personal regards. But she would not give them another chance to fly for the Army.

Jackie was crushed by the decision to end the experiment so soon but kept a brave public face, even claiming that it had been her idea in the first place. She spent the next several months discouraging the women pilots who were desperately trying to keep flying. Some were writing their representatives. Others were contacting AAF headquarters. All of them felt the weight of guilt and embarrassment as they contemplated going home before the war was over. Jackie stubbornly stuck to General Arnold's pronouncements, determined that even Nancy's ferry pilots would be leaving in December with all the others.

The Ferrying Division desperately wanted to keep their women pilots. By now Nancy's champion, General Tunner, had left on assignment to the China-Burma-India theater, replaced by a new general, Robert Nowland. General Nowland did what he could to save the program. As late as November, he wrote to Arnold explaining how difficult it would be to replace the women, as they constituted close to half of the Ferrying Division's "frozen" pursuit pilots (those who were locked into flying only pursuits). He went so far as to put a dollar amount on how much it would cost to replace the 117 women ferry pilots: $1,085,312.

When it became clear that the women ferry pilots would not be able to continue to serve, Nancy was furious. She had counted on

Jackie's clout and connections to push militarization through. She had discouraged her women from pursuing other routes to staying in their jobs, telling them to be patient and to wait it out. She had counted on her elite group being able to fly even if the WASP ended. And it had all come to naught. In the years to come, she rarely spoke about this time—it was too painful to recall—and when she did, she blamed Jackie for the program ending and cursed General Arnold. Even so, she must have wondered what she might have done differently: if she should have done more, or maybe if she should have done less.

Tragically, while training had ended, fatal accidents had not. Just before Thanksgiving, Hazel joined a flight of four WASP and seventeen male pilots from their base in Romulus, Michigan, to the Bell factory in Niagara Falls, New York. There she picked up a P-63 Kingcobra and headed toward Great Falls, Montana, where it would be handed off to the Russians. It was a long trip to Montana at that time of year, and Hazel spent a day or two with other WASP ferry pilots waiting out bad weather, eating Thanksgiving dinner, bowling, and making plans for the future.

When the skies cleared, Hazel, along with dozens of other pilots who had sat out the weather in nearby towns, headed to Great Falls. There were several other P-63s in the landing pattern when she arrived. She was on her final approach when another P-63 came in above and slightly behind her and lowered his landing gear, clearly not seeing her. The control tower frantically called to both planes but received no answer. They flashed the red light from the tower, telling them both to abort the landing, but neither pilot took action. The other pilot collided into Hazel just short of the runway. His right fuel tank exploded and engulfed both planes in flames as they crashed to the ground.

An officer who watched the accident in horror bravely climbed into Hazel's plane and pulled her from the flames, but as they hurried her into the ambulance, they neglected to take off her still-smoking leather jacket. She continued to burn all the way to the hospital. She died the next day. When her body was sent home to her family on the West Coast, the local funeral home and cemetery both refused it. She was Asian; they served whites only. After a prolonged battle, the family ultimately was given permission to bury Hazel in a nonmilitary funeral. They buried her brother, who died in France three days after she did, alongside her.

When the news about disbandment arrived in October, class 44-W-8 was just days from graduation and quickly headed to bases to serve for the remaining time they had. This left two classes hoping to finish training in Sweetwater, and those women faced the reality that time was short and their service after training would be even shorter. The barracks were slowly emptying with each graduation, and the field was quieter by the day. Sweetwater had once been home to more than five hundred women pilots; there were now fewer than two hundred left. The food, which had become so wonderful by the time Dora arrived in the spring of 1943, was miserable again by late 1944, with the kitchen cooking powdered eggs the night before and warming them up for breakfast in the morning. As the program shrank, it lost its priority in the still-rationed nation, and most of the women filled up on milk.

On November 8, class 44-W-9 graduated. Maggie Gee, a Chinese American pilot from San Francisco, was among the graduates. Standing next to her that day was her good friend Elaine Harmon from Baltimore. Like the other women in the crowd, Elaine later recalled feeling a powerful mix of emotions: pride in having won her silver wings, and sadness for the loss of the program that had meant so much to so many women. She and Maggie had become fast friends and were happy they were going to be based at Las Vegas Army Air Field together—even if it was only for the last six weeks of the WASP.

The graduation ceremony was a relatively small, somber affair. Dedie Deaton was the master of ceremonies. Instead of a military band, the Sweetwater High School band played. There were no photographers and no newsreels. Jackie was the only distinguished guest and was supposed to speak, but when it came time for her to take her place on the podium, she simply couldn't get the words out. Overcome with emotion, tears streaming down her cheeks, she dejectedly sat back down. As one WASP later wrote home to her parents, Jackie looked as though she had "been through a terrific battle and lost." Lieutenant Colonel Roy Ward, the Avenger Field commander, said a few words instead, before introducing the main speaker, Colonel Schwartz. Lieutenant Colonel Ward, too, was flummoxed by Jackie's tears, praised the women pilots, lamented the "liquidation" of the WASP, and "offered hope that something might yet be done to keep them flying."

Jackie composed herself enough to hand the women their diplomas, while the colonel pinned on their wings. After the graduation ceremony was over, Jackie spoke to the women. Three weeks earlier, someone from General Arnold's staff had called her and asked her to close the program immediately. Jackie had protested, and as a result the women had been allowed to finish training and to graduate. While their leader may have lost the battle, she had won them this small victory.

Now that class 44-W-9 was moving on, that left only one class of women trainees: Marty's. She later described the final month of the program as a "rat race." The last class was pushed hard to finish quickly, and their flying was compressed, with little time off for rest. There was no room for error in their graduation date and no class to wash back to if they got behind. There were now fewer than eighty women pilots at Avenger Field, and the barracks that had once been filled with as many as five hundred women stood dark. There were no underclassmen to taunt, no one to brag to about how tough the AT-6 was to fly compared to that simple

Stearman. Marty had hoped her parents would come down for the ceremony, writing to them that "this graduation means more to me than any college degree could ever mean. It sounds like the whole Army is going to make something out of it too." But travel was just too difficult during wartime, and her parents were unable to attend.

The date of the final graduation—December 7, 1944—drew closer, and Jackie and the Army Air Forces decided to go out in style. The public relations officer with the AAF Training Command, Lieutenant Colonel Manning Sell, had been given free rein in planning the graduation and the publicity surrounding it, and he made it one for the history books. The Movietone News cameramen arrived the Monday before to shoot newsreel of the field and the women, keeping them up until 1:00 A.M. the night before graduation singing their class songs, and making them climb in and out of the planes over and over until they got just the right shot.

Nancy Love was invited but did not attend. Nonetheless, nearly one hundred WASP flew back to Sweetwater under orders to celebrate the final graduation so that the last class would not be alone. Along with the many WASP in the audience were a number of the men who had had a hand in their journey, including Lieutenant General Barton Kyle Yount, commanding general of the AAF Central Flying Training Command (the command in charge of Avenger Field) and General Henry "Hap" Arnold, commanding general of the entire U.S. Army Air Forces.

The Big Spring Bombardier School Band returned to provide the music, and the ceremony itself was poignant and celebratory. When General Arnold took to the stage, he told the women that when the program began, he didn't know if women would be capable of flying military planes. But he'd taken a chance, and the women had proven themselves:

> You and more than 900 of your sisters have shown that you can fly wingtip to wingtip with your brothers. If

ever there was any doubt in anyone's mind that women can become skillful pilots, the WASP have dispelled that doubt. I want to stress how valuable I believe the whole WASP program has been for the country... [We] know that you can handle our greatest fighters, our heaviest bombers; we... know that you are capable of ferrying, target towing, and test flying. So, on this last graduation day, I salute you and all WASP. We of the Army Air Force are proud of you; we will never forget our debt to you.

Jackie had her chance to speak at the graduation, too, and she did not cry this day. She was poised and professional, and clearly proud of what she and her women had accomplished. "It seems incredible a person can have so many different emotions," Jackie told the crowd. "Happiness, sorrow, pride, I have all three of those today. I'm very happy that we've trained a thousand women to fly the Army way ... I think it's going to mean more to aviation than anyone realizes ... this program that will go down in history ... not only in history, but I'm sure it's going to do something that is so vital and has been so badly needed in aviation for so many years ... And I'm sure that if there's a reason to call you girls back up after December 20, that all of you will respond and that we'll have probably 95 percent of you back in the Air Forces anyway."

Marty walked away from the day with one thought in mind: "Those wings are certainly beautiful."

Shortly after the graduation ceremony, Jackie went back to the hospital for surgery for her abdominal adhesions. From her hospital bed she tried to maintain control of events, nervous that Nancy and her women ferry pilots might still find a way to stay on even as the rest of the women were disbanded. Jackie's devoted husband, Floyd Odlum, was at her side, doing his best to help her as she struggled to recover after her operation.

On December 14, 1944, Floyd wrote to one of Jackie's assistants at the Pentagon, asking her to release an enclosed press statement about disbandment. He also mentioned an article by the writer and aviator Gil Robb Wilson that had been published only a few days before. In the article Wilson, a founder of the Civil Air Patrol, praised the skilled women ferry pilots and made the point that it would be costly and time-consuming to replace them, arguing that these women should be allowed to stay on even if others were to be demobilized. Jackie clearly wanted to stamp out this kind of message in the press right away. "The point about this is she thinks that the small clique that has been anti everything and nearly came out with an interview in the Pittsburgh paper recently may be holding their fire until the 20th (hoping to end the Wasps as such, but keep themselves in)," Floyd wrote. "A short official statement before this time giving the reason for demobilization might stop some of the other misinformation from coming out or at least from becoming the first impression with the public or editors to be overcome with much greater effort than otherwise." Then he added: "By tomorrow Jackie should be through the worst of the aftermath of the operation."

On December 14, 1944, Nancy Love took her last flight as a WASP, picking up a C-54 Skymaster (a four-engine transport) from Chicago that needed to be ferried to California. Before she left Ferrying Division headquarters in Cincinnati on this final mission, she gave an interview to the press. In the interview, which was syndicated in newspapers throughout the United States, Nancy, who had always insisted on the women's equality with men, made a last-ditch case for women pilots flying for the military, insisting that the women were in fact not only equal but actually superior to their male counterparts. "Women," she explained to the reporter, "are physically and temperamentally suited for fighter plane operation. They are smaller, hence more comfortable in a tiny crowded cockpit. They are quicker to react under many circumstances and are supposed to have a lighter, more deliberate touch and thus are better able to surmount emergencies when they arise."

Then she sounded a note of pride in her pilots:

> They definitely have proved that women are useful in military flying and can replace men for combat. The theory that women "can't take it" physically, has been thoroughly disproved. I have it in writing, from excellent authority, that the women's physical record is equal to, if not better, than men over a two year period . . .
>
> We have an expression, "eager beaver" to describe anyone who is always willing and anxious to do a task. The WASP really have been "eager beavers." Their conscientiousness has been marvelous—in part I daresay, because they know that, as women, they "had to make good."
>
> It hasn't been an easy job, or highly paid, or glamorous . . . You can't be glamorous when, on a one or two-week trip away from base, you have room in your fighter plane for only one clean shirt, a toothbrush and maybe a pair of pajamas.

She went on to reflect on what would happen now that the WASP was coming to an end. The idea of returning to work as a flight instructor would be "humdrum" by comparison. Airlines had plenty of men in their pilot pools, and the war wasn't over yet, so it wasn't as if the airplane factories were ready to do sales promotions again, as they had done in peacetime.

When asked about her own postwar plans, Nancy laughed—"a laugh without much mirth," according to the reporter. "I have none," she replied. "I'm leaving today, flying a C-54 to California . . . Going to fly all night. I want to get away and think what all has happened to me . . . And to us."

After the C-54 was safely delivered, Nancy immediately returned to New Castle Army Air Base. There were just four days left before disbandment, and women pilots across the country were holding dinners and parties to commemorate the end of the program. Nancy chose to be part of the farewell dinner for the 2nd Ferrying Group, where it had all begun. The setting was the officers' club, a place that had been a home to the women since their arrival two years earlier. Since then, the club had grown from a one-room meeting place to a much larger structure that was comfortably furnished and appointed. Even though the WASP had never technically been members of the military, they had always been welcome at the officers' club, with their own bottles behind the bar waiting for each of them at the end of a long day of flying.

In preparation for the evening ahead, the women arranged tables together in the shape of a horseshoe, put boards over wooden sawhorses, then laid white tablecloths across them. A basket of flowers and long, white tapered candles served as centerpieces. Nancy carefully assigned seats around the table: Betty Gillies to her left, Teresa James, Helen Richey, and other "originals" seated nearby—forty-one women in total, so familiar to one another after months of flying side by side. Everyone wore their formal blue uniforms: dress jacket, skirt, crisp white shirt, black tie, and their hard-won silver wings over their heart.

The women called the gathering the "Last Supper," and it was a bittersweet affair. They were happy to be reunited, regaling one another with tales of flights they had taken and experiences they'd shared. Nonetheless, the loss weighed heavily, and the air in the dark, wood-paneled room of the officers' club grew thick with cigarette smoke and chagrin. The women contemplated what to do next. Teresa planned to return to her family in Wilkinsburg. Helen was also heading back to Pennsylvania, to her family in McKeesport. It was as if their lives, which until now had been propelled by forward motion, were suddenly going in reverse. A few of the women held back from drinking that night, knowing they had one last P-47 to deliver out of Farmingdale, Long Island, in the morning. But others were happy to drown their sorrows. The war was still being fought. Planes sat on ramps from Farmingdale all the way to Long Beach, California, waiting to be ferried. But the women were being sent home, caught on the losing side of a political battle, common sense be damned.

The WASP's collective achievement had been remarkable. By December 1944, 1,102 women were wearing those silver wings. They had flown more than seventy-seven different types of planes and had covered over 60 million miles. They had served as test pilots, flown personnel, and trained ground gunners to find planes as they strafed them. With the exception of combat flying, the women were doing every single type of assignment their male counterparts performed. Thirty-eight of them had given their lives.

In large part, the women were being sent home because an Allied victory was almost certain at this point. The prevailing wisdom was that the women were no longer needed because the men would be coming home soon. But what no one seemed to remember was that the WASP had been vital to ending the war in the first place. They had released 1,102 men to fly in combat. They had trained men on the ground and in the air to find and fire at planes. They had taught men how to fly trainers and how not to be afraid to fly temperamental bombers. They had test-flown planes after repairs. They had proven, without a doubt, that women could be counted on as pilots, whatever the job, whatever the emergency. They had all played a part in winning the war.

The women at New Castle were asleep in their beds, their bags packed, when they were startled awake by shouts of "Fire!" One by one they climbed out of bed, wrapped themselves in robes and blankets, and walked outside to see their beloved officers' club engulfed in flames. A brisk wind sent terrifying cascades of sparks into the night air. Crowds of officers and other personnel from the base were beginning to gather, with one of the men bravely attempting to get into the building to rescue cash and papers kept in a safe inside. Soon enough, firefighters from the base were joined by three additional fire companies in an attempt to tame the blaze, with men stationed on rooftops to extinguish flaming pieces of wood that were coming dangerously close to falling on neighboring buildings. Huge columns of smoke billowed up into the starless sky. It was clear to the women that the officers' club where they had spent their "Last Supper" three days earlier—that had been their home for the past two years—could not be saved.

The firefighters struggled on until 7:00 A.M., when the fire was finally brought under control and they were able to leave. The date was December 20, 1944, the women's last day as pilots for the U.S. Army Air Forces. The sun rose on a cold and snowy morning, the acrid scent of smoke still in the air. The women trudged from office to office after their sleepless night, turning in their uniforms and equipment, everything from parachutes to watches, and signing out. Then they put on their civilian clothes—for many of them the same clothes they had arrived in—picked up their bags, and walked out of the base for the last time.

Decades later Teresa recalled the moment like it was yesterday: "After flying for 27 months with the women like you were sisters, flying around the country and then coming back and chatting about it—just like a big family, and then all of a sudden you lose that. How do you go home to people who didn't understand? You became a part of each other because you could talk about what happened, the scary moments, and bolster each other. You became very close and then all of a sudden, this association has ended . . . Something died right there."

Teresa stepped through the gate at Wilmington for the last time, and then, as she remembered, "I just stood there and cried."

In this portrait from 1950, Caro Bayley wishes her father a Happy Father's Day in front of the new Pitts Special he had bought to help facilitate her aerobatic pursuits. She would become the Women's International Aerobatic Champion in the plane the following year. *Courtesy of Caro Bayley Bosca*

CHAPTER TWENTY-TWO

The End of the Experiment

Teresa made straight for the train station in Wilmington, where she bought her own ticket home: she had arrived on her own dime and would leave the same way. It had been two years since she sat in her train from Pittsburgh, writing excitedly in her diary about her hopes of being accepted into Nancy's program. Back then she never could have imagined the planes she would get to fly or the friendships she would form. She hoped they would continue even now that the women were going to be scattered in every direction. She tried not to think about what she would do without flying and friends to distract her as she waited for word of Dink.

The other WASP left their bases in those days before Christmas

1944 feeling shaken and uncertain. For months they had been told they were about to join the military. Now they had been abruptly deactivated. It was confusing and even galling. Why were they being sent home when there was still a war on? The Battle of the Bulge was raging in Europe; the papers were filled with news of the struggle. Many of the women pilots felt a kind of embarrassment. How could they go home and explain to family and friends why they were no longer needed? For some, even the process of getting home was a bumpy experience. The WASP were stationed at bases all across the country, many of them situated hundreds of miles from their families, and with just a few days to make it home before the winter holidays. Travel during wartime was already a challenging business, but to make matters worse, the women weren't an official part of the military and thus had no automatic travel privileges. The civilian pseudo-military status that had hindered them at every step while they were serving continued to inconvenience them now that the program was over.

General Arnold must have felt bad for the women, because not long before the December 20 deactivation his office issued a memo with the following order: "WASP in good standing will be given the opportunity to ride in military aircraft to their homes or to the vicinity of their homes, provided space is available and no additional expense to the Government is incurred." Hundreds of WASP made it home in time for the holidays thanks to the memo. At some bases the commanding officers even allowed WASP to fly with the copilots of their choice. Ethel Meyer, who had been one of two women flight instructors at Shaw Field in South Carolina, flew home to Maryland with her new fiancé, James A. Finley, Jr. He met the family and stayed for Christmas. They were married in March 1945.

But not all of the WASP had such a smooth ride. At the time of disbandment, Florence Shutsy was based at Merced Army Air Field in California, test-flying planes after mechanical repairs. On December 20, she and a fellow WASP, Caroline Shunn, boarded separate BT-13s with two young lieutenants who had agreed to take them home to Pennsylvania. Their first stop of the trip was in Las Vegas, and, as Shutsy later recalled, "for some amazing reason, both aircraft were grounded. It didn't take much to figure that out." A weekend in Las Vegas sounded much more appealing than flying two women to the East Coast in December. Shutsy had just $10.35 to her name, most of which she spent on a hotel room for herself and Caroline, who had even less money than she did. After begging a series of rides on military planes, Shutsy finally borrowed money from an aunt and caught a bus out of Akron, Ohio, arriving home exhausted but in time for Christmas.

Teresa spent the holidays at home with her family and started the new year without any news of her husband. She knew she wanted to find a way to continue to fly, but the only work available involved flying "junkers"—battle-weary airplanes that had returned from the war and needed to be flown to junkyards, or "boneyards." Teresa knew that some of her fellow WASP were taking on this kind of work, but because the planes were in such poor condition, flying them was risky. "I lived this long . . . to hell with it," Teresa thought. "I'm not going to." Instead she found a job as a flight instructor at a local airport but quickly realized that demand for flying lessons had dropped dramatically. It was the middle of winter, it was still wartime, fuel and rubber were still rationed, and hardly anyone was flying for pleasure or sport. There were times when she'd have only two students in an entire day. Teresa simply wasn't making enough money to support herself.

In need of income and wanting to help out her folks, she went back to work in the family flower shop. Growing up, Teresa had worked with her parents at the store, and she was a good floral designer, able to put together a bouquet for a wedding or a wreath for a funeral. That first week she helped her mother and father prepare floral arrangements for six weddings, the heady scent of the blooms in the air reminding her of her childhood. She was grateful that working with her hands gave her mind a rest at least. "I didn't have time to think," she later recalled. Soon it was Valentine's Day, then Easter, and with each passing holiday, the shop was flooded with orders. Teresa kept busy with work, waiting and praying for the day she finally received word of Dink.

Across the country, former WASP like Teresa were left to assimilate into day-to-day life as best they could. During their time in the Army Air Forces they knew that their work was important and that they were needed: they were helping America win the war. Now they found themselves stripped of purpose, frustrated by their own idleness, and missing their WASP sisters. Back home, the WASP quickly discovered that their friends and family didn't really understand or appreciate what they'd been doing during their time away. It was hard to talk about their flying experiences with people who didn't know about airplanes. If they could celebrate the end of the war, that would be different. Instead, that December and January they sat at home, reading the newspaper headlines about the Battle of the Bulge in Europe and kamikaze attacks in the Pacific.

Even those same newspapers, which had been so critical of the WASP during their battle for militarization the previous summer, seemed to sympathize with the sadness, disappointment, and sense of loss so many of the WASP experienced that winter. Now that the women were no longer a threat to male pilots and traditional gender roles, favorable articles were suddenly common, with General Arnold lauding in both the *New York Times* and *Time* magazine the good work the women had done. The actor and comedian Bob Hope, who had spent time with Teresa James the year before, wrote an article describing his experience aboard a plane flown by a WASP—supposedly leading a formation of B-17s—while he was performing for the troops as part of the USO.

"We should all make them take a bow," Hope wrote, "because any time a girl can pilot the lead ship of a formation of Flying Fortresses it certainly makes a sucker out of that phrase, 'weaker sex.'"

The press and the public may have applauded the contribution of the WASP now that the experiment was over, but they were clear about their expectations for the women going forward. Not a single article questioned the program's deactivation even though the war continued; if the AAF had enough men to do the job, all the better. The women were simply expected to go home—and remain there. Soon enough, "Rosie the Riveters" across the country, who had been working in industry jobs throughout the war, would face the same fate. The WASP experience might have served as a warning to working women across the country that they were on borrowed time.

As Teresa and the other women were finding their way home, Jacqueline Cochran was heading back to Washington, where General Arnold had assigned her to write a report on the WASP. The document she produced is a testament to the women and their achievements. Of the 1,102 women who had earned their wings, 916 had stayed with the program through disbandment. Jackie laid out the results of medical and aptitude testing, skill evaluations and flying records, all of which led to an inevitable conclusion: women could fly military planes just as well as men. The experiment had been a success.

At home in Wilkinsburg, Teresa waited. Throughout early 1945 the American forces continued to beat back the enemy. In January they finally claimed victory at the Battle of the Bulge, and Germany began its slow retreat. Soviet troops started to beat back the Germans from the east, capturing Warsaw. On the Pacific front, progress was also being made, even if the conflict was far from over. American troops, especially naval and Marine forces, defeated the Japanese island by island, retaking the Philippines in February, invading Iwo Jima, and ruthlessly firebombing Tokyo that spring. By March, the Allies in Europe were crossing the Rhine and entering Germany at last. On May 8, 1945, with Hitler dead in his bunker, Germany surrendered. The war in the Pacific raged on, but the fight for Europe was finally over. As the news became official, crowds thronged in public squares across the Western world to celebrate.

Then, in late July 1945, Teresa finally received the telegram she had been dreading more than anything: her husband had indeed been killed when his plane crashed in France. Teresa simply refused to believe it was true. As the rest of the country read about the bombings of Hiroshima and Nagasaki that August, Teresa kept praying that Dink had been captured, going to mass as often as she could, hoping against hope that he would be found in some prisoner of war camp. He was such a good pilot, she was certain he had figured out a way to land that plane.

By the fall of 1945, the war was over, but Teresa remained in a shocked limbo. She decided to enroll in a floral design school in Houston, where she kept working with her hands, distracting herself as she had done at her family's flower shop. After Houston, she attended an advanced school of design in Cleveland, Ohio, always hoping but knowing that as time went on there was less and less chance she would hear from Dink.

Elaine Harmon and Maggie Gee were in downtown San Francisco when the news came in that the war was finally over. As members of 44-W-9, the second-to-last class, they hadn't had much time to serve. After the graduation ceremony, when Jackie had gotten so choked up she was unable to speak, the two friends left Sweetwater by train, paying for their own tickets to their new station in Las Vegas on the promise that if they would submit their voucher they would be reimbursed. Upon arrival they found nearly forty other WASP—some, like Blanche Osborn, flying the enormous B-17, while others, like Betty Wall, flying the P-39 Airacobra fighter plane to train pursuit pilots readying for combat. It was challenging, dynamic flying. Elaine and Maggie didn't have the time or experience to pilot the more sophisticated planes of their fellow WASP, so they flew their old familiar BT-13s and AT-6s, taking up pilots who needed to practice their instrument flying skills. They had been serving for only six weeks when disbandment arrived.

Maggie had decided to head home to California. Elaine wasn't sure what to do, so she'd decided to tag along. She'd never been to California before. And since her husband had left for the war in the Pacific, she figured he might come back via the West Coast, which would make her that much closer upon his return. While Maggie headed back to college, Elaine found a job as an air traffic controller at Oakland Municipal Airport. If she herself couldn't fly, at least she could direct the airplanes as they came in.

Years later Elaine remembered the day the news arrived that the war was finally over: "They were building bonfires in the streets and everybody was hugging everybody and kissing them. One of the soldiers that was staying at the same hotel where we were climbed out on a flagpole from about the fifth floor of the hotel and was just hanging there cheering." The change in mood was immediate. "During the war everybody seemed to be in a bad humor or gloomy," she remembered. "After the war, oh, people were friendly, like a big load had been lifted off of them."

Soon enough, Elaine's husband did return. "Of course, I got pregnant the first night he was here," Elaine admitted. A new chapter was beginning for the nation, and for many of the WASP, too.

In the immediate postwar years, the WASP were scattered across the country, but they found ways to keep in contact—and to push against those limitations society was setting for them. The Order of Fifinella, the organization the women had formed as disbandment loomed over them, now had more than eight hundred members, totaling over 70 percent of the women who had served. Its newsletter arrived by mail every month, then twice a month, to all of the women who joined and provided a current address. The 1946 newsletters were full of news about what the members were doing, including announcements about marriages and babies, and discussion about how best to promote the role of women in aviation. Each issue also listed pages and pages of jobs.

Some of those listings came from branches of the AAF. The rest were from aircraft manufacturers or commercial airlines. The only problem was that very few were for pilots. The AAF was clear: the WASP could work as civilians, but the AAF would not allow them to fly their military aircraft now that they had been deactivated. Several of the women took the AAF up on its offer of non-flying jobs, but most persisted in their search for ways to remain in the air.

In August 1946, the Order of Fifinella held its first national convention. It took place in Lock Haven, Pennsylvania, home of the Piper Cub factory where so many of the women had worked before the war. William "Papa" Piper, the owner of the Piper Aircraft Corporation, hosted the event, which included a tour of his factory and contests in spot landing and "bomb-dropping" in which the women dropped water balloons or bags of flour on targets from the air. They concluded the second day with a cocktail party; prizes of nylons were given as rewards for the contests. At least two hundred women attended the final banquet, where Piper invited them to hold the next year's reunion at his other plant, in Ponca City, Oklahoma.

The following morning, the WASP joined together for a formation flight over the National Air Races in Cleveland, which had just resumed after a wartime hiatus. Four flights of twenty-five Piper Cubs flew the trip from Pennsylvania to Ohio in three-ship formations. It was the "largest civilian formation ever flown, the largest mass delivery ever attempted, [and was] accomplished entirely by women pilots." Not a single Cub was scratched. When they arrived at Akron—there wasn't room for all of their planes at Cleveland—Goodyear hosted the women with sandwiches and drinks as the media swarmed them for pictures. Nearly two years after they were deactivated, the women of the WASP had proven they still had it.

The women found other ways to stay in touch, too. In the immediate postwar years there were a number of homes across the country that the women designated as "WASP's Nests" with an open-door policy for any WASP who happened to come through town. In some, WASP floated in and out, and they threw parties almost every night, talking about airplanes and hoping to find flying jobs. They were not ready to give up on their dream of flying for a living.

In 1946 several WASP, including Caro Bayley and Kaddy Landry, decided to put on an air show in Tampa. They sat around their WASP nest in Coconut Grove, Florida, drinking beers and making plans. There would be an air race, with trials for speed and altitude records, along with stunts and novelty acts. It would be reminiscent of the aviation events of the 1930s that had drawn all of them to flying in the first place. But all of the events, races and acts alike, would be solely for women pilots. They would call it the All-Woman Air Show. In February 1947, Caro wrote in to the Order of Fifinella newsletter to promote it: "What we are trying to do is have an airshow in which the girls will feel free to race and participate. You know yourself that a lot of girls will race if it's not against men or right after a man's race. Nobody realizes (I didn't myself) what fun racing can be . . . We're trying to sell more American women on the sport and practicability of flying and also to give the girls who do fly something to use their skill for. We can't make a living at it, we might as well have fun with it."

The following month, a whopping 13,000 spectators showed up to watch the women fly. In their programs they read about the ATA, the WASP, and the Ninety-Nines—about all the important flying women had done during the war. The pilots themselves made a good showing: Caro Bayley flew a sail plane act. Marge Hulburt set a new international women's speed record. Kaddy Landry won first place in the aerobatic competition and second place in the Military Pilots' Association fifteen-mile closed-circuit race. All in all, "it was a rousing success." According to the next newsletter, the day's events ended with "a fine cocktail party where we saw Wasps we hadn't seen in years."

The WASP reunion and the air show marked high points for the women who wanted to fly. Beginning in 1947, the vast majority of the WASP were getting married and having children. Nearly one hundred of the women were married in the first year after the WASP ended and babies often quickly followed. With more women busy with new families, and fewer and fewer opportunities in the aviation industry, they turned their attention away from flying and from the Order of Fifinella. The 1947 reunion held at the Piper factory in Oklahoma was poorly attended, leading the board members to wonder if low attendance was due to finances or perhaps because of the "husband and wife problem," meaning if a family got only one vacation per year, it was unlikely to be used to attend the wife's WASP reunion.

Still, the WASP continued to celebrate one another's successes, especially in aviation. Some, like Caro Bayley, Kaddy Landry, and Dorothy "Dot" Swain, flew in air shows and continued to compete in aerobatics. Caro won the Women's International Aerobatic Championship in a Pitts Special and gained an altitude record, taking a Piper Cub to 30,203 feet on the same day, winning the Fifinella Award from her fellow WASP for her efforts. Teresa, too, joined an early air show, finally getting a chance to experience the thrill of racing after so many years of being left out of the fun before the war due to lack of funding. It must have been a welcome distraction as she continued to wait for word of Dink.

———

For years after receiving the telegram informing her of Dink's death, Teresa continued to believe that her husband was coming home. General Jimmy Doolittle himself had confirmed that there was every chance he was alive. What's more, Teresa was sure that she had seen Dink's photo on the cover of the newspaper along with other POWs. Then, in 1949, she received a letter from the military that should have dashed all her hopes. The letter stated that Dink's remains had been found in France. They were going to be "casketed" and shipped to the Jefferson Barracks National Cemetery in St. Louis. Soon after, another letter arrived explaining what had happened. Dink had been a crew member on a B-17 mission in France. His plane was hit by antiaircraft fire and went down in a small town named Joinville-le-Pont, in the Paris suburbs. Even after the arrival of the letters and her brain knowing it must be true, her heart still couldn't shake the feeling that Dink would come walking through the flower shop door any day now, saying it had all been a horrible mistake.

Then, in early 1950, a man came into the store and asked to speak to Teresa Martin. It was the waist gunner from Dink's B-17. He told her that for years he'd had no recollection of the crash, but then the memories started coming back to him, and he knew he needed to find Teresa. Overcome with emotion, she asked him what had happened the day Dink went missing. The waist gunner said he remembered the plane being hit by antiaircraft fire. He believed the impact had blown off the front end of the plane entirely. He didn't think Dink or the copilot or navigator ever knew what hit them. His last memory was of jumping out of the damaged bomber and feeling his parachute open. The man told Teresa that he would come back soon so they could talk some more—that he was headed to New York City. Teresa never heard from him again.

The meeting with the man in the flower shop was a turning point for Teresa. After his visit, she knew she could no longer continue to hope that she would see her husband again. On April 1,

1950, she joined Dink's family in St. Louis at a formal military funeral for George and the six crew members who died with him that June day in 1944. She clung to the carefully folded flag she'd been presented—all she had left besides memories. Although she rarely spoke about her grief for Dink, there is no doubt it was profound and lasting. The future she had planned with him—a marriage, a home, a family—had been violently ripped away from her; everything they had planned and hoped for was gone. There would never be another.

A few years later, on a trip to New York City, Teresa happened to walk past a hair salon that had put a sign outside: BLONDES HAVE MORE FUN. On a whim, she decided to find out if that was true. She emerged with her dark, curly hair dyed a bleached blond. She was going to have to make a new life for herself now.

In the years after the war, some WASP worked to encourage women in aviation, including by telling their own story at airshows and other events. *Betty Jane Williams Collection. Courtesy Texas Woman's University*

CHAPTER TWENTY-THREE

Finding Their Way

After disbandment, Dora Dougherty did her best to adjust to life on the ground. Although she was happy to be home with her parents in Illinois and able to help with her dad, who had lost a leg in an accident earlier in the year, she couldn't shake her desire to get back in the cockpit. For Dora, flying was now her vocation, and before long she began applying for pilot jobs with the commercial airlines.

Dora was the definition of a qualified pilot. During her time with the WASP, she had flown every type of military plane, even the B-29 Superfortress bomber. She'd spent her last two months as a WASP at Wendover Field in Wendover, Utah, reunited with Colonel Paul Tibbets and several of the men who'd been a part of her B-29 crew earlier that summer. There, she flew in support of a group of male pilots and scientists who were training to drop the first atomic bomb. She had amassed hundreds more hours of flying time, and she had her new commercial pilot's license and a 12,000-horsepower rating to boot. Surely someone would hire her.

But Dora was rejected everywhere she went. Now that pilots were beginning to come home from overseas, the airline industry had its pick, and it did not pick women. Qualified WASP were repeatedly and consistently turned down by an industry that would not hire women pilots, explaining that their customers were already cautious enough about getting into the air and that if women were flying the airplanes, the passengers would simply be too nervous to fly.

Dora continued to read the WASP newsletter, scouring it for piloting jobs and finding few. If she or any of the other women were hoping to get help from their former leaders, they were soon to be disappointed. In the spring of 1945, Jackie sent out a disheartening letter to the WASP: "I have been in touch with airline companies, aircraft manufacturers, and have exhausted all possibilities of utilization—and everywhere the answer has been the same: 'We have more pilots at present than we can possibly use and the manpower reservoir is so great that there is no possible use in sight for women pilots.'" The training programs the government established before and during the war, including the Civilian Pilot Training Program, had been hugely successful. Between 1939 and 1945, the CPTP had trained more than 435,000 pilots, and the number of commercial licenses—the license needed to be paid to fly—had risen dramatically, from 68,449 in 1944 to 162,873 in 1945. The reality was, not every pilot from the war was going to be able to make flying a career now that the war was over.

Facing a surplus of pilots, companies could be choosy. When several of the women applied to be test pilots at Boeing—a job many of them had done as WASP—they learned they would need both a bachelor's degree in engineering and qualification as a four-engine pilot in order to even be considered. They had more luck in Alaska, where at least twenty-four companies indicated they might employ the women as pilots. In a large, mountainous state where cities and towns were spread out and infrastructure was limited, aviation was (and continues to be) an invaluable mode of transportation, opening up more opportunities for pilots. A few of Dora's friends received job offers in Alaska and encouraged Dora to join them. But Dora felt responsible for her parents and didn't want to be so far away from them, so her friends went without her.

For those who could not find flying jobs, getting a job in another area of aviation seemed like the next best thing. At least they would be close to airplanes, even if they were not able to fly them. In the 1945 newsletters, WASP reported holding 202 aviation-related jobs, with another eleven working in the office of an aviation-related business. Many worked for the CAA in some capacity, often in the control tower at an airfield. Others taught on Link Trainers, investigated accidents, or worked in operations or dispatch for various airlines. At least two WASP became stewardesses.

Dora kept in touch with friends she made while serving, including some of the male pilots who had stayed on at Wendover Airfield in Utah, her last station as a WASP. One of them, her good friend Mac, had shared a final steak with Dora on her last night at Wendover and had flown her home to Illinois personally. In the spring of 1945, Dora wrote to him, explaining just how much she was missing her time in the WASP. She kept his response.

"I have heard complaints, screams, bitches, tirades for and against, but never have I read such a pathetic letter," Mac wrote, tongue in cheek. "I am for you, I wish I were with you, I halfway understand you, but that's where it ends . . . Thou art of human flesh, and a woman to boot. Do you realize what that means. You are of the earth born. Especially in the eyes of men. They say, 'no,

not for you my sweet. There are dishes in the sink, stockings that
need mending. That's for you dear.' But still you dream of stick
and throttle. Foolish girl."

Then Mac tried to cheer her up by reminding her of the hard-
ships that flying for the Army brought with it: "Think of the days
in the soup when your gyro's went out, of the nights when you
were lost, of the moments when an engine threatened to quit. Remember that funny feeling in your stomach when the wheels
wouldn't come down, the lovely thought of having to bail-out in a
rain swept night . . ." But despite his attempts to shake Dora out of
her sadness, Mac couldn't keep it up:

> Aw, Dora, I tried to break it down and say it's no damn
> good, but I can't. I like that scared feeling, I like the not
> really knowing, and I know you like it too . . . I guess you
> are not alone in your clipped wing dilemma, there must be
> other WASP's who are feeling the same thing. As far as I
> know there is no cure. It's a burden you must bear every-
> day that you look at the sky . . . and I worry at times
> whether or not I shall be feeling the same way when my
> turn comes . . . it makes me think. What's next? There
> can't be anything that will be able to replace this. This has
> just gone on too long. But it isn't just us, you and me, its
> thousands like us. The poor fish who will lift a bloodshot
> eye every time an engine whines in the sky.

Mac was trying to be kind, reassuring Dora that they were in
the same boat and that he was going to miss flying as much as she
did after his own discharge. But Dora would have been aware that
this wasn't strictly true. In all likelihood, Mac would at least have
a shot at getting a job flying after the war. He wasn't going to be
turned down for jobs because of his sex.

That same spring Dora signed up for classes at Northwestern
University, keeping her promise to her mother that she would fin-

ish her education. For a few months she worked in a short-term job for Defense Plant Corporation flying old military planes to civilian buyers on an as-needed basis. In between trips she returned to her studies. As a student at Northwestern, Dora soon found the campus quickly filling up with male veterans returning from the war. These men were often utilizing G.I. Bill benefits that Dora, as a civilian, couldn't access. Even so, she guessed she would feel more comfortable around them than with wide-eyed young college girls who'd only just left home. Dora had served on military bases for two years, she'd flown military planes, and in large part she'd been treated as an equal by those around her. She missed her days as a WASP intensely, and, in search of camaraderie, she decided to go to the campus veterans' club. But she was denied admission: after all, she was a woman, and not a "true" veteran.

In November 1946, Dora heard that the Chicago chapter of the Order of Fifinella was holding a meeting. She made sure to attend, eager for a chance to connect with people who actually understood her. Later she reported on the gathering in a letter for the WASP Newsletter: "We escaped from our pink chiffon civilian world for a few very enjoyable hours to talk of better days and compare notes of friends who have continued in the ozone industry and those who have gone on to better things." Dora wrote that she was joining the Chicago chapter women in planning a memorial party for the anniversary of their disbandment, December 20, "the dear, lovely, repulsive 20 of broken dreams. This is the second anniversary, oh weeping ones, and we are going to have a beautiful blow-out . . . and we'll all be on instruments before the evening's through."

Four and a half million women had gone to work during the war. Afterward the country remained uncertain about women's place in the workforce. In the postwar years the nation continued to debate its "woman question": What did they want to do, what would they do, what should society allow them to do? Everyone from economists, sociologists, and psychologists to *Life* magazine weighed in on the appropriate role for women in the new atomic age. Entire issues of academic journals devoted themselves to the topic, speculating about the function of women in society. The U.S. Department of Labor urged that "readjustment and re-employment of men *and* women must be worked out," asserting that "wage rates should be based on occupation and not on sex." The vast majority of Americans agreed. A 1946 *Fortune* magazine survey on "Women in America" asked whether "women should always be paid the same as men." Nearly 65 percent of men and over 70 percent of women believed they should. The Americans who had so recently lived through the Great Depression were not necessarily advocating for equal economic opportunity for all women, however. Many feared, and had long feared, that a double wage standard would create unfair competition, encouraging companies to displace higher-waged male breadwinners with lower-paid women.

The fear of women "taking" men's jobs persisted. When *Fortune* asked: "Do you think a married woman who has no children under sixteen and whose husband makes enough to support her should or should not be allowed to take a job if she wants to?" on average 46 percent of men and 38 percent of women declared those economically stable women should not be allowed to work. (Thirty-four percent men and 41 percent women thought they should.) There was also concern about the state of the American family and the role of women in that family. *Life* magazine explored the "American Woman's Dilemma" and worried about the "typical young lady of 1947," who, with "a good education, [and] a range of interests," had "a more complicated situation" than her mother's generation. *Life* wondered, "She wants a husband and she wants children. Should she go on working? Full time? Part time? Will housework bore her? What will she do when her children are grown?" The women of the WASP were facing similar dilemmas. They held licenses in the skilled profession of aviation.

They were passionate about flying, but for those who had children, family life was expected to take precedence and any work activity outside of the home was viewed with suspicion.

Meanwhile, children and family experts pointed fingers at inattentive mothers and "delusional" feminists for the "increasing incidence of obvious and flagrant disorders in the adjustment of children and young people as reflected in the figures on delinquency . . ." Women, it seemed, could not win. The solution for the "woman question," according to the experts, was to simply better educate young women about the inevitable limitations ahead.

For many WASP—skilled, passionate pilots who had found profound meaning and adventure during wartime—the impact of the loss of that work was devastating. One WASP was hit particularly hard. After the war, Helen Richey had returned to her hometown of McKeesport. This pioneering pilot had broken records in the 1930s and had flown with Jackie in the Air Transport Auxiliary in England before returning to the United States to train and fly with the WASP. When the program ended, she felt grounded and restless. Before long she moved to New York City, where she stayed with a friend and was briefly able to ferry war surplus planes. In 1945, Helen flew on a surplus ferrying trip with another WASP, Avanell Pinkley. Avanell lived in Manhattan as well and had plans to be away for the summer, so she offered her apartment to Helen and even gave her some money to purchase furniture. Helen moved in, although she never did buy any furniture, instead sleeping on a Japanese straw mat on the floor.

Avanell wanted to help Helen and found several office jobs for her, but Helen refused to take them. For someone who had spent her life as a pilot—who had broken records with her daring feats and whose greatest dream was to fly commercial aircraft—the thought of sitting behind a desk must have seemed a torment. Avanell remembered, "All her background and training was in flying and she didn't want to do anything else. But, other than an occasional ferrying job, there was nothing in that line available."

"If this sounds grim, it really wasn't," Avanell added. "Helen had so much humor that she was always amusing and fun to be with. I became very fond of her in the short time I knew her." Helen, whose father was sending her money regularly, soon moved into a fifth-floor walk-up in Chelsea near another former WASP, Mary Parker.

As 1946 came to a close, Helen went home to McKeesport to spend the holidays with her family. Her sister, Lucille Gamble, thought Helen seemed unusually quiet and depressed, even somewhat detached from reality. When Lucille inquired about Helen's health, Helen admitted that she'd been under the care of a doctor. Lucille remembered Helen remarking several times that, at the age of thirty-seven, her flying career was over and she didn't know what she was going to do. Their father had become seriously ill, and Helen went to visit him in the hospital. Afterward, Helen told Lucille that she never expected to see her father again.

After the holidays, Helen returned to Manhattan. Early in the new year she threw a party that Mary Parker, her fellow WASP, attended. Mary remembered that Helen had seemed preoccupied and mentioned suicide, but no one took her seriously. In the coming days Mary became worried that Helen wasn't answering her calls. On January 7, Mary went to Helen's apartment. Getting no answer, she found the building superintendent and got him to let her in. Helen's lifeless body was stretched out on a cot. She was wearing red-and-white-polka-dot pajamas in her neatly made bed, with one arm drawn up to her forehead. An empty drinking glass sat on the floor. She had taken an overdose of sleeping pills. Her death was ruled a suicide. No note was ever found.

WASP Helen Mary Clark, Janet Beasley, and Avanell Pinkley escorted Helen's body home to McKeesport. There was a simple service in which, in lieu of a eulogy, the minister read poems about flight: "Oh, I have slipped the surly bonds of earth . . ." At nearby Bettis Field, where Helen had first earned her wings some seventeen years earlier, four planes took off, flying over Helen in an aerial salute as she went to her grave.

The following year, in early January 1949, Dora Dougherty received a letter from Jacqueline Cochran letting her know that former WASP were invited to join the new U.S. Air Force Reserve, whose mission was to prepare combat-ready forces in the event of another war.

"Dear Ex-WASP," it read:

> At long last, the United States Air Force has agreed to offer to all ex-WASP who meet the standards and qualifications a commission of 2nd Lieutenant in the United States Air Force Reserve on a *non-flying* status [emphasis added]. The rank of commission in the Reserve will be predicated on the length of service you had in the WASP, exclusive of training periods.

The same letter made its way across the country to WASP in every state. Dora and the other women were thrilled to hear from Jackie again, and they were excited by the potential of enlisting in the reserves and serving their country once again. Nonetheless, they were deeply disappointed that they would not have the chance to fly.

They couldn't have known that Jackie herself had stood in the way of their gaining that opportunity. After the war, Jackie had been active in campaigning for the Army Air Forces to become independent, registering as a lobbyist and raising over $100,000 to pay writers and advertisers to promote the cause. In July 1947 those efforts bore fruit. President Truman signed the National Security Act, creating the new United States Air Force and fulfilling General Arnold's dream. This, in turn, paved the way for the Women's Armed Forces Integration Act, which authorized "the enlistment of women in the Regular and Reserve components of the four services." While a leader in the effort for an independent air force, Jackie had actively testified against women flying for the military, arguing that while women pilots were just as capable as men, they were a poor long-term investment: "By the time you've got them ready to go into the higher echelon of flying, they would already be married, and therefore they would be on their way to having a family." Once again, Jackie stood in the way of the women pilots' advancement when she felt it would move them too far outside of traditional gender roles.

Despite the fact that they would not be allowed to fly, a total of 156 WASP took their commissions as officers in the Air Force Reserve, including Dora, Nancy Love, Jackie Cochran, and Teresa James. The Order of Fifinella newsletters were full of articles on how to join, as well as news of those who had already signed up and at what rank. But while WASP joined up in large numbers, only 112 were able to serve for any length of time: the Air Force had not realized when they sent out their invitation to join that many of the women had young children and later discharged them for "dependency." (Needless to say, men were not discharged for the same reason.)

Now a reservist, Dora completed her bachelor's degree in 1949 and got a temporary job as a flight instructor at the University of Illinois's Institute of Aviation. She later recalled that the university was willing to hire her even though she was a woman because they thought she could be a role model for female students and that "she'd keep the men on their toes." Dora became the first instructor to get all of her students through the course within one semester. But when she asked for a permanent, full-time position, she was told a contract wasn't in the cards—not for her and not for any other woman pilot. Luckily for Dora, the university's Aviation Psychology Laboratory was more open-minded. She spent the early 1950s working as a pilot and research assistant there, gathering flight data and organizing and evaluating it. It wasn't always as exciting as flying the B-29, but it was interesting work that kept her involved in aviation—and it paid the bills.

Nancy Love flies her girls in their family plane from their home in Martha's Vineyard to the mainland, for doctor appointments and other mundane things. The girls find it a very normal part of life. *Courtesy International Women's Air and Space Museum*

CHAPTER TWENTY-FOUR

Moving On

The last Order of Fifinella reunion of any size was in September of 1948. By 1951 the order was no more: there was no president, no board, and no organization. Its members were now forging other paths in life. Throughout the 1950s the majority of the WASP married and had children. As they changed their names and moved about the country, many in the group lost touch.

Nancy Love was a prime example. Immediately after the war ended she had become determined to find out why she and Bob hadn't been able to conceive a baby in their ten years of marriage. She went to see a specialist, who discovered she had a blocked fallopian tube caused by a flawed appendectomy she'd had as a child.

She was able to have the problem fixed, and by the end of 1946 she was at last pregnant. Their first child, Hannah Lincoln Love, was born on August 1, 1947. Another daughter, Margaret "Marky" Campbell Love, followed the first, and then came a third, Alice "Allie" Harkness Love. For the Loves' children, the 1950s were filled with time spent sailing, riding horses, and going on family vacations, often flying to the destination in the family's Bonanza airplane. In a 1955 article Nancy wrote that she thought the time had come for more people to have personal planes: "I find on my trips with the children that we create no more curiosity arriving in our airplane than we would in a station wagon and that's as it should be. I believe that more and more women will take to private flying as they learn the practical utility of it." But besides recreational flights such as these, for the first time since Nancy had started flying as a teenager, airplanes were no longer her primary focus.

Along with so many of the WASP, Nancy had tried—and failed—to find flying work after the war. As the women packed their bags to go home in December 1944, Nancy quietly packed hers for an opportunity of a lifetime. Nancy's friend General C. R. Smith, deputy director of the Air Transport Command, arranged for Nancy to go with him to Calcutta in January "for the purpose of looking over our operation." Nancy's job once she arrived in India was to assess the efficiency of the ATC's China-Burma-India supply route and to write up reports. General William Tunner, who had been so instrumental in founding the WAFS, was now in command of the "Hump" operation, in which cargo planes flew supplies over the Himalayas and Burma to China, where troops were fighting the Japanese from the Chinese mainland. The Hump was a range of mountains in the eastern end of the Himalayas, 16,000 feet high and incredibly dangerous to fly over, with unpredictable changes in weather. More than 1,200 men were killed flying the route, with 500 of the 700 planes lost during the war never found. Despite the risks involved, on January 8, 1945,

Nancy became the first woman to pilot an American C-54 over the Hump.

After weeks of flying in the region, Nancy left with General Smith and his aide to fly the route home. Nancy flew the C-54 for twenty of the fifty-four hours it took to fly across Australia, to Dutch New Guinea, Indonesia, Tarawa, and finally Honolulu. General Smith was clearly bending every rule for Nancy. Less than two years earlier she had been prohibited from flying a B-17 across the Atlantic; now she was piloting a military plane thousands of miles across the South Pacific in a war zone. It was an indication of Smith's appreciation for Nancy and everything she had done for the Air Transport Command.

On February 6, 1945, Nancy arrived back in Cincinnati, where her husband, Bob, was now stationed and where she was quickly brought back to reality. She was now only the wife of an Army Air Forces officer and had no privileges on the airfield or with the airplanes. Her final report from her trip, dated February 9, 1945, was the last time her name ever appeared in the records of the Ferrying Division to which she had devoted the past four years of her life. But she hadn't given up on flying yet.

In May 1945, Nancy arranged to ferry three twin-engine C-53 transport planes to Madrid for Iberia Airlines, enlisting the help of five of her former WAFS pilots to help her complete the job. But then the war in Europe ended, and the mission was scrapped: the airline was no longer desperate for the airplanes and certainly wasn't desperate enough to have women fly them over. Nancy and Barbara Erickson London—one of the women who was supposed to join her on the Spain trip—then attempted to start their own business, a fixed base operation (FBO) supplying gas, repairs, and airplane rentals, but failed to secure an airfield. In 1946 the Army Air Forces awarded medals to both Nancy and Bob for their wartime service: Nancy the Air Medal and Bob the Distinguished Service Medal—the first time a husband and wife had been jointly decorated by the AAF. But while Bob continued to fly for his living, taking a job as president of a freight airline that hoped to move into passenger flights, Nancy did not. Soon she was busy with her three girls, enjoying a new kind of adventure.

Although the majority of the WASP were like Nancy, married with children, as a group they were still not completely typical of their generation. Two-thirds of the WASP, even those with children, worked outside the home throughout the 1950s when the vast majority of their peers—and especially their white peers—did not. While many of these women held what might have been considered "traditional" jobs as teachers, librarians, or office workers, others continued to break boundaries. Ten percent of them were flight instructors, the one aviation field in which women were able to succeed, albeit still in relatively small numbers. More than a third of the WASP worked or attended college while their youngest child was under the age of five. Many others did not marry or have children at all, despite the constant messaging coming from the government and the media encouraging them to do so.

Jackie Cochran continued to be the exception to every rule. Despite serious health issues, including numerous abdominal, bowel, and even sinus surgeries throughout the 1950s, her competitive nature would not let her rest. When Jacqueline Auriol of France broke Jackie's speed record in late 1952 and won the Harmon Trophy for her efforts, Jackie was determined to regain her status as the fastest woman alive. The generals and Air Force leaders who were her friends couldn't help her get what she needed—a jet—so Floyd provided instead. By the end of the year he had gotten her a job with Canadair as a test pilot, and Canadair manufactured the Air Force's variant of the F-86 Sabre jet. To prepare to fly the plane, Jackie called on a friend: Chuck Yeager, the pilot who had broken the sound barrier just five years earlier. Yeager trained her to fly a jet at Edwards Air Force Base, home of some of the best test pilots in the world. Then after only six hours and thirteen takeoffs and landings in the F-86, Jackie dove through Mach 1 and broke the sound barrier three separate times. She also broke three world records, handily reclaiming her title as "fastest woman in the world" and winning the Harmon Trophy back.

Since the end of the war, Jackie had been in perpetual motion. After finishing her reports for General Arnold in the summer of 1945, she had hoped to travel to England. Her plan was to expand her business, but she was also likely curious about how the country had changed since her time there earlier in the war. When she learned she couldn't get clearance to travel in Allied-occupied Europe, Floyd decided to do something about it. At the time, journalists were among the few people who were allowed to travel in Europe, so Floyd bought a magazine—*Liberty*—and pressured its editors to hire Jackie as a war correspondent. General Arnold, who knew a good ally when he saw one, appointed Jackie as a consultant and gave her priority-one traveling orders, affording her the freedom to travel wherever she wanted to go in the war-torn world. Floyd's debilitating arthritis forced him to stay home. Instead, he wrote letters telling Jackie that wherever she went she carried with her his "all-enduring and complete love" and his "wholehearted and all consuming affection."

Soon enough, Jackie was in Guam, fishing and playing poker with Barney Giles and other American generals stationed there. She was in Manila as the war ended in the Pacific, witnessing the surrender of the Japanese general Tomoyuki Yamashita. From there she went to Japan, touring Kyoto and flying low over Emperor Hirohito's palace. Jackie then went to China and, through connections Floyd made for her through his cousin who was the Canadian ambassador to China, met with Madame Chiang Kai-shek (Soong Mei-ling) and with Mao Tse-tung. While other war correspondents were set to become civilians again as of November 1, 1945, General Dwight Eisenhower gave Jackie clearances to go to France and Germany. She headed that way via Cairo, where on November 7 she again met with General Giles, who was now posted there. Giles took her to Iraq and Iran, where she paid a visit to Shah Mohammad Reza Pahlavi, then on to Rome in a B-25 for an audience with Pope Pius XII. Jackie then went to Germany, where she toured the recently liberated Buchenwald, bribed her way into Hitler's bunker, and took a doorknob from the Chancellery after bribing the Russian guards with cigarettes. After that, she went shopping for furniture in London as she awaited her December flight home.

When Jackie returned home, five months after she left, she found Floyd was not well. His arthritis had gotten so bad, he was hardly walking at all. When business associates came to visit him at the ranch in Indio, they'd soak with him in the heated pool as they worked. Worried about Floyd but never one to sit on her heels, Jackie decided it was time to return to air racing. She competed in the 1946 Bendix Trophy Race in a P-51 Mustang with Lockheed wing-drop tanks for extra fuel. The only woman to fly the race that year against sixteen men, she took second place and donated her $6,500 prize to the Army Air Forces Aid Society. She spent the rest of the 1940s racing, promoting her cosmetics business, and hosting and attending parties with generals, politicians, and other national leaders.

In 1953 Jackie published her autobiography, *The Stars at Noon*, which she would later admit was largely written by Floyd (although it is likely he had help, too). In it she put on paper the story that she had told for so long: that she was an orphan who had made good on her own. Even though she was financially supporting several members of her family while they lived on her ranch, she refused to acknowledge them as blood relations in her book, still running away from her origins so many years after leaving the Florida Panhandle behind her. In 1955 she decided her next challenge would be politics. After narrowly winning a brutal primary campaign, Jackie lost the congressional seat for California's Twenty-Ninth District after an even uglier battle with Democrat

Dalip Singh Saund, who called her "that woman" and whom Jackie called "that Hindu" throughout the election.

Jackie and Nancy did not maintain any kind of friendship after the disbandment of the WASP. Their relationship, once tense but cordial, had deteriorated horribly as the end of the WASP experiment had drawn to a close. After the war these two talented women, who could have been allies in the advancement of women in aviation, could hardly stand the sight of each other. Nancy blamed Jackie for the end of the program, and her animosity toward her would sharpen and last for the rest of her days. As for Jackie, although she initially admired Nancy and hoped to fit in with her country club crowd, she was convinced that Nancy had deliberately worked to undermine her and the program as a whole.

Jackie had finally revealed her animosity for Nancy in a "very personal and confidential" letter she had written to General Arnold while at the Pentagon, writing her final report in the spring of 1945, just as Nancy was flying in Asia. The trouble with the WASP program, Jackie wrote, was "first, last and all the time generated in the Air Transport Command." She went on to explain the problems she believed had plagued the program from the beginning, including what she thought was a purposeful delay of her return from England so the ATC could announce Nancy as leader of women pilots without Jackie's interference. Five pages into the letter she got to Nancy directly:

> So far as Nancy Love was concerned she was ambitious, got the help of her husband, C.R. Smith and others to build something up around her and I arrived home just in time to be an interference. That only intensified the deep hatred she admitted to me and others that she held toward me increasingly over ten years because as she expressed it, "I had done the things she wanted to do" . . . Later on she and her close friend [Betty Gillies] were given special transition to fly a B-17 across to Europe and this was stopped

because it was against the policy to use women pilots other
than in the United States and Canada. She blamed that on
me and her hatred grew to the explosion point where she
lost her sound reasoning powers and was against everything I tried to do . . .

The truth was that Jackie was right about Nancy's growing bel-
ligerency, although there is little evidence that jealousy was at the
heart of it, as Jackie suggests. In her letter she also described the
efforts of Nancy, Betty Gillies, and others to sabotage the militarization effort, writing that she believed they had deliberately tried
to spread discord "in numerous continual ways . . . It was like having two or three rotten apples in a barrel." Although Jackie's letter
was clearly written in anger, she ended it with a note of surprising
insight: "If I had been empowered to fire her [Nancy] she would
either have quit her activities or quit her job. As it was I suffered
along rather than have anyone think it might be a personal scrap
between two females." Just as Nancy had spent the two years of the
program determined to suppress any rumors of a "catfight" between the two women, Jackie had been doing the same. In this, at
least, Jackie and Nancy were united.

We know of one occasion when the two women were together
in the same room after the disbandment. It took place in April of
1946, when they were invited to attend the same conference at
Stephens College, a women's college in Columbia, Missouri, that
had its own aviation department. Members of the WASP and the
Ninety-Nines were in attendance, along with women writers from
aviation magazines and representatives of government agencies
and the airline industry. One can't help but wonder how organiz-
ers reacted when they realized these two outstanding women in
aviation did not want to talk to each other. But despite the chill
between them, there is no doubt that Jackie would have heard the
news that Nancy had started a family. Although she never com-
mented on it, it must have been painful for Jackie to see. She

longed to have children with Floyd, but it wasn't to be. Her continuing health issues, including abdominal adhesions, seemed to have led to at least two miscarriages and other fertility challenges. Despite Jackie's strong desire to be a mother again, the little boy she lost when she was just a teenager was her only child.

Marty Wyall, pictured here with her plane in 1965, spent much of her time in the 1960s flying for her aviation company and bringing the WASP back together again. *Courtesy John Wyall*

CHAPTER TWENTY-FIVE

Reunited

In December 1963, the former Mary Anna Martin sat at her kitchen table writing out her Christmas cards. Much about Marty's life had changed since disbandment. Her name was Marty Wyall now and she was a married mother of five children, about to turn forty-two. But one thing had stayed the same: her lingering sense that her WASP years were unfinished business.

As a member of the last class of trainees, Marty had graduated just weeks before the disbandment of WASP and so she'd never had a chance to serve in active duty. While she would remain forever grateful that she'd been allowed to finish her seven months in Sweetwater, she still felt disappointed—and even a little guilty—

that she had undergone the most extensive training of all the women without the chance to do anything with it. With the WASP, she had found something that she loved and that she was really good at. She had met a group of friends who loved and respected her for who she was, who didn't care that she was the pastor's daughter, and who just wanted to fly like she did. Marty's time at Sweetwater had been a little piece of heaven for her, and leaving it behind had felt a lot like being exiled from Eden.

After the disbandment, Marty returned to her hometown of Fort Wayne, Indiana, where she tried to find work as a pilot. There, she wrote letters to her representatives in an attempt to get a flying job overseas; they thanked her for her patriotism but had nothing for her. She applied for a job with TWA, which had sent letters to all the WASP inviting them to interview for non-flying jobs. Marty was hoping she might be hired as a stewardess, so at least she'd get to be up in the air. She was likely deemed too short to be a stewardess, because they instead offered her a position in reservations, which she declined. Soon after, she found work flying old Army trainer planes, or "junkers," from the Des Moines depot to Indianapolis, where the planes were then sold to civilians; but the work was unpredictable, and she eventually had to find something more stable. After a brief, miserable stint as a church secretary for her father, she finally found work as a flight instructor at Franklin Flying Field, about twenty miles south of Indianapolis.

It was at the Franklin airfield that she met Eugene Wyall. Gene had been a Seabee (a member of the U.S. Navy Construction Battalions) during the war and was injured when his ship was torpedoed, then was drafted into the Army Corps of Engineers. He'd arrived at Franklin hoping to learn to fly and soon began taking lessons with Marty. Gene didn't talk much about his time in the war, but that was okay with Marty: he was a nice guy, good-looking, smart, and seemed to like airplanes. He was also smitten with Marty. Less than two months after they met, Gene proposed, and Marty said yes. Newly engaged, Marty was blissfully happy;

the only problem was that when her boss found out she was getting married, he fired her on the spot. "I didn't hire you to be looking for a husband," he said flatly. Marty didn't mind too much: it was September, and flight lessons were slowing down for the season. Besides, she was too busy thinking about her future with Gene to care.

In January 1946 she and Gene were married. "After that," Marty later remembered, "it was quite a different life. It took a long time to get adjusted to married life." She had five children in quick succession: four sons and a daughter. Then she and Gene bought a small farm in Fort Wayne, Indiana, with plenty of room for the kids to play. For Marty, life in the 1950s was consumed with running the small Wyall farm and raising her babies. It would be eleven years before she flew a plane again.

Then one day in 1957 opportunity came knocking. Marty was sitting at her family piano—not playing, as the former piano major could have, but instead cleaning gooey hand lotion out of the keys after her son had poured it there. As if to rescue her from that demoralizing task, Marty's friend Margaret Ringenberg appeared at the door. Margaret was a fellow WASP who lived nearby and still kept up with her flying, working as a flight instructor and competing in air races. Marty assumed Margaret was going to ask her to babysit her daughter while she flew. Instead, Margaret asked Marty if she wanted to go with her to California.

It turned out Margaret had signed up to compete in that year's Powder Puff Derby—the annual transcontinental air race for women—with her sister-in-law as her copilot. But now the sister-in-law had to bail out, and Margaret was looking for a substitute. She planned to leave in the morning and she wanted Marty to join her. Marty's youngest baby, Martha, was only seven weeks old. Could Marty really leave her newborn child and four other young kids? After casting a frustrated eye at her ruined piano, Marty decided that, yes, she could. She hastily called her mother, who agreed to babysit, and then talked to her doctor about getting the nursing baby on formula. Marty's husband, Gene, thought the whole thing was a terrible idea, but Marty's mind was stubbornly set, and the next morning she and Margaret took off for the West Coast. Upon arrival, Marty was thrilled to meet up with other WASP convening for the race: "All these gals that I had heard about and wanted to know more about, and here they were," she would recall. It had been nearly thirteen years since disbandment, and now, suddenly, Marty was getting a taste of the old days.

The race took the women all the way from California to Philadelphia, straight across the country. Margaret did the flying, with Marty as her navigator and general assistant. By the second stop Marty was leaking breast milk, taking pills in an attempt to dry herself up, and wondering, *What the hell am I doing?* But it was too late to turn back now. Being in an airplane again felt good, natural. The feeling of being in the air, looking down on the earth, renewed her. It reminded her how much she loved to fly— reminded her who she was besides mother and wife. Over the course of nearly two weeks, the women worked their way east, and by the time they made it to the North Philadelphia Airport, Marty's mind was made up. She knew she wanted to fly again. The following year she found a copilot of her own, rounded up sponsors despite her husband's resistance, and began flying in as many air races as she could.

Five years later, in 1963, Marty's youngest child, Martha, started school, leaving Marty with a few extra hours in the day to herself. At long last she was able to reflect on her life and what she wanted for the future. The twentieth anniversary of the WASP's disbandment was the following year. As she sat in her kitchen writing Christmas cards, many of them to her WASP friends, she became determined to commemorate the occasion. As a member of the last class at Sweetwater, she didn't know very many of the WASP and was aware she had done very little flying compared to the other women. But even so, she wanted to reconnect—not just with her classmates, but with WASP from all classes. During her time training in Sweetwater, Marty had kept a scrapbook chronicling her experiences and those of her fellow WASP. All these years later she continued to believe the women's collective flying work was important, and she remained devoted to collecting and preserving the record of it all.

Marty knew there was a Ninety-Nines convention taking place on August 7, 1964, in Cincinnati. She decided to encourage as many WASP as she could track down to attend the event and reached out to Betty Gillies and the Ninety-Nines, who agreed to host a dinner for the WASP to mark the anniversary. Marty also wrote to Jackie and asked her to speak at the dinner. Marty didn't really know Jackie—back at Sweetwater, Jackie was often busy with Dedie Deaton and the administrators, not the trainees—but Marty had never been one to be shy. She waited until July for a response, and when she didn't hear back from Jackie, she began to look elsewhere.

Marty decided to ask Dora Dougherty instead. Dora and Marty hadn't overlapped at Sweetwater, but Marty knew her by reputation. Unlike Marty and so many of the WASP, Dora had stayed single, did not have children, and had spent the past decade focused exclusively on her career. After graduating from Northwestern, she had gone on to earn her master's degree and her doctorate, completing her PhD in aviation education in 1955, all while serving as an officer in the U.S. Air Force Reserves. Dora worked for a few years as an engineer in Baltimore before getting offered a job at Bell Helicopter in Fort Worth in 1957. Bell had a major research program on helicopter instrument flying. Dora became a test pilot, and only the twenty-seventh woman in the world to earn her helicopter license. She immediately joined the Whirly-Girls, an organization of women helicopter pilots founded in 1955 by WASP trainee Jean Ross Howard Phelan, finding a new community of women who "got" her. In 1961, with only nine solo hours, Dora had set two international records in Bell helicopters.

Given Dora's many achievements, Marty thought she would be

the perfect person to speak at the reunion dinner. Dora said yes, and Marty thought the matter was settled. Then one day not long before the dinner, Marty and her sons were out baling hay when someone shouted from the shop that she had a telephone call. It took her a few minutes to get out of the hay and to the phone. When Marty finally picked up the receiver, she could hear a woman on the other end of the line "cussing a blue streak" and complaining, "I've waited long enough, dammit, who does this Marty Wyall think she is? I don't have the time for this!"

It was Jackie. Marty apologized for taking so long to get to the phone, and Jackie yelled back that she'd been about to hang up. She'd just returned from the Paris Air Show and now had Marty's letter of invitation and wondered what arrangements had been made. Marty told her about the WASP dinner at the Ninety-Nines meeting and then, after a moment's hesitation, boldly asked Jackie to pay $400 for the WASP wings charms Marty was having designed to give to the women attending the gathering. Jackie told her she could take care of that and, yes, she thought she'd be able to attend and speak. As Marty didn't want to take back her invitation to Dora, she decided there would just have to be two speakers.

That August, Jackie arrived in Cincinnati for the dinner, flying her own Beech D-18 with her copilot, hairdresser, and secretary in tow. Thanks to Marty's efforts, eighty-six WASP gathered at the dinner, along with Jackie and Dedie Deaton—the first major gathering of the women since the 1940s.

At the dinner, Jackie asked Marty why there were two speakers. Marty quickly explained that Dora worked in the field of aviation—in fact, Dora had just been appointed to the FAA's new Women's Advisory Committee on Aviation by President Johnson—and Marty thought she would be a nice "opener" for Jackie. Dora had prepared a longer talk, but she graciously kept her remarks short. Over the years Dora had corresponded with Jackie, each woman congratulating the other on her aviation achievements, with Jackie even inviting Dora out to the ranch for a visit. As a result, Dora felt confident teasing Jackie a little bit. During her speech, she made sure to mention that the WASP had a pet name for Miss Cochran. Jackie's face immediately took on a stoical expression, and Dora knew she was expecting the worst. When Dora revealed that the nickname was "Goldilocks," Jackie smiled in relief. For her part, Jackie seemed to take real pride in Dora's successes and later bragged about her to others as one of "her girls" who was doing so well.

After the dinner, several of the WASP came up to say hello to Jackie. Marty watched as her classmate and friend Jean Terrell Moreo introduced herself and thanked Jackie for coming. When Jackie asked Jean what she was doing with her life, Jean told her she was driving a school bus and raising her ten children. Jackie's face lit up. "Well, that's the most wonderful thing a woman can do anyway," she said. "Motherhood is what we're here for and it's probably the greatest career that you could have ever chosen."

That night Jackie invited a group of women up to her room, ordering snacks and drinks for everyone, and they all sat around on the floor and talked, just like the old days. Marty joined them; Dora likely did, too. Jackie seemed pleasant and relaxed, regaling them with tales of her exploits and hearing about theirs, too. The WASP had spent the past two decades busy living their lives—and, like so many of the World War II generation, they didn't spend much time dwelling on the past. Marty and others like her weren't about to sit down at the dinner table and start telling flying stories to their families. Years later, when asked why not, Marty became exasperated and made it crystal clear: "Have you ever been at a dinner table with five little children? The conversation is not about Mother. The conversation is 'Now, why did you hit John out there in the yard with a big brick . . .'" Many WASP simply didn't talk about the war years because they felt their friends and family members wouldn't be interested or were too busy to care. As Marty put it, "They were not the kind of people that would understand what we were talking about." Reunited, they were eager to share memories that had long lain dormant.

All told, the 1964 reunion was a success. Marty was able to build a list of WASP that included both the names they had had in training and their married names. With the encouragement of those who had attended the reunion, she also decided to put together the first WASP newsletter since 1951. It came out in October 1964, and although it was only one eleven-by-seventeen-inch sheet of paper, printed front and back—primarily made up of one-sentence reports from forty-eight women—it was a start.

Marty spent the coming years gathering more and more information about the WASP and building up her roster of current names and addresses. She decided to revive the Order of Fifinella, creating regular newsletters, gathering news from designated class secretaries, reporting on activities, and growing the membership. She continued flying, too. Despite her husband Gene's initial resistance to her air racing, he had come to support her flying again and even occasionally joined her as her copilot. In the 1960s the couple turned Marty's piloting skills into a business venture, with Marty becoming a certified air taxi and commercial operator out of Baer Field near their home in Fort Wayne. Gene had a road construction business and was helping to build Interstate 69 but often found he had to wait for the right parts to be shipped, which caused delays. That's where Marty came in. Gene would call Marty from the road and say, "I need a part in Milwaukee." Marty would get in her plane and go. The factory would bring the part out to the airport, where Marty would pick it up and take it where it was needed, sometimes landing on the unfinished highway to complete the delivery. Gene encouraged Marty to grow her business, but she didn't particularly want to be a manager; she wanted to be a pilot.

When she wasn't flying or taking care of her children or working on the farm, Marty was working on reconnecting the WASP. When she started out, she knew only a handful, most of them classmates. Before long, she knew all their names and all their addresses—and they knew her and were grateful for her. The 1965 newsletters grew longer, including four pages of roster corrections and a brief financial statement, with the Order of Fifinella reporting $172.35 cash on hand. By June 1968 the newsletters had become longer still, with the latest one beginning with six pages of class news about who had moved where and whose children were graduating, along with more and more talk of the women who were flying. Perhaps the newsletters themselves encouraged some of the women to renew their licenses, now that careers had stabilized and children were older and needed them less. The June 1968 newsletter concluded with a note that the cash on hand was $784.45 and announced that WASP Betty Jo Reed was planning a 1969 reunion in Denver to commemorate the silver anniversary of their deactivation.

When Jackie Cochran learned of the plans for the reunion, she stepped in, inviting the WASP to hold the event at her ranch in California. While Jackie was the hostess and arranged the hotel, golfing, and tours, Marty and Betty Jo did much of the work. Years later Marty's son John remembered marching round and round the family's kitchen table, collating paper itineraries for the event and stuffing them into envelopes. This reunion would be more than three times as big as the one held just five years earlier, with 275 WASP in attendance.

Elaine Harmon, from class 44-W-9, felt particularly fortunate to attend. After disbandment, she stayed close with her WASP classmates, beginning a class newsletter right after the war that helped everyone to keep in touch. She had loved the 1946 reunion in Cleveland (she wasn't a part of the fly-in, as she was pregnant with her first child), and since then had been busy raising her family. When her husband died of heart disease in September 1965, she had four kids still in school to support. She found work as a real estate appraiser and watched every nickel and dime. When she learned of the 1969 reunion and told her children about it, they responded, "What are the WASP?"

Elaine began to tell them about her time during the war training at Sweetwater and her brief active duty. Her children decided it was time for Elaine to do something for herself, and all pitched in what little money they had to buy her a plane ticket to California. Elaine would later recall their gift as a highlight of her life. At Jackie's ranch, she was able to decompress from the last few years of struggle and spend time with good friends like Maggie Gee, who was now a physicist in the University of California, Berkeley, Radiation Laboratory.

It was, Marty later remembered, a "very, very good reunion." On Saturday morning, fifty WASP played golf at the Cochran Golf Course while the rest took a bus tour of the Coachella Valley. In the evening Jackie and Floyd hosted a big barbecue at the ranch under a tent. Jackie wore a yellow lace dress and string of pearls, and made sure to visit with everybody at their tables. She had invited her friend Chuck Yeager to speak. Dedie Deaton gave a speech at the banquet, too, charming the women by pointing out that she was the only person ever to meet every one of the WASP. The WASP recognized Marty for her efforts in preserving the Order of Fifinella and their history, too, with an award presented to her by General Yeager. For years she'd been accumulating WASP records, storing the papers and paraphernalia, knowing it was important to telling their story. At the end, the women elected officers for the first time in nearly twenty years, choosing Dottie Young—a member of the first class of "guinea pig" trainees at Houston—as their first president since 1951. Marty was voted in as historian, a permanent position, gaining official sanction for the work she had been doing for years. Later, the final cash-on-hand report was $2,839.89. The Order of Fifinella was not only reborn; it was thriving.

There was one notable absence from the reunion. Out on Martha's Vineyard, Nancy Love kept herself at arm's length from the reunions and gatherings. She had a life centered on her family. Although many of her originals and former ferry pilots visited her on the island, she seemed disinclined to dwell on the war years.

When her girls reached their teens, she bought a little Cessna 150 so they could learn to fly. Nancy, who had once flown some of the most challenging military planes ever created, was too nervous to teach her girls herself. Instead, she made sure to stay at home when they went to the airport on Martha's Vineyard to take lessons with their instructor, WASP Carolyn Cullen. At home, Nancy would quietly watch them from the front porch, anxiously noting when they took off and landed but never wanting her girls to see how fearful she was for them.

When she was not working to help the WASP gain recognition as veterans, Dora Dougherty Strother was working as chief over all human-factors engineering research and project work for the Bell Helicopter company. *Dora Dougherty Strother McKeown Collection. Courtesy Texas Woman's University*

CHAPTER TWENTY-SIX

The Fight Begins

After Dink's funeral, Teresa James had done her best to make a new life for herself. At the end of the 1940s, when the WASP were offered the chance to join the Air Force Reserve, Teresa leapt at the opportunity, joining the 375th Troop Carrier Wing at Pittsburgh. Thanks to her WASP service during the war, she was commissioned as a major, serving as a special services officer. Despite the fact that she was not allowed to fly, she was happy to finally join the military proper and to take advantage of its regular pay and benefits. Throughout the 1950s and into the 1960s, Teresa continued to serve in the reserves while working in her day job as a florist. She kept teaching flying lessons in the evenings and on weekends when there wasn't a wedding to work, but there weren't enough students for her to make a living at it. If she could put enough money together or find someone to fly with, she took part in a few air races, enjoying the thrill of the sport and the sense of competition and camaraderie she found in flying circles.

Around 1961 she went to visit some WASP friends who were living in Alaska. She found herself enthralled by its beauty and by the incredible flying over the mountains and into isolated lakes. Still blond—now covering a few grays hairs in addition to her natural brown—and wanting to have some new fun, she decided to take the leap and move there. In Anchorage, Teresa found a job managing a flower shop at a hotel and started befriending local pilots, flying Piper Super Cubs and Cherokees, some with skis. She also continued to serve in the reserves and was assigned to the Red Carpet Committee, in charge of meeting visiting dignitaries. In 1963 her work for the Red Carpet Committee led to a renewed acquaintance with Jacqueline Cochran, who she ended up flying to remote lakes to go fly-fishing and to search for a possible homestead.

By now Teresa had spent over a decade and a half in the reserves. She was in her early fifties and had begun to think about her retirement. She knew that although the two years she had spent in the WASP had gotten her commissioned as a major, they weren't being counted toward her retirement. Why wasn't the work the women had done during the war being officially recognized? Teresa wasn't even supposed to wear her wings on her uniform, although many of the WASP who continued to serve did, in spite of the rules. Teresa was well aware that attempts at militarization and recognition for the WASP had failed in the past. The bill to militarize the women during the war had been pushed aside and a brief postwar attempt at recognition by the WASP, which would have made such a difference in her life, had withered in the congressional committee in 1947. Even so, many WASP like Teresa never lost their will to gain some kind of official recognition for their service during the war. With the military refusing to take her two years in the WASP into account, Teresa felt she was being shortchanged.

With the twentieth anniversary of WASP disbandment on the horizon, Teresa decided it was time to try to start up the fight for military recognition again. The war had changed her life forever. It had claimed her husband. Her job. Her livelihood. It had now been twenty years since she'd lost Dink. How different would her life have been if she and the other WASP had been recognized as veterans in the years after the war? If she had been eligible for the G.I. Bill, who knew what she might have achieved? "Hell, I could have gone back to school; I could have done a lot of things," she later pointed out.

In 1963, Teresa decided to start a campaign to credit the WASP for the time they served during the war, so that the women could get retirement benefits based on *all* of their service. She asked the Reserve Officers Association to pass a resolution supporting her effort so that it could be submitted to Congress the following year. She also sent letters to as many WASP as she could find, urging them to get petitions signed and send them to their members of Congress. Teresa valiantly attempted to push a bill through Congress in 1964, timed with the twentieth anniversary of WASP disbandment. But there was not enough support, and it didn't go far before faltering.

After her Alaska adventure and the failed attempt to push the bill through Congress, Teresa kept moving, first to California, then to Florida, attending WASP reunions whenever she could. At one such gathering she ran into Jackie Cochran, who she had gotten to know well in the years since the war, and started to tell her about her attempt to have the women recognized for their service. Jackie told Teresa in no uncertain terms that her militarization efforts were a waste of time. Jackie had tried it in Washington, D.C., and if she couldn't do it, no one could. When Jackie changed her mind and wanted to talk with Teresa about it the next day, Teresa, annoyed with her from the night before, couldn't be bothered. She was forging her own path.

Teresa was pleased to find another important ally for her cause. Dora Dougherty had been serving in the reserves since the late 1940s, just like Teresa. Although their paths hadn't really crossed during the war, the two women began to run into each other at the various WASP gatherings and reunions and discovered they shared the goal of veteran recognition. Dora and Teresa began communicating via letters and phone calls and quickly became a united front.

Dora's life had changed dramatically since she had earned her PhD and gone to work for Bell Helicopter in the 1950s. Although she had remained single through her twenties and thirties, one day in 1963 a journalist named Lester Strother walked into her office in Fort Worth to interview her for a story about her time in the WASP and her extraordinary career since. Three years later, just a few days shy of her forty-fifth birthday and much to Dora's delight, they were married.

A few months after the wedding, Dora wrote to her old friend Izzy, her classmate during her WASP training, about her new unexpected joy at finding herself happily married in her mid-forties. "Tomorrow will make the fourth month of our marriage," she wrote. "We are both so grateful for each day together. Although there is a lot to be said for marrying young there is also a lot to be said for waiting. I don't believe in waiting as long as I did—I don't think—at least you couldn't have convinced me of the advantages when I was younger, nevertheless it is a delightful way of life."

In March 1972, with Dora's support, Teresa again renewed her fight for recognition. She sent a letter to the WASP encouraging them to join her in "an all out concentrated effort to get credit for the time they spent in the service." Teresa's idea was for the women who served in the active or reserve military in the years since the war to also be credited for the time they spent in the WASP, so that it could go toward retirement and promotion. The credit given to male reservists included their World War II service. Shouldn't that be the case for WASP as well? In a publicity letter, Teresa pointed out that the WASP had lost their effort to join the military in 1944 by only 27 votes. (It was actually only 19.) "The narrow margin indicates sentiments were in favor of the WASP but the WASP *simply had no lobby*," Teresa wrote. "*Now* is the time for terminating that unfinished MILITARY business in an equitable and honorable manner. Give the members of the WASP their just dues, full benefits for the time of active duty."

Teresa worked diligently, with Dora sending documents and materials in support of the cause. On May 17, 1972, Representative Patsy Mink of Hawaii introduced House Resolution 15035 on behalf of the WASP. Teresa handwrote (she never had learned to type) to every member of the House and Senate, as well as to all the Ninety-Nines and WASP, asking them to "focus the urgency of a concerted effort to work quickly and in unison toward the correction of the overlooked WASPs during World War II."

The end result of Representative Mink's bill, H.R. 15035, was another rejection of the WASP. Teresa, Dora, and the other WASP were sorely disappointed. The report from the Armed Services Committee repeated the same arguments the women had heard in the 1940s. Opponents feared giving the WASP veteran status would open a "Pandora's box" of other civilian organizations clamoring for the same. The concern both in the immediate postwar years and in the economically strapped decade of the 1970s was the practical question of who would pay for it all. In order to succeed, the WASP would need to prove that they were different from other civilian groups—that they had indeed earned the title of "veterans."

Teresa had worked so hard to get the bill introduced, but the reality was that there had been a decided lack of coordination among the WASP in support of it. The lesson of the failed 1972 campaign was that if the WASP wanted to win, they needed more extensive coordination, more strategic outside support, and more media coverage. They were going to have to win over the attention of the American public and gain the sympathy of lobbyists and Congress in the process. The 1972 defeat put into motion a massive five-year effort on behalf of the WASP to earn recognition once and for all, with Teresa at the forefront. In the fight for WASP recognition, she became one of its most outspoken advocates.

The WASP reunion of 1972, memorializing their thirtieth anniversary, took place at their old training base of Sweetwater and was attended by more than three hundred WASP, their biggest reunion yet. Women from across the country were reunited, some of them returning to Sweetwater for the first time since their disbanding, happily reconnecting with old friends, shouting and laughing as they found one another, squinting to see the young friend in the older face, quickly shedding the years as they "hangar flew" together once more. Marty Wyall traveled down from Indiana for the reunion, excited to reconnect with her classmates in 44-W-10 and to take her new position as historian.

The event also gave Teresa James and Dora Dougherty Strother a chance to meet up again in person after months of corresponding about the Mink bill. Their love of flying coupled with their common goal of achieving veteran status had created a powerful bond between them. At the reunion Teresa and Dora saw an opportunity to enlist a powerful ally to their cause. The guest of honor that weekend was Colonel Bruce Arnold, son of General Henry H. Arnold, head of the U.S. Army Air Forces and the man who had given the orders for both the formation of the WASP and its disbandment. General Arnold had passed away in 1950, and so the WASP had invited Bruce to accept the Order of Fifinella Award on his behalf. Bruce Arnold had served in the Air Force since 1949 and now held the rank of colonel. Teresa had been trying to persuade the younger Arnold to support the WASP cause for several years, knowing if they could persuade him to join their fight for military benefits, they'd gain some much-needed sway in Washington. Together with Dora, she decided to ask him for his help.

On Saturday evening, at a banquet attended by more than 1,000 people (and aired on local television), Bruce Arnold gave a speech accepting the Order of Fifinella Award on behalf of his father. He explained that General Arnold had been very proud of his role in the WASP's formation, telling the women, "Your performance not only surpassed his expectations, it exceeded his wildest dreams." Dora had the idea to give Arnold a copy of the speech his father had given to the final graduating class in Sweetwater, and as Bruce Arnold read his father's words aloud, he became choked with emotion.

By the end of the weekend, Teresa, Dora, and the small committee they'd put together earlier that year had secured his support. Later, Arnold himself recalled: "There was a parade and lots of hell-raising, and in a weak moment, after three martinis, I volunteered." Jokes aside, he seemed committed. "Seriously, I felt responsible in a way," he said. "I wanted to finish up some thirty-year-old business my old man didn't have a chance to finish." During the reunion, Teresa and Dora and their small committee also met with Nancy Crews, the president of their organization, formally deciding to expand their efforts to fight for militarization. Along with the colonel, they began to make plans.

In 1973 the WASP militarization committee, which now included Marty Wyall, clarified their goal. They would propose legislation that would declare that the time the women had served in the WASP counted as military service and that they were therefore all "entitled to an honorable discharge from the Air Force of the Army." The committee believed that if their proposal was adopted by Congress, they would immediately be recognized as World

War II veterans, eligible for "all benefits afforded same." Now the challenge was to convince Washington.

For many of the WASP the timing was right. By now the women were in their fifties; most of their children were in high school or out of the house, and the working women were well established in their careers. They were beginning to recognize that the friends they'd made during World War II were important to them and that the jobs that they'd done back then were important as well. It was a new period in their lives, when they had the time, good health, and energy not only to renew those friendships but to correct past wrongs. As they reconnected with one another and began to remember who they were and what they'd done during the war, the WASP were realizing they did not want to be forgotten—and they didn't want the thirty-eight women who had been killed serving in the WASP to be forgotten, either.

The women had their work cut out for them. The WASP records were scattered, but they got to work gathering as much information as possible. Dedie Deaton was called upon to provide institutional memory. Dora Dougherty worked to gather official records from the Air Force. Marty Wyall was asked to excavate the records and materials she'd been storing in her barn over the decades since deactivation. Teresa James did most of her work from her home in Florida but enjoyed coming to Washington as often as she could. When she was in town, Teresa joined the Washington, D.C.–area WASP at their new "office," at the prestigious Army and Navy Club, just blocks from the White House. Bruce Arnold had used his connections to secure the women space in the building, albeit in a room that, until they arrived, had been a broom closet.

The broom closet office was regularly manned by five or six WASP who lived in the D.C. area. One of them was Elaine Harmon, who lived in nearby Silver Spring, Maryland. Elaine worked in the office and often hosted visiting WASP at her home. Lucile Doll Wise, who had served with the Weather Wing, flying inspectors to various weather stations during the war, rode to the Pentagon with her husband each morning and then took the Metro to the office, working nearly every day of the week. She set up an extensive filing system, keeping track of the paperwork and getting to know women beyond her own class, typing out letter after letter. Lee Wheelwright, a ferry pilot out of Long Beach, took care of the phone calls, treating it like a daily job. Dorothy Deane Ferguson, who served as an engineering test pilot in Greenwood, Mississippi, was now a Washington area attorney and helped the WASP with their legal arguments.

The D.C. women had to do a bit of decorating to turn their new office into a functional workspace. It had a lone desk with a seafoam-green rotary telephone and a typewriter that was often moved to the top of the small bookcase when the desk was in use. The closet did have a large window, but it overlooked a brick wall, so one of the women brought in a white banner emblazoned with their Fifinella mascot to help brighten the place. This was to be their headquarters for their fight to be recognized as veterans of World War II.

Unlike during the war, the women would have to undertake this fight without the help of their leaders. Although supportive of the women's efforts in spirit, Jackie and Nancy were facing their own struggles. Jackie, the traveler and adventurer, had become increasingly limited by her physical health. In 1970 she went to the Mayo Clinic complaining of muscle cramping, night sweats, headaches, and weight gain. She bore surgical scars from an earlier breast reduction, multiple abdominal operations, and lumbar disc disease. The year before she had sold her Lockheed Lodestar with her lucky N number: N13V. Until now Jackie had always transferred the number to each of her new planes. The fact that she sold the plane with the number meant she didn't plan to buy another one. In May 1971, Jackie suffered a major heart attack and was given a pacemaker. She failed to pass her FAA medical exam later that year and lost her medical, meaning she could no longer legally fly. Floyd was also suffering with health problems, and his finances had taken a downturn, so they decided to sell their ranch to a developer and move to a smaller home on the land. Although the couple still traveled in the motor home they owned and attended rocket launches at Cape Kennedy, Jackie entered a period of decline. At the age of sixty-five, Jackie Cochran was done flying for good.

On Martha's Vineyard, Nancy Love was also going through her own decline. By now her daughters had left for boarding school, leaving Nancy without a focus. Together with her husband, Bob, she took the opportunity to travel; they started a charter boat business, but she was uninspired. She continued to smoke relentlessly, as she always had, and instead of at her usual 2:00 P.M. cocktail hour she began drinking her martinis earlier and earlier in the day. Moods that might had been brushed off as mere melancholy in the past developed into depression.

In 1971, Nancy's close family and friends confronted her about her drinking, which had gone from bad to worse. Nancy was receptive and apologetic. She decided to start writing her thoughts down as a form of therapy but never allowed anyone to see what she wrote. Nancy and Bob began splitting their time between Martha's Vineyard and Florida, where they bought a house and sailboat. Nancy was still in touch with Teresa James, Betty Gillies, and a number of her original WAFS pilots, but was too busy struggling with her own demons to do more than privately cheer the women on.

In Washington, the women of the broom closet continued their work. Bruce Arnold had helped the WASP set up three subcommittees, each tasked with proving the women had earned the right to be called veterans. The first committee was charged with finding evidence to prove the WASP had been treated as military personnel—rather than as civilians—throughout their time in the program. The second committee was going to compare the WASP's wartime service to that of other organizations in the military. The third committee was tasked with preparing opening testimony for hearings that would hopefully be held in both the House and Senate. Dora was assigned to this last committee and took on the task with her usual rigor and determination.

Meanwhile, WASP Bernice "Bee" Falk Haydu, who had recently been elected president of the Order of Fifinella board, got to work to coordinate efforts and make it happen. In 1975 she announced: "The policy of the O.O.F. Board is going to be PUBLICITY." Smart, determined, intolerant of error, and always careful in her word choice, Bee was the ideal person to helm the WASP press relations effort. Both she and Bruce Arnold knew that they had to be cautious about the kind of publicity the WASP received, drawing a distinction between what they would call "Remember us" publicity and "We want veteran status" publicity, revealing the fine line the women walked. They knew they would be better off sweetly reminding Americans of their war effort than appearing to actually want something.

Nonetheless, this was a very different time from the war years, when the women had faced such unrelenting resistance. The civil rights movement of the 1960s had created all kinds of challenges to the status quo. The women's rights movement was also underway, with women's organizations coming together and becoming more vocal about the ability of women to do all kinds of work, even jobs that had long been off-limits to them because of their sex. This in turn put pressure on the military to finally admit women as equals to men.

With the passage of the Equal Rights Amendment in 1972, the U.S. Air Force Academy began "contingency planning" about "actions necessary to admit women," as they fully expected that, with the ratification of the amendment, women would become a part of the academy. There was plenty of opposition to this. Jacqueline

Cochran testified against it in 1975, arguing that women's primary role should be in the home, even sadly claiming, "If I had been so fortunate as to have had my children live, I don't think I would have gone [air racing]. I don't think there is any question about it." Despite Jackie's assertions and the protest of others, in October 1975, President Ford signed Public Law 94-106, ordering the service academies to admit women. In the summer of 1976, 157 women entered the Air Force Academy, 119 entered the U.S. Military Academy at West Point, and 81 entered the U.S. Naval Academy.

While many of the WASP were careful not to define themselves as vocal "women's libbers," they nonetheless felt their work flying for the military had helped to set many of these changes in motion. And yet their work during the war seemed to have been overlooked. In early 1976, when the Air Force announced that they were accepting twenty young women for undergraduate pilot training, an article appeared in the newspapers announcing it as "the first time the Air Force has accepted women as pilots." The first time for women pilots? While the WASP had technically been a part of the Army Air Forces—the Air Force didn't become an independent branch of the military until 1947—they felt particularly stung by the omission. General Arnold had promised the final graduating class in Sweetwater, "We will never forget our debt to you." But clearly the Air Force had, indeed, forgotten the WASP.

"Nobody seemed to remember about us," Dora later reflected. "No books were written about us, and we were sort of a forgotten page in history. We just wanted to set that straight. We wanted them to know that we were the first women military pilots . . .

"When the WASPs started, the military didn't know whether we were emotionally stable enough to be military pilots," Dora observed.

> A lot of the military brass felt that we weren't. Women were hysterical, they said. They didn't know whether we could physiologically and biologically meet a mili-

tary schedule and [thought] that we would have to take four days off every month. They didn't know whether we would be capable of taking commands received or give them . . . I think had it not been for our program that the military probably would have been delayed longer for women to fly. Because of our program—some of the findings that came out of it— we opened the door.

When the WASP saw the article about the new young women military pilots, they began calling up their local newspapers with a firm but polite correction. The newspapers loved it and began running stories with headlines like "HEROINES FLEW DANGEROUS FLIGHTS" and "AMERICA'S FORGOTTEN HEROINES KEEP FIGHTING." One article read: "They are the forgotten heroines of World War II, some 1,000 spunky young women who flew warplanes on thankless but dangerous missions at home so the men could go to battle on the enemy's turf." The media often portrayed the WASP as sacrificing themselves for their nation in its time of need and now wanting nothing more than to right a past wrong. "Today, many of them are grandmothers, but they are still fighting for a status denied them since 1944 when male civilian pilots helped defeat a bill before Congress which would have made them military officers." These portrayals of the WASP, first as "spunky young women," then as "grandmothers" who had been wronged, helped present the women as nonthreatening. Even in 1976 the women still had to be careful not to appear too "pushy" or risk alienating public support.

Meanwhile, WASP around the country sent Marty every newspaper clipping or other bit of publicity about the Women Airforce Service Pilots they could find. While her family rolled their eyes at the full post office box and the little scraps of paper that spilled out of envelopes into their neat home, Marty kept saving it all in a giant scrapbook, knowing it might ultimately aid the cause. In total, the women sent Marty news clippings from thirty states and sixty-six cities, impressive numbers for a purely grassroots campaign.

Nancy Love was supportive of the women's efforts to win veteran status and helpful when asked specific questions, but she was not a part of the fight. In 1974 she was diagnosed with breast cancer and underwent a radical double mastectomy. That same year she wrote letters to all her children apologizing for the sorrow her drinking had caused the family. She also wrote about her love for Bob: "As you know, Daddy has been my salvation—sounds funny, but it's really true, as I'd have gone off in every possible wild direction—even more than I did—without his steady and understanding tolerance of my vagaries. Having respect for a man sounds mid-Victorian, but it's true, and is an important element in loving him. Mutual respect is a necessity."

In June 1976, Nancy fell into a coma. Her daughters were called home. They thought they'd lost her, but when they arrived at the hospital, Nancy was sitting in a chair, asking for her reading glasses. Her weight was down to ninety-five pounds, but she claimed she felt fine and enjoyed "a marvelous reunion" with her girls filled with laughter and sharing of memories. As Nancy's cancer spread to her larynx and esophagus, it became increasingly difficult for her to communicate verbally. Many friends stopped calling. But Teresa James didn't give up on Nancy, going to visit later that summer, bringing with her another Florida-based WASP, Kay Rawls Thompson. "I remember her standing in the door saying goodbye to us, still puffing on that infernal cigarette," Teresa later recalled. It was the last time Teresa and Nancy saw each other.

In 1976 the WASP voted Nancy Woman of the Year. They hoped to give her the award in person at their reunion in a few weeks. But Nancy couldn't make it; she was very near the end. "All my life, I thought I would go down in a blaze of glory in an airplane," she observed. "Here I am hardly able to do anything at all." The plaque was mailed to Nancy instead, and her daughter shared Nancy's thanks and appreciation with the rest of the WASP.

Nancy died on October 22, 1976, at age sixty-two. Her daughter Marky asked the WASP not to send flowers to the private family funeral on Martha's Vineyard but to instead make a donation to the American Cancer Society in her honor.

Nancy, with her quick, friendly smile and determination to gain opportunities for women to fly, was gone.

The WASP gather in Washington, D.C., with signed petitions supporting their efforts from across the nation. Bee Haydu is on the right. Elaine Harmon can be seen in the middle, looking to the left. *Courtesy Texas Woman's University*

CHAPTER TWENTY-SEVEN

The Year of the WASP

The women dubbed 1977 the "Year of the WASP." When they gathered for their reunion in Hot Springs, Arkansas, it was with a new determination. They knew that if they were to be successful, they had to mobilize in even greater numbers. The time for remaining silent was over. Silence was what Jackie had demanded of them in 1944 when she had forbidden them to speak out or take action during the first attempt to militarize the WASP, fearful that they would seem too pushy. The women all knew where that had gotten them. At the time, Congress wondered if the WASP even wanted to be in the military, as none of them were writing and calling to support the bill. Now the women were determined to use their voices and their smarts to finally achieve their goal of veterans' recognition.

Dora, Marty, and Teresa were at the reunion, where they helped the committee develop a new communication plan: a calling tree, which would enable them to get out information to one another quickly. When he received word about hearings, Bruce Arnold would phone Bee Haydu. Bee would call designated WASP "captains," who then instructed as many WASP as possible to act. Those WASP would quickly write or send Mailgrams to the chairs of the House and Senate veterans' affairs committees while seeking as much newspaper, radio, and television publicity as possible and encouraging other sympathetic groups to do the same.

The women also redoubled their efforts to compile as much evidence as possible to prove that they had, indeed, been a part of the military during the war. The veteran recognition committee asked WASP to send them information about any dangerous or near-death experiences they'd had during their service, along with any time they were reprimanded or threatened, asked to guard or protect their planes, or asked to take an oath, verbally or in writing, to defend their country. In the process, they found hundreds of "lost" WASP, helping rekindle friendships and gather even more data. "I am certain that if each and every one of you will do his or her share, we *will* receive the proper recognition from Washington this year," Bee wrote to everyone. "It is so close; let's not let it slip from our fingers."

Meanwhile, the WASP story was being shared in newspaper articles from Los Angeles, California, to Rochester, New York. Most vitally, the WASP gained an invaluable supporter when *Stars and Stripes*—the one-hundred-year-old weekly paper for active military, veterans, and their families—endorsed the women's fight for recognition. The paper hired WASP Patricia Collins Hughes to write a weekly article covering the campaign. Each week Pat published articles with calls to action, which became a game changer for the WASP. Bee told everybody to subscribe to *Stars and Stripes* so they could see all the updates; now no one had to wait for the WASP's quarterly newsletter for the latest.

In addition to *Stars and Stripes,* the women found another, much more unlikely ally: the champion of conservatism Senator Barry Goldwater. Although Goldwater had lost his 1964 presidential bid, he continued to be a major force in the conservative movement and remained a hero to many in the Republican Party. He was, however, not the most obvious supporter for a group of women. Goldwater voted against the Equal Rights Amendment— one of only eight senators to do so—and was strongly against women in the military serving in combat. Yet Goldwater had also served in the Air Transport Command during World War II, where he had flown with some of the WASP, including as an instructor pilot. Thanks to that direct contact with the women pilots, Goldwater understood and respected the WASP. When Bruce Arnold approached him to ask him to join the WASP in their cause, he agreed, becoming an instrumental force on behalf of the women in Congress. In 1977 it was Goldwater who extracted promises from the chairmen of the House and Senate veterans' affairs committees that they would at least hold hearings on the WASP issue that year.

With the women's extensive publicity, Bruce Arnold's lobbying, and Senator Goldwater prodding his colleagues to support the WASP, the new bill began its slow journey through Congress. This time around, the bill had two very important cosponsors: Congresswomen Margaret Heckler, a Republican from Massachusetts, and Lindy Boggs, a Democrat from Louisiana, picked up the women's fight in the House. Both Heckler and Boggs were ardent supporters of the WASP and worked across the aisle to sponsor the bill.

The WASP were nervous. The year before, a bill for WASP veteran status had come before the House Committee on Veteran Affairs but had failed to go any further. Olin "Tiger" Teague, the congressional representative for Texas's Sixth Congressional District and the chairman of the committee, was a distinguished World War II veteran, having participated in the D-Day invasion of Normandy. Teague told the women that as far as he was concerned, they had served as civilians, and he would never let the bill out of committee. This time, when the bill reached Teague's committee, it stalled once again. Teague simply wouldn't allow it to go forward. He continued to object on principle: Why should women who had served as civilians be given the same benefits as "real" veterans like himself? As the women presented more and more evidence to support their cause, members of the committee were handed a copy of one of the WASP's discharge papers. It was a lightbulb moment for Teague: the papers were identical to the ones he had been given. Teague finally understood that the women had been members of the military in everything but name and finally allowed the WASP bill through.

In May 1977 the women got their long-awaited hearing. The WASP needed to choose one woman who would testify on behalf of the group, first before the Senate and then before the House. Teresa James was the natural choice. She had been one of the earliest advocates of the legislation, diligently writing and organizing since the 1960s and continuing to play an important part in the efforts throughout the 1970s. Sharp, witty, and articulate, Teresa knew the WASP story inside and out—and she had been there from the very start. But Teresa declined, insisting that she worked better behind the scenes. "I'll do my thing with a pencil," she said.

Instead, she recommended Dora for the job.

Dora humbly accepted the role of chief witness. The once self-described "country girl" from Illinois who had dropped out of college to become a WASP and then gone on to earn her bachelor's, master's, and PhD—all without the support of the G.I. Bill—prepared to give testimony at a Senate hearing. She'd spent several years researching the WASP's history while serving a tour at Wright-Patterson Air Force Base in Ohio as a reservist, and those efforts now paid off. Together with Bruce Arnold, she wrote a forty-two-page statement, then practiced with him to sharpen her presentation, anticipate questions, and prepare for possible attacks. The whole process reminded Dora a bit of preparing her doctoral dissertation defense, although this time, the stakes felt higher. "To say it was not a high stress condition would be a gross understatement," she admitted.

The morning of the Senate hearing, May 25, 1977, Dora got up early and readied herself for the day ahead. She put on a collared yellow dress with a feminine striped tie, looking professional but, she hoped, friendly. She made her way over to Capitol Hill and up the steps of the Russell Senate Office Building, where she was led to a large room and asked to sit at a small desk covered in green baize. In front of her was a large silver microphone and beyond the microphone members of the Senate committee were seated in a large semicircle at a distance of about twenty feet. As Dora looked up at them, the men seemed to loom above her. To the far right, photographers aimed their lenses in Dora's direction. To the left sat the reporters. With Dora at the table were WASP Margaret Kerr Boylan and Bee Haydu, with Bee in her Santiago-blue WASP uniform, there to help with the testimony. Dora was happy to turn around and see Teresa and Marty along with nearly forty other WASP in the visitors' section, a dozen of them also dressed in uniform.

Even with Dora's decades of academic, professional, and aviation achievement, she had never felt so intimidated. When the moment came, she began to read from her statement. After her brief introduction she asked that the committee "remove all extraneous and emotional issues to arrive at the true merits of the WASP bid for militarization." She continued: "The 78th Congress rejected the WASP case for militarization by the slim margin of 19 votes. It is my fervent hope this Congress will overturn this vote—and by a large majority." With the Senate committee—and the press—looking on, Dora recounted the story of the WASP. Her statement was full of detailed time lines, charts, pictures of the women in uniform, and illustrations of their wings.

In closing, she read the women's official request. "We hope that this committee, after its investigation, will find that we are worthy of the recognition promised to us so many years ago," Dora said. "We ask that you retroactively grant us recognition as military pilots of this great republic through the passage of the bill before you."

Next it was Senator Goldwater's turn to testify. Wearing his signature thick black glasses with his close-cropped hair, Goldwater, the anti-ERA conservative, leapt to the women's defense, pointing out that the women had been discriminated against:

"Now, I don't want to overdo this aspect, but it is a fact that these girls did bear extra burdens simply because they were women," he stated. "The very reason they were not militarized was their sex. The law allowed the Air Forces to commission men as flight officers, but not women."

He also addressed the primary concern of many who opposed the bill: that recognizing the WASP as veterans would set a precedent for other civilian groups who served with the military to be recognized as veterans, too. "My argument is that the WASPs are entitled to veterans' benefits because of the nature of their duties," Goldwater testified. "These benefits should not be given merely to offer recognition to the women. The benefits are due to them because they were a part of the military." The WASP bill was not another "women's issue," Goldwater argued. It was righting a historic wrong.

Opponents of the WASP were given the chance to voice their views as well. The most significant opposition came from the Veterans Administration's new chief benefits director, Dorothy Starbuck. Starbuck, who had served as a WAC in England during World War II, argued that there had been fundamental distinctions between the WASP and members of the military. She cited the fact that, as civilians, WASP could resign at any time; that, as civil servants, they were eligible for Federal Employees Compensation for job-related injuries; and that, in the event of deaths, their surviving spouses and children became eligible for benefits under this same program. Starbuck was, of course, wrong on this count. Many survivors of the thirty-eight WASP killed while serving never received compensation; the Civil Service Commission claimed the women were military, and the military claimed they were civil service.

Despite Starbuck's opposition, Dora and the other WASP left feeling cautiously optimistic. In the coming weeks they worked on their rebuttal and hoped for the House to hold its own hearings on the matter.

On August 15, 1977, WASP's telephones began ringing all across the country as Bee's captains dialed every number on their list. It was a red alert. Hearings before the House had been scheduled for September 20 and 21. An "Action Now" flyer followed, asking the women to make a strong showing at the hearings. "We hope each and every one of you can be there. No one can do this alone. It takes a mass effort. Put down your knitting and quit canning your home-grown vegetables or ask your boss for the day off and get yourselves HERE! Take a plane, take a bus, take your car, but get here."

This was it: one final push—the last stand. WASP traveled from across the country to support Dora at the hearing. Again Dora carefully delivered her testimony. It was more familiar to her now, but even so, the experience was unnerving. Some representatives stood up in the middle of her speech. At other times their aides came in and spoke to them over their shoulders. *Are they listening to me?* Dora thought. *I'm here; I've got something to say!* Colonel Bruce Arnold testified, as did Senator Goldwater. But a turning point came with the testimony of Antonia Handler Chayes, assistant secretary of the Air Force for manpower, reserve affairs, and installations, and one of the highest-ranking women in the Air Force at the time.

Chayes had been earmarked as a potential WASP ally by Margaret Heckler and Lindy Boggs, the bill's cosponsors. They knew that Chayes had been involved in a number of contemporary fights for women in the Air Force—including easing the restrictions on women missile officers and pilots—and that she would likely be a positive witness for the women. Until now the Air Force had maintained its official position that it wasn't appropriate for them to even consider the idea that the WASP could be veterans because the women had served as civilians. It was the same argument Teresa had heard over and over again since the 1960s. She hoped Chayes might help provide an effective counterargument.

The start was not auspicious. When Representative G. V. "Sonny" Montgomery of Mississippi, a World War II veteran, introduced Chayes, he reminded everyone in the room that, despite the efforts of the women's rights movement, chauvinism was still alive and well. "Besides being such an attractive person, she's also a very capable person," he said of the Air Force leader. The WASP were introduced in opening remarks as "charming witnesses," and Montgomery had earlier announced that during the war he had gone to the WASP training areas because "they were the most attractive persons in that part of the country." Goldwater had responded, "You can find pretty girls any place you go in Texas." One WASP supporter later vented about the language the congressmen used, saying it "symbolized to me . . . how these men feel about women. *No* ideas, *no* arguments will ever penetrate their attitudinal wall."

The WASP sat in the balcony, anxious to hear what would happen next.

In her initial responses, Chayes stuck to the Air Force's official policy of neutrality. Then it was Congresswoman Heckler's turn to question Chayes. Sticking to the plan she had worked out with

Chayes in advance, Heckler gave her a chance to voice an opinion besides the official Air Force position: "What is your view, as one who has studied the issue?" Heckler asked.

Opponents of the WASP continually argued that giving the women veteran status would set a precedent for other civilians to demand a similar status, but Chayes, in another strategic move, suggested that the WASP story had in fact already set another, more troubling precedent. The promise to the WASP of militarization had not been kept: What did this say to present-day and future volunteers? Chayes insinuated that to deny the WASP their recognition would risk losing the trust of all potential volunteer military personnel, particularly the greatest untapped pool for the new, post-Vietnam all-volunteer force: women. "There is an implied promise, today, of equal opportunity for everyone in the Armed Forces. It is part of a new environment to recognize women as persons today, as well as pilots. And these considerations tell me personally to look favorably on the legislation, again, speaking only for myself, understanding that the administration has had a position and that position has not officially changed."

Oppositional testimonies came from the Veterans Administration and other veterans' groups, who were worried about resources running thin. Representative John Paul Hammerschmidt read into the record letters from some of the civilian flight instructors who had fought to obstruct WASP militarization in 1944. When John Sommer, Jr., spoke on behalf of the American Legion, he went so far as to argue that giving the WASP benefits "would denigrate the term veteran so that it will never again have the value that presently attaches to it."

The women left the hearings that day not knowing what to expect. Their champions had presented strong evidence of support, and it seemed like Secretary Chayes's testimony was a turning point, but it was unclear how it had all been received. The WASP held a cocktail party the evening after the hearings, with several members of Congress in attendance. Bee was most optimistic, pointing out that three different veterans' groups, including the American Legion, had told the women that "if we got the green light from the Department of Defense they would back us." Elaine Harmon saw things differently, writing to Marty that "the hearings don't look too hopeful. Everyone is for us . . . but everyone is passing the buck to the Defense Department."

In the weeks after the hearings, the WASP waited and watched, prodding for support and action. Both of their bills languished in committees.

Committee chairman Ray Roberts was not a supporter of the bill but he continued working on it, asking a variety of individuals for their views on the issue, including Jacqueline Cochran. At seventy-one years old and in poor health, Jackie couldn't attend the hearings, but she responded to Roberts's request for comments in an October 10 letter in which she blamed the failure of the 1944 bill on WAC colonel Oveta Culp Hobby. She urged, "I think that at long last they [the WASP] deserve some recognition for the work they have done and I hope that they get the bill passed."

Then the WASP got a series of lucky breaks. Senator Barry Goldwater had promised that if the WASP bills got bottlenecked in the committee, he would attach a WASP amendment to every piece of legislation until it got pushed through. Sure enough, in October, the WASP request got attached to a bill increasing educational benefits for veterans. The WASP celebrated the move and waited anxiously as the bill with their amendment moved through the chamber.

Next, the WASP got a momentous vote of support from the Department of Defense, in part thanks to the efforts of Chayes behind the scenes. In a letter written by Deputy Secretary of Defense Charles Duncan, Jr., to James T. McIntyre, Jr., acting director of the Office of Management and Budget, Duncan boldly copied members of Congress and stated: "The Department of Defense supports recognition of the WASP's service to their country during World War II. We believe their service should be treated as active duty in the Armed Forces of the United States for purposes of laws administered by the Veterans Administration." It was a huge turning point for the WASP. The *Stars and Stripes* printed the letter in its entirety, and the women rejoiced at their good fortune.

Days passed. As Congress debated the bill with their precious amendment attached, Bee, Elaine, Teresa, and dozens of other WASP nervously waited, many of them watching from the balcony wearing their blue uniforms and silver wings. Congresswoman Heckler kept pushing, and finally the bill came before the House for a vote on November 3, 1977.

After so many years of hoping and waiting—and the failure of so many other bills in the past—it must have seemed to the women as if they would never win, that they would be trapped forever in the limbo of committees and hearings. Yet this time was different. On November 3 the bill was approved by Congress. The next day it was also approved by the Senate. The women had achieved their long-awaited victory.

The WASP who had gathered in D.C. laughed out loud and hugged one another, later offering toast after toast to their heroes of the fight. Patricia Collins Hughes wrote in the *Stars and Stripes* that week that "our clamor for recognition is nearing an end. Our triumphant journey will be climaxed by the President's signature affirming our precious status."

Teresa could hardly believe it. She'd written hundreds of letters and made hundreds of phone calls over the past two decades. Now it was over. She only regretted that Nancy Love hadn't lived long enough to see the bill pass. Dora, for her part, was proud—and relieved.

On November 23, 1977, President Carter signed H.R. 8701, which carried the amendment "officially declaring the Women Airforce Service Pilots as having served on active duty in the

Armed Forces of the United States for purposes of laws administered by the Veterans Administration." After the signing, Bruce
Arnold and his wife invited the women to their home to celebrate.
That night someone asked Elaine Harmon how much the WASP
had spent on the effort. She replied, "Not much," to which the individual informed her that he had never heard of a bill going
through Congress that didn't cost "at least seventy-five thousand
dollars." The women had done the job for just $12,000.

Although the WASP were jubilant, the reality was that their
recognition as veterans was late in many ways. By 1979, when the
Department of Defense finally issued their discharge certificates,
most of the World War II G.I. benefits were long gone. At least the
women could now be admitted to Veterans Administration hospi-
tals and buried in military cemeteries, and Teresa and others who
served after World War II assumed their time in the WASP counted
toward their retirement benefits.

"We were sent the ribbons and medals to which we were entitled," Dora recalled. "I received the American Campaign Medal,
WWII Victory Medal and Honorable Service Lapel pin . . . But, I
believe that for all of us, the most important aspect of the recognition was just that . . . the recognition. No longer did we hold the
title of 'forgotten women pilots.' Our Uncle Sam had recognized
us as his first military women pilots. We could now take our place
proudly, and with honor among those who served, fought, and
died for their country."

In 2014, family and friends of the WASP joined sponsor Wingtip-to-Wingtip Association to share the WASP story with a float in the Tournament of Roses Parade. *Photo by and courtesy of Katherine Sharp Landdeck*

CHAPTER TWENTY-EIGHT

The Final Flight

Jackie was surprised but pleased for the women when the news of their veteran status came in—but she was too sick to celebrate with them. In her final years she retreated from the public eye, from her frenetic travel schedule, and from her social life. Floyd, who had suffered for years with debilitating arthritis, had died on June 17, 1976, and Jackie never fully recovered from his death. Floyd had been her staunchest ally. He'd used his money and power to help her achieve her goals, but perhaps even more vital was the constant encouragement and emotional support he offered her. He had been in every way her ideal partner. After Floyd died she lost a piece of herself. She never held another party.

Although she remained close with her good friend Chuck Yeager, she saw less and less of the WASP and no longer attended reunions and events. She continued to have stomach troubles, heart trouble, and possibly arthritis. By the summer of 1980 Jackie's pacemaker was not functioning well. She'd been through at least three of them, none of them able to keep up with her hectic schedule. She was swollen with fluid and her legs were cracked and bleeding. Stubborn to the end, she refused to lie down because she was terrified of dying in bed. Her illness had been protracted, but in the end she died peacefully, while sleeping in her wheelchair, on August 9, 1980.

The service for Jackie three days later was a small, private ceremony at Coachella Valley Public Cemetery near her home in Indio. Jackie was laid to rest in a simple casket with a large spray of yellow roses, her favorite, laid over the top. The beautiful doll she won back in the 1920s—the one that had been taken away from her and then returned in exchange for her financial support of the family—was placed in her arms. She had told friends she wanted the doll with her if she went to heaven—but she wanted the sword the U.S. Air Force Academy cadets had given her in 1975 as well, so she could fight her way out if she went to hell. In the end she sent the sword to the academy, where today it sits in their exhibit to her accomplishments.

After the success of the 1977 bill, the WASP believed that their fight was over. It was only when some of the women began to apply for new civil service jobs or process their retirements from the military that they realized there was a problem: their service during the war still did not count toward veterans' preference in jobs or toward retirement.

When Teresa first began her battle for recognition, she was largely motivated by the desire to include the time she spent in the WASP toward her retirement from the military, and for others to be eligible for job preference in federal or state employment. But it turned out that the language of the amendment limited the benefits the WASP could actually receive. Their bill "provided that WASP service shall be considered active duty for the purposes of all laws administered by the Veterans Administration." Since the bill specifically said "Veterans Administration," this meant that other offices—such as the Office of Personnel Management—were within their legal rights to deny the women benefits from their department.

Elaine Harmon was one of the women directly affected by the language of the bill. She had joined the reserves after the war and then lost her commission when the Air Force realized she had children under the age of eighteen. She was widowed in 1965 and hoped for veterans' preference in the competitive 1980s job market, which was particularly challenging for a woman in her early sixties. Elaine applied for a civil service position, but quickly realized that she wasn't being given veterans' job preference points as she should have been. When she asked about it, a manager in the Pittsburgh branch of the Office of Personnel Management (OPM) told her that WASP service was not considered active duty "under the veteran preference laws." The OPM felt it was not obliged, or even allowed, to offer Elaine veterans' preference.

Elaine was frustrated—and furious at being denied the very advantages the WASP had worked so hard to secure. She decided to do something. In 1981 she went back to Congress to fight for full veterans' benefits. Despite the support of a handful of WASP, including a frustrated Teresa, Elaine felt very lonely in her fight. The women who had rallied together to be remembered in 1977 believed the victory had been won. Very few even realized another battle was being fought on their behalf. Elaine made certain the women's champion Barry Goldwater learned about the narrow way departments like the Office of Personnel Management were interpreting the law. Goldwater was livid:

"You will recall the very reason WASPs did not qualify initially for active duty service was a discriminatory government ruling that women were not 'persons,'" Goldwater wrote to Elaine. "If women were 'persons' under the law, they would have been eligible to be commissioned as officers during World War II. This is the error Congress knowingly overturned by enacting PL95-202. Any effort to revive this kind of narrow thinking to disqualify women in 1981 is unconscionable and must be rejected."

On September 29, 1981, Elaine appeared before the House Committee on Veterans' Affairs. She spent much of her testimony again justifying the WASP's veteran status and describing her own experience in the job market. Another WASP, Jeanne L. McSheehy, testified about having been denied retirement credit for her service in the WASP, as well as a denial from the Social Security Administration that had even ended in a request for Jeanne to issue them a refund check.

After the testimonies were over and the hearings concluded, Elaine, Teresa, and their supporters waited. Nothing happened. No one followed up with Elaine; no decisions were made. Without the loud collective voice of the WASP, the press, and their political supporters, Congress simply moved on. In July the following year, she finally received a letter from Sonny Montgomery, chair of the House Committee on Veterans' Affairs, who declared her issue should be taken up with the Post Office and Civil Service Committee and recommended she request the committee consider amending the veterans' preference laws to include the honorably discharged WASP. In other words, the Committee on Veterans' Affairs felt the WASP were no longer their problem. The political climate had changed substantially by the 1980s. That same year, 1982, the Equal Rights Amendment expired, with only thirty-five of the thirty-eight states needed voting in favor of ratification. It seemed that Elaine had reached a dead end. "How many closed doors can you go up against?" she later asked.

Unable to rally enough support for another fight, Elaine and Teresa moved on. Teresa had retired from the reserves in 1976, expecting that her two years as a WASP would count toward her pension. With this interpretation of the law, her retirement pay was half what it would have been with those years added in. The lack of fairness was familiar, but the women, proud and determined not to be seen as victims, moved forward, embracing their veteran title despite the limited actual benefits. At least they would receive some medical assistance and a flag on their coffins at their funerals. That was going to have to be enough.

The WASP spent the next few years focused on submitting the proper paperwork to receive the benefits for which they were eligible. Now that the women were in their sixties and seventies, they also began thinking about their legacy. WASP Bee Haydu and Sara Payne Hayden created a new nonprofit, which became the Women Military Aviators, an organization that today is made up of modern military women pilots inspired by the WASP and their work. Young women pilots who had come into the military in the 1970s and after were now being allowed to train with men, but they still had to fight for the chance to fly each and every plane—and they often found themselves serving on bases where they were the only women. They were facing challenges because of their gender, just as the WASP had, but without a community of women pilots to sustain them. The goal of the WMA was to provide that much-needed sisterhood and offer young women pilots resources to help sustain them. After much, often cantankerous debate, the WASP also decided to set aside the name Order of Fifinella for their organization. In the fall of 1982, they elected a new board under new bylaws and a new name: Women Airforce Service Pilots, Inc.

Nineteen eighty-four marked the fortieth anniversary of the disbandment of the WASP, and the fortieth anniversary of the year Teresa James lost her husband, Dink. Teresa was in her seventies now, and despite having lived a lifetime without Dink, she still had so many unanswered questions. The military had only given her minimal information about the crash, and although Teresa had spoken briefly with the gunner on Dink's plane a few years after the war, there was so much she didn't know about his final moments. Was Dink killed instantly when the plane was hit by antiaircraft fire? Did he die when the plane crashed? Did he somehow survive the crash and succumb to his injuries later? Forty years after Dink's death, Teresa finally got the chance to lay some of these questions to rest when she received an invitation to travel to France to commemorate the fortieth anniversary of D-Day.

The invitation came from the International P-47 Thunderbolt Pilot's Association, a group wanting to honor women like Teresa who had worked to deliver P-47 airplanes during the war. When Teresa learned the reunion would take place in Paris, she dug up her old telegrams and confirmed the name of the town where Dink's plane had gone down. It was Joinville-le-Pont, less than ten miles outside of the city. Teresa decided to go to Paris for the reunion and visit the town where Dink's plane crashed while she was there. She wrote to the mayor of Joinville-le-Pont to let him know she would like to come and why. The mayor contacted the president of the local veterans' association. A few weeks later Teresa received another letter saying that eyewitnesses to the crash had been found. They were still living in the same small town all these years later.

On May 27, 1984, Teresa arrived in Joinville-le-Pont, a pretty town on the banks of the river Marne. After a full reception at the city hall, Teresa was taken to the crash site. There she stood in front of a house that had been hit by the B-17's wing as it came down. The same woman who had been living in the house forty years before was still there, and Teresa was able to speak to her about her memories of the event. The woman explained that it felt like a miracle that the large bomber had crashed in the middle of the narrow street, largely avoiding people's homes and preventing further casualties. Teresa felt certain that the miraculous landing was Dink's doing. On the wrought-iron fence in front of the house was a plaque that read in French: IN HONOR OF THE NINE AMERI-CAN AIRMEN WHO GAVE THEIR LIVES FOR FREEDOM. It was marked June 22, 1944. Teresa was overcome with emotion; the last letter she'd received from Dink bore the same date.

That same day Teresa met with two other eyewitnesses. They were men in their fifties now, but in 1944 they had been seventeen-year-old boys. The day of the crash, they had been sheltering in a garage after the air-raid siren had gone off. They showed Teresa their hiding place, describing for her the roar of the plane over-head as it came, the terrifying sound of the aircraft shattering on impact. When the two young men emerged from the garage, they saw the smoldering plane and a body that had been thrown from it, landing between two trees. They rushed the man to the hospi-tal, but he was already dead. It was Dink.

After the visit to the site of the crash, Teresa returned to the city hall with the mayor. There he presented her with a large piece of landing gear that had been recovered from the downed B-17. On it was a gold plate that read, IN MEMORY OF GEORGE L. MARTIN. She was also given a dog tag from one of Dink's crew members and a coin that had been found where Dink's body was discov-ered. The man who gave her the coin explained that his father had carried it with him ever since the war as a talisman. It was clear that the town of Joinville-le-Pont had not forgotten Teresa's hus-band, and now they were honoring her for her loss. She stood to thank them, but all she could do was cry.

On her way home to Florida, Teresa reflected on her visit and all it had meant to her. Although her eyes were still misted with tears, she could see the streets and gray-roofed buildings of Paris below. Had Dink seen the city like that as he flew over it, or was it always covered in clouds that spring? During her long flight home, Teresa wrote down a record of everything that had happened in France, detailing all she'd learned, just as she'd once written in her diary all those years ago. In her elegant, curling script she pre-served her story, and Dink's, over sixteen pages.

"He was an excellent pilot," she wrote. "We both had two loves—each other and flying."

After returning from France, Teresa James lived another two decades. She never even came close to remarrying; no one had touched her heart like Dink had. She died in hospice care, in Florida, after a brief illness, in August 2008 at the age of ninety-seven. Teresa had always loved to laugh and make others laugh along with her, and she kept her sense of humor to the very end. It had been a good life, filled with friends, flying, and plenty of stories. It had not been everything she'd wanted, but it had been more than enough.

After testifying before Congress in the late 1970s, Dora Dougherty Strother continued to work at Bell Helicopter for another ten years, until her retirement in 1987. During the course of her outstanding career, she had broken records and barriers and served on presidential committees, fulfilling every dream her suffragette mother could have had for her emancipated daughter.

Dora continued to do all she could to advocate for the WASP and to preserve their legacy. She began working on her memoirs, describing her time during the war. In the early 1990s, together with Marty and their fellow WASP Pat Pateman, Dora helped to find a home for Marty's WASP archives and Dora's own extensive collection. The three women visited universities across the country, including several women's colleges. In the end they all agreed the best home for their collection was at Texas Woman's University in Denton, Texas. Just three hours from Sweetwater and five from Houston, the university was a public institution primarily for women, and the head of the library, Elizabeth Snapp, was dedicated to preserving the WASP's story. In 1993 the WASP formally voted and declared their home within the Woman's Collection at TWU, and the women began sending the library materials that would help preserve their story.

In 2001, Dora's beloved husband, Lester, passed away. Although she had married late by the standards of the time, the couple had spent three and a half decades together—happy years. Dora was still grieving for Lester when her association with the WASP brought another important man into her life. His name was Harry McKeown. Dora and Harry had first met very briefly at Clovis Army Air Force Base back in 1944, when she was touring with Colonel Tibbets in the B-29. In 1995, Harry came across an article about Dora that mentioned her service, and he decided to write to her, letting her know he remembered her from her WASP days. "You came to show us that the B-29 plane was not one to be feared," Harry wrote. "You were the pilot that day and demonstrated your excellent flying skills and convinced us the B-29 was the plane that any pilot could be proud to fly. From that day on we never had a pilot who didn't want to fly the B-29." Since then, Harry and Dora had stayed in touch.

"Harry McKeown turned out to be the second love of my life," Dora wrote in her memoirs. He had lost his wife to cancer several years before. Together, Harry and Dora, a widower and a widow, former pilots, and veterans, started a new life together. They married in November 2002, ten days before Dora's eighty-second birthday.

The final WASP reunion took place in September 2008 in Irving, Texas. The women were in their eighties and nineties now, and old age was catching up with them. The leaders were all gone—Nancy, Jackie, and even Betty Gillies. Teresa had passed away earlier in the summer. Brilliant, generous Dora had recently been diagnosed with Alzheimer's and could not attend.

Only one hundred of the three hundred WASP remaining were able to make it to Irving, some in wheelchairs, many with canes, most with family alongside lending a hand when needed. But many of the women were still in remarkably good shape, astonishing the staff at the hotel, who couldn't believe this boisterous crowd was the group of "old" ladies they had expected.

Marty Wyall was there, as spry as ever, running from group to group, catching up with friends.

Betty Blake—who had witnessed the attack on Pearl Harbor from her balcony and then joined the first class of WASP in Houston—attended, her long hair up in a bun as she laughed and told stories of flying those pursuit planes. Maggie Gee and Elaine Harmon from class 44-W-9 were reunited, comparing stories of their days in training and active duty. Nell "Mickey" Bright was there and, while missing her classmates Caro and Kaddy, was sure to tell everyone stories of class 43-W-7, "the best class there ever was!"

There were ice sculptures of the WASP wings and an AT-6 plane after BJ Williams said it wouldn't be a party without ice sculptures. Sponsors who were old friends of the WASP helped out, and dozens of aviation supporters filled the hospitality room with flowers as the women spent time walking from wall to wall, looking at the hundreds of wartime photos that had been pinned up for them to remember the planes they'd flown and to show their families what they had done during the war.

The highlight of the reunion took place at the banquet dinner on the final night. Friends of the WASP arranged for eighty-six U.S. Air Force reservist women to attend the event to assist the women and their families. Led by Colonel Sandra Opeka of the U.S. Air Force Reserve, the women marched into the banquet room in two flights, one wearing their class A (dress) uniforms, the other wearing flight suits. As the WASP looked on, the reservists lined up precisely on either side of the banquet stage and remained at attention. Then several of them took turns stepping forward and reading a quote from a WASP, something that had inspired them. The crowd smiled and mumbled the names of the WASP when they recognized their words. "Honor is everything." *Shutsy*. "The harder you work, the luckier you get." *Bee Haydu*.

They read some twenty quotes, then the reservists stepped back into place and together presented arms to—or saluted—the women. Stunned by the honor, the WASP solemnly saluted back. The room was filled with goosebumps and tears.

The night ended with an address by Major Nicole Malachowski—the first female U.S. Air Force Thunderbird pilot. Nicole explained that her call sign was "Fifi," in tribute to the WASP's mascot Fifinella. She described how important Fifi was to her and other women pilots she knew. Some of them wove the mascot into their own patches or painted her on the seats in their cockpits. Others wore bracelets or other symbols of the WASP, channeling the strength and pioneering spirit of the earlier generation. The WASP legacy was clear.

There was one final honor in store for the women. In June 2009, Congress voted to give the women of the WASP the Congressional Gold Medal, the highest civilian honor that Congress can bestow. The following March, more than two hundred WASP, all in their eighties and nineties, traveled to Washington, D.C., to personally accept the medal. The WASP and their supporters gathered in Emancipation Hall, in the Capitol Visitor Center, as members of the House of Representatives gave tributes. In her speech, House Speaker Nancy Pelosi pointed out that the women had gone unrecognized for far too long. "Women Airforce Service Pilots, we are all your daughters; you taught us how to fly," Pelosi said. After the ceremony each WASP was formally presented with her own medal by a female member of the U.S. Air Force or the U.S. Air Force Reserve.

Finally, their service—and their sacrifice—had not been forgotten.

Elaine Harmon grins as she waves goodbye during a flight in a Stearman biplane. *Photo by Don Sloan. Courtesy of Terry Harmon*

Epilogue

As the women began to pass away in greater and greater numbers, the remaining WASP attended as many of their funerals as they could. On September 7, 2016, Marty Wyall was one of three WASP who traveled to Arlington National Cemetery in Virginia for Elaine Harmon's funeral. Elaine had died the year before, in April 2015, but it had taken over a year to arrange for her interment. When her family had originally reached out to the cemetery to make arrangements, they received stunning news. As of 2015, WASP were no longer eligible to be placed at Arlington.

Simply put, the cemetery was running out of room. As the

Vietnam generation began to reach their sixties and seventies, Secretary of the Army John McHugh became concerned about capacity. He made the decision that the WASP, and the thirty-seven other groups who tagged along on Public Law 95-202, were no longer going to be eligible to be interred at Arlington. His argument was that the way the 1977 law was written, the WASP had served on "active duty in the Armed Forces of the United States for purposes of laws administered by the Veterans Administration." Since 1973, Arlington National Cemetery has been run by the secretary of the Army, not the Veterans Administration. So while the WASP were still eligible to be laid to rest at VA cemeteries, they were not allowed at Arlington. Once again the WASP were being denied on a technicality.

Elaine herself had attended funerals at Arlington for other members of the WASP and had made clear that she wanted the same when her own time came. When her family learned that Arlington would no longer honor the WASP, they decided they weren't going to take no for an answer. They used social media to circulate a petition, earning over 178,000 signatures, and walked the halls of Congress talking with as many people as they could, getting the attention of Senator Barbara Mikulski of Maryland, who had introduced the legislation to get the women the Congressional Gold Medal in 2009, and Senator Joni Ernst, the first female combat veteran in the Senate. Representatives Martha McSally of Arizona, a U.S. Air Force pilot and friend of the WASP, and Susan Davis of California joined the cause. McSally took the battle personally and met with Arlington administrators to try to find a solution but was told only a law specifically allowing the WASP to be interred at Arlington could fix the problem. So her office worked to write the legislation that would do just that. In May 2016 it was passed and signed into law by President Obama. One year and five months after her death, Elaine's place at Arlington was finally assured.

Marty made her way from Indiana for the funeral, traveling alone. This time, at least, she allowed the airport personnel to push her in a wheelchair to baggage claim. She didn't really need the wheelchair, she said, but it made the airport staff feel good to help her and so she let them. There were so few of the women left. Dora Dougherty Strother McKeown had passed away in 2013 at the age of ninety-one from complications from Alzheimer's. Elaine's classmate and dear friend Maggie Gee had died the year after that, in 2014.

The day of the funeral, Marty, along with her fellow WASP Shutsy Reynolds and Shirley Kruse, gathered with the rest of Elaine's family and friends around a small tent up the hill from the Arlington columbarium. There was a radiant blue sky overhead. Elaine's family took their places, seated in chairs in a formal, quiet mood. An Army chaplain gave a brief service, then seven men and women gave a twenty-one-gun salute. A bugler stood away from the mourners, a little up the hillside, surrounded by gravestones, and somberly played taps as a young woman Air Force captain presented Elaine's family with her hard-won flag: "Day is done, gone the sun, From the lake, from the hills, from the sky; All is well, safely rest, God is nigh."

Elaine's ashes were interred in the columbarium behind a little green curtain. After the interment, a service was held at the nearby Women in Military Service for America Memorial, a beautiful museum at the doorstep of Arlington National Cemetery. The tributes to Elaine at the service were lively and celebratory. She had lived a life of adventure, from her time as a WASP to bungee jumping while she was in her eighties. Elaine was kindhearted and much loved, especially by the WASP, who knew she had spent much of the past forty years working to make certain they were not forgotten. The service ended with a rousing rendition of the official song of the U.S. Air Force: "Off we go into the wild blue yonder . . ."

The room was filled with emotion. It was almost as if Elaine and the rest of the WASP could be heard singing along, "Climbing high into the sun . . ."

Mary Anna Martin Wyall, the pastor's daughter from Indiana, the last to join, was there to witness it all, keeping the memory safe, loyal WASP historian to the end.

The author with Caro Bayley Bosca and Curtis Pitts, in Bartlesville, Oklahoma, June 5, 1993.

Author's Note

We cannot always trace the beginnings of a lifelong project to one moment in time, but I know the very day this book began. On a sunny June 5, 1993, I went to the Bartlesville Bi-Plane Expo and in a moment of luck and fate I met Caro Bayley Bosca, a WASP of World War II. It was one of those lightning moments, and I realized that this was what I wanted to do with my life. I spent the next three years reading everything I could about the WASP, who I'd never heard of before despite my bachelor's in history and love of aviation. I decided to go to graduate school at the University of Tennessee to learn how to study their history the "right" way, and in 1996 I started my initial oral histories with the WASP. When I began, the women were in their early seventies. They were sharp, funny, and eager to tell their stories. My little Radio Shack tape recorder (with pop-up microphone) recorded them all whether as formal oral histories appropriate for my professors to hear, or more casual reminiscences about planes, flying, personalities, and war told over evening cocktails. These personal histories, hundreds of them, flowed as I worked through my PhD and down through the years to an email I received just last week. And when the last WASP has made her final flight, I'll treasure new letters, diaries, and photographs shared by their sons and daughters. There are so many stories still to be told.

The women's own words, gathered either from my own or others' oral histories with them, as well as their letters, diaries, memoirs, and speeches, are at the heart of this book. But as a historian I know that despite their value, these sources are often only part of the story, so I turned to more traditional sources such as government documents, accident reports, newspaper articles, and photographs to help me understand a more complete history of the WASP. I have worked to corroborate all of my sources, following the rule of three whenever possible. That said, details can be missed despite due diligence, and I regret any mistakes that may be in this work.

As this is a work of serious nonfiction, the women and men profiled in this book are all real people and their real names have been used. You may note that the first names of many WASP are used throughout, while other people are referred to by their last names. This was a deliberate choice. I was fortunate enough to know most of the WASP named in the book. While I never met Jacqueline Cochran or Nancy Love, I knew Teresa James, Dora Dougherty Strother McKeown, and Marty Wyall personally. I interviewed most of the other WASP mentioned throughout the book as well. It felt awkward and distancing to call Marty, who I've known for over twenty years, "Wyall." More important, as many of the WASP in the book married during or after the war—

some of them, like Dora, more than once—using first names also allowed me to avoid the confusion of switching between maiden names and married names.

While my endnotes cite specific sources utilized in the text, they do not include the many sources that deeply influenced this work. Serious researchers and just the curious of heart may find a full bibliography along with comments about some particular sources on my personal website, katherinesharplanddeck.com. Notes on my methodology and other topics of interest to historians may be found there, along with stories about many of the other WASP I knew personally and studied but was unable to include in this book.

The Women with Silver Wings covers the lifetime of the women of the WASP. It was important to them and to me that their whole story, full of triumphs and reversals, be properly told. Thanks for following the WASP on their journey. They would hope that you walk away remembering that they were the first American women to fly for their country. And they would want to inspire you to find something you are passionate about in life and *go for it*.

Katherine Sharp Landdeck
Denton, Texas

Acknowledgments

How can I possibly begin to thank all of the people who have helped me learn and tell the WASP story over the past twenty-six years? It is overwhelming and humbling to reflect upon this journey. I cannot possibly name everyone, but please know that every question about my work, every bit of encouragement, every filled seat at talks, provided the fuel to reach this point. I am grateful to you whether your name is found in these pages or not.

My first thanks must go to the pilot of the red Pitts Special at the Bartlesville Bi-Plane Expo in June 1993 who, upon finding me on my toes peering into his plane, kindly pointed to the shade of the hangar where Curtis Pitts, the famed aircraft designer, sat, and then encouraged me to go say hello. I don't know your name, but Curtis introduced me to the woman at his side, Caro Bayley Bosca, and this adventure of my lifetime began. So thanks.

Years later Caro liked to tell the story of the day she "found" me, and how she was sure I was about thirteen years old (I was twenty-three). On the day we first met she was kind enough to write her name and address on an orange index card she had in her purse for note taking, and told me to write to her if I wanted to learn more. In 1996 I pulled out that card, which I'd carried in my bag for three years since Caro handed it to me, and wrote to her, beginning my letter with, "You probably don't remember me . . ." She invited me to the WASP induction into the National Aviation Hall of Fame in Dayton, Ohio, and, after help from WASP Nadine Nagle, to get the itinerary and into the right hotel (as well as a stern introduction from Nadine to her fellow WASP: "This is Katy. She is a history student who wants to learn more about us. Be nice to her"), I began my oral histories.

My professors at the University of Tennessee, particularly my mentors Susan Becker and Charles Johnson, had guided me on how to conduct the histories, and Elaine Harmon and Ruth Kearney were kind enough to be my first interviewees. I interviewed Caro along with Katherine "Kaddy" Landry Steele that weekend, too. Margaret Ray Ringenberg trustingly loaned me her roster so I could run to the local copy store and have the addresses of all the WASP so I could send them my questionnaires later that summer. From that Ohio gathering in the summer of 1996 I found my way to my first WASP reunion in California that fall. Violet Thurn Cowden befriended me there, and her encouragement and friendship continue to sustain me despite the fact that we lost her in 2011. Dawn Rochow Balden Seymour gave me the first of several interviews, which began years of friendship as well.

I was fortunate to get to interview so many WASP, traveling to their gatherings three or four times a year, in the beginning thanks to some financial support from the University of Tennessee's Department of History. Professor Yen Ping Hao always seemed to find a little extra Bernadotte Schmidt money to help me get where I needed to go. Susan Becker helped me shape my study of the WASP from the beginning—helping me see the women beyond their obvious cool factor and putting them into the context of women's and American history. William Bruce Wheeler, Steven Ash, and Vejas Liulevicius encouraged me throughout my time at Tennessee. Other faculty members who worked with me on my thesis or dissertation include G. Kurt Piehler, Janis Appier, Lorri Glover, Steve Pope, and Elizabeth Haiken. John Finger was particularly supportive as well. Fellow graduate students Nancy

Schurr, Brad Austin, and Stephen Berry helped me survive the realities of graduate school and continue to encourage me today. My work at the Center for the Study of War and Society brought me in touch with many inspiring veterans and writers, and best of all my good friend Cynthia Tinker. Thanks to you all.

While I got to know many of the WASP, those I became closest to were the "Oshkosh WASP"—those women who attended the Experimental Aircraft Association's annual fly-in in Wisconsin each summer. The day Scotty Gough gave me one of her peanut butter and orange marmalade sandwiches was the day I knew I'd been accepted as part of their group. Ethel Finley seemed to know I was in it for the long haul and quickly had me moderating talks with the WASP and promising to tell their story even when they were gone. There were so many others—Kaddy Landry Steele, Caro, Nell "Mickey" Stevenson Bright, Betty Brown, Betty Jo Reed, Betty Strohfus, Margaret Ringenberg, Dot Swain Lewis, Bee Haydu, and of course Shutsy Reynolds, whose trust and friendship meant so much to me. The volunteers at EAA, many of whom I still see year after year, made it easier for the WASP to attend, and thus for me to spend time with them. The fellows on the West Ramp who helped us set up and take down and kept our water jugs full were the WASP's heroes (and mine)—especially those years our tent flooded. Patrick and his tech crew in the museum, Mark Forss, Sue Anderson, Chris Henry, the "A" team, and countless others at EAA—thanks for all you did for us and continue to do.

The next generation of women military pilots have continued to motivate and inspire me to tell the story of the WASP. The late Captain Rosemary Mariner mentored and befriended me from my time in graduate school, and aided in my understanding of some of the realities of military life. Trish Beckman, a trailblazer herself, always made sure I was included at the WASP table, and asked, "So how's it going?"—making clear by her tone that she fully expected me to finish this book one day. Lucy Young has encouraged me for many years too. So many other of the Gen 2 women and members of the Women Military Aviators have encouraged and prodded me down this road. They have inspiring stories of their own still waiting to be told.

I was so fortunate to know the women who led us through the WASP story in this book. I chose them in part because I knew them (they were all alive when I began) and I could ask them questions as I worked. I also chose Teresa, Marty, and Dora because they traveled through the entire WASP experience, from beginning to end, and they all had letters or diaries from the war years. I am grateful for all three agreeing to be a part of the book, and for the time they spent answering my questions and pointing me to sources.

Other WASP who were particularly helpful over time include Mary Regalbutto Jones, Lois Hollingsworth Ziler, Betty Nicholas, Lucile Wise, Beverly Beesemeyer, Alyce Rohrer, Flora Belle Reece, Emma Coulter Ware, Iris Critchell, Kay Hillbrandt, Dorothy Lucas, and Charlyne Creger. Jeanette Gagnon Goodrum and Jean Terrell Moreo McCreery were particularly good to me. Mickey Bright and Bee Haydu continue to help me to this day. Tuskegee Airman Colonel Charles McGee has been a good friend for many years, too.

In the 1990s the WASP voted to place their group and individual collections at Texas Woman's University in Denton, Texas, creating the Official WASP Archive. I've been told I was the first researcher to utilize the new WASP Collection that summer of 1996. I can't thank enough the archivists and library staff, from the beginning with Nancy Durr, the late Dawn Letson, Elizabeth Snapp, and my dear friend Tracey MacGowan (and Marco too), to today with Kimberly Johnson, Shelia Bickle, and Corynthia Dorgan. Countless staff, student assistants, and even some of my own interns transcribed letters, scanned pictures, and made countless copies for me, and, while I may not have all of their names, they should know their work was important and I am grateful.

Archivists and colleagues at other research locations have

helped shape my study of the WASP over the years as well. The archives at the U.S. Air Force Academy in Colorado hold Yvonne "Pat" Pateman's papers, and the archivists were very generous in helping me early in my study. A chance meeting with Margaret Weitekamp when we were both graduate students led to a continuing friendship, and an eventual Guggenheim Fellowship and work with Dominic Pisano and Dorothy Cochrane at the Smithsonian National Air and Space Museum. The archivists at the NASM have been continually helpful to my work as well. National Archives II in College Park, Maryland, is one of my favorite places in the world. The archivists and staff encouraged my questions and forgave my whoops of joy when I found the boxes that held the more than 25,000 letters of inquiry—all from women who had hoped to join the WASP. It was a humbling moment to see their passion for aviation and for their country handwritten on personal stationery and carefully typed on onionskin paper. The Library of Congress—not the fancy one but the low-ceilinged one across the street, with old-fashioned lockers and smart, enthusiastic archivists who helped me find even more documents, all the way down to General Arnold's phone records—was a pleasure to work in, too. While I love the convenience of our digital age, being able to research in a physical archive and touch pieces of paper that shaped the past will never get old to me. The archivists who keep it all straight are my heroes.

I haven't always been able to travel and appreciate the work of those I have not yet had a chance to meet in person, and their superior finding aids. The ever-patient Mary Burzloff at the Eisenhower Library sent me copies of invaluable documents tied with a little bow, and noticed materials I didn't ask for that she thought might be—and were—helpful. Virginia Lewick, expert in all things Eleanor Roosevelt at the Franklin D. Roosevelt Library, put little notes on the documents she sent me, so I would know whose handwritten scribbles I was reading alongside the typewritten words. Michael Sharaba at the International Women's Air and Space Museum generously scanned the documents I needed, always enthusiastically insisting "This is why we are here!" Shaylyn Sawyer at the Ninety-Nines Museum of Women Pilots and Stephanie Berry of the National Aeronautic Association helped corroborate details. Linda Barnickel and Elizabeth Odle at the Nashville Public Library were helpful with information about Cornelia. Renee Jones of the St. Louis Public Library went the extra mile and found some quite unexpected but incredibly helpful materials about Teresa and Dink. Debbie Seracini at the San Diego Air and Space Museum helped with documents and some terrific photos.

The work of other historians and archivists filled in details that helped my understanding and hopefully made this story of the WASP a bit more interesting. My friend Julia Lauria-Blum of the Cradle of Aviation Museum was particularly helpful with details about Teresa. Terry Mace of the United Kingdom generously shared information he had gathered about the American women who served with the ATA, particularly Helen Richey. Howard Kroplick opened my eyes to the existence of the Long Island Aviation Country Club, and then kindly scanned the full 1940 membership book and shared it with me, allowing me to confirm my suspicion about the small world that was elite aviation in the prewar years. Julia Scatliff O'Grady found a transcript of a phone call between Eleanor Roosevelt and CAA head Robert Hinckley during her own research, and very thoughtfully copied it and sent it to me. H. O. Malone shared his files on Nancy Love with me, and Deborah Douglas shared her materials, knowledge, and friendship as well. Sally Van Wagenen Keil donated her transcripts and notes to TWU and talked with me about them when I had questions. Maryann Bucknum Brinley kindly talked with me about the interviews she did for her work on Jackie. Doris Rich wrote fabulous, detailed footnotes in her biography of Jacqueline Cochran. Rob Simbeck shared some of his research on Cornelia Fort and encouraged me to keep after the WASP story. Sarah Byrn Rickman helped me get started on my research on Nancy.

What historian is so lucky as to get a job as a professor just a short walk across campus from the archive they need the most for their research? Some days I still cannot believe my luck and am so grateful for the support of my current and retired colleagues in the Department of History and Political Science at TWU: Lybeth Hodges, Barbara Presnall, Paul Travis, Val Belfiglio, Tim Hoye, Jim Alexander, Pat Devereaux, Martina Will de Chapparro, Jacob Blosser, Sara Fanning, Parker Hevron, Jon Olsen, Jennifer Danley-Scott, Wouter von Evre, Clare Brock, Vivienne Born, Donna Rizos, Cynthia Lewis, and the late Jeff Robb and Dorothy DeMoss. Special thanks to Mark Kessler, who told me to take time to think and helped me have the courage to write the book I wanted to write. Their continued support, encouragement, and patience over the years are much appreciated. Other constant supporters at TWU include Hugh Burns, who boldly interrupted my job interview to insist they must hire me, and Phyllis Bridges, who took me under her wing early and supports me to this day. Historian Linda Kerber (University of Iowa) encouraged my study of the WASP when I was a graduate student and most recently taught me the value of saying, "Alas, I cannot," as I struggled to find time to write. My thanks would be incomplete without a note to my students. Their questions, encouragement, and excitement kept me on my path on days I wanted to stop, and they helped remind me of who it was I wanted to know this story.

The kids of the WASP (they call themselves KOWs), including Albert "Chig" Lewis, Doug Durham, Emily Friend, Meg Farrell, Andy Hailey, Cybil Ewalt, Sherry Dunn, Art Roberts, Julie Englund, Helen Hall, Eileen McDargh, and many others have supported my work and told other kids of WASP that they could trust me as I talked with their mothers. You won't all find your mothers' names in here—but please know I haven't forgotten them. They are in here, even if they remain unnamed. Teresa James's nieces, Yvonne James and Catherine Mowry have been very helpful and I am grateful to them for their trust. Nancy Love's daughter Allie Love and great-nephew Nick Knobil both helped with my understanding of Nancy's personality and feelings post-war. While I'd known Elaine Harmon since 1996, I got to know her family, especially Terry Harmon, Whitney Miller, Tiffany Miller, and Erin Miller, in 2016 when we worked on the bill to get the WASP back into Arlington National Cemetery. I can see Elaine's smarts and stubbornness in all of them. A special note of thanks must go to Pat Thomas, whose mom, Audrey Tardy of class 43-W-7, I never had a chance to meet. Pat was among the very first of the kids to welcome me into their circle, and has been a friend ever since. She has read drafts of this manuscript, used her fabulous skills in genealogy to confirm my hunches, and sent me notes reminding me why I was doing this just when I needed them most. I will be forever grateful, Pat.

Friends helped me reach this point as well. WASP supporters Sherry Ringler, Sandra Opeka, Gina Louis, Lana Kraeszig, Wendy Cooper—thanks. Dr. Katie Allen, Buck Allen, Barry Holz, and the H2O gang, too. I know there are more, and I see you and thank you. Brian Krause encouraged me as I struggled through tough days in graduate school, and still calls and says, "Should I ask?" before asking how the book is going. Thanks so much, Brian. Misa and Carlos Ramirez sat on their porch and helped me navigate the ins and outs of contracts; Misa, a terrific writer of one of my favorite characters (Lola Cruz), has been irreplaceable as I've learned how to balance life with writing. Carrie Bell, thanks for all of our chats. Liane MacMillan is my very own cheerleader, telling complete strangers about me and my book everywhere, from football games to boat tours in Europe. My Essential Ingredients book club friends have asked me about this book for years, and have patiently not kicked me out as I've missed month after month because of impending deadlines.

Nicholas Fandos wrote a beautiful *New York Times* article about Elaine Harmon's funeral in 2016. He was thoughtful enough to quote me and use my name in the piece. The article drew the attention of the brilliant literary agent Jen Marshall. Her enthusiasm for the WASP and their story, and her faith that I was the right person to write it, changed the direction of my own story. She is also one of the nicest, funniest people I know, and I am grateful to call her my agent and friend. The same Fandos article brought tears to the eyes of Angela Christian, who was so touched by these women's story. It was my pleasure to introduce her to some of them in person. Thomas Kail saw the article too, and I am so thankful for his encouragement and belief that this is an important story. I am so happy for the time you took to come meet Shutsy, Mickey, and Millie.

My editor at Crown Publishing, Emma Berry, has believed in this book from the minute we met, and I've learned much from her guidance. Michael Morris patiently went through several versions of the cover until we reached this beautiful one. The copy editor, David Chesanow, saved me from myself and I can't thank him enough. Elizabeth Eno and Jennifer Rodriguez have made my words look beautiful. The enthusiasm and smart work of Sarah Breivogel and Melissa Esner are much appreciated. Thanks to Lydia Morgan for ably shepherding the paperback. Thanks to Gillian Blake, Annsley Rosner, and David Drake, too. Thanks to the entire Crown team who have worked on this book. After all these years it is humbling to have your help in sharing the story of these women.

The smart, ever-patient, and kind Eve Claxton signed on to help me learn how to shift from academic writing to narrative non-fiction. She got more than she bargained for with this complicated story of many women over many decades. Rolling up her sleeves, she helped me shape this story and find a way to cut hundreds of pages without losing the thread of the history. I learned so much from you, Eve. Thank you for sticking with me. I don't think I would have made it without our weekly calls, your guidance, patience, and hard work. Thanks for bringing Kelly Shetron in to help when time got tight.

My in-laws have helped with this study of the WASP immensely over the past two-plus decades. From loaning me a car to drive to Oshkosh for a week each summer, to tolerating a daughter/sister-in-law who missed dinner nearly every night of her visit because she was with the WASP, to asking thoughtful questions, and sharing my joy and grief, I am so thankful for your support all of these years. So thanks to John Landdeck, Melissa Meyer Landdeck, Jennifer Landdeck, Daniel Landdeck, Amy Scrobel, Brian Scrobel, and all my nieces and nephews, who have spent their entire lives listening to Aunt Kate talk about her WASP.

My mom, Carol Dahlgren Sharp, encouraged me to write ever since I was a kid. When I was young she taught me about family history, and proofread and typed out my school papers (at 90-plus words per minute), always telling me I could do whatever I set my mind to do. She read parts of drafts of this book over the years and always made sure I knew she believed in me. My younger (they would like me to say *much* younger) brother and sister, Richard Sharp and Sarah Sharp, have added so much to my life, and always seemed proud of their big sister, while I am so incredibly proud of both of them. They have offered practical help, too, whether sitting and talking through writing problems or taking on driving duties. My brother very cleverly married an even more clever historian, Libby Hearne, and I have so enjoyed talking through some of these ideas with her. Her notes on an early draft of this book were spot-on and incredibly helpful. I am beyond thankful for all of you.

When I got my PhD my dad, Randall B. Sharp, made T-shirts (many of them) that said "Dr. Kate's Dad" in the upper-left chest, and he wore them everywhere, all the time, just so he could brag about me to anyone who asked about it. He taught me about World War II as we watched the old movies together, helped me with some of my research on the WASP, and in general made it clear that he was very proud of me. I miss him every day.

Caroline and Alice have endured a lifetime of *the book* and put it all into perspective for me. Your encouragement and quiet some days, and your insistence that I have a life away from work on others, helped keep me balanced and happy. Thanks for being you.

Finally, words will never be enough to thank my husband, John. He has traveled by my side this entire journey. He has scheduled his life around WASP events for literally decades. He's talked through ideas big and small, listened to me read chapters out loud, asked questions, and offered tough but fair critiques, always with the goal of helping me feel good about my work in the end. He has been my local expert on all things aviation—whether planes or flying or basic mechanics. He has laughed with the WASP and mourned them with me when they've gone. He has been a true partner in every sense of the word. Thank you, John. Thank you.

As I drove home from the air show on that day in June so many years ago, I set my mind to learning about the WASP and telling their story to as many people as I could. I never want to walk into another roomful of people who have never heard of these inspiring women. As these pages should make clear, I've had a lot of good company along the way.

Katherine Sharp Landdeck
Denton, Texas

In Memoriam

Thirty-eight WASP lost their lives during their service. These are their names.

Jane Champlin	Dorothy Nichols
Susan Clarke	Jeanne L. Norbeck
Margie L. Davis	Margaret Oldenburg
Katherine Dussaq	Mabel Rawlinson
Marjorie Edwards	Gleanna Roberts
Elizabeth Ericson	Marie N. Michell Robinson
Cornelia Fort	Bettie Mae Scott
Frances Grimes	Dorothy Scott
Mary Hartson	Margaret J. Seip
Mary H. Howson	Helen J. Severson
Edith Keene	Marie Sharon
Kathryn B. Lawrence	Evelyn Sharp
Hazel ah Ying Lee	Betty P. Stine
Paula Loop	Marion Toevs
Alice Lovejoy	Gertrude Tompkins
Lea Ola McDonald	Mary Trebing
Peggy Martin	Mary L. Webster
Virginia Moffatt	Bonnie Jean Welz
Beverly Moses	Betty Taylor Wood

NOTES

PROLOGUE

3 **In the quiet early morning** This account of Cornelia Fort's experiences at Pearl Harbor is based on the following sources: Cornelia Fort, "At Twilight's Last Gleaming," *Woman's Home Companion*, July 1943, 19; Cornelia Fort Logbook, Official WASP Archive, Texas Woman's University, Denton, Texas; Cornelia Fort, as quoted in Rob Simbeck, *Daughter of the Air: The Brief Soaring Life of Cornelia Fort* (New York: Atlantic Monthly Press, 1999), 99. She flew an Interstate Cadet, N37345, with a 65-horsepower Continental engine. Thanks to Cornelia's grandnephew Trey Stokes for the word "escaped" to describe Cornelia's feelings about the debutante life. Trey Stokes, personal conversation, June 2019, Denton, Texas.

4 **As she later remembered** While those who restore airplanes and believe they have restored the plane Cornelia Fort flew that day say the plane was trainer blue and yellow, fairly standard for the Cadet, Pearl Harbor historian David Aiken said the plane was vermillion and cream in a detail-filled article about that day. Unfortunately, Aiken died in 2018 so cannot be asked about his sources. I have stuck with blue and yellow in the text until I can find Aiken's evidence. David Aiken, "Out for a Sunday Ride: Civilian Pilots Caught in History's Path," *Flight Journal*, July 2017. Online at https://www.flightjournal.com/wp-content/uploads/2017/07/SundayRide.pdf.

5 **The next day** Betty Guild Tackaberry Blake, interview with author, July 21, 2003, Dayton, Ohio.

CHAPTER 1: AIRMINDED

7 **Only a few short weeks** In addition to specifically cited sources, this account of Teresa James relies on her biography by Jan Churchill, *On Wings to War: Teresa James, Aviator* (Manhattan, KS: Sunflower University Press, 1992), 8–30.

9 **The couple had met** While Teresa's biographer says the couple got together in 1940, Teresa's scrapbook holds a photograph of Teresa and Dink dated 1937, along with several others of her and Dink, sometimes with others, over the next few years. Thanks to Teresa's niece Catherine Mowry for loaning me the scrapbook and allowing me to use the photos.

9 **Then an opportunity arose** Helen Richey and the other women joined two hundred American men who had joined the ATA in September 1941. After Pearl Harbor the vast majority of those men left to join the U.S. Army Air Forces, but twenty of the American men stayed with the ATA the duration of the war.

10 **Teresa wrote to Cochran** In this letter Teresa also said, "I am thirty-one years of age, weight 138, height, 5 ft. 6 in." This would mean Teresa was born in 1911—indeed her birth certificate shows her birth date as January 24, 1911—not the 1914 she would later consistently (to the point it is in her obituary) claim. After receiving Teresa's letter, Jackie did invite Teresa to join her group going to England. Sincere thanks to Mary Burtzloff of the Eisenhower Library who found these letters for me. Ms. Burtzloff was an immense help finding many, many, many documents and sending them to me tied with a little ribbon, clearly understanding the gifts that they were. In addition to Teresa's birth certificate, the 1920 census confirms her 1911 birth date. Letter from Teresa James to Jacqueline Cochran, February 4, 1942, Jacqueline Cochran Collection, Eisenhower Library; letter from Mary Nicholson, secretary to Jacqueline Cochran, to Teresa James, March 31, 1942, Jacqueline Cochran Collection, Eisenhower Library.

10 **It was in Colorado Springs** Teresa had helped form the Civil Air Patrol unit at their local airport the year before and even taught her younger sister to fly. With sixteen-year-old Betty's new private license there were four pilots in the James family. Teresa's older brother Francis had inspired her to fly and her brother Jack flew as well. "Taught Her Kid Sister to Fly," *Pittsburgh Sun-Telegraph*, September 20, 1941; another article, "Romance in the Clouds," appeared in the Colorado Springs paper.

11 **Then on September 6, 1942** Telegram inviting Teresa James to join the WAFS, September 6, 1942, in author's possession.

12 **Like the other women** See Joseph Corn's excellent book *Winged Gospel* for more on the importance of aviation to the American people in this period through the 1950s. Joseph Corn, *The Winged Gospel: America's Romance with Aviation, 1900–1950* (New York: Oxford University Press, 1983).

12 **Aircraft manufacturers wanted** Dora Dougherty Strother, Oral History Interview K239.0512-2018, by Hugh N. Ahmann, June 10, 1991, Fort Worth, Texas, transcript, 9.

13 **For Earhart** Susan Butler, *East to the Dawn: The Life of Amelia Earhart* (Boston: Da Capo Press, 2009), 99.

13 **She would joke** Teresa James, interview with author, March 20, 1999, Orlando, Florida.

14 **It took a handsome pilot** This section on Teresa learning to fly came from Teresa James, interview with author.

16 **That was a lot of money** B. F. Timmons, "The Cost of Weddings," *American Sociological Review* 4, no. 2 (April 1939): 224–33.

16 **"I'll be home for dinner"** Quote from Churchill, *On Wings to War,* 10.

17 **A group of active women pilots** There were 117 women pilots as opposed to some 9,000 male pilots. *The Ninety-Nines: Yesterday-Today-Tomorrow* (Paducah, KY: Turner Publishing, 1996), 11.

17 **One of the members** Glenn Kerfoot, *Propeller Annie: The Story of Helen Richey, the Real First Lady of the Airlines* (Lexington, KY: Kentucky Aviation History Roundtable, 2008).

18 **Even before meeting Helen** The plane, *Outdoor Girl,* was sponsored by a cosmetics company. These paragraphs on the endurance flight are based on the following sources: "First Woman Airline Co-Pilot Flies Plane from Capital to Detroit with 7 Passengers," *New York Times,* January 1, 1935, 22. Marsalis was breaking her own record she set with Lois Thaden in August 1932. "Women End Flight, Set 10-Day Record; Mrs. Marsalis and Miss Richey Set Women's Endurance Mark at 237 Hours 42 Minutes, Pass Old One by 41 Hours; Emerge from Craft at Miami Tired but Happy—Buffeted by Squalls Final Night," *New York Times,* December 31, 1933, 21; "Women 6 Days in Air, Weary on Christmas; Endurance Fliers Eat Hearty Holiday Dinner Taken to Them by Supply Plane," *New York Times,* December 26, 1933, 13.

18 **During one such refueling exercise** They had already moved from two-hour shifts flying the plane to one-hour shifts because they simply couldn't stay awake any longer than that. "Airwomen Near Endurance Mark; They Must Remain Aloft Until 6:09 Tonight to Set New Record in Florida; Defy Fog in Reloading; Both 'Feel Good,' Mrs. Marsalis Sends Word—Miss Richey Fixes a Damaged Wing," Associated Press story in *New York Times,* December 28, 1933, 15; "Women End Flight, Set 10-Day Record," 21.

19 **A year after her endurance stunt** "First Woman Airline Co-Pilot Flies Plane from Capital to Detroit with 7 Passengers," 22; W. B. Courtney, "Ladybird," *Colliers* 95 (March 30, 1935), 16.

19 **Despite the excellent press** "First Woman Airline Co-Pilot," 22; Susan Ware, *Still Missing: Amelia Earhart and the Search for Modern Feminism* (New York: W. W. Norton, 1993), 80; Claudia M. Oakes, *United States Women in Aviation, 1930–1939* (Washington, DC: Smithsonian Institution Press, 1991), 13; Glenn Kerfoot, "Lost Lady of American Aviation," incomplete citation, article from 1970s, via https://journals.psu .edu/wph/article/viewFile/4032/3849; Cindy Weigand, "Helen Richey: ATA Girl, WASP, Aviation Pioneer."

20 **At the time, Amelia Earhart** The Air Commerce Department later defended themselves, saying that "it was not an order, not an attachment to her transport license." They claimed their "informal suggestion" was not the cause of Helen's problems. In 1973, Emily Howell Warner was the first woman pilot to be hired by a regularly scheduled U.S. airline since Helen Richey in 1934. "Feminists Stirred over Woman Flier; Alice Paul Agrees with Amelia Earhart Sex, Not Inability, Cost Helen Richey Her Job . . . ," Associated Press story in *New York Times,* November 8, 1935, 25.

21 **In Buffalo, Teresa was** Teresa earned her advanced instructor rating not long after her primary so she could teach advanced and inverted flying. Teresa James, interview; Churchill, *On Wings to War,* 20–21.

21 **In June the British stood** Some 338,000 British and French men escaped via the English Channel.

21 **Dink soon joined Teresa** James, interview with author; Teresa James, autobiography, 1986, available at Official WASP Archive, Texas Woman's University, Denton, Texas.

CHAPTER 2: THE EXPERIMENT BEGINS

23 **On the three-hundred-mile journey** Teresa James, diary, Official WASP Archive, Texas Woman's University, Denton, Texas.

24 **She had seen photographs** Teresa James, interview with author, March 20, 1999, Orlando, Florida.

24 **With her 2,200 hours** Teresa James, diary; Churchill, *On Wings to War*, 44–45.

24 **At 6:30 A.M. she went** Aline Rhonie Hofheimer Brooks had her transport license by 1931. She flew with the Aéro Club de France. Find multiple primary sources concerning Aline Rhonie at http://www.dmairfield.com/Collections/Rhonie%20Collection/index.html; Sarah Byrn Rickman, *WASP of the Ferry Command: Women Pilots, Uncommon Deeds* (Denton: University of North Texas Press, 2016), 129.

24 **Aline was** The mural was originally 106 feet. In 1960, she removed it from Roosevelt Field before the hangar the mural was in was razed, then she restored it in Roosevelt Field mall and added twenty-five more portraits, bringing the total new length to 126 feet. https://www.airspacemag.com/airspacemag/artist-aline-rhonie-180956198/.

24 **But Teresa still found** Teresa James, interview with author.

24 **At the base, Teresa** This recollection of Teresa's interview for the WAFS based on Teresa James, interview with author.

25 **"This Base is new"** Churchill, *On Wings to War*, 45–46.

25 **Teresa hoped** Teresa James, diary, September 18, 1942. The 65-horsepower plane was similar to the Piper Cub. Teresa had over 1,000 hours of flight experience in the Cub.

26 **That afternoon** Rob Simbeck, *Daughter of the Air: The Brief Soaring Life of Cornelia Fort* (New York: Atlantic Monthly Press, 1999).

26 **Then there was Betty** At five foot one and 100 pounds, Betty Huyler Gillies was one of the smallest of the women pilots, but was also one of the most experienced and well-known. As president of the Ninety-Nines, she led a significant fight against the CAA to allow women to fly while pregnant.

27 **That same day** Adela Riek Scharr, *Sisters in the Sky*, vol. I, *The WAFS* (Gerald, MO: Patrice Press, 1986).

27 **After passing** Walter J. Marx, Captain, Ferrying Division Historical Officer, Historical Branch, Intelligence and Security Division, Headquarters, Air Transport Command, *History of the Air Transport Command: Women Pilots in the Air Transport Command* (Washington, DC: U.S. Government Printing Office, March 1945), Yvonne Pateman Collection, United States Air Force Academy, MS 31, Microfilm roll #8, A3003, 35; Sarah Byrn Rickman, *The Original: The Women's Auxiliary Ferrying Squadron of World War II* (Sarasota, FL: Disc-Us Books, 2001), 65.

27 **"I never was sure"** "Evidentally" is misspelled. Teresa James, diary, September 18, 1942.

27 **The women were assigned** The women began moving in on September 18, 1942. The men intended for BOQ 14 moved across base to an area known as "Mosquito Meadows." Jan Churchill, *From Delaware to Everywhere* (Dover, DE: Dover Litho Publishing, 2007), 39.

27 **Construction on the building** Teresa said of Nancy, "She was charming and she was so solicitous and said you're walking into an old barracks now and you're going to be sleeping on an iron cot. And the way she told us. She says it won't be forever. We'll get things straightened out. And that's the way she was." Teresa James, interview with author. There were forty-four rooms in the BOQ. Teresa James, diary, September 18, 1942; Teresa James, interview with author; Churchill, *From Delaware to Everywhere*, 48–49.

27 **"THINGS I BET"** Teresa James, diary.

28 **In the wake of the Pearl** David Kennedy, *Freedom from Fear Part II: The American People in World War II* (New York: Oxford University Press, 1999), 230–31.

28 **From the beginning** Marx, *History of the ATC,* 36.

29 **They also had to meet** Civilian men joining the Ferrying Division were required to have only two hundred flight hours and three years of high school, and could be between nineteen and forty-five years old; the bar was much higher for the women. *ATC History,* 35–37.

29 **Mornings began** Delphine Bohn remembers, "To 'stand formation and roll call at 8:00 A.M.' meant not as late as even 8:01 A.M.," in her unpublished memoir, "Catch a Shooting Star," available at Official WASP Archive, Texas Woman's University, Denton, Texas.

29 **As much as Nancy** *ATC History,* Bohn, "Catch a Shooting Star," iv–19.

29 **Although the women's living** Teresa James, interview with author; Churchill, *On Wings to War,* 49.

29 **Teresa later remembered** Teresa James, interview with Dawn Letson, June 16, 1998, Lake Worth, Florida, for the Official WASP Archive, the Woman's Collection, Texas Woman's University, Denton, Texas.

30 **Nancy had gone to Vassar** Nancy's youngest daughter Allie emphasized the unfairness of Nancy being labeled as wealthy. She had been well-off during her youth and did indeed attend Vassar but was forced to drop out when her father lost everything in the Great Depression. Allie exclaimed, "She was flat broke!" Allie Love, telephone call with author, October 31, 2018.

30 **Next it was Teresa's turn** This story can be found in Teresa James, interview with Letson.

30 **It wasn't until later** Teresa James, interview with author.

CHAPTER 3: SHE WILL DIRECT THE WOMEN PILOTS

32 **"All of us realized"** Fort, "At Twilight's Last Gleaming," *Woman's Home Companion,* July 1942, 19.

32 **Keeping the program small** The number of WAFS is often listed as twenty-five or twenty-eight. Nancy initially chose twenty-five women, but another three joined by January 1943 before all qualified women began to be funneled through Jacqueline Cochran's training program, bringing the total to twenty-eight. See Sarah Byrn Rickman's works on the WAFS for more detail; Marx, *ATC History,* 30.

33 **"No better choice"** Fort, "At Twilight's Last Gleaming."

33 **Indeed, in many ways** This description of Nancy Harkness Love as a youth is primarily drawn from Sarah Byrn Rickman, *Nancy Love and the WASP Ferry Pilots of World War II* (Denton: University of North Texas Press, 2008).

33 **Some barnstormers had sponsors** WASP Charlyne Creger grew up in Oklahoma and later claimed her flight with a barnstormer "set the direction for the rest of my life." Charlyne Creger, interview with author, October, 1996, Anaheim, California; one-page biography, 1996, given to author by Creger.

34 **"A ride in a barnstorming Fleet"** Nancy Love quote from an undated newspaper article.

34 That evening "Grandfather indulged Mum's enthusiasms. Grinny did not." Nancy's daughter Margaret "Marky" Love as quoted in Rickman, *Nancy Love,* 10.

34 On August 26, 1930 "Riding breeches" and "prop held together" quotes from Crocker Snow, famed Boston pilot, who gave her a check ride not long after her return to Milton. Crocker Snow, too, belonged to the Long Island Aviation Country Club. Crocker Snow, *Logbook: A Pilot's Life* (Washington, DC: Brassey's/Roger Warner Book, 1997), 77.

35 Nancy later remembered "Wasp Nest," *Cross Country News,* February 25, 1960.

35 "I wanted to fly" "Wasp Nest."

35 That fall, her mother Some believe she even "vicariously enjoyed and even envied her daughter's adventurous spirit." Rickman says Love's eldest daughter, Hannah, believes this. Rickman, *Nancy Love,* 15.

35 It was 1930 Department of Commerce, Aeronautics Branch, Form Fl-7, Notification to Miss Nancy Lincoln Harkness that she had officially received her private pilot's license, November 7, 1930, in author's possession; Rickman, *Nancy Love,* 11.

35 Nancy returned Rickman, *Nancy Love,* 15.

35 The academy had www.milton.edu/about/history/.

35 On a dare Upon her return to school Nancy was met by the chairman of the board of trustees, and the presidents of both the girls' and boys' schools. In punishment for her stunt she was sent home for two weeks. "'A Penny a Pound, Up You Go' Was Bug That Bit Nancy H. Love," *The Stephens Life,* April 26, 1946, 3.

35 She narrowly escaped When Nancy's daughter attended Milton in the 1960s, Nancy was still known among students for the flight. Quote from Marky Love in Rickman, *Nancy Love,* 13–14.

35 When she wasn't aloft Most of this paragraph is from https://vcencyclopedia .vassar.edu/alumni/nancy-love.html.

36 Even Nancy's first crash Her instructor was more seriously injured, losing an eye in the incident. Rickman, *Nancy Love,* 16–19; https://vcencyclopedia.vassar.edu /alumni/nancy-love.html.

36 Nineteen thirty-four marked a turning point https://vcencyclopedia.vassar.edu /alumni/nancy-love.html.

36 moved to New York Rickman, *Nancy Love,* 24.

36 "I do not want to take time" Nancy Harkness, letter to Uncle Tom, early 1934, in author's possession, Nancy Harkness Love file 13.

37 Nancy's job at Inter-City Rickman, *Nancy Love,* 45.

37 Throughout the 1930s She was a test pilot for the groundbreaking Hammond Model Y, a plane with tricycle landing gear, the first of its kind.

38 Some of Nancy's flying friends "Women Fliers Prepare for War-Time Service: Mrs. 'Teddy' Kenyon Reveals Clubs Being Formed for Such Service," *Lewiston Daily Sun,* March 28, 1936, via https://news.google.com/newspapers?nid=1928&dat= 19360328&id=e84gAAAAIBAJ&sjid=6moFAAAAIBAJ&pg=3795,6652746. Teddy Kenyon was one of Nancy's roommates.

38 **His name was** He was also the father of famed World War II and Vietnam-era pilot Brigadier General Robin Olds. General Robert Olds would die of heart disease and pneumonia in 1943 at the age of forty-six.

38 **Lieutenant Colonel Olds** Major S. L. Zamzow, USAF Historian, *Ambassador of American Airpower: Major General Robert Olds* (Maxwell Air Force Base, Montgomery, AL: Air University, 2008).

39 **She placed stars** Letter, Nancy H. Love to Lieutenant Colonel Robert Olds, U.S. Army Air Corps, May 21, 1940, in author's possession.

39 **Nancy was confident** Letter, Nancy H. Love to Lieutenant Colonel Robert Olds, U.S. Army Air Corps, May 21, 1940, in author's possession. Some quotes from the letter can be found in Captain Walter J. Marx, *History of the Air Transport Command: Women Pilots in the Air Transport Command,* 1946 (declassified 1952), 3–4.

39 **In early June** This information about the flight in part from "Girl Pilots War Plane to Canada," *Boston Record,* June 5, 1940.

40 **Olds wrote** Olds mentioned the fact that H.R. 10030, the Naval Aviation Personnel Act, contained an amendment by the Navy to authorize the commissioning of women as pilots in the Navy and Marine Corps. The amendment seems to have been stricken from the final version of the bill, which was approved in Congress, August 27, 1940. *Congressional Record,* 864; Marx, *Air Transport Command History of Women Pilots,* 3–4.

40 **Despite the slight smile** Richard G. Davis, *Hap: Henry H. Arnold, Military Aviator* (Bolling AFB, Washington, DC: Air Force History and Museums Program, 1997), http://www.afhistory.af.mil/Books/Authors.aspx, 1.

40 **Whether or not** General Arnold was awarded the rank of major general on a temporary basis in September 1938, linked to his role as chief of the Air Corps. He would be made a permanent major general in February 1941. One week after the Japanese attack on Pearl Harbor, he became a lieutenant general. In March 1943 he became a four-star general (full general). In December 1944 he became a five-star general of the Army. And with the creation of the United States Air Force he became the first and only five-star general of the USAF in 1949.

40 **Despite the growing crisis** Davis, *Hap.* Cites Craven and Cate plans and early operations, 104–16.

40 **Arnold believed** J. Merton England, CWO, AAF Historical Office, Headquarters, Army Air Forces, *Army Air Forces Historical Studies No. 55: Women Pilots with the AAF, 1941–1944.* (Washington, DC: U.S. Government Printing Office, March 1946), 3–4.

41 **Both Nancy and Bob** Allie Love, telephone interview with author, October 31, 2018.

41 **Out on base** Letter to her friend Mac postwar, Iwasm.

42 **In March** Olds suffered his first major heart attack in March 1942. He returned to lead the Second Air Force until heart disease and another heart attack finally led to his untimely death in April 1943 at the age of forty-six.

42 **General Harold George took over** This section on Tunner learning of Nancy Love is based on Rickman, *Nancy Love,* chapter 6.

43 **Nancy's idea** ATC History, 14.

43 **Colonel Tunner was equally anxious** This section on Tunner, Baker, and Love making plans about the 2nd Ferrying Group is based on the following sources: Marx, *History of the ATC,* 18–21; England, *Army Air Forces Historical Studies No. 55: Women Pilots with the AAF, 1941–1944.*

44 **They even came up with** What to call various women's auxiliaries and organizations was a serious matter. The Women's Army Auxiliary Corps was the WAAC, which opponents ridiculed by making the sound of a duck's quack. This unfortunate precedent clearly made leaders think twice before choosing a name. In a time of fierce competition for women's participation, something as seemingly inconsequential as an unfavorable acronym could be off-putting to future recruits.

44 **But in July 1942** General Arnold had been hearing from members of Congress, including Democrat W. R. Pogue of Texas, who'd asked whether women couldn't be utilized as pilots in the WAAC. Arnold responded, explaining the bill that had just passed creating the WAAC had neglected to authorize flying officers or a way to pay them. *ATC History,* 18; England, *Army Air Forces Historical Studies No. 55.*

44 **At least he seemed** Marx, *History of the ATC,* 21.

44 **At the White House** Virginia Troutman, letter to Eleanor Roosevelt, August 14, 1942, National Archives.

44 **On September 1, 1942** Eleanor Roosevelt, "My Day" column, September 1, 1942, United Feature Syndicate, https://www2.gwu.edu/~erpapers/myday/displaydoc .cfm?_y=1942&_f=md056279.

45 **Two days later** According to the Army Air Forces official history on the women pilots, a day or two after Roosevelt's column came out, General Arnold told a group of his air staff that "Women pilots would be used to the maximum in the ferrying of light trainer planes from the factory to the schools. . . ." He then ordered them to work out the details of the women pilots with General George, head of the Air Transport Command. Arnold later denied that Eleanor Roosevelt had any influence on the matter. England, *Army Air Forces Historical Studies No. 55,* 16.

45 **On September 5** In a postwar oral history, Kuter was asked about his role with the WASP. "Only as a staff officer, but very violently at one moment. Arnold was away—the chief of staff was away, and I was the senior deputy chief of staff. Harold George charged in with an elaborate staff study, obviously coordinated all over the place. It just had to be signed that day because something was going to happen the next day and it couldn't wait. 'Arnold would surely sign it,' he told me; he had been on this from the beginning. I looked it over and it seemed bona fide." The form would set up the WAFS with Nancy Love in charge. Nancy's husband Bob was one of General George's senior staff officers. Kuter explained that "with Hal's enthusiasm and pressure and evidence of coordination and assurances, I signed it." Nancy Love was sworn in that very day. Drama soon ensued.

   Kuter continued in his oral history: "General Marshall very shortly thereafter called me, 'What in the hell have you done?' Naturally, I went to see him quickly and asked him in what area was he concerned. The President, the Secretary of War, General Marshall, apparently, General Arnold had been in complete agreement that they would form a WAF organization, and it would be headed by 'Jackie' Cochran. I had jumped the gun here and formed something else headed by someone who wasn't Jackie Cochran. Jackie was in England demanding priority on the first airplane back to really get this thing straightened out. General Marshall told me that I had messed it up like all hell (laughter). I had." He concluded, "So that is my association with women in the Air Force. I did participate in a big way at the wrong time with the wrong women."

When asked whether General George had taken advantage of him, Kuter dodged the question: "Just remotely possible, he did. On the other hand, General Arnold may never have given Hal George a clue of these other ideas. I think that is quite possible. Coordination was not really at its very best when Hap Arnold was responsible." General Lawrence Sherman Kuter, USAF Oral History, October 3, 1974, pg 421–23. Available AFHRA, Call Number: K239.0512-810 v.i c.i and IRIS Number 01015373. Sincere thanks to Dr. Brian D. Laslie, NORAD, and USNORTHCOM Deputy Command Historian for telling me about this oral history.

45 **That same day** ATC History, 22–23.

45 **On September 11, 1942** "Women Will Form a Ferry Command," New York Times, September 11, 1942.

46 **By the time** "First of the WAFS Pass Ground Tests," New York Times, September 12, 1942.

46 **Throughout the summer** ATC History, 14–18.

CHAPTER 4: OUTSTANDING WOMAN FLIER OF THE WORLD

48 **When she noticed** See Doris Rich, Jackie Cochran: Pilot in the Fastest Lane (Gainesville; University Press of Florida, 2007), 100–103. Quote from Radio Script, June 17, 1940, AFSS, Box 9, Eisenhower Library, as cited in Rich.

48 **Throughout the spring** Lettice Curtis, The Forgotten Pilots: A Story of the Air Transport Auxiliary, 1939–1945, 4th ed. (Olney, UK: Lettice Curtis, 1998).

48 **Jackie had been in England** Telegram from Jacqueline Cochran to Marjorie E. Hook, January 23, 1942, recruiting her into the ATA, Box A94.392c, Folder 4, ATA Collection, Texas Woman's University.

49 **Wanting to avoid a diplomatic crisis** Jackie was being watched closely to make certain our allies were not upset. Robert Hinckley, Civil Aeronautics Authority, one-page transcript of telephone conversation with Mrs. Roosevelt, December 5, 1941. Box 38, Folder 18, Robert Hinckley Collection, University of Utah, J. Willard Marriott Library. Many thanks to Julia Scatliff O'Grady for sharing this with me. For more information on Hinckley see the Robert H. Hinckley Institute of Politics at the University of Utah. Interestingly, after serving in numerous public service positions during the 1930s and the war, he went on to cofound the American Broadcasting Company (ABC) in 1946.

49 **The next day,** "Women Will Form a Ferry Command," New York Times, September 11, 1942; "First of the WAFS Pass Ground Tests," New York Times, September 12, 1942.

49 **He informed everyone** All of this leads Jackie to believe that Arnold didn't know anything about the work Nancy and the Ferrying Division were doing, but she was wrong. He was well aware of their actions and in fact authorized them to begin the program before Jackie's return. Arnold's response to Cochran's comments, page 17, footnote 41, in J. Merton England, Army Air Forces Historical Studies No. 55; Women Pilots with the AAF, 1941–1944 (Washington, DC: U.S. Government Printing Office, March 1946); ibid., 17.

49 **The day after** This section of George's views and Cochran's response are based on Major General H. L. George, Air Transport Command, memorandum to General Ar-

nold, September 12, 1942, of *History of the Women Airforce Service Pilots Program and Activities in the AAF Training Command: A Summary of the Women's Flying Training Program, 16 November 1942 to 20 December 1944.* Headquarters AAF Training Command, Fort Worth, Texas, March 1, 1945, appendix.

50 **On September 15** "Named to Direct Women's Air Work," *New York Times,* September 15, 1942, 26.

51 **These two women** The information on the Long Island Aviation Country Club is in large part thanks to Howard Kroplick, beginning with his website www .vanderbiltcupraces.com. Kroplick generously shared with me the Long Island Aviation Country Club 1940 membership book, 1940, which included these names.

51 **When people who knew** Delphine Bohn, "Catch a Shooting Star," unpublished memoir, Official WASP Archive, Texas Woman's University, Denton, Texas.

52 **Throughout her life** In addition to specifically named sources, the description of Jacqueline Cochran's backstory is based on the following sources: Jacqueline Cochran, *The Stars at Noon* (Boston: Little, Brown, 1954); Rich, *Jackie Cochran;* Billie Pittman Ayers and Beth Dees, *Superwoman Jacqueline Cochran: Family Memories About the Famous Pilot, Patriot, Wife and Businesswoman* (1st Books Library, 1999); and Jacqueline Cochran and Maryann Bucknum Brinley, *Jackie Cochran: The Autobiography of the Greatest Woman Pilot in Aviation History* (New York: Bantam Books, 1987).

53 **Then in late May** The historical record gives conflicting evidence of how long Jackie, her husband, and son may have lived together before living apart. Perhaps up to a year, perhaps more or less. "Five Year Old Child Is Fatally Burned Friday," DeFuniak Springs *Breeze,* June 4, 1925; Ayers and Dees, *Superwoman,* 39–40; Rich, *Jackie Cochran,* 11–12; Cochran and Brinley, *Jackie Cochran: The Autobiography,* 49.

53 **They buried him** Ayers and Dees, *Superwoman,* 39–41.

54 **By the time she arrived** Her niece wondered if Jackie had also been inspired by her fondness for a preacher named Jack Hamilton: "An old family friend, Jennie Daw, is convinced Bessie chose Jacqueline out of her fondness for the preacher named Jack Hamilton who led the congregation—including the Pittman family—at the Hamilton Baptist Church back in Gateswood. She often signed her name 'Jack' in the many letters she wrote to us before Mother died." *Superwoman,* 44.

54 **The stories she told** Cochran, *The Stars at Noon,* and every newspaper and magazine article written about her from 1932 forward.

55 **Some of her clients** Clifford and Molly Hemphill, the couple who had invited Jackie to the party where she met Floyd, were members of the Long Island Aviation Country Club. Long Island Aviation Country Club membership book, 1940.

55 **"There are so many"** Cochran, *The Stars at Noon,* 45.

56 **On August 11, Jackie passed** Jacqueline Cochran Log Book, 1932–1934, Jacqueline Cochran Collection, Eisenhower Library.

56 **Stories of girl fliers** Cited in Ayers and Dees, *Superwoman,* 45.

57 **Although in many ways** As Floyd's daughter-in-law Judith Odlum later explained, "There was a symbiotic relationship there that was truly hard to figure out. They were totally dependent on each other." Judith believed Jackie "needed his support . . . and . . . he really adored her admiration." Doris Rich quotes Judith Odlum, Chuck and Glennis

Yeager, and others in her descriptions of the relationship between Jackie and Floyd. Rich, *Jackie Cochran,* 57–58.

57 **"Those first few days"** Rich, *Jackie Cochran,* 64.

57 **Amelia often visited Jackie** Jacqueline Cochran, interview with Kenneth Leish, Oral History Research Office of Columbia University, New York, May 1960, Transcript 33; Rich, *Jackie Cochran,* 64–65.

58 **After Jackie learned** This paragraph, including quotes, is from the following sources: Cochran, interview with Columbia University; Rich, *Jackie Cochran,* 66–69.

58 **A month later Jackie flew** "F.W. Fuller Breaks Bendix Race Mark, San Franciscan Defeats Competitors with 260-270 mph Speed, He Wins $13,000 in Prizes, Jacqueline Cochrane Takes 3rd Place in Burbank–Cleveland Flight Winning $5,500," *New York Times,* September 4, 1937.

58 **That September she won** By the late 1930s she was recognized in various national publications as "queen of the skyways." Helen Waterhouse, *Popular Aviation,* December 1938, as cited in Rich, *Jackie Cochran,* 88.

59 **There's a photograph** Jacqueline Cochran won the National Trophy in 1937 along with Howard Hughes. Lieutenant Colonel Olds had shared the stage with Jackie in 1938 when she won her first Harmon Trophy for best international woman pilot and Olds won the National Trophy for outstanding American aviator. (Jackie had won the National Trophy the year before.) Original photo caption: "Mrs. Eleanor Roosevelt today presented the Harmon Trophy to Jacqueline Cochran as America's outstanding aviatrix during 1937. This trophy is awarded annually by the Ligue Internationale des Aviateurs to perpetuate the memory of the famous World War Lafayette Escadrille Corps. Photo shows Mrs. Roosevelt shaking hands with Miss Cochran, while in the back row are Mrs. Helen MacCloskey Rough, one of America's outstanding woman flyers and Mrs. Alexander de Seversky, wife of the President of the Seversky Aircraft Corporation." Nancy Love is not named. Photo by George Rinhart/Corbis via Getty Images: https://www.gettyimages.com/detail/news-photo/mrs-eleanor-roosevelt -today-presented-the-harmon-trophy-to-news-photo/530725978.

60 **Immediately following France** Jacqueline Cochran, letter to Mrs. Franklin Roosevelt, September 28, 1939, available at Official WASP Archive at Texas Woman's University and President Franklin D. Roosevelt Library, Eleanor Roosevelt Collection.

60 **Eleanor Roosevelt received** The historical record tells us that the president saw it but not how he responded. Cochran letter to Roosevelt, September 28, 1939. The letter has handwritten notes on it from Eleanor Roosevelt to her secretary. She soon wrote Jackie back supporting her idea and promising to forward it to the Army, Navy, and Coast Guard. In Eleanor Roosevelt's papers at the FDR Library are letters from Rear Admiral R. R. Waesche, Commandant of the U.S. Coast Guard, and Secretary of War Harry H. Woodring, each acknowledging the notes about Jackie's ideas from Mrs. Roosevelt. Woodring's letter said: "The interest of women pilots in aviation and in national defense is gratifying. Undoubtedly their services in time of emergency would be helpful, particularly in those activities where they might relieve Air Reserve officers for active military duty. In this connection the utilization of their services would seem to be primarily a matter of interest to the Civil Aeronautics Authority rather than the War Department." He continued, "The organization of the Air Corps and the Air Reserve does not provide for or contemplate the organization of units including women pilots."

Letter from Eleanor Roosevelt to Jacqueline Cochran, October 11, 1939; letter from R. R. Waesche to Miss Malvina C. Thompson (Eleanor Roosevelt's secretary), October 13, 1939; letter from Harry H. Woodring, secretary of war, to Miss Malvina C. Thompson, October 27, 1939. There is a note in the same file: "Return to Mrs. Roosevelt. The President has seen." All from the Eleanor Roosevelt Collection at the Franklin D. Roosevelt Library. Many thanks to the fabulous archivist Virginia Lewick for her above-and-beyond assistance in finding these documents and helping me understand the notes on them.

61 **In June 1941, Jackie began** Jackie had gotten to know General Henry "Hap" Arnold the year before when seated next to him at a White House luncheon. It was Arnold who suggested she fly to England. See Rich, *Jackie Cochran*, 100–103; Cochran, *The Stars at Noon*.

61 **In England, Jackie met** Jacqueline Cochran, "They Call Them 'Ata-girls' and 'Waafs'—the Women of the R.A.F.," *Vogue*, August 15, 1941, 71–72, 107; Cochran, *The Stars at Noon*, 103–4; Curtis, *The Forgotten Pilots;* "Miss Cochran Back, Urges U.S. to Train Women Fliers for War," *New York Times*, July 2, 1941.

61 **The morning after her return** There is no notation of this private meeting in FDR's calendar, but it seems possible. President Franklin D. Roosevelt's daily calendar can be found digitally as part of his presidential library at http://www.fdrlibrary.marist.edu /daybyday/daylog/june-30th-1941/; "Miss Cochran a Guest: Flier Has Luncheon with the Roosevelt's at Hyde Park," *New York Times*, July 3, 1941.

61 **Jackie was invited** Eleanor Roosevelt, "My Day" column, *Washington Daily News*, July 3, 1941.

61 **Not long after her visits** This is a time of great organizational transition as the U.S. military begins to prepare seriously for war. The Air Corps, a minor part of the U.S. Army up to this point, became the U.S. Army Air Forces, a strong arm of the Army, in July 1941. The Air Corps still exists within the USAAF. Wesley Frank Craven and James Lea Cate, eds., *Plans and Early Operations, January 1939 to August 1942* (Chicago: University of Chicago Press, 1948).

62 **The purpose of the meeting** England, *Army Air Forces Historical Studies No. 55*, 5.

62 **Olds immediately encouraged** England, *Army Air Forces Historical Studies No. 55* and Cochran, *The Stars at Noon*.

63 **Jackie labored for some weeks** Letter and survey from Colonel Robert Olds, Air Corps Ferrying Command, to "All women holders of licenses," July 29, 1941. Jacqueline Cochran Collection, Eisenhower Library.

63 **On August 1, 1941** Unsigned copy of memo for C/AAF, prepared by Colonel Olds, August 1, 1941, in ATC 321.9 as found in Walter J. Marx, *History of the Air Transport Command: Women Pilots in the Air Transport Command* (Washington, DC: U.S. Government Printing Office, March 1945), 9, and England, *Army Air Forces Historical Studies No. 55*, 7.

63 **not realizing** Even Eleanor Roosevelt was pressuring General Arnold. In her August 5 "My Day" column she wrote about the women pilots in England after having talked with Jackie and concluded, "It would seem to be wise to give women pilots this opportunity" to help their country as pilots. Eleanor Roosevelt, "My Day" column, *Washington Daily News*, August 5, 1941, http://www.gwu.edu/~erpapers/myday /displayco.cfm.

63 **After months of preparation** According to a letter from the British Air Commission in January 1942, Jackie's arrangements were "arrived at after discussions or correspondence with representatives of your State Department, General Arnold of the United States Army Air Corps, General Olds of the United States Ferry Command, and Honorable Robert Hinckley of your Civil Aeronautics Authority," as well as Jackie herself. Letter to Jacqueline Cochran from A. H. Self, Director General, British Air Commission, January 24, 1942. True copy to be found in the Jacqueline Cochran Collection on the Eisenhower Library website, https://www.eisenhower.archives.gov. Cochran donated her extensive professional and personal papers to the Eisenhower Library in the late 1970s. She was an ardent supporter, credits herself as one of the leaders of the group that convinced the general to run for president, and hosted him on her California ranch for golf and the writing of his memoirs.

64 **It was Arnold who gave** *History of the Women Airforce Service Pilots Program and Activities in the AAF Training Command*, 19. It is unclear why Esther Nelson, who joined Nancy before Teresa did, was not on the flight. Catherine Slocum had resigned when the care she had planned for her four children fell through and she had to go home.

CHAPTER 5: FERRY PILOTS

65 **Betty Gillies** Captain Walter J. Marx, Ferrying Division Historical Officer, Historical Branch, Intelligence and Security Division, Headquarters, Air Transport Command, *History of the Air Transport Command: Women Pilots in the Air Transport Command* (Washington, DC: U.S. Government Printing Office, March 1945), Yvonne Pateman Collection, United States Air Force Academy, MS 31, Microfilm roll #8, A3003; Betty Gillies, interview with Dawn Letson, Official WASP Archive, Texas Woman's University, October 6, 1996; Rickman, *Nancy Love*, 92.

65 **Since then, they had traded** "Gray-Green Uniform Is Adopted for WAFS: Women Pilots to Get Costume Adapted to Flying," UP story in *New York Times*, September 16, 1942.

66 **When the women finally received** Teresa James, interview with Dawn Letson, Lake Worth, Florida, June 16, 1998, Official WASP Archive, Texas Woman's University, Denton, Texas.

66 **Ferry pilots weren't allowed** This description of their first trip is based in large part on Teresa James, diary, Official WASP Archive, Texas Woman's University, Denton, Texas.

66 **Cornelia wrote** Cornelia Fort, letter home.

67 **To celebrate** Betty Gillies, Nancy Love, and Jacqueline Cochran were all members of the Long Island Aviation Country Club. Before they caught the 6:30 train home to Wilmington, Cornelia hurried into New York to hear Bruno Walter conducting at Carnegie Hall, then met Mrs. McCain (the mother of a boyfriend) at '21' for a quick drink. Cornelia Fort, letter home, October 24, 1942, in Doris Tanner Collection, Box 3, Folder 77, Texas Woman's University.

68 **When it was too rainy** When clouds are too low for the limitations of the plane or pilot—they would quickly be into the clouds after takeoff—it is called a low ceiling. Delphine Bohn, "Catch a Shooting Star," unpublished memoir, V-8-9, Official WASP Archive, Texas Woman's University, Denton, Texas.

68 **Teresa didn't care** Teresa James, diary, October 12, 1942; Bohn, "Catch a Shooting Star," V-8-9.

69 **It didn't help matters** Teresa James, diary, late September 1942. The U.S. Army Corps of Engineers transformed New Castle from unspoiled countryside to a 1,600-acre airport with four runways and 250 buildings between 1942 and 1945. Churchill, *From Delaware to Everywhere*, 8.

69 **She decorated** She had this radio until the end of her life.

69 **Before long** Teresa James, interview with Dawn Letson, June 1998, Lake Worth, Florida, Official WASP Archive, Texas Woman's University, Denton, Texas.

70 **It was dancing** Rickman, *Nancy Love*, 100.

70 **The reality was** See Leisa D. Meyer's excellent work, *Creating GI Jane: Sexuality and Power in the Women's Army Corps During World War II* (New York: Columbia University Press, 1997).

70 **In early December** "The WAFS: A Squadron of 25 Girls Is Leading the Way for U.S. Women Fliers," *Look*, February 9, 1943.

71 **One of the most frustrating** The Ferrying Division later claimed they "were simply an attempt to forestall any possible criticism by scandalmongers of the morals of the WAFS." They feared "the least breath of scandal, the most remote cause for gossip, an innuendo in the daily column of a popular columnist," which they worried "could have done irreparable harm to the entire WAF organization." They validated the "wisdom of this policy" with the fact that "not once did a report of any laxity on the part of a WAF ever reach the press." *ATC History*, 73–75.

71 **The women did end up** Although this may have been the rule, anecdotal evidence from the women themselves suggests it was not strictly followed as they moved through the war. Delphine Bohn reveals that "on a rare occasion or two a few of us even acquired a minimal knowledge of weightlessness." It would seem that "fun-and-games" were practiced in the bulky Curtiss C-46 when the flight crew would fly to altitude and enter a partial outside loop, allowing the passengers in the empty cabin carefully lined with safety quilts and pads to experience momentary weightlessness. Bohn, "Catch a Shooting Star," iv-21-22.

72 **Pilots were expected** *ATC History*, 71.

72 **By December, WAFS pilots were being** This section on the trip to Great Falls is based in large part on Teresa James, diary, December 1942.

75 **By the end of 1942** *ATC History*, 78.

75 **Plans were already in motion** The women eventually served with the 2nd Ferrying Group (Wilmington), 3rd Ferrying Group (Romulus, Michigan), 5th Ferrying Group (Dallas), and 6th Ferrying Group (Long Beach, California). *ATC History*.

75 **Nancy, too, was ready** As Nancy began to expand to new bases, she was short one of her women pilots. Aline Rhonie either resigned or was discharged (the historical record is unclear) at the end of her ninety-day contract. She may have taken an extra night to get back to the base after a flight, and although this type of delay was fairly common for male pilots, it was not acceptable for Nancy in her efforts to create a reputation of efficiency. Whether it was by choice or by force, Aline left Wilmington and the twenty-eight WAFS pilots were down to twenty-six. Rhonie left Wilmington and,

using her own connections, went to England to fly with the Air Transport Auxiliary. *ATC History,* 78.

75 **Teresa knew this** Teresa James, diary, December 11, 1942.

76 **In the new year** Five women went to each base to serve as a foundation when Jackie's women began to join them in April 1942. The WAFS pilots who headed to Dallas with Nancy included twenty-two-year-old Florene Miller from Texas, twenty-one-year-old Helen Richards from California, twenty-three-year-old Dorothy Scott from Seattle, and finally Betsy Ferguson, a farm girl from Coffeyville, Kansas.

CHAPTER 6: THE FABULOUS FIRST

77 **With her usual bravado** Jane Sincell Straughan, interview with Nancy Durr, October 4, 1996, Anaheim, California, Official WASP Archive, Texas Woman's University, Denton, Texas; Mary Lou Colbert Neale, interview with author, October 3, 1996, Anaheim, California.

78 **In Houston** Leni Leoti "Dedie" Clark Deaton, interview with Doris Tanner (WASP), March 20, 1982, found at Official WASP Archive, Texas Woman's University, Denton, Texas.

79 **Leoti Deaton was in the middle** Deaton, interview with Tanner.

80 **After stepping off** The Army Air Forces Flying Training Command became the Army Air Forces Training Command on July 31, 1943, after the Flying Training Command merged with the Army Air Forces Technical Training Command.

80 **Jackie's instructions to Dedie** These quotes are Deaton's recollections of her conversation with Jacqueline Cochran. Leoti "Dedie" Deaton, Chief Establishment Officer, Women Airforce Service Pilots. Oral history interview with Ziggy Hunter, March 18, 1975, edited by Dawn Letson and Nancy M. Durr, available at Official WASP Archive, Texas Woman's University, Denton, Texas.

81 **Clearly, Jackie had been** Deaton earned a Civil Service Commission classification of CAF-6 (clerical-administrative-fiscal) under some duress. The quotes are based on Deaton's retelling of the conversation, but the sentiment is clear. Doris Brinker Tanner, Oral history with Dedie Deaton, March 20, 1982, available at Texas Woman's University. Information on civil service classifications can be found at https://www.historians .org/about-aha-and-membership/aha-history-and-archives/gi-roundtable-series /pamphlets/who-should-choose-a-civil-service-career/what-is-federal-civil-service -like-today.

81 **With her rating secured** Doris Brinker Tanner, *Arnold, Cochran, Deaton: Women Airforce Service Pilots, WWII.* Private publication in author's possession. Doris Tanner was a WASP and is a historian who has written several small booklets on different aspects of the WASP history. Most of her work is available in the Official WASP Archive at Texas Woman's University, Denton, Texas; Dedie Deaton, interview with Doris Brinker Tanner.

81 **Thankfully,** The couple helped Dedie when others wouldn't because they felt a special need to help the war effort. Deaton, interview with Tanner; Tanner, *Arnold, Cochran, Deaton.*

82 **As Dedie was soon** Deaton, interview with Hunter, 1975.

82 **Now that Dedie** Jane Sincell Straughan, interview with Nancy Durr, October 4, 1996, Anaheim, California. Official WASP Archive at Texas Woman's University.

82 **The Rice was the busiest hotel** New recruit Marjorie Kumler remembered that the hotel had "more men in uniform per square inch in the lobby than any other hotel in the city." Nearby Ellington Field alone had more than 5,000 cadets. Marjorie Kumler, "They've Done It Again," *Ladies' Home Journal*, March 1944; Mary Lou Neale, interview with author, 1996.

83 **She made certain** The women, as were the men, were organized by training class: "43" stood for the year they would graduate, "W" stood for women, and "1" stood for the first class. Subsequent classes would follow (43-W-2, 43-W-3, etc.) There were eighteen classes total, ending with 44-W-10, the last class.

83 **"You girls are the first"** Kumler, "They've Done It Again," 28.

83 **Jackie then introduced** Straughan, interview with Durr, October 4, 1996.

84 **The heiress Marion Florsheim** Kumler, "They've Done It Again." Marion did not graduate from the flight training. According to Neale, Marion became run-down and her husband, Manny, came from New York to take her home. Neale, interview with author, 1996.

84 **Twenty-seven-year-old Mary Lou Colbert** Rear Admiral Colbert was a part of the Coast and Geodetic Survey, today known as NOAA. It had ranks similar to naval ranks (until it was absorbed by the Navy) and foreign assignments, taking Mary Lou to Alaska, Hawaii, the Philippines, and Washington, D.C. Rear Admiral Colbert, was director of the Coast and Geodetic Survey for over ten years and on the board of directors of *National Geographic* magazine. Mary Lou Colbert Neale, oral history, October 4, 2002, Texas Woman's University; Mary Lou Colbert Neale, interview with author, October 1996, Anaheim, California. Available at Woman's Collection at Texas Woman's University.

84 **Others, like Marylene Geraldine "Geri" Nyman** Geri Nyman, class 43-W-1, interview with Dawn Letson, October 4, 1996, available at Texas Woman's University; Geri Nyman, personal email with author, September 18, 1997.

85 **Each of the women** Mary Lou Neale, interview with author.

85 **As Mary Lou later recalled** Mary Lou Colbert Neale, interview with author. Other WASP have anecdotally reported that they were told to say they were a baseball team or other such untruths.

85 **Now that the women were housed** Byrd Howell Granger, *On Final Approach: The Women Airforce Service Pilots of World War II* (Scottsdale, AZ: Falconer Publishing, 1991), 72–74. Granger was a WASP in class 43-W-1.

86 **Food was another problem** Leni "Dedie" Deaton, "Supplementary History of the Women's Airforce Service Pilot Training Program at 319th Army Air Forces Flying Training Detachment, Municipal Airport, Houston, Texas, 318th Army Air Forces Flying Training Detachment, Later Designated 2563rd Army Air Forces Base Unit, Avenger Field, Sweetwater, Texas," in Dora Strother Collection, Texas Woman's University. Geri Nyman, class 43-W-1, interview with Dawn Letson, October 4, 1996, available at Texas Woman's University.

86 **Food was another problem** Dedie Deaton, interview with Ziggy Hunter; Dedie Deaton, interview with Doris Tanner.

86 **She tackled the transportation** Eventually the Army found trucks with trailers attached to the back filled with "home-made" seats. The women called them "cattle trucks," which gives some idea of their comfort. Deaton, "Supplementary History."

87 **There were twenty-two** The twenty-two different types assigned to the 319th in December 1942 included "nine BT-13As, six L-38s, five L-3Fs, five L-4As, and four PT-19As. Of the remainder there were fewer than three of a kind. The Gulf Coast Headquarters recommended that these be removed and replaced with standard military planes." Dora Dougherty Strother, Lt. Col. USAF Reserve, *The WASP Training Program: An Historical Synopsis,* Air Force Museum Research Division, January 1973, 5–6. Dora wrote this report as part of her active duty work with the Air Force Reserve.

87 **Jackie had been** Jacqueline Cochran, *The Stars at Noon* (Boston: Little, Brown, 1954), 120.

87 **As Geri later** Nyman, interview with Letson, 1996.

87 **Dedie did her best** Deaton, interview with Hunter.

88 **Mary Lou later admitted** Neale, interview with author, October 1996.

CHAPTER 7: A CHANCE TO SERVE

89 **Dora Dougherty was reading** *Chicago Herald American,* December 3, 1942. This section on Dora learning about the WASP and getting into training comes primarily from Dora Dougherty Strother McKeown's unpublished memoir.

90 **At the Palmer** At the time Ethel Sheehy was vice president of the Ninety-Nines, Jacqueline Cochran was president.

90 **Dora was young** Dora Dougherty Strother McKeown, memoir, 12–14; Dora Dougherty Strother, interview with author.

90 **Airplanes had been** Dora Dougherty Strother, Oral History Interview K239.0512-2018, by Hugh N. Ahmann, for USAF, June 10, 1991, Fort Worth, Texas, Transcript page 9. Oral history available at Official WASP Archive, Texas Woman's University.

91 **Roosevelt Field** The same field Lindbergh flew out of, and where Jacqueline Cochran had gotten her license. https://www.cradleofaviation.org.

91 **In 1931 they** Dora, memoir, chapter 1.

91 **After eight days of nonstop** *New York Times,* July 2, 1931. There are numerous stories, including the majority of the front page, on pages 1 through 7 of this issue. There is coverage of the flight in the *New York Times,* on page 1 and often additional pages, for the entire eight days of the flight.

92 **Later that year** Dora called it Curtiss-Wright, probably for the flight school, but it was really Curtiss-Reynolds and only a few miles from her home in Winnetka. It became Navy Glenview. http://www.airfields-freeman.com/IL/Airfields_IL_Chicago_N.htm.

92 **Each week there was a parachute** Dora Dougherty Strother, USAF Oral History Interview K239.0512-2018, by Hugh N. Ahmann, June 10, 1991, Fort Worth, Texas.

92 **But when the pilot** Before every flight, the pilot figures out the weight and balance. Every plane has a weight limit, and the weight distribution must be placed in certain parts of the plane. This is why, when a plane is full, pilots will sometimes ask for people to volunteer to get off (even after boarding) and why luggage sometimes is left behind. If the plane is too heavy, it simply won't fly.

92 **Dora's mother wouldn't** Dora Dougherty Strother, USAF Oral History Interview K239.0512-2018, by Hugh N. Ahmann, June 10, 1991, Fort Worth, Texas.

92 **Lucille had lived** Dora Dougherty Strother McKeown, memoir, chapter 1.

93 **Lucille didn't mind** Dora Dougherty Strother McKeown, memoir.

94 **After the CPTP was established** Most of the WASP CPTP students were in the first nine classes. The percentage of WASP who learned to fly in CPTP has been determined via oral histories and questionnaires developed by the author, as well as official military documents. For more of this type of detail, see Katherine Sharp Landdeck, *Pushing the Envelope: The Women Airforce Service Pilots and American Society*, doctoral dissertation presented for the doctor of philosophy degree, University of Tennessee, 2003.

94 **The program was conceived** Much of this section on the CPTP is based on the good work of Dominick A. Pisano, *To Fill the Skies with Pilots: The Civilian Pilot Training Program, 1939–46* (Chicago: University of Illinois Press, 1993; Washington: Smithsonian Institution Press, 2001 [reprint]).

94 **The isolationist movement** Charles Lindbergh was a leading and loud member of the isolationist America First movement.

94 **Another way to send** Women were admitted at a ratio of one woman for every class of ten. By June 1941, CPTP trainees had to sign legal obligations to join the military if the United States went to war. Subsequently women were excluded from joining the CPTP. When women protested this action, they received a letter from Robert Hinckley that stated, "If, or when, the time comes when trained girls are needed in non-combat work to release men for active duty, that will be a different situation." Eleanor Roosevelt received numerous letters from women imploring her to help, and she complained to Hinckley directly. The response from the CAA was clear, stating: "It is generally recognized that male pilots have a wider and more varied potential usefulness to the armed forces than female pilots," and it maintained that it was acting accordingly. Despite the limited time women were eligible for the CPTP, the number of women pilots in the United States jumped from 675 in 1939 to almost 3,000 by July 1, 1941.

95 **That fall Dora** Dora Dougherty Strother, interview with USAF, 1991.

95 **The college administrators** Dora Dougherty Strother, interview with USAF, 1991.

96 **After leaving Cottey College** Dora, memoir.

96 **In the early fall** Letter from Jack Goldberg to Dora Dougherty, 1942, as quoted in memoir: "Something is going on here at New Castle Army Air Base that you would be interested in . . . They are signing up women as civilian ferry pilots. You should look into this."

97 **After a long train** Dora Dougherty, diary, January 12–14, 1943.

97 **One woman worked** Dora Dougherty, memoir, 21–22. Lois Hollingsworth Ziler had a degree in aeronautical engineering from Purdue University despite being orphaned before the age of twelve and raised by her older sisters "rather loosely." She was working in the research division of United Aircraft when she learned about the WASP. Lois Hollingsworth Ziler, interview with author, May 25, 1997.

97 **Commanding officer Garrett's mood** Dora explains in her memoir that Captain Garrett gave a speech similar to this to all three of the first classes of women. She provided these quotes on page 21 of her memoir and borrowed them from an article, "They've Done It Again," in the *Ladies' Home Journal*, March 1944, written by Marjorie Kumler of class 43-W-1 (article in author's possession).

98 **These cottages typically** Some of the women reported the rooms at the Alamotel were "swell," and "right up to date." Betty Deuser Budde and Dora Dougherty, letters home.

98 **Jackie had been horrified** Jackie reluctantly asked permission from the AAF to have the women stay in the courts. They agreed but, mindful of the reputation, for no more than sixty days. Doris Brinker Tanner, *Arnold, Cochran, Deaton: Women Airforce Service Pilots, WWII,* 63. The full telegram from the Training Command can be found in Granger, *On Final Approach,* 79. Private publication in author's possession.

98 **Dora was sharing** Based on Dora's recollection of cold showers and Fleishman's mention of them in his orientation speech, it isn't hard to imagine that the hotel's "running ice water" was a sly mention of the water in the shower. Betty Deuser Budde, letter home to family, January 15, 1943, available at Texas Woman's University; Dora Dougherty, diary, January 14, 1943; Dora Dougherty, letter home, January 18, 1943; Dora Dougherty, letter home, January 19, 1943; Dora Dougherty Strother, *The WASP Training Program: An Historical Synopsis,* Air Force Museum Research Division, January 1973, 8.

98 **Following a sleepless first night** Dora Dougherty, letter home, January 15, 1943.

99 **Dora glanced around** Dora Dougherty Strother McKeown, memoir, 22.

99 **Fleishman began his speech** The speech became very popular across the Training Command. Letter from Mrs. Cliff Deaton (Dedie Deaton) to Miss Nora McSweeney, Pentagon, October 8, 1943. McSweeney worked in Cochran's office in the Pentagon. Available at Texas Woman's University, WASP Collection, MSS 384, Doris Tanner, Series 10, Box 2, Folder 41. Lieutenant Alfred Fleishman, Orientation to class 43-W-4, Women's Flying Training Detachment, Houston, Texas, February 16, 1943. Available at the WASP Collection, Texas Woman's University.

100 **If your father is a General** Fleishman wasn't just speaking hypothetically here. The first two classes had daughters of both an admiral and a general. Fleishman, orientation, February 1943.

100 **"My heart and my determination"** Dora Dougherty Strother McKeown, memoir, 23. A transcript of Fleishman's speech is over nine pages long.

100 **They filled out Civil Service** Marjorie Kumler, "They've Done It Again," *Ladies' Home Journal,* March 1944.

101 **Betty Deuser** Betty Deuser Budde, class 43-W-3, letter home to family, January 15, 1943, available at Texas Woman's University.

101 **That evening the women waltzed** Betty Deuser Budde, class 43-W-3, letter home to family, January 15, 1943, available at Texas Woman's University; Dora didn't get a leather jacket, but didn't mind as she thought it was too warm anyway. She got a size 40 sweater but Marge (who is normally a 13) got a 42 and they "got a big laugh when she tried it on," Dora, letter home, January 15, 1943.

102 **Now Dora and her classmates** The third class seems not to have shared the first two classes' skepticism about Fleishman. When he was promoted to first lieutenant in late January, "everyone was very happy" (Dora, letter). Betty Deuser Budde, letters, January 18, 1943; Dora, diary, January 20, 1943; Dora, letter home, January 27, 1943; Dora, memoir, 25.

102 **After the rain** Betty Deuser Budde, letters, January 15–20, 1943.

102 **Dora, never one to complain** Dora, letter home, May 9, 1943.

103 **Then there was ground school** Dora, letter, January 29, 1943.

103 **He was in his late twenties** Budde, letter home, January 18, 1943. Budde names him in her February 1 letter.

103 **He sat behind Dora** While most aircraft enthusiasts think of the Taylorcraft as a side-by-side airplane, during World War II the company developed a tandem plane for the U.S. Army Air Corps, producing more than 2,000 of the tandem L-2 liaison planes. It was this plane that Dora flew that day.

103 **She had never** Dora, letter home, January 15, 1943; Budde, letters, January 20, 1943.

103 **She flew for an hour** Dora, diary, January 18–23, 1943; Dora, letter home, January 15, 1943; Budde, letters home, January 15–20, 1943.

104 **Dora began writing home** Dora, letter home, January 25, 1943. They practiced many of their landings and procedures at an auxiliary field, Dado Field, but all of their initial takeoffs and final landings were at the Houston airport—often in between Braniff Airlines' commercial flights.

104 **At the end of a long day** Betty Budde, letters, and Dora, letters home.

104 **Diaries and letters home** Dora, letter home, January 25, 1943.

104 **One of the women** The historical record has not revealed who.

104 **"We get up at six"** Dora, memoir, 28.

CHAPTER 8: CARRYING ON

106 **Before long** These stories about Betty Gillies are from Teresa James, interview with Dawn Letson, June 1998, Lake Worth, Florida, Official WASP Archive, Texas Woman's University, Denton, Texas.

107 **On February 15, 1943** Teresa James, diary, February 15, 1943.

107 **The plane needed to be delivered** Teresa later believed she had delivered it for use in the movie *Ladies Courageous;* while that is possible, she is likely mistaken. The film was shot at Long Beach from August to November 1943. It is unlikely they would have asked her to fly an open-cockpit PT-19 across the country in February when principal photography didn't begin until late summer. It is even more unlikely that the AAF would have let go of one of their planes for that long.

107 **The plane Teresa was assigned** This story of Teresa's flight and experiences in California come primarily from Teresa James, diary, March 1943.

109 **Teresa spent the rest** Teresa James, diary, March 3, 1943.

109 **Betty Gillies was there** Teresa James, interview with Dawn Letson. The story goes that Betty was allowed to check out in the P-47 because Nancy had been frank with the commander at Wilmington, telling him that she was tired of flying light planes and she was leaving as a result. No doubt the Ferrying Division didn't want to lose Betty and the other experienced WAFS pilots at their base, so—despite the official line that women were restricted to trainers—the division began to give the women a chance with the pursuits.

110 **While Teresa continued flying** WAFS initially based with the 6th Ferrying Group, Long Beach, included Cornelia Fort, Barbara Jane Erickson, Evelyn Sharp, Barbara

Towne, Bernice Batten, and soon Nancy Love. Cornelia's family home, Fortland, had burned beyond saving, particularly the wing with Cornelia's room, just a few weeks earlier. She lost all of her family pictures, including those of her father, who had died only three years before, and all of her diaries that she had kept since childhood and throughout her time flying in Hawaii and in the WAFS. Simbeck, *Daughter of the Air,* 196–203.

110 **The 6th Ferrying Group** Captain Walter J. Marx, Ferrying Division Historical Officer, Historical Branch, Intelligence and Security Division, Headquarters, Air Transport Command, *History of the Air Transport Command: Women Pilots in the Air Transport Command* (Washington, DC: U.S. Government Printing Office, March 1945), Yvonne Pateman Collection, United States Air Force Academy, MS 31, Microfilm roll #8, A3003, 79.

110 **In a letter** Cornelia Fort, letter home, February 17, 1943, in Doris Brinker Tanner files, Official WASP Archive, Texas Woman's University, Denton, Texas.

110 **Besides the balmy weather** The officers' club was often frequented by movie stars who had been drafted into the service. The club also boasted one of the best bands in the country, along with "silver chafing dishes filled with fried oysters and cheese." Cornelia Fort, letter home.

110 **Cornelia wrote** Cornelia Fort, letter home to mother, February 17, 1943. (Also cited in Simbeck, *Daughter of the Air,* 208–9.)

111 **"Any girl who has flown"** Cornelia Fort, letter home, February 17, 1943. https://www.pbs.org/wgbh/americanexperience/features/flygirls-cornelia-fort/.

111 **The women flew their first** Cornelia Fort, letter home to mother, February 22, 1943.

111 **Cornelia and the others** Cornelia Fort, letter home to mother, February 22, 1943.

112 **Cornelia described the experience** Cornelia Fort, letter home to mother, February 23, 1943. Madge Rutherford Minton, letter home, September 8, 1943, Official WASP Archive, Texas Woman's University, Denton, Texas.

112 **The P-51 had been designed** Teresa James later called it a "little jackrabbit" and struggled initially to fly it compared to the heavier, 2,800-horsepower P-40. Teresa James, interview with author, March 20, 1999, Orlando, Florida.

113 **Up in the clouds** Nancy Love, logbook, courtesy the International Women's Air and Space Museum; Delphine Bohn, unpublished memoir "Catch a Shooting Star," chapter 10; Rickman, *Nancy Love,* 111.

113 **Bob wrote to her that night** Letter from Robert Love to Nancy Love, as cited in Rickman, *Nancy Love,* 113.

113 **Within one month** While the Ferrying Division technically limited the women to flying light trainers, it was the commanders at each base who really determined what and how much the women could fly. The workload at each base influenced their flying as well. The Long Beach base, for example, was surrounded by numerous factories, which were busily building new, sophisticated aircraft for the war. For example, more than 10,000 P-51s were built in North American Aviation's Inglewood, California, factory and another 5,000 at their factory near Dallas. The P-51 was vital to the war effort, with some arguing it was the most important plane of the war. The 6th Ferrying Group was responsible for getting the new planes to points of debarkation on the East Coast

as quickly as possible. The high levels of productivity meant that Long Beach desperately needed competent pilots, and the commanding officers did not care what gender the pilots were as long as they delivered the planes quickly and safely. Love, logbook.

113 **Nancy much preferred** Allie Love, telephone call with author, October 31, 2018; Margaret "Marky" Love, interview with Deborah G. Douglas, Aeronautics Department of Smithsonian National Air and Space Museum, interview in 1986, transcript from September 16, 1986, in author's possession.

114 **Other WAFS pilots quickly** A. J. Merton England, CWO, AAF Historical Office, Headquarters, Army Air Forces, *Army Air Forces Historical Studies No. 55: Women Pilots with the AAF, 1941–1944* (Washington, DC: U.S. Government Printing Office, March 1946), 39–41.

114 **She had been flying** The male pilot, Stamme, reported that he pulled his plane up in order to tear the two planes apart into a "slightly stalled attitude and the engine was sputtering due to having my mixture leaned out and the sudden pull up." He nosed back down to prevent the stall and looked around for the other plane. His right strut was sprung and towed in, his right fuel tank was damaged, and the center lower cockpit fairing was damaged. Stamme thought he had struck Cornelia's cockpit. It seems he also hit her wing. The odd thing about some BT-13s was that the left wingtip was wooden while the right wingtip was metal. Upon impact the wooden wingtip peeled up six feet of the leading edge of Cornelia's left wing toward the center of the plane and the cockpit. She didn't have a chance. Official AAF Report of Accident, Cornelia C. Fort, March 21, 1943. This report contains descriptions of the accident, reports of aircraft accident, reports of damage to Stamme's plane, witness statements, aircraft clearance records, pictures of Cornelia Fort's plane, and telegrams notifying various commands about the accident, and is available at the Official WASP Archive, Texas Woman's University, Denton, Texas; For another description of the accident see Simbeck, *Daughter of the Air*, 226–36.

114 **According to witnesses** She also did not cut the switch and turn off the gas, something she would have done if she had been conscious to try to avoid fire, suggesting she was unconscious from the initial contact. Letter from Nancy Love to Cornelia Fort's flight instructor; Simbeck, *Daughter of the Air*.

114 **The young male pilot's plane** Lieutenant Biggio, also on the flight, watched the plane on the right "suddenly break off to the right as though on a snap roll. It seemed to go over about one and one-half times and then the nose fell through and it went into a spin to the right." Local farmer Joe Seymour heard the planes flying overhead and looked up. He watched Cornelia's plane in its final moments: "The ship leveled, then rolled over two or three times, then it turned South gradually going up and rolled over two or three more times, and the last time it stayed on its back and started down. After a smart piece it started spinning to the left. It spun all the way to the ground." Report of Accident, Cornelia C. Fort, March 21, 1943; Simbeck, *Daughter of the Air*, 226–36.

114 **Cornelia** Cornelia Fort, letter home to mother, March 10, 1943; Cornelia Fort, letter home to mother, March 16, 1943.

114 **Cornelia's funeral** It was the only funeral for her pilots that Nancy would attend.

115 **At the church** Later, women would not have the same honor. Simbeck, *Daughter of the Air*.

115 **Because the WAFS pilots** The women were covered by the very small Civil Service

Commission death benefit, but not all of them received it and how much they received seems to have varied. While Cornelia's biographer Rob Simbeck reports that her mother received $250, Mary Howson's mother received a cold, formal letter and a check for $171.50 to pay for her daughter's funeral. Granger says they were all eligible for only $200. Granger, *On Final Approach*, 1991, 475.

115 **It was bad enough** Margaret Love, interview with Douglas, 1986.

115 **"My feeling about the loss"** Rickman, *Nancy Love*, 119.

115 **Cornelia's death haunted** Cornelia Fort was a wonderful observer of the world around her, and her writings told the stories of the women pilots and the beauty of the sky. The tragedy was theirs but is without a doubt ours as well. Simbeck, *Daughter of the Air*, 234.

CHAPTER 9: THE ARMY WAY

117 **On January 27, 1943** Dora Dougherty Strother McKeown, letter home, January 27, 1943, Official WASP Archive, Texas Woman's University, Denton, Texas.

118 **The following afternoon** Dora Dougherty, letter home, January 28, 1943.

118 **A week after her initial visit** The AAF Training Command spent weeks looking for a location for a second school for women. AAF Training Command History; Leni Leoti "Dedie" Clark Deaton, interview with Doris Tanner (WASP), March 20, 1982, found at Official WASP Archive, Texas Woman's University, Denton, Texas.

118 **Ten days after** Dora wrote home a bit annoyed by it all: "We were supposed to get a lot done but I can't see that we accomplished anything." Dora Dougherty, letter home, February 8 and 9, 1943.

118 **While promises were made** "Cochran Visits Brain Child," *Fifinella Gazette* no. 1, February 10, 1943. Available at Official WASP Archive, Texas Woman's University, Denton, Texas.

119 **Aviation Enterprises** *Fifinella Gazette* no. 1, February 10, 1943.

119 **That February** Byrd Howell Granger, a member of class 43-W-1 from New Rochelle, New York, was the founding editor of the *Fifinella Gazette* and had learned about Dahl's creatures the year before, after Walt Disney released artwork for an animated movie based on the book. Byrd wrote to Disney himself to ask for permission to use the Fifinella name and image, and permission was granted. *Fifinella Gazette* no. 1, February 10, 1943.

119 **Dora offered to help** Dora Dougherty, letter home, February 6, 1943.

120 **As the days went on** Dora Dougherty, letter home, February 8, 1943.

120 **Three days later** Dora Dougherty, letter home, February 11, 1943.

121 **Again she wrote home** Dora Dougherty, letter home, February 22, 1943.

121 **But Dora was** Dora happily wrote in her diary, "*PASSED ARMY CHECK* with St. Shepherd and was I happy. Gosh." Dora Dougherty, letter home, April 25, 1943; Dora Dougherty, diary, April 25, 1943, available at Official WASP Archive, Texas Woman's University, Denton, Texas.

122 **Only weeks after** Dora, letter home, March 14, 1943. Margaret was the first of the women to die. Cornelia would die eleven days later but is most often remembered, as she was flying on active duty and Margaret was a trainee.

122 **She went up** Margaret Oldenburg, USAAF official accident report, available at Official WASP Archive, Texas Woman's University, Denton, Texas.

122 **At about 5:45 P.M.** "Woman Student Pilot, Man Die in Plane Crash: Trainer Craft Falls in Pasture South of City," *Houston Post*, March 8, 1943.

122 **Dora had been in a different** *Fifinella Gazette* no. 3, April 1, 1943. Marge Oldenburg official USAAF accident report, available at Texas Woman's University, Denton, Texas; Norris G. Morgan, https://www.findagrave.com/cgi-bin/fg.cgi?page=gr&GRid =35560870.

123 **That night Dora** Dora Dougherty, diary, March 7, 1943.

123 **Following Dedie's advice** Dora Dougherty, letter home, March 24, 1943.

123 **Dora would sit grounded** Betty Budde, letters home, March 1943, available at Official WASP Archive, Texas Woman's University, Denton, Texas; Dora, letter home, March 24, 1943.

124 **When Margaret Oldenburg's body** "Woman Student, Man Die in Plane Crash"; *WASP: In Memoriam*, booklet dedicated to the 38 WASP who were killed, available Official WASP Archive, Texas Woman's University, Denton, Texas; Norris G. Morgan, 1901–1943, https://www.findagrave.com/cgi-bin/fg.cgi?page=gr&GRid=35560870; Granger, *On Final Approach*, 107-8.

124 **Margaret's family** There is some discrepancy in the historical record regarding how much the women received. Granger says $200.

124 **After Margaret's death** Betty Budde, letter home, February 4, 1943; Dora Dougherty, letter home, February 4, 1943.

124 **Despite it all** Jack H. Oldenburg, condolence response note, MSS 807c Oldenburg, Official WASP Archive, Texas Woman's University, Denton, Texas.

CHAPTER 10: THE HOPEFULS

126 **"THE WAFS"** "The WAFS: A Squadron of 25 Girls Is Leading the Way for U.S. Women Fliers," *Look*, February 9, 1943.

126 **All Marty had ever wanted** This discussion of Mary Anna "Marty" Martin Wyall's story is based on these sources: Mary Anna Martin Wyall, interview with Dawn Letson, June 28–30, 1992, Fort Wayne, Indiana. Official WASP Archive, Texas Woman's University, Denton, Texas; and Mary Anna Martin Wyall, interviews with author, 1996–2017.

129 **She could have her pick** While in 1940 just 6 percent of the general white female population had some college (at least one year) and 4 percent had four or more years, 80 percent of the WASP had at least one year, 54 percent had a four-year degree, and 7 percent had coursework at the graduate level. Fifteen percent of the WASP clearly attended private colleges or universities. WASP statistics based on data gathered by the author for the Landdeck, "Pushing of the Envelope." General data from Bureau of Census, *Historical Studies of the United States, Colonial Times to 1970, Part 1* (Washington, DC: U.S. Department of Commerce, 1975), 380.

129 **In 1942** Nancy Love had been concerned that a black woman might apply for her squadron and that she would have to turn her away. As far as we know, Nancy did not have any African American women applying to join the WAFS, but she would have likely struggled to find a place for them even if they had applied. Later in the war, the

Tuskegee Airmen trained at Mather Field in California along with some of the WASP. Delphine Bohn, unpublished memoir, "Catch a Shooting Star," Official WASP Archive, Texas Woman's University, Denton, Texas; Caro Bayley Bosca, interview with author, June 1996, Dayton, Ohio.

129 **Entire towns** Many black Americans carried *The Negro Motorist Green Book* with them when they traveled across the United States. The book noted the names and locations of friendly hotels and restaurants and warned of those dangerous "sundown" towns.

130 **Furthermore, the women** The Navy's WAVES did not admit black women until over two years after it was founded, under the argument that there were no black men going to sea for the women to replace; even at the height of the war, nearly all black men in the Navy were relegated to positions as cooks or waiters. The Navy's policy reflected the standard view that women in the military were in a support role, releasing men for more important duties, such as combat; the WASP struggled against this view in 1944. The argument that black personnel in the WAVES were unnecessary held sway until President Roosevelt, under pressure from black leaders, ordered the Navy to admit them. Seventy-two black women ended up joining the WAVES and were trained alongside white women; because there were so few of them, segregation was considered too difficult logistically. The former director of the WAVES, Mildred McAfee Horton, asserted that she did not see the integration of the black women as a problem. In her memoir, *The Stars at Noon,* Jackie argued, "I do not believe this country can have second class citizenship for any of its people . . ." Jacqueline Cochran, *The Stars at Noon* (Boston: Little, Brown, 1954); Cochran, interview by Kenneth Leish, Oral History Research Office of Columbia University, May 1960, page 46 of transcribed interview; Jacqueline Cochran, interview with Natalie Stewart Smith, Indio, California, 1977, available at U.S. Air Force Academy archives. Brenda Moore, *To Serve My Country, To Serve My Race: The Story of the Only African American WACS Stationed Overseas During World War II* (New York: New York University Press, 1996), 2–3.

130 **Instead, she actively** Janet Harmon Bragg had a commercial pilot's license and worked to promote desegregation of the armed forces in part through her column, "Negroes in Aviation," for the *Chicago Defender,* a prominent newspaper by and for black Americans. She was likely one of only two—with Willa Brown being the first— black women to hold that license. She applied to join, likely in the early days of the program, when Ethel Sheehy came to the Palmer House in Chicago. As Janet later described the meeting, Ethel didn't quite know what to do with her. They met and talked it over, with Ethel explaining the difficulties of bringing an African American woman into an all-white program training in the South. While race was undoubtedly the major factor in Janet's rejection, one other issue worked against her. She turned thirty-five years old in March of 1942. The top age for training was thirty-five. Depending on when she applied, she might have been too old.

130 **Mildred had learned to fly** https://www.nps.gov/tuai/and-there-were-women .htm.

131 **Thank you for your letter** Letter from Jacqueline Cochran to Sadie Lee Johnson, August 19, 1943. WASP Historical Subjects, "African American Applicants" file, National Archives II, College Park, Maryland. Sadie wrote her letter applying on August 4, 1943. Thanks to Pat Jernigan, who initially found this letter and generously shared it with author.

131 **"However I would suggest"** Cochran may have believed what she said about it simply being too difficult to bring black women into the already tenuously organized WASP, but other military branches made some effort to incorporate black women, however forced. The WAAC quickly admitted African American women, thanks to the efforts of black political organizations, and gave them their share of officer positions, but the women remained segregated. The WAAC, eventually the WAC, was a large enough organization that the black women could be segregated from the white women and still be a large enough group to be effectively utilized. Other branches of the military were not so willing to incorporate black women. The Marines did not admit African American women until 1949, four years after the end of World War II. Moore, *To Serve My Country, To Serve My Race*, 2–3.

131 **Mildred was furious** The actual letter addressed to Mildred Hemmons Carter has been lost to time, but the letter to Sadie Lee Johnson fits the description Carter has given of the letter, and as it was essentially a form letter with date and name changed, it is safe to assume this is the letter—or very similar to the letter—that Carter received. https://www.cnn.com/2012/01/22/us/tuskegee-airmen-first-couple/index.html.

132 **Ola Mildred Rexroat** Ola M. Rexroat, telephone interview with author, February 3, 1997; Margaret Chamberlain Tamplin, telephone interview with author, February 3, 1997; Charlyne Creger, interview with author.

132 **There were also very few** Julie Jenner Stege, interview with author, July 27, 2001, Oshkosh, Wisconsin; Bee Falk Haydu, questionnaire 1996, in author's possession; Bee Haydu, interviews with author, 1997–2016.

132 **Hazel Ah Ying Lee** "How to Tell Japs from the Chinese: Angry Citizens Victimize Allies with Emotional Outburst at Enemy," *Life*, December 22, 1941, 81–82.

132 **Hazel had learned to fly** Kay Gott, *Hazel Ah Ying Lee: Women Airforce Service Pilot*, self-published, 1996, in author's possession; https://chineseexclusionfiles.com /tag/virginia-wong/.

CHAPTER 11: EARNING THOSE WINGS

134 **Nancy sent the first letter** Nancy Love, letter to Jacqueline Cochran, November 4, 1942, Jacqueline Cochran Papers, Eisenhower Library.

135 **Jackie wrote back** Jacqueline Cochran, letter to Nancy Love, Jacqueline Cochran Collection, Eisenhower Library.

135 **On February 24, 1943** This detail about the telephone call is in the official history of the WASP in the Air Transport Command. The historian who wrote it cites a letter Nancy wrote to Tunner on March 3, 1943, about it. Captain Walter J. Marx, Ferrying Division Historical Officer, Historical Branch, Intelligence and Security Division, Headquarters, Air Transport Command, *History of the Air Transport Command: Women Pilots in the Air Transport Command* (Washington, DC: U.S. Government Printing Office, March 1945), Yvonne Pateman Collection, United States Air Force Academy, MS 31, Microfilm roll #8, A3003.

135 **By February 1943, Jackie** Madge Rutherford (Minton), letter home, March 3, 1943; Ruth Lindley, letters home, April 6, 1943.

136 **In March of 1943, Congress** Oveta Culp Hobby, as head of the women, faced unexpected resistance to the new status, with one reporter claiming the women of the WAC were going to be given prophylactics before they left to serve, an untrue claim

suggesting that the women were serving as prostitutes for the male soldiers, representative of the type of negative views some had about the women who volunteered to serve their country. Meyer, *Creating G.I. Jane;* Judith Bellafaire, *Women's Army Corps: A Commemoration of World War II Service,* Center for Military History Publication 52-15, http://history.army.mil/brochures/WAC/WAC/.htm.

137 **With a history** Rich, *Jackie Cochran.*

137 **In late March 1943** Marx, *ATC History,* 74; A. J. Merton England, CWO, AAF Historical Office, Headquarters, Army Air Forces, *Army Air Forces Historical Studies, No. 55: Women Pilots with the AAF, 1941–1944* (Washington, DC: U.S. Government Printing Office, March 1946), 40.

137 **And just days after** Marx, *ATC History,* 82.

138 **With no science to support them** Marx, *ATC History,* 83, quoting Civil Aeronautics Authority, *Handbook for Medical Examiners,* July 1, 1940, part II, p. 34, para. 3.

138 **At that time** Only forty years after the Wright brothers' first flight in 1903, aviation medicine was still in its relative infancy and women pilots were such a small segment of the flying population that they constituted an even greater unknown.

138 **Betty and the Ninety-Nines** Marguerite Jean Terrell Moreo McCreery, questionnaire, August 12, 1996, in author's possession; *Medical Consideration of the WASP,* August 21, 1945, 5–12, available at Official WASP Archive, Texas Woman's University, Denton, Texas; Delphine Bohn says, "She took a short leave, delivered a beautiful baby, left him with her family, and returned to fulfill her contract to fly airplanes." Delphine Bohn, unpublished memoir, "Catch a Shooting Star," V-17, available at Official WASP Archive, Texas Woman's University, Denton, Texas; Teresa James, interview with author, March 20, 1999, Orlando, Florida.

139 **That same month** Rickman, *Nancy Love,* 123–24.

139 **But she was even** Director of operations Colonel George D. Campbell penciled in a note stating, "Mrs. Love objected to this directive" on a copy of the Romulus directive limiting the women's flying. England, *Army Air Forces Historical Studies No. 55,* 40.

139 **Finally, under pressure** Marx, *ATC History,* 85–86.

139 **Although the women had** England, *Army Air Forces Historical Studies No. 55,* 43.

140 **Fortunately, the WAFS' track record** Marx, *ATC History,* 86.

141 **In his new capacity** *Fifinella Gazette* 1, no. 4, April 23, 1943; "We've been drilling so much those brown C.A.P. shoes of mine sure wore through fast," April 24, 1943. Betty Budde, letter home, March 25, 1943

141 **But there weren't any wings** Dora Dougherty, memoir; Granger, *On Final Approach;* Dora Dougherty, letters; Doris Brinker Tanner, *Arnold, Cochran, Deaton: Women Airforce Service Pilots, WWII.* Private publication in author's possession.

141 **The jeweler embellished** The WASP wings can cause confusion, as they are so different. The WAFS wore standard-issue Air Transport Command wings. Classes 43-W-1 and 43-W-2 had the same wings, with the exception of the shield reading "W 2," of course. The wings for 43-W-3 were made by a different manufacturer, Balford, and the shield and wings themselves were different: they lacked the "sweep" of the original GEMCO wings. Regulation pilot wings were unavailable for classes 43-W-4, 43-W-5, and 43-W-6, so they were modified from observer wings. Their shield is slightly differ-

ent and the sweep of the wings is different. Class 43-W-7 wings are pilot wings but a bit bigger than in earlier years. This is the last class with the shield. By the time class 43-W-8 graduated, the AAF decided the women should have official wings. and a special wing was designed for them with a "lozenge" in the middle instead of the shield. Unfortunately, the wings did not arrive in time for graduation. A rushed effort found enough AMICO-built pilot wings, the shield was cut away, and the "lozenge" or diamond was placed on the shield. Classes 44-W-1 through the final class, 44-W-10, all had the same "official" WASP wings. See Appendix C: "Wings" of Granger's *On Final Approach* for more information.

141 **Jackie left St. Vincent's** Cochran, *The Stars at Noon*, 120.

141 **On graduation day** Jacqueline Cochran description from photos from the day. Details of the graduation from the following sources: "Graduation Ceremony, First Graduating Class: Women's Flying Training Program, Army Air Forces (April 24, 1943)," PR Office, Ellington Field, Texas, as cited in Granger, *On Final Approach,* 114, 117, 119; Lieutenant Colonel Dora Dougherty Strother, USAF Reserve, *The WASP Training Program: An Historical Synopsis,* Air Force Museum Research Division, January 1973, 10.

143 **Jackie presented herself** Jackie also reminded the general, "You and I had this job in mind for myself from 1941 on when you recommended this set-up to General George." General George seemed to be worried that no one person should be in charge because the women would report to their sector commanders. But Jackie believed one person needed to keep track of all of the women and make sure they did their jobs well and were treated fairly. Jacqueline Cochran, memo to General Henry Arnold, Box 6, "WAC Data," Eisenhower Library, as cited in Granger, *On Final Approach,* 119.

144 **By all accounts** Teresa James, interview with author; Jane Sincell Straughan, interview with Nancy Durr, October 4, 1996, Anaheim, California, Official WASP Archive, Texas Woman's University, Denton, Texas; Margaret Ray Ringenberg of class 43-W-5 suggested it took a bit longer to fit in when she joined the WAFS. Margaret Ray Ringenberg, interview with author, June 1996.

CHAPTER 12: AVENGER FIELD

145 **Sweetwater was quite** Madge Rutherford (Minton), letter home, February 25, 1943.

146 **Although Hazel** Story from Dedie Deaton in interview with Doris Brinker Tanner, 1982.

146 **The reputation of women** See Meyer, *Creating G.I. Jane.*

146 **Dedie was put on high alert** This explanation of Avenger Field before the men left is based on the following sources: Doris Brinker Tanner, *The Sweetwater Experience and Leni Leoti,* privately published, copy available at Official WASP Archive, Texas Woman's University; Leni Leoti "Dedie" Clark Deaton, interview with Doris Tanner (WASP), March 20, 1982, found at Official WASP Archive, Texas Woman's University, Denton, Texas; Madge Rutherford (Minton), letters home, February 27, 1943; "the instructor's hands" quote from Madge Rutherford (Minton), letters home, March 11, 1943.

148 *Life* **magazine** "How to Tell Japs from the Chinese: Angry Citizens Victimize Allies with Emotional Outburst at Enemy," *Life,* December 22, 1941.

148 **One day Hazel found herself** Story from Hazel's classmate Faith Buchner Richards, as told in Gott, *Hazel Ah Ying Lee,* Madge Rutherford (Minton), letters home, June 5, 1943.

148 **Dedie Deaton soon learned** These paragraphs on good relations with Sweetwater are based upon these sources: Caro Bayley (Bosca), letter home, May 28, 1943; Caro Bayley (Bosca), letter home, June 15, 1943; Leoti "Dedie" Deaton, Chief Establishment Officer, Women Airforce Service Pilots, interview with Ziggy Hunter, March 18, 1975, edited by Dawn Letson and Nancy M. Durr, available at Official WASP Archive, Texas Woman's University, Denton, Texas; Deaton, interview with Tanner, 1982.

149 **It wasn't long** Description of the women's lives in Sweetwater is drawn from the following sources: Winifred Wood, *We Were WASPs* (Coral Gables, FL: Glade House, 1945), 21; Dora Dougherty, letter home, May 17, 20, 28, 1943; Caro Bayley Bosca, letter home, May 28–30, 1943; Dora Dougherty, letter home, May 17, 1943; Dora Dougherty, diary, May 28, 1943; Madge Rutherford Minton, letter home, May 28, 1943; Granger, *On Final Approach,* A-73 D, 121. The women brought with them the last of the planes from the 319th: AT-6s and twin-engine AT-11s. Liquor story from Granger, *On Final Approach,* 121.

151 **The hotel, built in 1927** Inez Woodward Woods, class 43-W-4, letters home, April 24, 1943, http://www.texasescapes.com/MikeCoxTexasTales/Bluebonnet-Hotel .htm.

151 **Most new recruits** Caro Bayley Bosca, letter to Page, letters home, Official WASP Archive, Texas Woman's University; Caro Bayley Bosca, questionnaire, 1996; Caro Bayley Bosca, interview, October 4, 2003, Official WASP Archive, Texas Woman's University, Denton, Texas; Wood, *We Were WASPs,* 12–14.

152 **The next morning** Caro Bayley Bosca, letters home, May 28, 1943; Madge Rutherford Minton, friend letter home to Madge's parents after a visit to base, with Minton's letters home, 1943; Wood, *We Were WASPs,* 15–16.

152 **By June of 1943, Dedie** Army Air Forces Gulf Coast Training Command Delinquency List, June 1943, available at Official WASP Archive, Texas Woman's University, Denton, Texas.

153 **An Army officer** Caro Bayley Bosca, letter home, May 29, 1943.

153 **Dedie wasn't merely** Deaton, interview with Tanner, March 20, 1982.

154 **Soon she had them** Ann Russ Holaday, 43-W-7, letter home, August 1943, available at Official WASP Archive, Texas Woman's University, Denton, Texas.

154 **On base and at the pool** Dora Dougherty, letter home, January 25, 1943: "She has that rare but essential ability for this job of being everywhere at once."

154 **But beyond those areas** Not all of the women drank. Some, like Florence Shutsy Reynolds, were so afraid of being washed out that they followed Dedie's rules to the letter. Florence Shutsy Reynolds, interviews with author, 1996–2017; Dorothy Swain Lewis, interview with author, Oshkosh, Wisconsin; Betty Jo Reed, interview with author, Oshkosh, Wisconsin; Dora Dougherty, letter home, May 28, 1943, and diary, May 28, 1943; Madge Rutherford, letter home, May 28, 1943; Caro Bayley, letter home, May 29, 1943; Granger, *On Final Approach.*

154 **Meanwhile the newsreel crews** Caro Bayley Bosca, letter home, August 17, 1943; Madge Rutherford Minton, letters home.

154 **Another consequence** Lucile Doll Wise, email with author, September 27, 2017; Shirley Kruse, email with author, October 12, 2017; Caro Bayley Bosca, letters home, 1943; Madge Rutherford Minton, letters home; Nell Stevenson Bright, interviews with author.

155 **She began keeping records** Board Hearings, Spiral Notebooks, 1943–1944, available at Official WASP Archive, Texas Woman's University, Denton, Texas.

155 **She sent the woman** The instructor was soon sent away, too. Board Hearings; Deaton, interview with Hunter.

155 **Dedie was especially intolerant** Deaton, interview with Tanner, March 20, 1982.

156 **Several of the women reported** Madge Rutherford (Minton), letter home, May 1943; Caro Bayley Bosca, letter home, May 27, 1943.

156 **And while the *Avenger*** "Officers Leave," *Avenger* 1, no. 2, June 28, 1943.

157 **"We got word that"** Inez Woodward Wood, letter home, postmarked June 7, 1943; Madge Rutherford Minton, letter home, May 26, 1943; Dora Dougherty, letter home, May 28, 1943.

157 **Dedie would later claim** Deaton, interview with Doris Brinker Tanner, 1982. While no one corroborates the pregnancy stories, it makes sense that Dedie was one of the only people to know about it.

CHAPTER 13: EXPANSION

158 **Under pressure from Jackie** Granger, *On Final Approach*, 119.

159 **Not everyone was happy** Jackie's new position meant she could "determine where and in what capacities women pilots could best be used, allocate them to the using agencies, decide upon the number to be trained and the standards for acceptance and graduation, formulate rules governing their conduct and welfare, draw up plans for militarization, and make inspection trips and maintain liaison with using agencies." A. J. Merton England, CWO, AAF Historical Office, Headquarters, Army Air Forces, *Army Air Forces Historical Studies No. 55: Women Pilots with the AAF, 1941–1944* (Washington, DC: U.S. Government Printing Office, March 1946), 44–46; "Coup for Cochran," *Newsweek*, July 19, 1943, 40–42.

159 **In mid-June 1943** Arnold wrote that he expected to have 500 women flying for the Army Air Forces by December 1943 and 1,200 in the air by the end of 1944. General H. H. Arnold, Commanding General of the Army Air Forces, Memorandum for General Marshall, June 14, 1943, Jacqueline Cochran Collection, Eisenhower Library.

159 **General Arnold strongly advocated** Arnold was a noted advocate for an independent air force, which may have made him particularly reluctant to hand over control of the women pilots to the WAC.

159 **There were, in fact** General H. H. Arnold, Commanding General of the Army Air Forces, Memorandum for General Marshall, June 14, 1943, Jacqueline Cochran Collection, Eisenhower Library.

160 **Ever the pragmatist** They were commissioned into the Army or the Naval Reserve and received "the same pay and allowances and [were] entitled to the same rights, privileges, and benefits as members of the Officers' Reserve Corps of the Army and the Naval Reserve of the Navy with the same grade and length of service." Public Law 38—78th Congress, Chapter 63—1st Session, H.B. 1857. Approved April 16, 1943. Attached

to General H. H. Arnold, Commanding General of the Army Air Forces, Memorandum for General Marshall, June 14, 1943, Jacqueline Cochran Collection, Eisenhower Library.

160 **Less than two weeks after** "Conversation Between Miss Cochran, Colonel Hobby and Colonel Carmichael," transcript, June 25, 1943, Jacqueline Cochran Collection, Eisenhower Library.

161 **It was a gamble** Madge Rutherford Minton, letter home, July 5, 1943.

161 **That same July** Madge Rutherford Minton, letter home, June 17, 1943; Dora Dougherty, memoir; Dora Dougherty, letter home, June 16, 1943; Dora Dougherty, diary, July 2, 1943.

161 **The ATC made phone calls** Captain Walter J. Marx, Ferrying Division Historical Officer, Historical Branch, Intelligence and Security Division, Headquarters, Air Transport Command, *History of the Air Transport Command: Women Pilots in the Air Transport Command* (Washington, DC: U.S. Government Printing Office, March 1945), Yvonne Pateman Collection, United States Air Force Academy, MS 31, Microfilm roll #8, A3003, 100–101.

161 **Soon, twenty-five graduates** Dora Dougherty Strother McKeown, unpublished memoir, in author's possession; Dora Dougherty, diary; Betty Budde, letter home.

163 **After the meeting** This discussion of the meeting in Washington and plans for Camp Davis are based in part on these sources: Dora Dougherty, memoir; Dora Dougherty, diary, July 21, 1943; Betty Budde, letter home, July 21, 1943; and Lois Hollingsworth Ziler, interview with author, May 25, 1997.

163 **They would live** After her arrival Dora wrote: "We were brought to our bare barracks in the nurses quarters & then taken to one of the small mess halls—looks dismal but not too." Dora Dougherty, letter home, July 22, 1943.

164 **The women had fun** Dora Dougherty, letter home, July 23, 1943.

164 **They ended up landing** Dora Dougherty, memoir, chapter 6.

164 **Finally, Camp Davis** Dora Dougherty, memoir, chapter 6.

164 **Commanding officer Major Lovick Stephenson** Dora Dougherty Strother McKeown, memoir, chapter 6, 68. Stephenson commanding the 4th Tow Target Squadron of the Third Air Force.

165 **It was hard not to feel** Betty Deuser wrote home about it on the condition that her family keep it to themselves, as Jackie had emphasized the secretive nature of their mission. Betty Deuser Budde, letter home, July 22, 1943.

165 **The Army base was home** Camp Davis as it was in 1943 can be seen in *Something About a Soldier,* a Columbia Pictures film directed by Alfred E. Green and starring Tom Neal and Evelyn Keyes, which was filmed just before Dora's arrival. Dora Dougherty Strother McKeown, memoir, chapter 6.

165 **The women later found out** Dora Dougherty Strother McKeown, memoir, chapter 6.

165 **While the pilots** Dora Dougherty, letter home, July 21, 1943; Dora Dougherty, letter home, July 23, 1943; Betty also excitedly wrote home that a unit of British combat pilots were at Camp Davis and touring the United States, "exchanging ideas on antiaircraft with our men." Betty Deuser Budde, letters home, July 26, 1943.

165 **As Betty Deuser wrote** Betty Deuser Budde, letters home, July 26, 1943.

166 **This required the pilot** The ammunition was color-coded to make clear which guns were hitting the targets and which were missing them.

166 **Although flying the route** None of the women were shot down during their work.

166 **Dora knew it would be** Dora Dougherty, letter home, July 25, 1943.

166 **The women's transfer to Camp Davis** Unless otherwise noted, this explanation of the trouble with the transfer is based up these sources: Marx, *History of the Air Transport Command,* 100-104; England, *Army Air Forces Historical Studies No. 55.*

167 **The battle continued** Technically to the 3rd Tow Target Squadron, part of the Third Air Force.

167 **The suspicion about Jackie** Additional conflicts of this sort arose throughout the life of the women pilots to the point that after the war the official ATC History wrote, "The peculiarity of this series of events hardly needs stressing. The ineptness of the methods used, the entire failure to protect the interests of the personnel involved, and the violations of normal military procedures, give an observer the impression of the intervention of an authority who was totally unacquainted with those procedures if not with the problems involved in any very large organization." *ATC History,* 107.

167 **Now the women were stuck** Dora Dougherty Strother McKeown, memoir.

168 **Some ten days into** Betty wrote home, "She gets things under way better than anyone." Dora Dougherty, letters home, August 5, 1943; Betty Deuser Budde, letters home, August 3 and August 9, 1943.

168 **The women were finally allowed** Dora Dougherty Strother McKeown, memoir, chapter 6, 77.

168 **She was going to** The U.S. Army Air Forces' Douglas A-24 was very similar to the Navy's SBD Dauntless, which had gained fame as the hero of the Battle of Midway in 1942 and was also on the field.

168 **At this point in the war** The planes were so bad that even the Marines wouldn't fly them. In late December 1943, Dora and four others each flew an A-24 to a Marine squadron in North Carolina. It should have been an easy day, but the Marine commander refused to accept the planes because they were in such "terrible condition." He was eventually forced to begrudgingly accept them, but only after hours of Dora and the others waiting and watching the debate between commands. Dora Dougherty Strother McKeown, memoir, 77.

168 **Despite the war-weary plane** Betty Deuser Budde, letters home, August 15, 1943; Dora, letters home, August 12, 1943; Dora, memoir, 6.2–6.9.

169 **In the following weeks** Dora, letters home, July 25, 1943; Betty Deuser Budde, letters home, July 26 and August 6, 1943.

169 **Jackie had warned them** Some of the romances at Camp Davis worked out. Dorothea "Didi" Johnson met fellow pilot Hank Ditto Moorman there. After they had dated awhile he gave her the gift of a war bond made out to Henry Dean Moorman with Mr. and Mrs. Henry Ditto Moorman as beneficiaries. Dean was the name of Didi's brother. It was a marriage proposal. Their first child, Henry Dean, was born after the war. Betty Deuser Budde, letter home, July 22, 1943; Dora Dougherty, diary, July 22, 1943; Dora Dougherty Strother McKeown, memoir, 5.7, 6.11, 13.

170 **The evening of August 23, 1943** Dora says she presumed they received the night training in an effort to get them familiar with the terrain for their cross-country flights. Dora remembers that the moon did not rise until after midnight. She only remembers the B-34s, a twin-engine plane the women weren't flying at the time, doing the night searchlight missions. Lois Hollingsworth Ziler remembers doing searchlight missions, saying, "They would put the light on the airplane and radar was just coming in, and we did a lot of the flying at night to see without seeing us if they could find our position and all." Lois could have been thinking of later flights. Dora Dougherty Strother McKeown, memoir; Dora Dougherty Strother, "Remembrances of the Accident Which Killed Mable [sic] Rawlinson," Texas Woman's University, Denton, Texas; Lois Hollingsworth Ziler, WASP class 43-W-3, interview with author, May 25, 1997.

170 **However, as Marion got** https://www.npr.org/sections/thetwo-way/2016/05/11 /477716378/congress-approves-arlington-cemetery-burials-for-female-wwii-pilots; Strother, "Remembrances."

170 **With hundreds of pilots** WASP Pat Pateman, who served in both Korea and Vietnam with the U.S. Air Force in addition to her time in the WASP during World War II, did extensive research in the 1970s to 1990s on the WASP experience, paying particular attention to the women's accidents and rumors concerning those accidents. Pat Pateman, letter to Christine Koyama/Saturday Productions, May 25, 1988, Pat Pateman Collection, U.S. Air Force Academy.

170 **It was twenty or twenty-five minutes** Dora Dougherty, letter home, September 3, 1943. In her May 2007 interview with me, Dora said it was about three-quarters of a residential block from the flight line where the planes were to the operations office and guessed the time to walk back and forth and get the new plane assigned would have taken twenty to twenty-five minutes. Dora Dougherty Strother, interview with author, May 2007.

170 **A plane coming in too low** We know from Lieutenant Robillard's later report that he and Mabel had entered the traffic pattern as usual and at about 1,100 feet she had pulled back on the throttle and lowered the landing gear. As she pushed the throttle back in to recover the power lost from the drag of the wheels, nothing happened. Mabel quickly pushed the throttle in and out, trying to make the motor catch, but it refused. Robillard tried to take over. He scrambled to put the emergency throttle that was stored for the instructor in the back seat into the appropriate slot so he could try to engage the throttle from there. He reported that he screamed at Mabel to jump despite the fact that they were at a dangerously low 700 feet. Mabel could not get the front hatch open. She was trapped. Robillard struggled to bring the powerless plane in for a landing but turned too tightly and the A-24 did what it was known to do in this situation: it quit flying. Robillard felt the plane shudder as it stalled, then could "remember no more." Mabel Rawlinson, War Department, USAAF Accident Report No. 44-8-23-11, Camp Davis, North Carolina, August 23, 1943, includes official determination of cause, description of accident, witness statement from Second Lieutenant Harvey J. Robillard, the check pilot on the flight; others who saw the accident; photos of the accident scene; and a copy of Jacqueline Cochran's report after she visited Camp Davis the next day. Official WASP Archive, Texas Woman's University, Denton, Texas.

171 **The nose of the plane hit** When asked about the hatch lever, Dora said, "I don't think that with the impact they could have gotten out even if the hatch was good." Dora Dougherty Strother, interview with author, May 2007; Dora Dougherty Strother,

"Remembrances"; Lois Hollingsworth Ziler, oral history, 1997; Didi and Hank Moorman, WASP class 43-W-4, interview with Ziggy Hunter, 1976; Rawlinson accident report.

171 **While some witnesses** It is most likely that the happy young woman from Kalamazoo, who had only a lap belt with no shoulder straps to hold her back, struck her head on the gunsight directly in front of her upon impact and never felt the flames that consumed her.

171 **Lois and her young** Lois Hollingsworth Ziler, interview with author, May 25, 1997.

171 **Meanwhile, Dora stood** Dora Dougherty Strother McKeown, memoir; Dora Dougherty Strother, interview with author, 2007.

171 **It was the first time** But it wouldn't be the last. On September 23, exactly one month after Mabel's death, Betty Taylor Wood—a newlywed who had married her flight instructor at Sweetwater—was killed when her own Dauntless crashed. A near mutiny occurred in protest of the poorly maintained plane. After fighting with Jackie Cochran about it, two of the women quit. The next month, on the twenty-third, commanding officer Colonel Stevenson grounded the WASP for the day, determined to break the jinx. Dora Dougherty Strother McKeown, memoir, chapter 6.

172 **As she opened** Over the years, stories began to circulate that Mabel had been shot down. This is unequivocally untrue. It was a tragic accident caused by a malfunctioning plane that could have been flown by any of the hundreds of pilots on the field at the time—not just the women. This section about Mabel Rawlinson's accident is based on Dora Dougherty, interview with author, May 2007; Dora, memoir; Dora Dougherty Strother McKeown, letters home; Dora Dougherty, diary; Dora Dougherty Strother, "Remembrances"; Lois Hollingsworth Ziler, interview with author, May 25, 1997; Helen Snapp, interview with author, March 20, 1999; Hank Moorman, interview with Ziggy Hunter, October 24, 1976; Rawlinson, War Department, USAAF Accident Report. No. 44-8-23-11, Camp Davis, North Carolina, August 23, 1943.

CHAPTER 14: THE WOMEN AIRFORCE SERVICE PILOTS

173 **On August 5 the women** The full name of the WASP changed slightly over the course of the war with the final official name, Women Airforce Service Pilots, confirmed by AAF Reg. 40-8 of April 3, 1944, and confirmed by that regulation's revision, December 30, 1944.

174 **Undeterred, Tunner continued** While admitting that some of Tunner's "objections" seemed "well-founded," the official postwar history of women pilots in the Air Transport Command revealed that "the generalization should be made that the Ferrying Division under General Tunner's command had somewhat of a reputation for jealously guarding its prerogatives." Captain Walter J. Marx, Ferrying Division Historical Officer, Historical Branch, Intelligence and Security Division, Headquarters, Air Transport Command, *History of the Air Transport Command: Women Pilots in the Air Transport Command* (Washington, DC: U.S. Government Printing Office, March 1945), Yvonne Pateman Collection, United States Air Force Academy, MS 31, Microfilm roll #8, A3003.

174 **"Women, I found"** Lieutenant General William H. Tunner, oral history with U.S. Air Force, K239.0512-911, October 5–6, 1976.

175 **Tunner decided** Nancy had checked out in the powerful P-51 in February 1943, and that May, when Betty Gillies, after fourteen hours of training, ferried a P-40 Thunderbolt, she became the first woman to ferry a pursuit (a fighter plane designed to fly at high speeds to pursue enemy aircraft).

175 **First designed** A total of 12,731 B-17s were built during the war.

175 **After thirty-one hours** They flew for 31.8 hours while training in the B-17, including a series of four-hour flights in the hectic, challenging traffic pattern, completing some sixteen landings, including at least one two-engine landing—not an easy feat in a four-engine plane. They also underwent night landings and instrument training—everything the women would need to ferry a B-17 across the country or even farther. Betty Gillies said, "I admire anybody who can survive that traffic pattern at Lockbourne . . . [I]t was a hectic traffic pattern." Betty Gillies, interview with Sally Van Wagenen Keil, 1977; Nancy Love, logbook; Betty Gillies, interview with Dawn Letson; Texas Woman's University, Denton, Texas, October 1996; Memo from Colonel George D. Campbell, Jr., Subject: Qualified Crew for B-17 Type Aircraft, August 16, 1943, Nancy Love Collection, International Women's Air and Space Museum.

175 **But General Tunner** Part of the reason Tunner wanted Nancy and Betty to fly the B-17 to England was that they had far more flight experience than most of the young men being sent overseas as pilots. The women were reliable, and as Betty later explained, "It was to make the boys think 'surely the work can't be that hard' . . ." Gillies, interview with Keil, 1977; Nancy Love's logbook shows she had 1,487 hours just before they were to take the flight to Europe. Betty Gillies had even more. Nancy Love, logbook, International Women's Air and Space Museum. Tunner, interview with USAF, 1976; Gillies, interview with Letson, 1996.

176 **On September 1** Betty Gillies, interview with Dawn Letson, 1996; Betty Gillies, interview with Keil, 1977; North Atlantic Wing, Air Transport Command, Official Aircraft Clearance, September 4, 1943; Nancy Love, logbook.

176 **That evening Nancy** Betty Gillies, interview with Keil; Gillies, letter to Bohn; pictures of Nancy, Betty, and crew, USAF; Official Orders, ATC; letter from Colonel Robert M. Love to Major Roy Atwood, September 1, 1943, as copied in Rickman, *Nancy Love,* 142.

176 **Meanwhile, unbeknownst to them, their careful plans** Betty Gillies, interview with Sally Van Wagenen Keil, 1977; Nancy Love, logbook; Aircraft Clearance, North Atlantic Wing, Air Transport Command, Operations Office, Presque Isle, Maine, September 4, 1943.

176 **Only then was General Arnold** Betty Gillies, interview with Keil; Gillies, letter to Delphine Bohn; Tunner OH USAF, K239.0512-911, 1976; Colonel Robert M. Love, letter to USAF Historian Lieutenant Colonel Oliver La Farge, November 10, 1945, as cited in Rickman, *Nancy Love,* 145; Message to Commanding Officer, EWATC, London, ATC Message Number 0135, September 4, 1945, Official WASP Archive, Texas Woman's University, Denton, Texas.

177 **Arnold's response was swift** Memo from Arnold stamped "Operational Priority," From: London, To: CG ATC, September 5, 1943, Official WASP Archive, Texas Woman's University, Denton, Texas. For more about this North Atlantic crossing during the war, you absolutely must read Ernest Gann's classic, *Fate Is the Hunter* (New York: Simon & Schuster, 1986).

177 **Betty's reaction was** Betty Gillies, interview with Keil, 1977; Rickman, *Nancy Love*, 149; Tunner, OH USAF, K239.0512-911, 1976; Gillies, interview with Letson, 1996; Gillies, interview with Keil, 1977.

177 **A dozen years later** Betty Gillies, interview with Keil; Gillies, letter to Bohn; Gillies, interview with Letson, October 6, 1996; Colonel Robert M. Love, letter to USAF Historian Lieutenant Colonel Oliver La Farge, November 10, 1945, as cited in Rickman, *Nancy Love*, 145; Nancy is quoted in "Noted Aviatrix Flies 'Aerial Taxi' from Island Home near Boston," *The Beechcrafter* (Beechcraft company magazine), Wichita, Kansas, October 27, 1955.

177 **Over thirty years later** Tunner OH USAF, K239.0512-911, 1976; letter to Major General Barney M. Giles, USA Chief of the Air Staff, Room 3E989, Pentagon Building, Subject: WASP Flight to U.K., From: Brigadier General C. R. Smith, Deputy Commander, September 7, 1943.

177 **Once the message had** Betty Gillies, interview with Dawn Letson, 1996; Iris Cummings Critchell, interview with author, March 16, 2008, San Diego, California; Rickman, *Nancy Love*, 144.

178 **Jackie's response** The training of the women at Lockbourne has been written about elsewhere, with the best explanation by Sally Van Wagenen Keil, whose aunt was one of the thirteen who graduated as first pilot, in her 1978 book, *Those Wonderful Women in Their Flying Machines: The Unknown Heroines of World War II* (New York: Four Directions Press, 1979); "Station WASP History: The Story of Women Airforce Service Pilots at Lockbourne," Lockbourne Army Air Base, Columbus, Ohio, November 24, 1944; Blanche Osborn Bross, letters home, October 1943, Official WASP Archive, Texas Woman's University, Denton, Texas; Dawn Rochow Balden Seymour, interview with author, 1996, Anaheim, California.

178 **Jackie, ever aware** Dawn Seymour, interview with author; Blanche Osborn Bross, letters home, October 1943; memo with subject: WASPs Qualified on Four-Engine Aircraft, to Air Forces Group, War Department, Bureau of Public Relations, Thru: Commanding General, Air Transport Command, November 20, 1943, with CC to Director of Women Pilots; "Station WASP History"; Betty Gillies interview, with Sally Van Wagenen Keil, 1977.

CHAPTER 15: ENGLAND

179 **Like the other women** Class 1 included the Tiger Moths and Messengers; Class 5 included the Lancaster, Fortress, and Liberator. There was also a Class 6—seaplanes or flying boats, including the Catalina, Sunderland, and others—but relatively few pilots were checked out in those, and only 967 were delivered out of over 300,000 total planes. Curtis, *The Forgotten Pilots*, appendices.

180 **Helen quickly moved** Rosemary du Cross, *ATA Girl* (London: Frederick Muller, 1983), 34.

180 **They weren't exaggerating** Joan Bradbrooke, "Atta Girls! American Girls Join the ATA to Ferry Britain's Fighters," *Skyways* 2 (January 1943): pp. 34–35, 44–45, 73.

180 **By July, Helen was flying** Ernie Pyle, "Girl Fliers," *Columbus Citizen*, October 20, 1942. During World War II, Ernie Pyle was the most followed journalist in the world. He knew Helen Richey well from his old beat as an aviation reporter.

180 **Helen was a superb pilot** du Cross, *ATA Girl*.

180 **While Helen was glad** Curtis, *Forgotten Pilots*, 143.

181 **Perhaps most troubling** During the war, 153 men and women flying for the ATA were killed—including twenty-six Americans. Curtis, *Forgotten Pilots*, Appendix 16.

181 **Helen's early reports back** Helen Richey, letter to Jacqueline Cochran, October 12, 1942, Jacqueline Cochran Collection, Eisenhower Library.

181 **By the end of October** Helen Richey, letter to Jacqueline Cochran, October 23, 1942, Jacqueline Cochran Collection, Eisenhower Library.

181 **The following month** Helen Richey, cable (RCA Radiogram) to Jacqueline Cochran, November 19, 1942, Jacqueline Cochran Collection, Eisenhower Library.

181 **On January 8, 1943, Helen** Helen Richey, Western Union cable to Jacqueline Cochran at Blackstone Hotel, Fort Worth, Texas, January 8, 1943, Jacqueline Cochran Collection, Eisenhower Library.

181 **Jackie who had kept** Jacqueline Cochran, overnight cable to Helen Richey, January 8–9, 1943, Jacqueline Cochran Collection, Eisenhower Library.

182 **It seems that after** On January 20, Jackie had sent Helen a cable telling her she'd talked with Helen's father and he said there was nothing Helen could do and she should stay in England. Jackie said she could not advise Helen either way but that passage to the United States was still next to impossible. Jacqueline Cochran, night cable to Helen Richey, Jacqueline Cochran Collection, Eisenhower Library.

182 **She'd had her** Helen had four minor accidents/incidents while in the ATA. She had a forced landing on December 14, 1942, because of a broken hydraulic pump, deemed not her fault. Her third faulted accident was on January 3, 1943. Helen Richey, personal file, ATA, Royal Air Force Museum, London, courtesy Terry Mace.

182 **On January 23, 1943** Jackie learned of Helen's dismissal from Peter Beasley, the husband of one of the American ATA women and friend of both Helen and Jackie. He cabled her explaining that the ATA was justifying canceling her contract because of "three accidents, nervous physical condition, unsatisfactory report class four checks." He suggested Jackie take no action. Peter Beasley, postal telegraph cable to Jacqueline Cochran, January 24, 1943.

182 **The chief medical officer** A. Barbour, Chief Medical Officer ATA, letter to Jacqueline Cochran, February 13, 1943, Jacqueline Cochran Collection, Eisenhower Library.

182 **Helen's sister had to wire** Martha Richey Smith, cable to Jacqueline Cochran Odlum, February 22, 1943, Jacqueline Cochran Collection, Eisenhower Library.

182 **Eventually, on March 19, Helen** We know when Helen left based on this form in which her pilot's handbook was detained. In the remarks was a note: "Civilian air pilot ATA returning home for good." Helen Richey, Form I.P.D.4 Articles Detained, Travellers' Censorship Office, Glasgow, March 19, 1943, Jacqueline Cochran Collection, Eisenhower Library.

182 **The following month** Jackie also asked Helen questions about how she left the ATA—including any funds she might have left behind—making it clear that there had not been any transition after Helen's departure. Jackie closed with "There are so many things I am anxious to know about." Jacqueline Cochran, letter to Helen Richey, April 27, 1943, Jacqueline Cochran Collection, Eisenhower Library.

182 **Then, on June 7, 1943** Helen Richey, cable to Jacqueline Cochran, June 7, 1943, Jacqueline Cochran Collection, Eisenhower Library.

183 **In July 1943, the *Avenger* ran** On January 23, 1943, while she was visiting Romulus, Nancy Love interviewed and accepted Lenore McElroy—a thirty-five-year-old

flight instructor with 3,500 hours of flight time—as her final WAFS member. On January 25, General Arnold sent a message to Tunner that from that point forward the Ferrying Division could only hire women who had gone through the WFTD, Jackie's training program. Betty Gillies later said, "This was a big blow to the Command," who had hoped to hire more of the experienced women pilots directly. Rickman, *Nancy Love*, 109; "A Page of Personalities," *Avenger* 1, no. 3, July 26, 1943, 7; Dawn Rochow Balden Seymour, telephone call with author, 2015.

183 **At thirty-four, she was** "A Page of Personalities"; "Miss Helen Richey, Flier, Found Dead," *New York Times*, January 8, 1947. Detailed, authoritative website on the ATA: http://www.airtransportaux.com/members/richey.html.

183 **In a letter on August 27** Dedie Deaton, letter to Jacqueline Cochran, August 27, 1943, Jacqueline Cochran Collection, Eisenhower Library; Helen Richey, letter to Jacqueline Cochran, Cochran Collection, Eisenhower Library.

184 **That same fall, Teresa** This section based on the following sources: Churchill, *On Wings to War*; Teresa James, letter "D-Day Plus 40 Years," in author's possession; Teresa James, interview with author, March 20, 1999, Orlando, Florida. Photographs of Teresa and Dink as well as Dink's brother (wearing Service Pilot wings) can be found in the Adela Riek Scharr Collection, St. Louis Public Library (special thanks to Renee Jones, Librarian, Rare Books and Manuscripts, St. Louis Public Library, for her above-and-beyond research into materials about Teresa). Teresa's mother kept the photo in a prominent place in her home the rest of her days. Catherine Mowry, niece of Teresa James, email with author, June 21, 2019.

CHAPTER 16: AERIAL DISHWASHERS

186 **On September 17, 1943, Jackie** This discussion of the uniform selection is based on these sources: "Telephone Calls," Records of Calls to General Arnold's office in the Pentagon, September 14, 1943. "Miss Cochran: Said General Arnold and Gen. Giles wanted to see her with her girls in uniform Friday morning. Gen. Arnold mentioned also showing them to Gen. Marshall. Called to make an appointment for Friday morning." Handwritten note, "8:45 Saturday—ok—notified," General Henry H. Arnold Collection, Library of Congress. Thanks to the staff at the Library of Congress and to Lieutenant Colonel Wendy Cooper for her help going through these phone logs; Cochran, *The Stars at Noon*, 123–24.

187 **That same month** U.S. Congress, House, House Committee on Military Affairs, Proposed Bill for Appointment of Female Pilots and Aviation Cadets in the Air Forces of the United States, H.R. 3358, Congress, House, 78th Cong., 1st session, *House Journal*, September 30, 1943.

188 **When the bill was made public** Betty Deuser Budde, letters home, November 14, 1943.

188 **Dora, still under the impression** Dora Dougherty, letter home, November 11, 1943.

189 **In every respect** This would change between January and June 1944 to three equal phases of ten weeks, but no real change in the number of hours for either flying or ground school. They seem to have just wanted a little more breathing room for weather and other circumstances. (Dedie Deaton was based at Randolph Field in the months following the WASP disbandment and likely helped work on this report.) *History of the WASP Program Army Air Forces Central Flying Training Command*, Historical Section,

A-2 (Personnel) Army Air Forces Central Flying Command, Randolph Field, Texas, January 20, 1945, 52–57.

189 **The reason for the extra** The flying time in training increased from 115 hours for the first class to 210 hours for the latest. Ground school, which the Training Command called the "academic program," increased from 180 hours to 309 hours. The course work expanded to include forty-two hours on engines and propellers, fifty hours on weather, a new eighteen-hour instrument course, ten hours minimum on aeronautical equipment maintenance, and twelve hours on forms and procedures. There were also sixty new hours on military training, including forty-two hours of close-order drill and ceremonies. *History of WASP Program Army Air Forces Central Flying Training Command*, 52.

189 **The bill that Jackie kept promising** Jackie visited Dora's base and told her they would be in the Army within eight weeks "for certain," Dora Dougherty, letter home, October 22, 1943; Madge Rutherford Minton, letter home, July 5, 1943.

189 **This new bill was more complicated** U.S. Congress, House, Hearings Before the Committee on Military Affairs: on H.R. 4219, 78th Congress, 2nd session, March 22, 1944 (Washington, DC: U.S. Government Printing Office, 1944).

190 **She'd worked so hard** "Girl Pilots: Air Force Trains Them at Avenger Field, Texas," *Life*, July 19, 1943, 73–81.

190 **However, in January 1944** U.S. Congress, House, Hearings Before the Committee on Military Affairs: on H.R. 4219, 78th Congress, 2nd session, March 22, 1944 (Washington, DC: U.S. Government Printing Office, 1944).

191 **Hundreds of WTS men** Just a couple of months later the Navy announced they would no longer use WTS as of the summer of 1944 as well. H. K. Reynolds, "Navy Dept. to Reduce Number of Pilots to Be Trained During Next 3 Years," *Contact*, April 1944, 4; "AAF Chief Urges Legislation to Commission Women Pilots: General Arnold Wants to Make the WASP Part of the Army—His Comment on Idle Men Pilots Seems Evasive," *Contact*, April 1944, 4.

191 **In January 1944 the editor** "Editor's Comment Arouses Wrath of Women Pilots: They Point to Record of Ferrying Ships for Army," *Cincinnati Times-Star*, January 31, 1944, 16.

191 **Ramspeck was active in the airline** Ramspeck resigned from Congress in 1945 to go on to help lead Eastern Airlines, including serving as its vice president from 1953 to 1961.

192 **They already held a letter** Henry L. Stimson, letter to Andrew J. May, Chairman of the House Committee on Military Affairs, February 16, 1944, Official WASP Archive, Texas Woman's University, Denton, Texas.

192 **After Arnold's hour** Jacqueline Cochran sat alongside Arnold throughout his testimony, available for questions but not speaking. U.S. Congress, House, Hearings Before the Committee on Military Affairs: on H.R. 4219, 78th Congress, 2nd session, March 22, 1944 (Washington, DC: U.S. Government Printing Office, 1944), 2–8; *Congressional Record*, June 21, 1944, 6398.

192 **In fact, the women had** Caro Bayley Bosca, letters home, March 1944; Madge Rutherford Minton, letters home, March 19, March 21, and March 26, 1944. Both available at Official WASP Archive, Texas Woman's University, Denton, Texas.

193 **Throughout the spring of 1944** Representative James Morrison of Louisiana reported that he had received "numerous inquiries from my people of Louisiana." U.S. Congress. House. *Appendix to the Congressional Record,* 78th Congress, 2nd session, 1944 (Washington, DC: U.S. Government Printing Office, 1944), A1969. The American Legion's efforts are documented on page A4017. Ruth Sarles, "Lay That Airplane Down, Babe, Cry Grounded He-Man Pilots," *Washington Daily News,* March 31, 1944, 24.

193 **The women worried** Caro Bayley explained to her mother that they had heard the same debate she had about the women pilots versus the men flight instructors, "but I think they'll just keep arguing because the bill putting us in the Army is almost passed." Madge Rutherford wasn't too excited about the idea of joining the military but was convinced nothing would really be decided until after the November elections anyway. She did believe, however, "that dear Jackie has gone too far. She's still recruiting girls in spite of rapidly growing adverse public opinion. The Woman's insatiable. It's a big mistake." Caro Bayley, letters home, February and March 1944; Madge Rutherford Minton, letters home, March 19 and March 21, 1944.

193 **Jackie continued to drop** Madge Rutherford Minton, letter home, April 15, 1944; Ruth Lindley, letters home, March 26, 1944; Madge Rutherford Minton, letters home; Betty Budde, letters home, November 14, 1943; Dora, letter home, November 11, 1943.

193 **Finally, the War Department** As early as mid-March 1944, Congressman A. J. May, chair of the Committee on Military Affairs, was calling General Arnold, as he was *"very anxious"* to talk with him about "some legislation." The increasingly troubled WASP bill? Phone logs, March 15, 1944. "WASP Militarization Favored by Stimson," *New York Times,* May 5, 1944, 2.

194 **But as the male WTS pilots** AAF letter to Honorable Andrew J. May, House of Representatives, May 2, 1944, at National Archives, Record Group 18, Entry 54A, Box 25. Declassified: NND 770089.

194 **Meanwhile, the articles** *Idaho Statesman* article found in: U.S. Congress. House. *Appendix to the Congressional Record.* 78th Congress, 2nd session, 1944, 2879; Austine Cassini, "These Charming People," *Washington Times-Herald,* May 23, 1944, also in House, *Appendix,* 3093.

195 **In January 1944, just before** The four women were Betty Gillies, Barbara Jane Erickson, Delphine Bohn, and Esther Manning. Betty Gillies, diary, January 6–10, 1944, in which Betty transcribed a letter to Delphine Bohn, February 3, 1984; Betty Gillies and Betty Jane Erickson London, interview with Dawn Letson, October 6, 1996, California.

196 **When Nancy found out** Delphine Bohn, "Catch a Shooting Star," unpublished memoir, in author's possession.

196 **When a member of Representative Ramspeck's** Nancy Love, letter, in ATC "Resumé of Conversation Between Mrs. Love and Colonel McCormick of Ramspeck Committee," April 17, 1944, copy from Pat Pateman collection, USAF Academy, Delphine Bohn, unpublished manuscript, "Catch a Shooting Star," in author's possession.

196 **What she didn't tell Betty** It was the A-1 of the Air Staff who stopped the letter. The Office of the Assistant Chief of the Air Staff—A-1 was Personnel, A-2 Intelligence, A-4 Matériel and Services; Delphine Bohn, "Catch a Shooting Star," unpublished memoir, in author's possession; Captain Walter J. Marx, Ferrying Division Historical Offi-

cer, Historical Branch, Intelligence and Security Division, Headquarters, Air Transport Command, *History of the Air Transport Command: Women Pilots in the Air Transport Command* (Washington, DC: U.S. Government Printing Office, March 1945), Yvonne Pateman Collection, United States Air Force Academy, MS 31, Microfilm roll #8, A3003, 283.

196 **Soon enough, General Hall** Betty Gillies and Barbara Jane Erickson London, interview with Dawn Letson, October 6, 1996.

198 **Right away Jackie** Margaret Kerr Boylan, WASP class 43-W-2, told this story to Maryann Bucknum Brinley as part of her autobiography with Jackie. Cochran and Brinley, *Jackie Cochran: The Autobiography;* Maryann Bucknum Brinley, telephone call with author, summer 2018.

198 **General Giles had issued a directive** Dora Dougherty, letter home, June 4, 1944; Delphine Bohn, "Catch a Shooting Star," unpublished memoir, in author's possession; letter from First Lieutenant E. A. McDonald, chief of the WASP Training Section of the AAF School of Applied Tactics, to Dora Dougherty, as quoted in Dora Dougherty Strother McKeown, memoir, chapter 11.

CHAPTER 17: A SECRET LITTLE DEAL

200 **At Camp Davis the previous fall** Dora Dougherty Strother McKeown, unpublished memoir, in author's possession; Betty Deuser Budde, letter home, July 22, 1943, and Dora Dougherty, letter home, July 23, 1943.

201 **At Dora's new station** Eglin Field was only thirty miles or so from Jackie's hometown of DeFuniak Springs, Florida; Dora Dougherty Strother McKeown, memoir, chapter 9.

201 **When the newly designed** Allen had heroically maneuvered the crippled plane to narrowly avoid Seattle's downtown but tragically crashed just short of the runway and into the Frye Meat Packing Plant. He was a conservative, well-respected test pilot and this crash, not the first for the new plane, sealed the reputation of the B-29 as deadly.

202 **Tibbets had to find a way** Unless otherwise cited, this discussion on the B-29 is based on the following sources: All Tibbets quotes from Brigadier General Paul Tibbets, interview with author, August 2, 1999, Oshkosh, Wisconsin; Jean Ross Howard, interview with Sally Van Wagenen Keil, 1976; Dora Dougherty Strother McKeown, interview with author, 1999, 2006; Dorothea "Didi" Moorman, interview with author, 1998; Dora Dougherty Strother, interview with Dawn Letson, August 28, 1992, Official WASP Archive, Texas Woman's University; quotes from Dora Dougherty Strother McKeown, memoir, chapter 10.

203 **The responsibility** "I think all of the women of the WASP felt this at all times as we did that day," she later recalled. "We felt we were representing all of the women pilots of the world, and that we had to do the very best that we could to uphold the reputation of women pilots. We were so intent on everything we did." Dora Dougherty Strother, interview with Dawn Letson, August 28, 1992, Texas Woman's University, Denton, Texas.

203 **While the crew later** War Department, U.S. Army Air Forces, Report of Aircraft Damage (Accident), June 24, 1944. National Archives, Record Group 18, Ent 294, Box 400, Declassified: NND 730061.

205 **"After lunch a test flight crew"** Dora Dougherty, diary, June 29, 1944, available at Official WASP Archive, Texas Woman's University, Denton, Texas.

205 **Tibbets would later laugh** I had the opportunity to meet with Paul Tibbets on several occasions, and in addition to our formal interview in 1999 I heard him laugh and tell the story of how Dora and Didi showed those boys how to do it on each occasion. He was very proud of them and had great respect and affection for both.

CHAPTER 18: THE LOST LAST CLASS

206 **Marty had worked hard** Mary Anna Martin Wyall, multiple interviews with author, 1997 to 2017.

207 **"Gee, what a long day"** Mary Anna Martin (Wyall), letter home, May 28, 1944, available at Official WASP Archive, Texas Woman's University, Denton, Texas.

208 **They have a lot of cute** WASP songbook, a booklet of WASP wartime songs put together by WASP for postwar reunions, available at Official WASP Archive, Texas Woman's University, Denton, Texas.

209 **Marty's class was determined** Marty Martin (Wyall), letter home, June 1, 1944.

209 **"Yesterday I got to land"** Marty Martin (Wyall), letter home, June 4, 1944.

210 **After two weeks** Marty Martin (Wyall), letters home, June 1944. Liquor story from Jean Ross Howard, class 43-W-3 trainee and WASP executive officer in Houston and Sweetwater; interview with Sally Van Wagenen Keil, 1976.

210 **For someone who lived** Marty Martin (Wyall), letter home, July 24, 1944.

211 **Like the rest of the women** Marty Martin (Wyall), letters home, July–September 1944.

211 **The Navy** This article was right next to the article on Arnold's testimony to get the WASP militarized. H. K. Reynolds, "Navy Dept. to Reduce Number of Pilots to Be Trained During Next 3 Years: Fewer Pilots Needed Because Rate of Loss Has Been Less Than Expected," *Contact,* April 1944, 4; the WASP article was "AAF Chief Urges Legislation to Commission Women Pilots: General Arnold Wants to Make the WASP Part of the Army—His Comment on Idle Men Pilots Seems Evasive," *Contact,* April 1944, 4.

211 **The media—once so positive** "Unnecessary and Undesirable?," *Time* 43, (May 29, 1944): 66; "Pictures Male Fliers Doing WASPS' Chores," *New York Times,* June 20, 1944, 11; *Contact* 8, no. 3 (April 1944), 5; Ruth Sarles, " 'Swoose' Thinks WASP Program Smells of 'Some Kind of Racket,' " *Washington Daily News,* May 13, 1944, 14.

212 **The committee indicated** U.S. Congress. House. *Appendix to the Congressional Record.* 78th Congress, 2nd Session, 1944, 3058–3059.

213 **The fact that the AAF** Just one example is the accelerated dismantling of many New Deal programs that began in 1943 with the influx of newly elected Republicans. John Morton Blum, *V Was for Victory: Politics and American Culture During World War II* (New York: Harcourt Brace Jovanovich, 1976), 234–35.

213 **Citing the costs of training** House, *Appendix,* 2937.

213 **Throughout 1944, most** Maureen Honey, *Creating Rosie the Riveter: Class, Gender and Propaganda During World War II* (Amherst: University of Massachusetts Press, 1984).

214 **Still, not everyone** "End of Wasp Training Plan Recommended by Committee," incompletely cited news clipping, June 6, 1944, in author's possession; "A Suggested Minority Report in the Event Chairman Ramspeck Persists in His Intent to Issue an Unfavorable Report," Jacqueline Cochran Collection, Eisenhower Library.

214 **They argued that** In the years after the war, AAF historian Walter La Farge says of the fight for the women that he could figure out why the AAF would not admit the male flight instructors into the Army. He concludes, "Congress was cantankerous and the Army Air Forces were politically stupid." Walter La Farge, *The Eagle in the Egg: The Story of the Coming of Age of Military Air Transport Which Produced the Berlin Airlift* (Boston: Houghton Mifflin, 1949), 138.

214 **"I think it is time"** Walter Brehm, Republican from Ohio, House, Debate on H.R. 4219, "Appointment of Female Pilots and Aviation Cadets in Army Air Forces," *Congressional Record*, 6413.

214 **The debate went on and on** Izac had worked hard against Arnold during the Billy Mitchell trial in 1925 and Jackie Cochran thought Izac's work to kill the WASP bill was personal. Jackie Cochran, interview with the Lyndon Baines Johnson Library and Museum, 1976.

214 **He wanted to move on** "Congress Rushing to Quit This Week," *New York Times*, June 19, 1944, 21; *Congressional Record*, House, Debate on H.R. 4219, 6414.

214 **The enacting clause** *Congressional Record*, House, Debate on H.R. 4219, "Appointment of Female Pilots and Aviation Cadets in Army Air Forces," 6398. One can find a list of the yeas and nays in the following: House, *Appendix*, 2938. Of those voting (73 abstained), 145 Democrats voted nay (supporting WASP), and 131 Republicans voted yea (opposing WASP). Six of the eight women voted in favor of the WASP. The veterans were split with 70 nays and 65 yeas.

215 **No one knew** Caro Bayley (Bosca), letter home, June 22, 1944.

215 **He didn't think** "General Arnold Regrets Prospective WASPs' 'Wild Good Chase,'" *Washington Star*, July 3, 1944.

215 **Marty wrote home** Mary Anna (Wyall), letters home, June 30, 1944.

215 **Marty knew** Mary Anna (Wyall), letters home, June 30, 1944.

215 **On June 27, telegrams** The Central Flying Training Command was apparently not consulted about the decision to end training. They were notified on June 28, 1944, that "the program would be terminated as soon as the students then in training had been graduated. The news came with little warning." It was this command that supported the women remaining at Avenger Field until the Air Transport Command could fly them home. *History of the WASP Program Army Air Forces Central Flying Training Command*, Historical Section, A-2 (Personnel) Army Air Forces Central Flying Command, Randolph Field, Texas, January 20, 1945, 23.

216 **When the Air Transport Command planes** "General Arnold Regrets Prospective WASPs' 'Wild Good Chase' "; "Army to Fly Home 42 Girls Stranded at Texas Field," *New York Times*, July 1, 1944; *Avenger* 1, no. 22, July 14, 1944; "Silver Wings on Blue" by Winona Jeanne Marsh of Omaha. The note accompanying the song said, "Miss Marsh was scheduled for class 45-W-1. Our appreciation for her interest in the program in spite of her disappointment." *WASP Songbook*, p. 13; Winona Jeanne Marsh, twenty-two, married John Joseph Cleary, February 27, 1946, https://omahamarriages. wordpress.com/m-1/. Dora Dougherty, letter home, June 21, 1944.

217 **Jackie tried to help** Telephone conversations, transcriptions, Elaine Scull, Joan Bogert, Emma Lou Fluke, Amy Falcon, Mr. Nevin, Mr. Smith, and others, dated June 27, 1944. Eisenhower Library.

CHAPTER 19: "I REGRET TO INFORM YOU . . ."

218 **Teresa James was** She received the telegram on June 25, 1944.

219 **Teresa agreed** Churchill, *On Wings to War;* Manhattan, KS: 143.

219 **Back on base, Teresa** Lieutenant George Martin to Teresa James Martin, June 21, 1944, printed in Churchill, *On Wings to War,* 141.

220 **Teresa spent the summer** Teresa James, interview with Dawn Letson, Lake Worth, Florida, June 16, 1998, at Official WASP Archive, Texas Woman's University, Denton, Texas.

220 **All of the other women** One of her fellow "originals," Delphine Bohn, later recalled that Teresa was never the same. Delphine Bohn, "Catch a Shooting Star," unpublished memoir, xvii–6.

220 **In September** "Racers Win 3rd E Award with 10,000th P-47: Jacqueline Cochran, WASP Chief, Christens Plane 'Ten Grand,' " *Republic Aviation News* 14, no. 8, September 22, 1944; Teresa James, interview with Letson.

221 **Betty Gillies pulled out** Nancy Batson Crews, interview with Dawn Letson, Odenville, Alabama, June 11, 1997, Official WASP Archive, Texas Woman's University, Denton, Texas.

221 **The day of the launch** Public Relations release, Republic Aviation Corporation, September 20, 1944; "First Woman Ever to Fly a Thunderbolt Is One of Two Girls Landing Here in P-47s," *Republic Aviation News—Indiana Division,* September 1943.

221 **Under Secretary of War Robert P. Patterson** Patterson was on hand to award Republic with their third Army-Navy E Award for excellence in production. Patterson described how the newly modified P-47 had arrived "in the nick of time," only months after the United States entered the war. "10,000th P-47 Fighter Rolls off the Line; Patterson Hails Republic Plant's Record," *New York Times,* September 20, 1944, ProQuest Historical Newspapers; "Racers Win 3rd E Award with 10,000th P-47."

221 **A bit bored** Thanks to Julia Lauria-Blum for sharing Teresa James's explanation of a photo of several of the women ferry pilots (Helen Richey, Teresa James, Betty Gillies, and others) while they sat listening to speeches that day. "Camera Glimpses of Great Day in the History of Republic," *Republic Aviation News,* September 22, 1944.

221 **Before they could spend** "10,000th P-47 Fighter Rolls off the Line."

221 **At the side** "10,000th P-47 Fighter Rolls Off the Line; Patterson Hails Republic Plant's Record," *New York Times,* September 20, 1944.

222 **It was a short** Churchill, *On Wings to War,* 102; Teresa James, interview with Letson; Betty Gillies and Barbara Erickson London, interview with Dawn Letson, 1996, California.

222 **She didn't mind** Teresa James, interview with author, March 20, 1999, Orlando, Florida.

222 **Before she knew it** Teresa James, interview with author; Churchill, *On Wings to War,* 138.

223 **In late October** Churchill, *On Wings to War,* 143–44.

224 **Around the same time** Teresa James, interview with author; Teresa James, interview with Julia Lauria-Blum, Cradle of Aviation Museum.

CHAPTER 20: SIMPLE JUSTICE

225 **In the days after** Record of telephone conversation, from Mrs. Thomas Wadlow, Pleasant Ridge, Michigan, to Miss Jacqueline Cochran, June 27, 1944, and June 29, 1944, Jacqueline Cochran Collection, Eisenhower Library.

226 **When one mother asked** Transcript of call with Mrs. Thomas Wadlow, Pleasant Ridge, Michigan, June 29, 1944, Jacqueline Cochran Collection, Eisenhower Library.

226 **On another call** Transcript of call with Mr. Nevin of Providence, Rhode Island, June 27, 1944, Jacqueline Cochran Collection, Eisenhower Library.

227 **The new bill in the Senate** "Civic Leaders Ask Aid of Congress, Women's Club to Help Save WASP," *Avenger* 1, no. 22, July 14, 1944.

227 **The Ninety-Nines rallied** Granger, *On Final Approach,*

227 **She refused and instead** She was most definitely in the program: we have oral history and photo evidence from her 44-W-4 classmates, and she wrote in to the postwar newsletter. Telephone conversation with Jane Doyle of class 44-W-4, and photos shared by Jane Doyle, April 2018. And postwar WASP newsletter.

227 **More pilots were surviving** A fascinating look at the early recognition of combat fatigue and the need for rotation out of combat theaters for aircraft crew can be found in "Combat Crew Rotation: World War II and Korean War," Historical Studies Branch, USAF Historical Division, Aerospace Studies Institute, Air University, Maxwell Air Force Base, Alabama, January 1968. Available online.

228 **Flying these planes** While in August 1942 the ATC took pilots with only 300 hours, by June 1944, the pilots doing most of the ferrying had over 1,000 hours of flight experience—whether they were men back from war or women pilots who had built up their time while serving. Captain Walter J. Marx, Ferrying Division Historical Officer, Historical Branch, Intelligence and Security Division, Headquarters, Air Transport Command, *History of the Air Transport Command: Pilots in the Air Transport Command* (Washington, DC: U.S. Government Printing Office, March 1945), 50.

228 **The AAF was still making** Marx, *History of the ATC.*

228 **On July 3, Jackie** Telephone call, Jacqueline Cochran and Nancy Love, July 3, 1944, Jacqueline Cochran Collection, Eisenhower Library.

228 **Soon, Jackie began visiting** Jackie sent Ethel Sheehy and Helen Dettweiler to visit additional bases that she did not have time to visit.

229 **During the debate** As Congress considered the WASP militarization bill in the summer of 1944, the AAF explained to Congressman Andrew J. May of Kentucky, chairman of the House Committee on Military Affairs, that one of the primary reasons the program was created, in addition to releasing men for combat duty, was to "determine the manner and extent that women pilots can be effectively used in the Army Air Forces" for any future need. They went on to make the second point that "if we are going to test the project completely and fully we must have enough WASP so that the groups allocated to various phases of non-combat service will be large enough for us to reach definite conclusions. Without the enlargement of the present WASP training program, we will have the numbers necessary early in 1945." AAF letter to Honorable Andrew J. May, House of Representatives, May 2, 1944. At National Archives, Record Group 18, Entry 54A, Box 25. Declassified: NND 770089.

229 **On August 1, 1944** Jacqueline Cochran, "Report on Women Airforce Service Pilots," To: Commanding General, Army Air Forces (Arnold), Through: Assistant Chief of Air Staff, Operations, Commitments, and Requirements, August 1, 1944, WASP Collection, Texas Woman's University, Denton, Texas.

229 **"Under a civilian status"** Jacqueline Cochran, "Report on Women Airforce Service Pilots," August 1, 1944.

230 **As soon as the report** Leoti "Dedie" Deaton, Chief Establishment Officer, Women Airforce Service Pilots. Oral history interview with Ziggy Hunter, March 18, 1975. Edited by Dawn Letson and Nancy M. Durr. Available at Official WASP Archive, Texas Woman's University, Denton, Texas; Ann Cottrell, "Fight to Give WASPs Army Role Renewed by Jacqueline Cochran: Report to Arnold Asserts Women Pilots Service Should Be Dissolved Unless It Is Absorbed by AAF, Cites High Rate of Resignations," Washington, D.C., August 8, 1944, 13. (Article in author's possession; no title to news clipping.)

230 **In it Jackie wrote** Cottrell, "Fight to Give WASPs Army Role."

230 **The Ferry Command immediately** Memorandum from Captain William R. Geddings, Public Relations Officer in the Headquarters of the Ferrying Division, Air Transport Command, to Nancy Love, August 9, 1944.

231 **One of the WASP, Caro Bayley** Caro Bayley Bosca, letter home, August 9, 1944, available at Official WASP Archive, Texas Woman's University, Denton, Texas.

232 **Jackie's report had dismissed** In her August report Jackie argued, "The usefulness of the WASPs cannot be measured by the importance of the types of planes they fly, for their job is to do the routine, the dishwashing flying jobs of the AAF, that will release men for higher grades of duty." Cochran, "Report on Women Airforce Service Pilots."

232 **Now it all seemed** Letter from Nancy Love, September 4, 1944; Barbara "BJ" Erickson London, interview with Sarah Rickman for Texas Woman's University, March 17 and 19, 2004, Long Beach, California. WASP Collection, Texas Woman's University, Denton, Texas.

232 **On September 4, 1944, Nancy** Letter from Nancy Love, September 4, 1944, as quoted in "Catch a Shooting Star," Delphine Bohn's unpublished memoir, Texas Woman's University, Denton, Texas, xvii–5.

CHAPTER 21: DISBANDMENT

235 **On October 1, 1944** General H. H. Arnold, letter to Jacqueline Cochran, Director of Women Pilots, October 1, 1944, Arnold Papers, Library of Congress, Manuscript Division, Container 294, Reel 205.

235 **The Army Air Forces had** AAF letter to Honorable Andrew J. May, House of Representatives, May 2, 1944. At National Archives, Record Group 18, Entry 54A, Box 25. Declassified: NND 770089.

236 **When they heard the news** Margaret Ray Ringenberg, interview with author, July 20, 1996; Violet Thurn Cowden, interview with author, August 4, 1996; Lois Hollingsworth Ziler, interview with author, 2002; Betty Gillies and Barbara Jane Erickson London, interview with Dawn Letson, October 1996.

236 **The next day Dedie** The AAF issued a letter listing what the WASP were allowed to keep and what they would have the opportunity to buy, including the prices. AAF

Ltr 40-34A, November 13, 1944, Dora Dougherty Strother McKeown Collection, Official WASP Archive, Texas Woman's University; Mary Anna Martin Wyall, letter home, October 8, 1944.

237 **Dora was stationed** Jacqueline Cochran, letter to all WASP, October 2, 1944, at Official WASP Archive, Texas Woman's University; Dora Dougherty, letter home, October 7, 1944, and October 29, 1944; Dora Dougherty Strother McKeown, memoir, chapter 12.

237 **When word of disbandment** Gott, *Hazel Ah Ying Lee;* Teresa James, interview with author, March 20, 1999, Orlando, Florida.

238 **On October 3, General Arnold** General Henry H. Arnold, letter to WASP, October 3, 1944, as quoted in Jacqueline Cochran, *Final Report on Women Pilot Program, 1945.* From Official WASP Archive, Texas Woman's University's WASP Collection, Denton, Texas. MSS 265, Byrd Granger Collection, Box 4, page 49.

238 **Jackie also wrote** Jacqueline Cochran, letter to "WASPs of 43-W-3, Biggs Field, El Paso, Texas," October 12, 1944, Jacqueline Cochran Collection, Eisenhower Library.

239 **As late as November** "Informational Bulletin, Subject: Inactivation of WASP, To: ALL GROUPS," November 6, 1944.

239 **When it became clear** Allie Love, telephone call with author, October 2018; Deborah Douglas, interview with Marky Love, 1986.

240 **In the years to come** Nancy's great-nephew Nick Knobil says his great-grandfather used to poke at Nancy, getting Nick to ask her what she thought about General Arnold. Nick says he learned all the best cusswords from Nancy raging about Arnold. Nick Knobil, emails with author, 2018.

240 **When the skies cleared** Army Air Forces Report of Major Accident, November 23, 1944.

241 **When her body was sent home** Gott, *Hazel Ah Ying Lee;* accident report of Hazel Ah Ying Lee, November 25, 1944. Mary Louise Webster was the last WASP to die when, on December 9, 1944, the plane in which she was a passenger accumulated ice on the wings and crashed, killing all aboard. She was twenty-five years old.

241 **The food** Marjorie Osborne Nicol, letter home, September 18, 1944.

241 **On November 8, class 44-W-9** Marjorie Osborne Nicol, letters home; Bob Peterson, letter to Marjorie Nicol's parents, November 9, 1944; Elaine Harmon and Ruth Kearney, interview with author, July 19, 1996, Xenia, Ohio; Maggie Gee, interview with author, October 1996.

242 **The graduation ceremony was a relatively small** The WASP's numbers had dwindled to such an extent that they were no longer a priority for an Army band or a wing review.

242 **As one WASP later wrote** Marjorie Osborne Nicol, letter home, September 11, 1944.

242 **Jackie composed herself** Marjorie Osborne Nicol, letter home, September 11, 1944; Elaine Harmon and Ruth Kearney, interview with author, July 19, 1996, Xenia, Ohio; Maggie Gee, interview with author, October 1996.

242 **Now that class 44-W-9** Mary Anna Martin (Wyall), letter home, November 14, 1944.

243 **The date of the final** I haven't found specific evidence of this date being chosen purposefully, but it is not surprising if it was. Jackie and the Army Air Forces were ever aware of publicity opportunities.

243 **The Movietone News cameramen arrived** Mary Anna Martin (Wyall), letter home, December 7, 1944. The Official WASP Archive at Texas Woman's University, Denton, Texas, has much of this film footage.

243 **Nonetheless, nearly one hundred** Mary Anna Martin (Wyall), letter home, December 7, 1944.

243 **But he'd taken a chance** You can find a bit of audio of his speech here: http://www.wingsacrossamerica.us/wasp/audio/arnold3.mp3.

244 **Jackie had her chance** You can find a segment of the speech and a link to audio of it here: http://www.wingsacrossamerica.us/wasp/Cochran_speech.htm.

244 **Marty walked away** Mary Anna Martin (Wyall), letter home, December 7, 1944.

245 **On December 14, 1944** Floyd Odlum, letter to Cecilia Edwards, December 14, 1944, Sally Van Wagenen Keil Collection, Official WASP Archive, Texas Woman's University, Denton, Texas.

245 **He also mentioned an article** Gil Robb Wilson, "WASPs to Be Demobilized Dec. 20: Of Nine Hundred of Them, Two Hundred Are Experts, Needed in War Work," *New York Herald Tribune,* December 13, 1944.

245 **"The point about this is"** Floyd Odlum, letter to Cecilia Edwards, December 14, 1944, Sally Van Wagenen Keil Collection, Official WASP Archive, Texas Woman's University, Denton, Texas.

245 **On December 14, 1944** Rickman, *Nancy Love,*

245 **In the interview** Paul B. Mason, "WASP to Close Their Careers as Army Pilots on Wednesday," *Baltimore Sun,* December 17, 1944, 15. (This was an Associated Press story that ran under different headlines across the United States.) Found at https://www.newspapers.com/image/373597388/?terms=wasp%2Bdisbandment.

246 **After the C-54 was safely** The "Farewell Dinner" program, as copied in Jan Churchill, *On Wings to War,* 156; *News Journal,* Wilmington, Delaware, "Air Base Fire," December 20, 1944; Teresa James, interview with Dawn Letson, June 16, 1998, Lake Worth, Florida, Official WASP Archive, Texas Woman's University.

247 **In preparation for the evening** Description based in part on photo from the evening found in Jan Churchill, *On Wings to War,* 154–64.

247 **The women called the gathering** Nancy Batson Crews, interview with Dawn Letson, Odenville, Alabama, June 11, 1997, Official WASP Archive, Texas Woman's University, Denton, Texas; Sarah Byrn Rickman, *Nancy Batson Crews: Alabama's First Lady of Flight* (Tuscaloosa: University of Alabama Press, 2009).

248 **The WASP's collective achievement** The breakdown was as follows: Headquarters AAF—1 (that's Jackie); Training Command—620; Air Transport Command—141; First Air Force—16; Second Air Force—80; Fourth Air Force—37; Weather Wing—11; Proving Ground—6; Air Technical Service—3; Troop Carrier—1—for a total of 916 serving the USAAF in December 1944. Cochran, Final Report on Women Pilot Program, *1945,* 28.

248 **The women at New Castle** *News Journal,* Wilmington, Delaware, "Air Base Fire,"

December 20, 1944. There was speculation that the fire had been the fault of an over-heated duct; Nancy Batson Crews, interview with Letson.

249 **Decades later Teresa recalled** Teresa James, interview with author, March 20, 1999, Orlando, Florida; Churchill, *On Wings to War*, 161.

CHAPTER 22: THE END OF THE EXPERIMENT

250 **The other WASP left** There were 1,102 WASP total: the 1,074 who graduated from AAF training (of 1,830 who entered) and the 28 original WAFS. Thirty-eight were killed either in training or on active duty. The remainder resigned or were let go for reasons varying from illness to family pressures to pregnancy. When disbandment was announced in October 1944, Jacqueline Cochran told the women they could resign with no negative marks on their records and a few did to pursue job opportunities, knowing the WASP would soon be no more. In all, 83 percent of the women remained on the job until the very last day.

251 **General Arnold must have** Arnold was trying to do the right thing, but he was also very aware of the fact that the Ramspeck Committee and the press were now watching his expenditures closely when related to the women, thus the "no additional expense to the government" piece of the memo. Memo, "Deactivation of WASP," Barney M. Giles, by command of General Arnold, November 1, 1944, Headquarters, Army Air Forces, Washington, D.C.

251 **Ethel Meyer** Ethel Meyer Finley, interview with author, July 1996, Oshkosh, Wisconsin.

251 **But not all of the WASP** Florence Shutsy Reynolds, interview with author, July 1996, Oshkosh, Wisconsin.

252 **Teresa spent the holidays** Teresa had flown planes like these in her last months as a WASP and knew the potential danger. Teresa James, interview with author, March 20, 1999, Orlando, Florida.

252 **In need of income** Before the war Teresa had worked in another shop besides her family store, Maxwell's Flower Shop. Ninety-Nines Amelia Earhart Memorial Scholarship application, an application for a $150 scholarship to earn her instrument rating, May 23, 1941, Teresa James Membership File, Ninety-Nines Museum, Oklahoma City, Oklahoma.

252 **That first week she helped** Teresa James, interview with author.

253 **Even those same newspapers** "WASP to Disband Dec. 20, Arnold Says; 1,000 Women Pilots Get Certificates," *New York Times*, October 4, 1944, 7. "Home by Christmas," *Time*, October 16, 1944, 68–69. Barbara Poole, "Requiem for the WASP," *Flying*, December 1944, 55–56, 146–47; Bob Hope, quoted in *WASP Newsletter*, January 25, 1945.

254 **The document she produced** Jackie also provided numerous comments on the AAF's final historical report, which came out in 1946. Jacqueline Cochran, *Final Report on Women Pilot Program, 1945*, 48. Located in the Byrd Granger Collection, Box 4, WASP Collection, Texas Woman's University, Denton, Texas.

254 **The experiment had been a success** I wrote my master's thesis on the effectiveness of the WASP as pilots for the AAF. Katherine Sharp Landdeck, master's thesis, "Experiment in the Cockpit: The Women Airforce Service Pilots of World War II," University of Tennessee, 1997; my dissertation "Against Prevailing Winds: The Women Airforce

Service Pilots and American Society," University of Tennessee, 2003, built upon the topic; Cochran, *Final Report, 1945.*

255 **Then, in late July 1945** Teresa James, interview with author.

255 **After the graduation ceremony** They never were; in fact, Elaine got a bill from the Army Air Forces a few years after the war saying she had never paid them for her trip. Elaine Harmon, interview with author, October 2, 2004, Williamsburg, Virginia.

256 **Maggie had decided** Elaine Harmon and Ruth Kearney, interview with author, July 19, 1996; Elaine Harmon, interview with author, October 2, 2004; Elaine Harmon, questionnaire, November 2000; Maggie Gee, interview with author, October 1996, Anaheim, California.

256 **Years later Elaine remembered** Elaine Harmon, interview with author, October 2, 2004, Williamsburg, Virginia.

256 **In the immediate postwar** The organization was first formed by WASP staff Clara Jo Marsh and Kay Dussaq, along with WASP Betty Jane Williams. Copies of all the newsletters can be found at the Official WASP Archive, Texas Woman's University, Denton, Texas. *WASP Newsletter,* November 24, 1944; *WASP Newsletter,* December 20, 1944; *WASP Newsletter,* October 1946.

257 **In August 1946** *WASP Newsletter,* October 1946.

257 **The following morning** Initially known as the Pulitzer Trophy Race, it was an annual event from 1920 to 1939. The war sent it into a hiatus from 1940 to 1945. Nineteen forty-six was the first year back and was filled with surplus warplanes and pilots.

257 **Four flights of twenty-five** *WASP Newsletter,* October 1946.

258 **The women found** There were WASP Nests listed throughout the immediate postwar newsletters, all across the country. Winnie Wood, Dorothy Swain, Caro Bayley, and Kaddy Landry all lived in Coconut Grove, Florida, sharing expenses and talking airplanes. Caro Bayley Bosca and Katherine Landry Steele, interview with author, June 1996, Dayton, Ohio; Caro Bayley Bosca, interview with author, 2000; Wood, *We Were WASPs.*

258 **In 1946 several WASP** *WASP Newsletter,* February 1947; Caro Bayley Bosca and Katherine Landry Steele, interview with author, 1996; Caro Bayley Bosca, interview with author, 2000; Caro Bayley Bosca, interview with author and Marty Wyall, Denton, Texas, 2003.

258 **The following month** It took place on March 16, 1947; program from air show in author's possession. Thanks to Albert "Chig" Lewis, son of Dorothy Swain Lewis, for getting me a copy; *The Ninety-Nines: Yesterday-Today-Tomorrow,* Google Books; Caro Bayley Bosca, interview with author, July 30, 1998, Oshkosh, Wisconsin; Katherine Landry Steele, interview with author, June 1996, Dayton, Ohio.

259 **The WASP reunion** In keeping with the mores of the times, the most common profession for the WASP after disbandment was housewife. Letter from Ann Lincoln Dennis to Clara Jo Marsh, February 13, 1945. MSS 249, Folder 24, WASP Collection, Texas Woman's University; *WASP Newsletters,* 1946, 1947. By the end of 1947, the Order of Fifinella reported its membership had dropped from eight hundred down to five hundred at the latest reunion, *WASP Newsletter,* October–December 1947; *WASP Newsletter,* 1951.

260 **For years after receiving** Churchill, *On Wings to War,* 144–47; James, "D-Day Plus 40 Years."

260 **Then, in early 1950** Teresa never officially changed her name to Dink's last name, Martin, but all who knew him called her Mrs. Martin.

260 **It was the waist gunner** Pat Pateman, "Rugged and Right—That's Teresa James," *Aviation Quarterly,* Winter 1989; Churchill, *On Wings to War,* 146.

260 **The meeting with the man** Photo of some of the Martin family at George's military funeral, April 1, 1950. In "Martin Research" in WASP Adela Riek Scharr's collection, St. Louis Public Library Special Collections. Sincere thanks to archivist Renee Jones for finding these materials for me. The gravestone marking his casket bears the names of all the crew members lost with Dink's plane that day: Robert Edinger, Michael D. Laytar, William A. MacDonald, George L. Martin, Raymond W. Pickett, Joseph A. Puspoki, James H. Wright, June 22, 1944.

261 **A few years later** I believe it was after 1955 because we have a photo of her in her reserves uniform in 1955 (if the picture is dated correctly) with her natural, dark hair. Thanks to Julia Lauria-Blum, close friend of Teresa's, for this story about how and when Teresa became a blonde.

CHAPTER 23: FINDING THEIR WAY

Much of the statistical information and even more details about the women's postwar lives to 1969 can be found in my doctoral dissertation: Katherine Sharp Landdeck, "Against Prevailing Winds: The Women Airforce Service Pilots and American Society," University of Tennessee, Knoxville, 2003.

262 **After disbandment,** Dora Dougherty Strother McKeown, unpublished memoir, chapter 12, in author's possession.

263 **But Dora was rejected** Beverly Beesemeyer, interview by author, October 5, 1996, Anaheim, California; Bernice Falk Haydu, questionnaire, 1997, in author's possession; Marianne Beard Nutt, in Betty Turner's book, *Out of the Blue and into History* (Chicago: Aviatrix 1999),43–45.

263 **In the spring of 1945** *WASP Newsletter,* March 15, 1945.

263 **In the spring of 1945** Dominick Pisano, *To Fill the Skies with Pilots.*

263 **When several of the women** Although a relatively small number of the women did fly four-engine aircraft during the war, none of those who applied for the Boeing job held both qualifications. *WASP Newsletter,* November 24, 1944.

263 **When several of the women** WASP Newsletters, 1945–1946.

264 **For those who could not** WASP Newsletters, 1945.

264 **Dora kept in touch** Letter from "Mac" (a pilot at Wendover Field) to Dora Dougherty, spring 1945, in Dora Dougherty Strother McKeown Collection, Official WASP Archive, Texas Woman's University, Denton, Texas; Dora Dougherty Strother McKeown, unpublished memoir, chapter 12.

265 **That same spring** Dora Dougherty Strother McKeown, interviews with author; Turner, *Out of the Blue and into History;* Eugenia Kaledin, *Mothers and More: American Women in the 1950s* (Boston: Twayne, 1984), 66.

266 **In November 1946** *WASP Newsletter,* November 1946.

267 **Everyone from economists** "American Woman's Dilemma," *Life,* June 16, 1947.

267 **The U.S. Department of Labor** Mary Anderson, Women's Bureau, U.S. Department of Labor, "The Postwar Role of Women," *American Economic Review* 34 (March 1944): 239–40.

267 **A 1946 *Fortune* magazine survey** "The *Fortune* Survey: Women in America—Part 1," *Fortune,* 34 (August 1946), 7.

267 **When *Fortune* asked** "American Woman's Dilemma," 101.

267 ***Life* magazine explored** "American Woman's Dilemma."

268 **Meanwhile, children and family** Marynia F. Farnham, "Battles Won and Lost," in "Women's Opportunities and Responsibilities," special issue, *Annals of the American Academy of Political and Social Science* 251, (May 1947): 114.

268 **The solution** Margaret Perry Bruton, "Present-Day Thinking on the Woman Question," *Annals of the American Academy of Political and Social Science* 251, no. 1 (May 1947): 14; Edward A. Strecker, *Their Mother's Sons* (Philadelphia: J. B. Lippincott, 1946); Philip Wylie, *Generation of Vipers* (New York: Pocket Books, 1942, 1955); Sidonie Matsner Gruenberg, "Changing Conceptions of the Family," *Annals of the American Academy of Political and Social Science* 251, no. 1 (May 1947): 132–33; Dr. Katharine Whiteside Taylor, "Women Face the Postwar World," *Marriage and Family Living* 7, no. 3 (August 1945): 58.

268 **After the war, Helen Richey** Unless specifically cited, much of this story on Helen Richey is from her strong but brief biography: Glenn Kerfoot, *Propeller Annie: The Story of Helen Richey, the Real First Lady of the Airlines* (Lexington: Kentucky Aviation Roundtable, 1988).

269 **There was a simple service** One of the poems he read was "High Flight" by John Gillespie Magee, original manuscript in John Magee Papers, 1941–46, Library of Congress Manuscript Division. More information on the poem and Magee can be found at https://blogs.loc.gov/catbird/2013/09/john-gillespie-magees-high-flight/.

270 **The following year** Letter from Jacqueline Cochran to ex-WASP, January 4, 1949, in author's possession and on file at Official WASP Archive, Texas Woman's University, Denton, Texas.

270 **After the war, Jackie had** Jacqueline Cochran, interview with United States Air Force Academy, March 11–12, 1976, Colorado Springs, Colorado; Rich, *Jackie Cochran,* 154.

270 **President Truman signed** Walter J. Boyne, *Beyond the Wild Blue: A History of the U.S. Air Force, 1947–1997* (New York: St. Martin's Press, 1997), 23.

270 **This, in turn, paved** Major General Jeanne Holm, USAF (Ret.), *Women in the Military: An Unfinished Revolution* (Novato, CA: Presidio Press, 1982), 120.

271 **While a leader in the effort** Jacqueline Cochran, interview with Kenneth Leish, Oral History Research Office of Columbia University, New York, New York, May 1960.

271 **Despite the fact** WASP roster, in author's possession; Margaret J. Ringenberg with Jane L. Roth, *Girls Can't Be Pilots* (Fort Wayne, IN: Daedalus Press, 1998), 120; letter from Headquarters Tenth Air Force, Selfridge Air Force Base, Michigan, to 1000 Lieutenant Margaret J. Ringenberg, July 3, 1951, in author's possession; Margaret Ringenberg, interview with author, June 1996; Barbara London Erickson, interview with Sarah Rickman, March 17 and 19, 2004.

271 **Now a Reservist** Dora Dougherty Strother, Oral History Interview K239.0512-2018, by Hugh N. Ahmann, June 10, 1991, Fort Worth, Texas; Dora Dougherty Strother, Curriculum Vitae, available at Official WASP Archive, Texas Woman's University, Denton, Texas.

CHAPTER 24: MOVING ON

272 **The last Order of Fifinella reunion** By the end of the year, the Order of Fifinella's membership had dropped to 375—about 400 fewer than they needed to stay financially viable. *WASP Newsletter,* January 1947. *WASP Newsletter,* December 1948; December 1949. Only a handful of WASP attended the 1951 reunion. *WASP Newsletter*s, 1951; Official Roster of the Women Airforce Service Pilots, 1994, in author's possession.

272 **Nancy Love was a prime** Rickman, *Nancy Love;* "Noted Aviatrix Flies 'Aerial Taxi' from Island Home Near Boston," *Beechcrafter* (Beechcraft Company magazine), Wichita, Kansas, October 27, 1955.

273 **Along with so many** Nancy Harkness Love, logbook, International Women's Air and Space Museum; Rickman, *Nancy Love.*

274 **In May 1945, Nancy arranged** Rickman, *Nancy Love.*

274 **Nancy and Barbara** Allie Love, telephone call with author, fall 2018.

274 **In 1946 the Army** Allie Love, telephone call with author; Rickman, *Nancy Love,* 233.

275 **Two-thirds of the WASP** Utilizing a database created out of questionnaires and oral histories gathered by the author, as well as the book of brief biographies by Betty Turner, the author was able to determine what became of the WASP in the 1950s and 1960s. Betty Turner, *Out of the Blue and into History* (Chicago: Aviatrix, 1999).

275 **the vast majority of their peers** In 1950, 23.8 percent of white married women worked. Cynthia Taeuber, ed., "Labor Force Participation Rates by Marital Status, Sex, and Age: 1947-1987," *Statistical Handbook on Women in America* (Phoenix, AZ: The Oryx Press, 1991), 102 (Table B3-2). Also, 28.3 percent of women with children ages six to seventeen worked. U.S. Bureau of the Census, *Historical Statistics of the United States: Colonial Times to 1970s, Part I* (Washington, DC: U.S. Government Printing Office, 1975), 134.

275 **"traditional" jobs** Other women held "odd" jobs that were not added in but could be considered "women's work," including waitress, school bus driver, etc.

275 **Ten percent of them were flight instructors** "Women Actively Engaged in Aviation—1959–1960," and "Active Airmen Certificates Held—1953–1961," *FAA Statistical Handbook of Aviation, 1961 Edition,* Federal Aviation Agency, 1961, 43–44.

275 **More than a third of the WASP** In 1950 11.9 percent and in 1955 16.2 percent of white American women with children under the age of six worked; 38 percent of the WASP clearly worked or went to college while their youngest child was under the age of five. *Historical Statistics. Statistical Handbook,* 37.

275 **Jackie Cochran continued** See Rich, *Jackie Cochran,* Chapter 22, for a much more detailed explanation of Floyd's efforts and Jackie's training and record-breaking flights.

276 **Since the end of the war** Rich, *Jackie Cochran,* Chapter 14, "War Correspondent."

277 **When Jackie returned** Rich, *Jackie Cochran,* 154–72.

277 **In 1953 Jackie published** Cochran, *The Stars at Noon;* Rich, *Jackie Cochran,* chapter 25.

278 **Jackie and Nancy** While Jackie did blame Nancy for sabotaging the efforts at the end, she primarily publicly blamed Oveta Culp Hobby of the WAC for the end of the WASP.

278 **Jackie had finally revealed** Jacqueline Cochran, "very personal and confidential" letter to General Henry H. Arnold, undated, but the content makes clear it is likely in the six months to a year after disbandment of the WASP. "ATC Rebuttal—Drafts, Working Papers," file 1, Jacqueline Cochran Collection, Eisenhower Library.

279 **We know of one occasion** Stephens College had heavily advocated to have the WASP flight school on their grounds and at the Columbia, Missouri, airport to the point that the AAF sent people to Columbia to consider it. But the surrounding terrain was too rolling, and when Avenger Field in Sweetwater came available, it was clearly a better fit. It was the Conference on Women in Aviation. Arlene Shoemaker, "Air Schooling for Milady," *Flying* 37, 1945; *History of the WASP Program Army Air Forces Central Flying Training Command,* Historical Section, A-2 (Personnel), Army Air Forces Central Flying Command, Randolph Field, Texas, January 20, 1945; *WASP Newsletter,* June 1946.

CHAPTER 25: REUNITED

281 **In December 1963** Unless otherwise cited, this discussion of Marty in the postwar years and the 1960s reunions is based upon Mary Anna Martin Wyall, interviews with author, 1997 to 2017.

285 **Marty decided to ask Dora** Dougherty Strother McKeown, interview with author; Dora Dougherty Strother McKeown, unpublished memoir, in author's possession, Dora Dougherty, Curriculum Vitae, Official WASP Archive, Texas Woman's University, Denton, Texas.

285 **She immediately joined** Today the Whirly-Girls is a thriving organization whose archives are held at Texas Woman's University, home of the Official WASP Archive; https://www.whirlygirls.org/about-us/; February 8, 1961—Federation Aeronautique Internationale Record: Altitude, 19,385 feet in Bell Model 47G3 helicopter; February 10, 1961—FAI Record: Distance in a Straight Line—Bell Model 47G-e helicopter—record distance 405 miles; Dora Dougherty, letter to Jacqueline Cochran, May 17, 1961, Official WASP Archive, Texas Woman's University, Denton, Texas; Jacqueline Cochran, letter to Dora Dougherty, July 10, 1961, Official WASP Archive, Texas Woman's University, Denton, Texas.

286 **That August, Jackie arrived** "Gals Wear 'General's Pants' as Wartime WASPs Gather," *Cincinnati Enquirer,* August 14, 1964, 4. Found at https://www.newspapers .com/image/100310978/?terms=jacqueline%2BCochran%2Bninety%2Bnines %2Bcincinnati

286 **At the dinner, Jackie asked** Dora Dougherty, letter to Jacqueline Cochran, May 17, 1961, Official WASP Archive, Texas Woman's University, Denton, Texas; Jacqueline Cochran, letter to Dora Dougherty, July 10, 1961, Official WASP Archive, Texas Woman's University, Denton, Texas; Mary Anna "Marty" Wyall, interview with Dawn Letson, June 30, 1992, Fort Wayne, Indiana; Marty Wyall, interviews with author; Dora Dougherty Strother McKeown, unpublished memoir and interview with author; Jacqueline Cochran, interview with United States Air Force Academy, March 11–12, 1976, conducted by the Department of History, United States Air Force Academy, Colorado Springs, Colorado.

287 **After the dinner** Jean Terrell Moreo McCreery from Ohio was in class 44-W-10. In addition to a bus driver and a mother, she was a skilled draftsman and good friend. After her first husband died, she married again in 1990 and became Jean McCreery. She was stubborn, funny, and smart and loved all of her kids very much. Marty Wyall, interview with author; Jean McCreery, interview with author.

287 **Jackie's face lit up** Jackie Cochran, interview with U.S. Air Force Academy, 1976.

287 **Years later, when asked** When asked why her kids were out of high school before they realized what she'd done in the war, Caro Bayley Bosca explained that she didn't talk about it in part because her husband had stayed stateside during the war and she didn't want him to feel bad because of her adventures flying B-25s and such. As to why her bridge and country club friends didn't know, she said, "Frankly, they would not have been interested." Caro Bayley Bosca and Marty Wyall, recorded discussion with author and WASP friend Sherry Ringler at author's home, 2003, in author's possession.

288 **It came out in October 1964** *WASP Newsletter,* October 1964, available at Official WASP Archive, Texas Woman's University, Denton, Texas.

288 **Gene encouraged Marty** Marty Wyall, interview with author, 1999; John Wyall, text message with author, June 20, 2019.

289 **The 1965 newsletters** All of these WASP newsletters are available at the Official WASP Archive, Texas Woman's University, Denton, Texas.

289 **The June 1968 newsletter** *WASP Newsletter,* June 1968; Betty Jo Reed, known lovingly by her WASP friends as "Birdlegs," had attended the WASP reunion in 1946 and others, and continued to stay active with the WASP organization, attending air shows and reunions until the very end. Betty Jo had kept flying some during the years after she and her husband opened one of the first McDonald's restaurants in the nation. *WASP Newsletter,* June 1968.

289 **Years later Marty's son John** Anecdote from John Wyall, son of Marty Wyall, 2016, Oshkosh, Wisconsin.

289 **Elaine Harmon** *WASP Newsletter,* December 1969; Elaine Harmon, interview with author, 2004, Williamsburg, Virginia.

290 **It was, Marty later remembered** *WASP Newsletter,* December 1969; Marty Wyall, Dora Dougherty Strother McKeown, and Elaine Harmon oral histories with author; reunion pictures, available at Official WASP Archive, Texas Woman's University, Denton, Texas.

290 **There was one notable** Two of Nancy's daughters ended up getting their private pilot's licenses. Allie Love, telephone call with author, fall 2018.

CHAPTER 26: THE FIGHT BEGINS

292 **After Dink's funeral** Churchill, *On Wings to War,* 165–67.

293 **Around 1961 she went** Teresa served in Alaska from 1961 to 1965. Churchill, *On Wings to War,* 164. The meeting with Jackie would lead to Teresa moving to California to manage Jackie's golf course for a few years. Teresa had never played golf but had never lived in California, either. Teresa James, interview with author, March 20, 1999, Orlando, Florida.

293 **She was in her early** Teresa James was born on January 25, 1911, *not* 1914, as she publicly claimed. Teresa James, letter to Jacqueline Cochran, February 4, 1942, Jacqueline Cochran Collection, Eisenhower Library; Teresa James birth certificate, State of Pennsylvania; Teresa James census records.

293 **Teresa wasn't even** Lieutenant Colonel Yvonne "Pat" Pateman, WASP class 43-W-5, served in the U.S. Air Force in Korea and Vietnam, proudly—and stubbornly—wearing her WASP wings on her uniform the entire time. Yvonne "Pat" Pateman, interview with author, 1999.

294 **How different would her life** Teresa wasn't alone in her sentiments. One of WASP Florence Shutsy Reynolds's greatest life regrets was that she was never able to go to college. She mourned the lost opportunities that the G.I. Bill would have brought to the WASPs. Multiple conversations with author over twenty-year friendship. Pat Pateman, "Rugged and Right—That's Teresa James," *Aviation Quarterly,* Winter 1989; Teresa James, interview with Dawn Letson, June 16, 1998, Lake Worth, Florida, Official WASP Archive, Texas Woman's University, Denton, Texas; Teresa James, interview with author, March 20, 1999, Orlando, Florida.

294 **In 1963, Teresa decided** Teresa James, letter with enclosures of petition and Reserve Officer Association resolution. TWU MSS 249, Folder 105. WASP Inc., Post War Organization; establishment of WASP Militarization Committee; Teresa James, interview with author.

294 **At one such gathering** Teresa James, interview with Letson.

295 **Dora's life had changed** It seems likely that Les was writing as a special correspondent for the St. Louis paper. Dora was set to present in St. Louis and they wanted a little pre-event coverage, so they must have contracted with Les to write the story. Les Strother, "She's Flying High in Copter and Lab," *St. Louis Post-Dispatch,* 76, found at https://www.newspapers.com/image/141963100/?terms=lester%2Bstrother%2Bdora %2Bdougherty%2BWASP.

295 **A few months after** Letter from Dora Dougherty Strother to Isabel Fenton Stinson, March 22, 1967, Official WASP Archive, Texas Woman's University, Denton, Texas.

295 **In March 1972** Teresa James, letter to WASP Membership, WASP Inc., Post War Organization; establishment of WASP Militarization Committee. MSS 249, Folder 105, Official WASP Archive, Texas Woman's University, Denton, Texas.

296 **Teresa worked diligently** According to a June 1972 letter from Dora Strother to Teresa James, there was a WASP militarization committee that included Francie Park, Jill McCormick, Eleanor Moriarty Beith, Alyce Stevens Rohrer, Pat Pateman, Marion Tibbets, and BJ Williams. There is no written evidence to suggest much of the concrete work they may have done. Anecdotal evidence suggests their talking about the issue made more WASP think about it, which led to the more vocal and active 1973 committee and eventual militarization. Letter from Dora Dougherty Strother to Teresa James, June 1972, TWU MSS 249, Folder 35, 1972 WASP Correspondence. Letter from Marty Wyall to Faith Buchner "Bucky" Richards, May 27, 1972. MSS 249, Folder 35, TWU.

296 **The end result** *Recomputation and Other Retirement Legislation,* Report by the Special Subcommittee on Retired-Pay Revisions of the Committee on Armed Services, House of Representatives, 92nd Congress, Second Session, December 29, 1972, page 17664. TWU MSS 362, Folder 3, and MSS 265, Box 6, Folder 8.

297 **The WASP reunion** *WASP Newsletter 5,* ed., December 1969.

297 **The guest of honor** After retiring from active duty in the Army in 1946, Henry H. Arnold became the first general of the new U.S. Air Force, five-star rank, in 1949, making him the only person to achieve five-star rank in two different branches of service. To this day he is the only person to achieve the five-star rank in the U.S. Air Force.

298 **On Saturday evening** "Thirtieth Memorial Reunion" pictorial directory, June 23–25, 1972, in author's possession.

298 **Later, Arnold himself recalled** Kathy Sawyer, "World War II Women Flyers Seek Equality," *Washington Post,* March 6, 1977, 1, 10.

298 **In 1973 the WASP militarization** Faith Buchner Richards, letter to Nancy Crews, March 11, 1973.

299 **The WASP records were scattered** The records were *not,* as some say today, closed or classified. The WASP records were classified immediately after the war, as were most war records, until they went through the normal procedural review. Some postwar reports were never classified and the wartime record declassification began in 1952. I know this from seeing the declassification stamps on the papers and a letter to me from the National Archives in 2007 confirming it.

299 **Bruce Arnold had used** Arnold initially allowed any WASP working on militarization to use his Washington, D.C., office whenever they were in town. This meant that the women on the committee could also use his WATS line, or "wide area telephone service," a long-distance telephone system that enabled the women to call their members across the country at fixed rates at a time when long-distance calls were prohibitively expensive. When Arnold's employer became aware of the time and resources being granted to the WASP, however, the women were told to leave. So Arnold used his influence to get the women their own office, literally an old broom closet, in the Army and Navy Club, signing for their temporary membership cards and guaranteeing payment of any bills incurred. Bee Haydu letter to author, January 17, 1997. Unfortunately, both Colonel Arnold and his wife are deceased, and so none of his personal recollections are available.

299 **The broom closet office** This discussion of the "broom closet" is based on the following sources: telephone call with Lucile Doll Wise, June 25, 2018; Sara Payne Hayden, Helen Schaefer, Mary Ellen Keil, and Emily Chapin (who'd served with the ATA in England before becoming a WASP) were all regulars in the office, too. Photograph, courtesy of Bee Falk Haydu in author's possession.

300 **Jackie, the traveler** Rich, *Jackie Cochran.*

301 **She failed to pass** Every pilot must pass the FAA's medical examination at regular intervals, depending on the "class" of medical and their purposes for flying. Once a medical is lost, the pilot is no longer legal to fly.

301 **On Martha's Vineyard** Rickman, *Nancy Love.*

301 **In Washington** They got off to a slow start. The ugly politics of the Watergate era had initially made it difficult for Bruce Arnold to find a sympathetic senator to come on board with the WASP cause, and the women's 1974 reunion had to be canceled because of the energy crisis and ensuing economic struggles. Nancy Crews, "President's Message," *WASP Newsletter 10,* December 1974.

301 **Bruce Arnold had helped** Bee Haydu, letter to author, January 17, 1997.

302 **Meanwhile, WASP Bernice** Bee Haydu, "Message from Your President," *WASP Newsletter 11,* November 1975.

302 **Nonetheless, this was** WASP Katherine "Kaddy" Landry Steele firmly believed that their efforts would not have been possible without the civil rights and women's movements paving the way for them. Interview with author, 1999, Oshkosh, Wisconsin.

302 **With the passage** "Air Force Academy Programs for Women Cadets," *Fact Sheet: United States Air Force,* U.S. Air Force Academy, Colorado, January 1977.

302 **Jacqueline Cochran testified** Jacqueline Cochran, testimony before congressional subcommittee hearing on admission of women to service academies, May 20, 1975, Texas Woman's University, Denton, Texas. Box 14, WEAL Collection.

303 **Despite Jackie's assertions** Letter from Bernice Chandler, chair of the Advisory Council on Women's Educational Programs, a group that worked to educate about and enforce Title IX, to Secretary of Defense Donald Rumsfeld, July 30, 1976. Texas Woman's University, Denton, Texas. Box 14, WEAL Collection.

303 **While many of the WASP** According to Kathleen Cosand, "The initial test group was 20, 18 active duty, 1 Air Force reserve, 1 Air National Guard. 9 active duty and 1 reserve (me), started UPT September 1976, UPT class 77-08. All ten of us graduated. The second group started 6 months later, I believe 78-03, 9 active duty, 1 ANG. 6 graduated." Email with Cosand, June 21, 2019; "Women Pilots OK'd by A.F.," UPI news report, January 18, 1976. Dated but title of newspaper only listed as "S.H.T." In MSS 827, Sally Keil, newspaper clippings. WASP Collection, Texas Woman's University, Denton, Texas.

303 **General Arnold had promised** General Henry H. Arnold, Farewell Speech to Graduates of 44-W-10, December 7, 1944.

303 **"Nobody seemed to remember"** Dora Dougherty Strother, Oral History Interview K239.0512-2018, by Hugh N. Ahmann, June 10, 1991, Fort Worth, Texas.

304 **When the WASP saw** Mary Regalbutto Jones, interview with author, 1997. Betty Jane Williams, interview and emails with author.

304 **The newspapers loved** Pat Kailer, "Heroines Flew Dangerous Flights: City Has WASPs," from an Albuquerque, New Mexico, paper, October 1976, MSS 827, Sally Keil Collection, WASP Collection, Texas Woman's University, Denton, Texas, David L. Langford, "America's Forgotten Heroines Keep Fighting," *Sarasota Herald-Tribune,* October 1, 1976, 2D.

304 **Meanwhile, WASP around** Marty Wyall, interviews with author and letter to author, in author's possession.

305 **Nancy Love was supportive** Unless otherwise cited, his segment on Nancy Love's end based in large part on Rickman, *Nancy Love,* 268–73.

305 **In 1976 the WASP** Bernice Falk Haydu, interview with author.

CHAPTER 27: THE YEAR OF THE WASP

307 **The women dubbed 1977** Unless otherwise cited, much of this chapter is based on interviews and correspondence between the author and the following WASP, gaining corroboration from them as well as written sources: Bee Falk Haydu, Marty Wyall, Dora Dougherty Strother McKeown, Elaine Harmon, Sara Payne Hayden, Mary Regalbutto Jones, Charlyne Creger, Teresa James, and Lucile Doll Wise, 1997–2017, in author's possession or donated to Official WASP Archive, Texas Woman's University, Denton, Texas.

308 **Dora, Marty, and Teresa** Minutes of October 23, 1976, General Business Meeting, Hot Springs, Arkansas. MSS 249, Folder 51, WASP Collection, Texas Woman's University; *WASP Newsletter 13,* Special Edition, December 1976.

308 **"I am certain that"** "Special Pre 'Red Alert' Notice" from Bee Haydu to WASP, February 1977, MSS 260, Box 2, Folder 11, WASP Collection, Texas Woman's University, Denton, Texas.

308 **Meanwhile, the WASP story** Bee Haydu, interview with author, October 2, 2004, Williamsburg, Virginia. In author's possession.

309 **In addition** Bart Barnes, "Barry Goldwater, GOP Hero, Dies," *Washington Post,* Saturday, May 30, 1998, A01. Bee Haydu, interview with author; Lucile Doll Wise, interview with author, 2004; Dora Dougherty Strother McKeown, interview with author, 2007.

310 **In May 1977** https://www.washingtonpost.com/archive/politics/1977/03/06/wwii -women-fliers-seek-equality/327281c1-d49a-474a-9945-09b7877c0c44/?utm_term =.dccdaa76d95f.

310 **But Teresa declined** Teresa James, interview with Dawn Letson, June 16, 1998, Lake Worth, Florida, Official WASP Archive, Texas Woman's University, Denton, Texas.

310 **Dora humbly accepted** Dora Dougherty Strother McKeown, unpublished memoir, chapter 13; Dora Dougherty Strother McKeown, telephone interview with author, May 25, 2007. Tape recording in author's possession.

311 **The morning of the Senate** Dora, interview with author; Bee Haydu, interview with author; https://archives.nbclearn.com/portal/site/k-12/flatview?cuecard=43773; Dora Dougherty Strother McKeown, memoir, chapter 13. A picture of the whole group on the steps shows Dora and Bee standing next to Bruce Arnold; Teresa James is in the back row, and Marty Wyall is in the middle.

311 **Even with Dora's decades** She explained that the WASP had lost the 1944 vote due to sex discrimination, peace syndrome, side issues (the men pilots), and pressure for adjournment. Dora gave the same statement to the Senate and the House committees. "Statement by Dora Dougherty Strother Before the Committee on Veterans' Affairs, House of Representatives," 95th Congress, 1st session, in support of H.R. 3321, introduced by Congresswoman Lindy Boggs, September 20, 1977; Dora Dougherty Strother McKeown, telephone interview with author, May 25, 2007. Tape recording in author's possession.

312 **Next it was Senator Goldwater's** "Senator Goldwater Supports WASPs Bill," *Stars and Stripes,* June 2, 1977.

312 **Opponents of the WASP** While Starbuck had worked with the VA since 1946, she was appointed as chief benefits officer in May 1977, the first woman to hold that position. https://weservedtoo.wordpress.com/2014/05/01/va-history-miss-dorothy-l -starbuck-became-the-first-woman-appointed-as-vas-chief-benefits-officer/.

312 **Starbuck, who had served** Patricia Collins Hughes, "Cleland's Letter Lacks Facts of Record," *Stars and Stripes,* June 30, 1977, 11; Hughes, "Senate Votes 91-0 for WASP Status," *Stars and Stripes,* October 27, 1977, 3.

313 **On August 15, 1977** "Red Alert," August 15, 1977. MSS 250, Legislation/Militarization 1942–1985, News Releases and Mailings. WASP Collection, Texas Woman's University, Denton, Texas; "Action Now" flyer. MSS 250 Legislative/Militarization, 1942–1985, News Releases and Mailings. WASP Collection, Texas Woman's University, Denton, Texas.

314 **Chayes had been earmarked** Chayes, who could have very easily toed the party line, said she admired the women but it wasn't appropriate for her to comment or support them. However, Chayes was touched by the women's story. Antonia Handler

Chayes, telephone interview with author, March 30, 2007. Tape recording in author's possession; Dora, memoir, chapter 13.

314 **Until now** Hearing Before a Select Subcommittee of the Committee on Veterans' Affairs, House of Representatives, Ninety-Fifth Congress, First Session, on Granting Veterans' Status to WASPs, September 20, 1977. Special thanks to WASP Elaine Harmon for loaning the author her personal copy, inscribed by Representative Heckler: "To Elaine Harmon, With Warmest Wishes and grateful thanks for your courageous and gallant service."

314 **The start was not** House Subcommittee Hearings, 261.

314 **The WASP were introduced** WASP Ann Tunner also gave testimony that day. House Subcommittee Hearings, 243, 252–53, 261; unsigned note from female, likely not WASP (possibly Sally Keil), supporter of the women to Pat Zell, September 27, 1977. MSS 827, Sally Keil Collection, WASP Collection, Texas Woman's University, Denton, Texas. To be fair, even Lindy Boggs, in her support of the WASP, used the women's physical appearance to demonstrate their strength. She pointed out that "the ladies were not only in uniform then, and well-disciplined then, but they obviously have been well-disciplined ever since, because they're able to fit into their uniforms today."

314 **In her initial responses** Antonia Handler Chayes, telephone interview with author, March 30, 2007. Tape recording in author's possession; House Subcommittee Hearings, 277.

315 **Opponents of the WASP** *Stars and Stripes*, October 6, 1977, 3.

315 **Oppositional testimonies** House Subcommittee Hearings, 445–46. See also "American Legion Opposes WASPs Bill," testimony of Robert E. Lyngh, Deputy Director, National Veterans Affairs and Rehabilitation Commission, the American Legion, before the Senate Committee on Veterans Affairs, May 25, 1977. *Stars and Stripes*, June 2, 1977, 15.

315 **Their champions had** After her statement, Chayes was confronted by the special assistant to the secretary of defense, who hotly accused her of not clearing her testimony. Chayes apologized but argued, "It seemed so obviously the right thing to do that it never occurred to me," and bluffed that perhaps she should go ask the White House. President Carter had recently pushed for women's equality, including an effort to have a woman in every department at the assistant secretary level or above, she had hoped that if her bluff was called he would be supportive. Antonia Handler Chayes, telephone interview with author.

315 **Bee was most optimistic** Bee Haydu, letter to Marty Wyall, September 22, 1977, MSS 249, Folder 45, WASP Collection, Texas Woman's University, Denton, Texas.

316 **Elaine Harmon saw** Letter from Elaine Harmon to Marty Wyall, September 1977, MSS 249, Folder 45, WASP Collection, Texas Woman's University, Denton, Texas.

316 **In the weeks after** Patricia Collins Hughes, "Roberts Vows to Keep WASP Bill Tied Up in Committee," *Stars and Stripes*, September 22, 1977, 3.

316 **Committee chairman Ray Roberts** House Subcommittee Hearings, 457.

316 **Next, the WASP got** Letter from the Deputy Secretary of Defense, Charles W. Duncan, Jr., to Acting Director, Office of Management and Budget, James T. McIntyre,

Jr., October 21, 1977, House Subcommittee Hearings, 453. The secretary of defense at the time was Dr. Harold Brown. He obviously authorized the department's new position and Duncan's letter; Hughes, "Senate Votes 91–0 for WASP Status," 3.

317 **After so many years** Patricia Collins Hughes, "WASPs Await President's Signature," *Stars and Stripes,* November 10, 1977.

317 **The WASP who had gathered** Ibid., 3.

317 **On November 23, 1977** Of Margaret Heckler, Patricia Collins Hughes asserted that without Heckler's "daring debate there would have been no victory," and credited Heckler as having "rekindled our faith in Congressional leadership." Hughes recognized Lindy Boggs as having been a "tower of strength to all the WASPs and to whom they will be eternally grateful for her skilled efforts on their behalf." The WASPs' gratitude toward Senator Goldwater and Bruce Arnold continues to this day. Patricia Collins Hughes, "Hallelujah! WASPs Are VETERANS at Last!," *Stars and Stripes,* December 1, 1977, 3.

318 **After the signing** While Bee Haydu had hoped they would be given one of the pens used to sign the bill, none of the WASP were invited to the signing. No one was sure why—if it was a snub or because they were only an amendment to a larger bill—but in any case they had been shut out. Bee Haydu, interview with author. Inquiries to the Carter Library have not answered this question.

318 **That night someone asked** *WASP Newsletter,* November 1978 and April 1979; Treasurer's Report, *WASP Newsletter*; Elaine Harmon, interview with author, October 2, 2004; Bernice Falk Haydu, interview with Dawn Letson and Elizabeth Snapp, September 12, 1992, Official WASP Archive, Texas Woman's University, Denton, Texas.

318 **By 1979, when the Department** Their bill, section 401 of Public Law 95-202, stated that the women would be treated as veterans *if* the Department of Defense considered their service during World War II to be active duty. The women still needed the Department of Defense to officially declare them discharged and issue certificates of honorable discharge. Once it finally did, in March 1979, the women had to find their paperwork and fill out a DD 214 to ask for their benefits.

318 **At least the women** For one WASP, the declaration came just in time. Irene Minter Brady was only fifty-seven, but she was dying when the Department of Defense at last began issuing discharges. She desperately wanted the American flag to cover her coffin so her son might have some memento of her service. Her 44-W-10 classmate Charlyne Creger was determined to make it happen and called Antonia Handler Chayes for help. Chayes's assistant Captain Pruitt flew from her office at the Pentagon to Irene's bedside to make certain she filed the proper paperwork. Her discharge was issued just in time. Irene died with her papers hanging on the hospital room wall for all to see. Randolph Field provided all female pallbearers for her military funeral, and an American flag was draped over Irene's coffin. It was exactly the kind of honor the women had fought for. The same story that described Brady's experience said of the military funeral: "The rules had changed and this may be our first and last such honor." *WASP Newsletter 18,* March 1980; Charlyne Creger, interview with author.

318 **"We were sent the ribbons"** Dora Dougherty Strother McKeown, memoir, chapter 13. In reality, they had to fight for those medals. Senator Goldwater pushed through a new bill to get the women their service medals, namely the World War II Victory Medal, honorable service pin, and, with over one year of service, the American Cam-

paign Medal. President Reagan signed Public Law 98-94 giving the women their medals in October 1983. *WASP Newsletter,* June 1984.

CHAPTER 28: THE FINAL FLIGHT

319 **Jackie was surprised** Jackie and Floyd's physician, Dr. Earl Thompson, said, "I think when Floyd died a little bit of her died. She never gave another party . . . just like she'd given up on life." Rich, *Jackie Cochran.*

320 **The service for Jackie** The WASP held a service of their own for her later that year, with over one hundred of the women in attendance. Memorial program and photos, Byrd Howell Granger Collection, Official WASP Archive, Texas Woman's University, Denton, Texas.

320 **Jackie was laid to rest** Several jets, unplanned, streaked low over her funeral service, as Chuck Yeager, Floyd's children and grandchildren, and some of her house staff—a total of thirteen people (her lucky number)—paid their final respects. I've thought the sword a bit ironic, since Jackie testified so adamantly against admitting women to the academy. It would seem she has been forgiven. https://www.legacy.com/obituaries/houstonchronicle/obituary.aspx?n=tony-marimon&pid=116247049. Jacqueline Cochran and Maryann Bucknum Brinley, *Jackie Cochran: The Autobiography of the Greatest Woman Pilot in Aviation History* (New York: Bantam Books, 1987), 345–48.

321 **Elaine Harmon was one** Elaine Harmon, interview with author, October 2, 2004.

321 **Elaine was frustrated** Goldwater wrote back to her assuring her that "Congress intended to make WASPs eligible for all veterans' benefits and programs just as any other person who served in active duty in World War II." Letter from Senator Barry Goldwater to Elaine Harmon, September 10, 1981. MSS 250, Official WASP Archive, Texas Woman's University.

321 **"You will recall"** Goldwater, letter to Harmon, September 10, 1981.

322 **On September 29, 1981** Statement of Elaine D. Harmon, WASP, Chairman of the WASP Veterans' Benefits Committee, before the House Veterans' Affairs Committee, Subcommittee on Oversight and Investigation with Respect to Implementation of Title IV of Public Law 95-202 on Benefits for WASP, September 29, 1981. MSS 250, Legislation/Militarization, Official WASP Archive, Texas Woman's University, Denton, Texas.

322 **Another WASP** Jean McSheehy had been a WAC when the WASP began, fought to be released so she could serve, then joined the military again after disbandment. By the 1970s she had retired from the military after being told her time in the WASP counted toward her service. Then she was told it didn't and she was not eligible for retirement pay because she had not served long enough. Letter from Jean McSheehy to Jacqueline Cochran, September 23, 1942, National Archives II, College Park, Maryland. Record Group 18, Central Decimal Files October 1942–May 1944, 324.5, Box 700 and 221.02, Box 496; Dayle D. Marshall, Director of Personnel Actions, Department of the Air Force, to Jeanne McSheehy, September 24, 1979; letter from Jeanne L. McSheehy, Lt. Col., USAFR Retired, to Elaine Harmon, September 9, 1981. MSS 250, Official WASP Archive, Texas Woman's University; Statement of Lieutenant Colonel Jean McSheehy, testimony before the House Committee on Veterans Affairs, September 29, 1981; Patricia Collins Hughes gave a statement at the same hearings as well.

322 **"How many closed doors"** Elaine Harmon, telephone interview with author, March 25, 2007, tape recording in author's possession.

323 **Nineteen eighty-four marked the fortieth** Unless otherwise cited, this story of Teresa's visit to France is based on Teresa James, "D-Day Plus 40 Years," her handwritten sixteen-page memoir of the trip and what it meant to her. In Madge Rutherford Minton Collection, Official WASP Archive, Texas Woman's University, Denton, Texas.

326 **She never even came close** I have confirmed her singleness with good friend Julia Lauria-Blum and Teresa's niece Yvonne James.

326 **She died in hospice** Teresa's obituaries say ninety-four, basing her age on the 1914 birth date, but in reality she was born in 1911, thus was ninety-seven. James letter to Cochran, February 4, 1942; Teresa James, birth certificate.

326 **In the early** Yvonne "Pat" Pateman served in class 43-W-5 and then went on to serve twenty-two years as a U.S. Air Force intelligence officer, including in Korea and Vietnam. During her time as an Air Force officer she proudly wore her WASP wings on her uniform despite it being against the rules. Pateman donated her materials to the U.S. Air Force Academy in 1983.

326 **In 1993 the WASP** One of the first collections in the WASP archive was that of Byrd Howell Granger, class 43-W-1. Byrd had been instrumental in gathering information for the 1970s effort and worked to put it all together in a book. When she died unexpectedly, Blanche Osborn Bross, one of the "lucky 13" B-17 pilots and best known as one of the women in the *Pistol Packin' Mama* picture, gathered Byrd's papers and sent them to Texas Woman's University. Blanche Osborn Bross, letter to author.

327 **"You came to show us"** Letter from Harry McKeown to Dora Dougherty Strother, August 2, 1995, Official WASP Archive, Texas Woman's University, Denton, Texas.

327 **"Harry McKeown turned out"** Dora Dougherty Strother McKeown, unpublished memoirs, in author's possession.

327 **The final WASP reunion** I was honored, as cofounder and vice president of The Wingtip-to-Wingtip Association, to be the chair of this final reunion.

329 **The WASP and their supporters** Emancipation Hall was packed with more than 2,000 of the WASP's family and friends, as well as dozens of reporters from around the world, to witness the women receiving the Congressional Gold Medal, March 2010.

EPILOGUE

331 **He made the decision** WASP Ruth Guhse's family was actually the first to discover the new policy. After nearly a year of fighting, the Guhse family finally had to give up. Ruth, who had always hoped to be buried at Arlington, was quietly laid to rest at a veterans cemetery in Virginia.

331 **When her family learned** To learn more about Elaine's family's fight for her and all the WASP, see her granddaughter Erin Miller's excellent book, *Final Flight, Final Fight* (Silver Spring, MD: 4336 Press, 2019), https://www.finalflightfinalfight.com/.

331 **So her office worked to write** It was my honor to work with her office in drafting the bill. For more of the backstory on the WASP and Arlington National Cemetery: https://www.theatlantic.com/politics/archive/2016/01/women-world-war-two -veterans-arlilngton/424158/. For more on the funeral: https://www.theatlantic.com

/politics/archive/2016/09/wasp-elaine-harmon-arlington-national-cemetery/499112/. Forgive the self-citation.

332 **The day of the funeral** Elaine Harmon, along with her classmate Ruth Kearney, was the first WASP whom I formally interviewed in June 1996. She helped and encouraged me immensely over the years and was a good friend. I was there at her service with Marty, Shutsy, and Shirley.

Index

Page numbers of photographs and their captions appear in italics.
Pilot surnames after marriage appear in parentheses.

THE WOMEN WITH SILVER WINGS

KATHERINE SHARP LANDDECK

Random
House
Book Club

Because
Stories Are
Better Shared ™

A BOOK CLUB GUIDE

A CONVERSATION WITH KATHERINE SHARP LANDDECK

RHBC: As the United States entered World War II, some 25,000 women applied to be part of the WASP so that they would have a chance to fly. Why did so few women, only 1,102, earn their silver wings?

KSL: The Army Air Forces planned for the WASP to be an experimental program that would allow them to test whether women pilots could be counted on in wartime. So there were very few slots, and the requirements for them were stiff: They had to be well-educated, have a significant amount of flying experience, meet the Army's strict physical standards, and provide letters of reference. Only 1,830 women were accepted for training. Once these pilots were accepted, they had to make it through challenging Army training. But of those women who made it into training, 70 percent graduated—the same ratio as male pilots. Their success encouraged those who supported the women to expand the experiment even further, and quieted some of their detractors. Still, one of the most heartbreaking parts of my research was reading the letters in the National Archives from women who were not accepted into the program. Tens of thousands of women, from farm wives in Iowa to school girls in Oregon and secretaries in South Carolina, desperately wanted to fly and serve their country.

Relatively few of them would make the cut. Meanwhile, African American women were shut out entirely, no matter their level of experience. For many of those women, some of whom I have met, the disappointment of not getting a chance to join the WASP stayed with them their entire lives.

RHBC: You're a private pilot yourself. In the process of your research, did you find that being able to connect with many of the women featured in the book over your shared love of aviation helped them to open up?

KSL: Oh, definitely! I often met with WASP at aviation events, and we did our interviews with the sound and smell of planes flying overhead. There was always a noticeable shift in their tone and attitude when they realized I was a pilot too. We shared not only the jargon of flying, but the passion for it. When they spoke of the power, peace, and sheer joy they felt as pilots, they knew I understood. Our conversations moved faster and went deeper because of that shared love. I know I got different—and I think better— stories because of it.

RHBC: There are so many fascinating stories interwoven throughout the book. How did you choose which ones to include?

KSL: Honestly, this was the hardest part of writing the book— there were so many amazing stories that ended up on the cutting room floor. In the end, I chose to focus on women who I myself knew personally and had done oral histories with. As a historian, I knew I could find plenty of facts about the WASP. But understanding their motivations is much more difficult. Oral histories can help us add that missing piece of the story. That said, our perspectives change over time, and memory can be imperfect. For that reason, I chose women who had primary sources—letters and diaries mostly—from the war years, so that I could understand what they were thinking and feeling during that time.

RHBC: The story of the WASP is a fascinating one, starting with the lead up to World War II and culminating with the women's fight to be buried at Arlington National Cemetery, in 2016. Can you tell us about that fight, which you helped spearhead, and what transpired?

KSL: Elaine Harmon, a WASP in the second-to-last class, died in 2015. She had been a big part of the fight for veterans' recognition in the 1970s, and wanted to be interned at Arlington National Cemetery, an honor she thought she had already won. When her family began planning her service, they were stunned to learn the cemetery had changed its policy and WASP were no longer eligible because of a technicality in the law that had cemented their status as veterans. I had helped with an earlier fight in 2002 to clarify the women's place in Arlington, and had known Elaine for nearly twenty years, so when they got the news from Arlington, Elaine's family contacted me for help. Eventually, it became clear that a new law was needed, and I worked with Representative Martha McSally's staff as they wrote the bill that eventually got the WASP, including Elaine, back into Arlington National Cemetery, where they belonged. It was a bit surreal to go from telling the WASP's story to helping shape the final pages of it, but I was happy to do it for Elaine, who was a terrific woman and a good friend. She would have been so proud of her family, who are pretty incredible in their own right, for fighting for her.

RHBC: Can you tell us a bit about the WASP's influence on the world today?

KSL: The WASP have been a huge influence on women pilots today, especially within the United States Air Force, where they are still a distinct minority. Many have adopted the WASP mascot, a winged gremlin named Fifinella, and have put her image on the seats of their cockpits. I've seen Fifinella jewelry and even tattoos.

RHBC: What do you hope readers will take away from *The Women with Silver Wings*?

KSL: The women of the WASP were independent, smart, and fallibly human. They faced adversity with open eyes and stubborn determination. They didn't achieve everything they wanted to, but they fought to have the chance to prove what they could do—and when given that chance, they proved themselves capable. They would want people to learn their story and remember them as the first women pilots for the U.S. military—and then to go out and fight for their own dreams, whatever they might be. I hope this book serves as an inspiration for new generations to follow in their footsteps.

QUESTIONS AND TOPICS FOR DISCUSSION

1. Before reading *The Women with Silver Wings*, what did you know about women's contributions to the war effort during World War II? Were you familiar with the WASP?

2. The WASP was the brainchild of two trailblazing pilots, Jacqueline Cochran and Nancy Harkness Love. What did they have in common? What set them apart?

3. Nancy and Jackie had strict standards for WASP applicants. They had to have logged significant flight time, attained a high level of educational achievement, and even—at least for Jackie's program—present a conventionally attractive appearance. Why did they insist on maintaining these standards, which were higher than those for men?

4. The women of the WASP grew up in a culture obsessed with flight, in which the fastest, most daring pilots—including women like Amelia Earhart—were as famous as film stars. What did flying represent for girls and young women in the 1920s and '30s? How did it influence them to apply to join the WASP?

5. In order to get the WASP off the ground, Nancy and Jackie needed the support of male allies in positions of power. Chief

among them was General Henry "Hap" Arnold. What was his motivation for helping the women? Was he ultimately a reliable ally? What about other prominent men, such as General Tunner, Bruce Arnold, and Barry Goldwater?

6. The WASP came from all over the country and from many different walks of life; they included both rural, working-class women like Teresa James, and daughters of the military and the social elite. How did they form friendships and develop camaraderie? Were there unbridgeable differences? How did they draw on these bonds when fighting for recognition as veterans in the 1970s and beyond?

7. Jackie and Nancy had very different visions of how women might contribute to the war effort. Nancy advocated hiring an elite group of pilots who would be fully integrated into the Army Air Forces, while Jackie wanted a larger group who, while part of the AAF, would be administratively segregated from men. What was their reasoning, and how was the conflict ultimately resolved?

8. In the early years of the program, the WASP became a media sensation, with reporters, photographers, and newsreel crews eager to capture stories and images of attractive young women flying military planes. How was it portrayed in early media coverage, how and why did this image shift as the tide of the war turned?

9. While the WASP counted two Chinese American pilots and at least one Native American pilot among its ranks, African American women were prohibited from joining, no matter how experienced. What might the opportunity to participate in the WASP have meant for Africa American pilots like Mildred Hemmons Carter? What did you think of Jackie Cochran's reasons for denying their applications?

10. While the WASP flew military planes and worked alongside military pilots, they were not officially members of the military themselves. What did this mean for their day-to-day lives in training and on base? How did it affect their lives after the war?

11. The WASP expected to become members of the Army Air Forces, a plan that Nancy Love, Jackie Cochran, and General "Hap" Arnold all supported. However, when the bill to militarize the WASP went before Congress, it failed. Why? Was there anything that might have changed its fate? What roles did Nancy, Jackie, and Betty Gilles play? Do they share some of the blame for its failure, or was it inevitable, given the politics of the time?

12. In the aftermath of the failure of the bill to militarize the WASP in June of 1944, the training program was closed immediately—and the whole organization shuttered by that December. Why were the WASP sent home while the war was still going on? Do you agree with this decision?

13. As a member of the last class of WASP trainees, Marty Wyall was able to serve for only a few weeks before disbandment, but she treasured this time and ultimately became instrumental in the effort to attain veteran status. What did this status mean for Marty and her fellow WASP?

14. After the war was over, many women, like Dora and Helen, had trouble finding jobs that would allow them to continue flying. What barriers to working as pilots did they and their classmates encounter after the war? How do these relate to the challenges faced by working women today?

15. *The Women with Silver Wings* follows the stories of several WASP—some of them famous, including Jackie Cochran and Nancy Love, and others with stories that are less familiar, like Te-

resa, Dora, and Marty. Was there a story you particularly liked, or one you found most interesting or relatable? Were there any you disliked?

16. Today, women military pilots serve alongside men, but their numbers are few. Commercial aviation, too, remains a male-dominated field. What does the example of the WASP mean for women in aviation? How might their story be used to encourage more women to fly?

TAKE YOUR READING FURTHER

Now that you've finished *The Women with Silver Wings*, check out these other inspiring books about women who did their part in World War II, as recommended by author Katherine Sharp Landdeck:

A Wasp Among Eagles by Ann Carl

A terrific personal memoir. Ann Carl was a pilot in the Women Airforce Service Pilots during the war. After graduating from training she was based at Wright-Patterson Army Air Field and became one of the few people, and the only woman, to fly the Bell YP-59A, the first American jet. I had a chance to meet Ann, and her humble demeanor is obvious throughout the book, despite her great flying abilities.

Band of Angels by Elizabeth Norman

While the important and tragic story of the men captured on Bataan in the Philippines inspired Americans to fight during the war and to remember the horror of it in the decades since, this book tells the story of the American nurses who were captured alongside them. In a riveting account, Elizabeth Norman, an RN herself, makes certain the harrowing experience of these women POWs is not forgotten.

D-Day Girls by Sarah Rose

In 1942 it was still unclear who would win the war, but it wasn't looking good for the Allies as Germany dominated the continent. Winston Churchill's Special Operations Executive (SEO) needed all the help it could get sabotaging the German efforts and turned to women. Utilizing diaries, declassified documents, and oral histories, Sarah Rose tells the story of three of the thirty-nine women who spent the war years ambushing the Nazis and helping lay the groundwork for the D-Day invasion.

A Woman of No Importance by Sonia Purnell

In another story of Great Britain's Special Operations Executive (SEO), Sonia Purnell focuses her attention on one woman in particular, American Virginia Hall. Talented in language skills, Hall was in Europe with various American Embassies before the war began. Despite losing her leg in an accident, she was determined to serve, and once the war began, to help. Purnell tells the inspiring story of her work to undermine the Germans and their determination to stop her.

The Unwomanly Face of War by Svetlana Alexievich

Ukranian-born Svetlana Alexievich won the Nobel Prize in Literature for this important work. Oral histories can reveal so much about the past on a very personal level, including not just facts but emotions, motivations, and reflections. Alexievich spent years interviewing hundreds of Soviet women who served and survived during World War II. Newly translated into English, her work reveals a deeper understanding of the work and sacrifices of Soviet women during the war.

Home Fires by Julie Summers

While perhaps less glamorous than stories of daring and intrigue, Julie Summers shares the important work of British women on the home-front during World War II. Members of the Women's Institute organized women to help run canteens, advised the government on evacuees, and made over 12 million pounds of jam and preserves from produce grown in home gardens to help ease food shortages. Summers stories of ordinary women making an extraordinary difference were the inspiration for the PBS *Masterpiece* series of the same name.

This essay was initially published in slightly different form on ReadItForward.com

KATHERINE SHARP LANDDECK is an associate professor of history at Texas Woman's University, the home of the WASP archives. She is also vice president of the Wingtip-to-Wingtip Association, a national nonprofit devoted to the accurate remembrance of the WASP. A graduate of the University of Tennessee, where she earned her PhD, she was granted a Gugghenheim Fellowship for her WASP research from the Smithsonian National Air and Space Museum. She has received numerous awards for her work on the WASP, appeared as an expert on NPR's *Morning Edition,* PBS, and the History Channel; and produced award-winning documentary films. Her work has been published in the *Washington Post, The Atlantic,* and *HuffPost,* as well as in numerous academic and aviation publications. Landdeck is a licensed pilot who flies whenever she can.

katherinesharplanddeck.com